W0115429

.

You Can't Always Have It All

Brittany Brown-Jackson

© 2022 Brittany Brown-Jackson All rights reserved. No part of this publication may
be reproduced, distributed, or transmitted in any form or by any means, including
photocopying, recording, or other electronic or mechanical methods, without the prior
written permission of the publisher, except in the case of brief quotations embodied in
critical reviews and certain other noncommercial uses permitted by copyright law.
ISBN: 978-1-66786-302-3

YOU CAN'T ALWAYS HAVE IT ALL

My condolences to anyone who has ever lost a loved one. My condolences to anyone who has ever felt as if they've never gotten over the death of a loved one. My condolences to those who felt they could never move on after the death of a loved one. I often would tell people I'm okay after my daughter's father died. Knowing on the inside I'm dying and crying not fully understanding why this happened to me. I would often tell people I'm a strong woman knowing I didn't feel like one everyday. I would often tell people I've moved past the situation knowing that I didn't and I still cant. I would often reminisce about how our life could've been had my daughter's father been here. But the thing we as humans forget is life is temporary. Our love for people is temporary, Our affection we have for people is temporary. Our feelings we have towards people are temporary. The people who come into our lives are temporary. The material things in our lives are temporary. The thing is we all forget everything in life is temporary and I love the temporary things, items, moments in life. I often have to remind myself of this life we have being temporary,However it saddens me because it's a life I don't want to end. However Life will end unfortunately,I've always been ecstatic with the temporary life I have. Between the happiness and the having a successful life. That temporary money I have I've come to conclusion wont even bring my daughter's father back. Life really is nothing but a dream and I've learned that in due time in my temporary life. Consequences ,choices ,decision, ,actions I had decided to make and act on have definitely made me happy but sad. But then when that happiness and those other emotions that were temporary go away.I'm back to thinking and wondering what else I can lose and who else I can lose.Rip to my daughter's father Februarytwenty fifth nineteen eighty four was when he was born but he died December third twenty seventeen. The only man whose ever made me happy the only man who showed me a different type of love that I had never had for the first time in my life. The type of love I took for granted and haven't been able to ever find since,That was a temporary love forever in my heart. A temporary love I cannot forget. A temporary love that will always have my heart broken and my mind blank. A temporary man who was put in my life to show me temporary love and happiness I've never had before but that I desired. A love that made me see nobody else or anything else. A love that cannot be replaced no matter how hard I tried to replace it and him. A love that will never make me love or view anyone to same. A love that will make me always have doubts towards other men. A love that has my heart shattered because it simply ended. A man who did anything and everything for me. Now I no longer have that desire for another temporary man or love in my life. My story is about a temporary man who was put into my life and taken away. About the life I now know without him.A life I now have searching for my next temporary love. My life pursuing to be a better woman and mother. A life where I have temporary encounters with men who meant no good and were temporary. A life in my mind just made sense to have a temporary companionship to feel complete and a whole. A life when I was always around others who meant me no good.

CHAPTER

1

I remember attending this one community college located in Orange Park,Florida. Where I was working on my computer science degree. I hated school so fucking much and computer science was had well some of the classes were hard and some were quite easy. The only motivation for me being in school was that the military paid for me to go to school and gave me a monthly check which was nice everyone didn't have that luxury and my father earned those benefits from being in the military for twenty six years. I hadn't even had a job yet but that check was nice and i was very god at saving my money and when i did spend money I was always a logical thinker just like my father. That was one thing my father and I had in common and I was glad to have got that trait from my dad my mom on the other hand wasn't good at managing money. The day I met the man would soon be my fiancé and the father of my child. I remember we had a spring event at the community college.Nothing but loud up to date pop and R&B music, I remember some kid was was dancing and singing on stage to a Bruno Mars song called "That's what I Like". I loved that song even though it was slightly annoying and very much overplayed. I remember there was different food stands and lots of students with happiness on their faces. Felt nice getting a break after my computer science class. I've always been quite intelligent when it pertains to electronics and fixing them. But lord knows those classes were difficult as hell. I remember sitting a table with the man who would soon be my boyfriend. I gave him the nickname of "Jay". That's what I called him because I didn't like his real name much. Mind you Jay was thirty two years of age when we met also Haitian-American. He was also dark-skinned and buff and bulky the way I like my men to be. Also at that time I was eighteen years of age when Jay and I had met. At the time I met him I was all worked up and ecstatic about a concert that was going to take place in Orlando,Florida.I was supposed to see of of my favorite R&B singers by the name of "Kehlani".Mind you this was Spring of twenty seventeen when I was supposed to attend that concert with some friends at the time from back home that lived in Virginia Beach,Virginia and another one that lived local in Jacksonville,Florida. We ended up not attending the concert because the date was changed due to a personal situation with the artist Kehlani. They changed date when my friends and I were supposed to go. A friend at the time who was going with us by the name of Nadja canceled because she wanted to attend water day at her summer camp job. I was very much pissed off because the bitch acted as if it were life or death. Like bitch your'e too old and grown to be ecstatic about water day at work with children. So I cut the bitch off a as friend, Meanwhile Nadja and Kay both requested on Ticketmaster for their refunds. And I don't ever recall receiving my refund but it was a thirty dollar concert ticket I said fuck it, plus my father paid for the concert ticket for me anyways. At the time I was residing with my father anyways. I was jobless and had no vehicle and I was attending community college. My father typically held my hand in life and he did everything for me. I didn't really have any friends in Florida all my friends were back home in Virginia. I was always an outgoing individual. As the saying goes closed mouths don't get fed,I was never shy or timid. I go after what I want and who I want. I started to notice Jay and I talking more and more as we started seeing each other more at the community college. Before I knew it he would take me to grab lunch quite often. Then I remember missing my networking class to be around him and see him more. My father was never overprotective but I could imagine what would happen If a guy came to pick me up from my father's house especially a grown ass man I was fucking every chance I could. My father was always very judging and cared about everything people said. Me on the other hand I could care less about what people have to say.But let's be real words do hurt and criticism especially when it's coming from people you love the most like your parents. I remember for the first time I showed up late my networking class. Jay had took me to lunch to get some food and I didn't have enough time to eat so he had to drop me off to class and I'm like no worries I can eat in class. As soon as I arrived to class I was kicked out by the ex military professor. He was fine as hell but an asshole. He told me it was unacceptable to arrive to class, I hate to say it but I was about fifteen minutes late! After getting kicked out of class I then call Jay back to come pick me up. Thank God he hadn't got too far away. He picked me up and we go to my father's house and in my room where we have unprotected sex. I wasn't even thinking about if I had gotten an STD or pregnant. We would drink an alcoholic beverage called mike's hard, that was our favorite drink and it was very strong it has twelve to fourteen percent alcohol in it. We also always drunk any kind of hardcore liquor for that matter ,we always had cups of ice from the gas station and we would put our drinks in it. I was really living in the moment of having someone temporarily in my life. We were so in the moment one time one out of my three classes were cancelled and I got Jay to take me home. I was really letting Jay come to my dad's house as if it was my house not even thinking about what would happen if we got caught having sex by my dad or even if he got caught being there in general. One time we were at his parents's house and he had to sneak me in and told me to be quiet. At the time he was house hopping and waiting to close n his house so he would stay at his brother and sister's duplex which they shared and or his friends from the military or his parents. had drunk a lot of alcohol but he he snuck me in the house he told me to sit in the car and wait until he comes back and I then thats when he brought me in the house. We had a lot to drink it was already late and my dad didn't really give me a curfew as far as he knew I was a good girl and I didn't do anything crazy. I had a few friends I hung out with from the community college that my dad had met anyways. So I didn't have a curfew plus living with my dad even as a kid or visiting during the summer time I didn't have friends I never did. I was always lonely and bored and I mean my father and I would go places together and have fun but theres nothing better than hanging out with friends. But that one night Jay had gave me his car and told me to take myself home and don't crash his car and to pick him up in the morning from his parents house so that he can do what he has to do. I wasn't that far away from home my dad lived in Orange Park and Jay's parents lived on one hundred and third street it was very close by and Iwasn't drunk so I could make it home. When I got in my dad's neighborhood I parked Jay"s car down the street. Then I got out and I jog home and open the door and go into the house my dad was in bed and had his room door open and I said hey dad and went into my bathroom in my room and went ahead and prepped everything so I could shower. I thengo in my room and grab my night clothes so I could get dressed in my bathroom which was so fucking annoying at times. That's the one thing that sucked about living with my dad there was no type of privacy and he would close his room door so I could come out the bathroom but I just preferred to get dressed in the bathroom. I was literally going out every day and night with Jay. I'm like damn i go out with him so much that I forget to see my actual friends. The one time I did go out with my friend Shelby we went to hamburger Mary's we had both never been there beforeI had met Shelby at a university in Jacksonville I had attended when I first graduated High School a college I didn't even want to go to but was really forced to by my dad because he was itching to send me to school when I wasn't ready and I was seventeen years old. But Shelby and I went to Hamburger Mary's my father knew her and I knew her family we always hung out since our college days at the university. Hamburger Mary's was a drag queen show but also restaurant and they were very affordable and it was fun and I remember how nice it felt to get out the house and really hangout with my friend instead of lying and using her as a excuse to get out of the house. Shelby had picked me up and she was in her early twenties and I always gave her gas money I didn't have a car but I could've also gotten one too I was really surprised my dad didn't get me a car especially since I had graduated high school early with a high GPA. But Hamburger Mary's was nice and fun and the food was cheap and good. It was very packed when we walked in and we were throwing dollars on stage. I had never been to a place like that before ever and I was all for going to new restaurants. Jay texted the whole time I was there and I would slowly but surely reply to him becauseI was trying to enjoy myself plus I was going to see him later anyways. I literally forgot about my friends although I was using them as excuses to go out because my dad didn't know I had a boyfriend and Jay even told me that eventually I needed to tell my dad I had a boyfriend because all the sneaking out reminded him on being in high school and I'm like well you knew my age and knew what you were getting into being with someone my age. Like Bev once told me he had no respect and didn't care about others and what they had to do for him and sacrifice. So the next morning as soon as my dad went to work which he left the house every morning at six thirty and got off work at three thirty so at times when we Jay and I hung out I would get him to drop me off before my dad got home so it didn't seem like I was always gone we had to switch it up at times so my dad wouldn't be onto me. I get up and get ready as soon as I heard my dad close the door and I called Jay and told him I could be on the way soon to get him and he said okay be careful. Meanwhile, I had been lying to my father telling him I've been taking uber home with the allowance he gave me. Knowing damn well Jay was taking me home anyways Jay took me home once and we had a few rounds of sex and had been drinking and my father called me saying he was on the way home so we had to clean up and hurry up and leave. I was shitting bricks while doing so because I didn't know if my dad was up the street and I didn't want to get caught. So we started to hang out at my sister's and brother's duplex which was in Jacksonville,Florida. He told them I was just a friend because of our age difference. We would drink and have sex every time we hung out and go out to eat a lot. One of the nice things about being with him is that he introduced me to so many new restaurants and we went everywhere in Jacksonville,Florida. Places I've never been before or heard of and I had never had that before. When school was over we started to hang out more and more and I remember he didn't have his own place yet because he was waiting to find a house to buy. Jay would often house hop between his parents house and his two friends apartment who he met in the military whose names I don't remember nor care to remember fuck them. He would also stay over his brother and sister's duplex. I remember we even had sex at his two friend's apartment. Jay and I lay in bed together talking then I asked him what if I get pregnant.He then quickly responds and says he'll take care of his responsibility. I'll give them the nicknames of Meatball and JR. One time we were finishing up having sex and Meatball came into the bedroom and started rubbing on me and I have this look on my face like are you going to stop, I look over at Jay he didn't say anything!! I was very pissed off and everything had been going great between us then I noticed how that temporary happiness started to go away very quickly. So Meatball is rubbing on me then ask JR if he wanted some pussy. Funny how Jay said nothing to his friends at all and he knew that I had been raped as a kid a few times and that I also had been raped in college when I was seventeen which i told him the full story of so the fact he said nothing to his friends like what the fuck. I asked Jay if he was okay with sharing with his friends because that was weird and how we just finish fucking and his one friend trying to fuck me. I'm like yea I'm good on this and I told him his friends had no type of respect for him. I then told Jay I wanted to go home so I grab my shit and we leave. In the car on our way to my home we argue and I ask him why the fuck didn't you say anything? I then say you know what we don't have to see each other anymore and he says that's fine we don't. I then asked him if he was going to let them run a train on me because that seems as if what Meatball had in mind with his short fat ass. He takes me home and we don't talk for a few days, I remember he was always on my mind and I thought about how good the sex was and how he always planned dates for us and then he reaches out to me first. Soon before my young and dumbass is back to seeing him it even got to the point of us hanging out and having sex at his parents house without them knowing. We did a lot of sneaking around which went on for months at a time. One time we had too much to drink and I had no choice but to stay with him so he got a hotel room and I remember sitting inside of his car it was pouring outside and he went inside the hotel to see if he could get a room when he comes back out he tells me a funny ass story on how he told the hotel receptionist that he goes on deployment tomorrow and needs a room and they give him a huge ass discount on the room and it was really nice too. It was hilarious to me I mean after all he was the one who had been in the military for ten years. We had sex all night long. It was so intense I've never had sex in the shower and on the floor and he taught me a lot of tricks. The next day its around twelve o'clock noon and we shower and get dressed. I remember thinking on the car ride home like shit my dad is going to kill me. I even told him when he drops me off don't pull into the driveway or wait for me to go inside. I didn't want my dad to see him. We began to sneak around more to the point where I was paying female acquaintances to pick me up and I'd give gas money so my dad could see I was out with girlfriends. Mind you school was over and my girlfriends would take me to Jay's brother and sister's duplex. Eventually I got a job at burger king which is in the back of my dad's neighborhood so Jay saw me less than before. He would come pick me up some nights from my dad's house. My six foot long and skinny ass is sneaking out the window, mind you my room and window shows on the front side of the house. There I was risking it all for a man and I knew that I could've been caught and my dad's neighbors could've told on me. Theneighbors in my dad's neighborhood watched me grow up. I was just thinking in my mind pleasedon't tell on me. I would always sneak out the window to go out with Jay while my dad was sleeping. One night we went out, and I met one of Jay's best friend's whose still in the military named Jacobi andI met Jacobi's girlfriend named Candace. They had a cookout with a bunch of people there and everyone was cool it was jay and I and I was talking to everyone i was always a people person. jay and I went outside to smoke weed on their patio with some others who were outside and I stayed with Candace and her daughter and some girls she was with talking just normal girl talk. We had al exchanged phone numbers. When we came back inside from smoking Candace and looked at me and said I looked high as hell and was walking slow and I laughed and I said hell I am. We ate some food they cooked which was really god i typically don't eat everyones cooking at all but it was pretty good food. Jay took me home after awhile then it was another time Jay and I went back to their house again. They lived in Orange Park they were very cool I also met their daughter who was close to being one year's old in age. I instantly clicked with Candace who informed me that Jay was fucking married!!!! My mouth instantly dropped and at the time of her telling me this our men were outside drinking and doing what men do. My exact words were "wait what"??? Candace then says to me but you have nothing to worry about because he doesn't care about her he told me he likes you and he's been telling me about you. Suddenly we both drink some of wine as we hear a male's voice come closer and sure enough it was Jay and he was on the phone with someone and based on his body language he seemed bothered and annoyed. Every time he got off the phone the phone kept ringing and I noticed he stopped answering. All I could think about if it was Jay's wife calling whose name was Carol. Candace showed me optics of Carol on Facebook an app I didn't have at the time by personal choice. Carol was latino and she was fat as hell she wasn't ugly but she had definitely let herself go after the military. Her and Jay were both in the military together. Candace also had told me how Jay had signed the divorce papers but Carol keeps playing games. Candace also tells me how Carol told Jay she didn't want kids and didn't want to marry him. In my mind I'm like wow and the motherfucker still marries him like damn I need to start being a ruthless bitch to these men because a man will really treat the bitch who doesn't want him better than the bitch who actually wants me. Dumb as hell and didn't make a bit of sense, the crazy part about it all was once Bev and I were talking and she told me the same thing about Carol that Candace did and Bev told me that Carol didn't want any kids and she also didn't want to marry Jay but he married her anyways. I was also told by Bev that Carol was always boring and bitchy she never wanted to do anything with the family and she's the one who left Jay and said she didn't want to be with him anymore. Candace even told me she told Jay how much she likes me and how he needs to keep me around. I didn't want to be mad at Candace for telling me becauseI mean I did need to know but I expected him to tell me and he didn't. I'm like damn even had Hibachi we were all on a double date then it was Jay,Candace,Jacobi and I celebrating Jacobi's proportion at work Jacobi was still in the Navy locally. I remember Jay getting all these texts messages and he had a look on his face of being bothered but i didn't know why nor did I want to ask and I'm like damn he could've been texting Carol and I have never ever been insecure or jealous of or towards any woman or girl. That wasn't my cup of tea if one looks good they look good I can't be hating that's not cute. But I also didn't want to be competing with any woman either, Carol was in her late twenties and Jay was in his early thirties. Jay was sitting beside me at Hibachi when he phone rings and he tells me that Niceyburned the house and I said what as I was drinking my beer. I remember being with Nicey outside when she was burning her school papers that she didn't need anymore and I was helping her burn the papers she was so ecstatic and it was funny but I didn't stay outside with her the whole time I had went back in the house and Jay and Ihad left to go to Hibachi. I kept thinking to myself as I drink my wine and fake a smile on my face am I now considered a mistress? Is he fucking her and me? Should I ask him about this? When Jay goes back outside I ask Candace questions that I didn't want to but I wanted to have my facts and details before confronting Jay about this marriage he's in that he chose to keep a secret from me. Embarrassed as fuck I swallowed my pride and I asked Candace if Carol lives here in Jacksonville or in Florida in general. Candace then tells me Carol is from Texas and lived in Texas at the time and to this day she still reside in Texas. I then found out that Carol and Jay are separated, then Candace says that Carol left Jay and said she didn't want him anymore . When Jay and I said our goodbyes and left on the car ride taking me home it was a silent car ride. I had all these thoughts and emotions going through my head. Out of nowhere I asked Jay if he was married. He made this face as I glance over to him from the side of my left eye. He takes a while to answer then, asks who told you? I say with an attitude Candace told me. This motherfucker said to me that she needs to keep her mouth closed telling his business and he's going to tell Jacobi about what she did. I'm like your'e lame as hell and you should've told me. Once again there goes another emotion and it's not that temporary happiness its more of a question to myself of why am I dealing with this shit from a man that I'm not obligated to deal with. It seemed like every time I would try to leave him If he would some how maneuver himself back into my life. It was a strong love I had for this man already mainly because I've never had that before and It felt nice to feel affection and wanted and loved even if I was only eighteen close to nineteen at this point. When Jay took me home once again I was thinking why am I with this man. I remember texting Jay saying I think I'm pregnant and telling me he needed to take me to the hospital. I was scared as fuck thinking what if I'm pregnant by this thirty two year old man and the next day he comes to pick me up and we go to the hospital and next thing I know the nurse comes in to collect a urine sample and Jay and I are laying in the hospital bed together few moments later the Dr. comes in to say I'm not pregnant. I was so relieved to hear this, Jay on the other hand didn't seem too ecstatic it was as if that's all he wanted from me was a baby. I mean all he talked about since

I had met him was wanting a baby and family. I noticed every time we would get into an argument Jay would tell Candace every fucking thing. I hated that shit like don't tell other people our problems.She would always tell Jay how she liked me and I was cool. Jay would also tell Candace he's done with me.Typically I am and always will be a nice, cool, outgoing person until you miss me off.

It is now May of twenty seventeen a few weeks before my birthday.Jay knows I'm a huge Aaliyah fan I grew up listening to her music and watching her movies. He ordered me some Aaliyah merchandise he told me but he couldn't say exactly what it was. I remember it like it was yesterday. He directly mailed my birthday gift to my home and Jay informs me that the package said delivered but there is another home around the corner from my dad's home and they have the same home number as my dad does. Later that day Jay takes me there to see if they possibly had my package and come to find out they in fact did. That shit instantly pissed me off. In my mind I'm like I know they can read that the package had my first and last name on it. They tried to steal my package on the low but they did give it back. The funny part about it all is that Jay thought he ordered me an Aaliyah backpack come to find out it was Rihanna. So eventually I started to hang out with Jay's family more and more. One time Jay's oldest sister Bev and I were driving together and she told me to play Jay like the other girls did. To get all I could get from him because her brother ain't shit. And she would tell me how Carol left Jay. For my birthday Jay and I went on a double date with Candace and Jacobi and everything was going fine again that temporary happiness. On the way back to dad's house which mind you I'm still sneaking out of my bedroom window. Jay told me I needed to grow up and tell my dad I have a boyfriend because he feels like we were doing high school shit. At this time days later my dad found out about me sneaking out the window because he noticed the screen was missing on the outer part which I had to take off in order to go through the window.

However, my dad didn't seem to be upset about me sneaking out. I was having the best time of my life and enjoying being around Jay. Me and my dad started to bump heads and Jay had finally closed on his nice one story house in Jacksonville. He offered to let me move in one night and surprisingly I stopped being scared of my dad and I moved in with this man. I remember we had sex on the floor the first few nights of being in the house and I had told my mom I was moving in with my boyfriend even though she lived all the way in Virginia which was ten hours away from Florida. My mom was more understanding and she chose to let me make my own mistakes, which I was completely fine with. When we invited Candace and Jacobi over to our new house to see how it looked. We were all hungry as hell and decided to have a crab boil at their house especially since we didn't have furniture yet. We all rode there together to the store and we went to their house we were drinking and talking waiting for the food to be ready. Candace and Jacobi had a neighbor who they were close with and she came over and was all over my man now mind you bitches always tried me and tried to downplay me because I had a baby face so they automatically assume you're "young". Even though I was nineteen I very much had a old soul I would often feel like I was older like in my thirties. Back to the neighbor she had to be in her thirties and looked like white trash mind you she was taken and ha a husband.Bitch had the nerve to ask me how old am I then tell Jay he's using me. Jay even told me the bitch asked to suck his dick!! Bitch has a husband out here trying to be a hoe and asked my man shit like that like I'm not in the other room. At that point I was ready to go home and one thing about it I was never scared of a little competition I was tall, pretty, skinny with abs and intelligent. I remember going home and fucking and feeling so under pressure because the man I'm with is now thirty three and he wants a baby so bad and is putting pressure under me to get pregnant. I even started back talking to my dad more on the phone even though he was upset that I chose to move out of his house to move in with a grown ass man. But telling myself this man loves me and we can make it work out and get married and have our family. Boy was I wrong when we had a small get together his cousin Jerry who lived with us a the time. Who also sold weed out of our house and I had never been accustomed to that lifestyle before. But I was for some reason loving every moment of that lifestyle. I felt like we were in a movie or music video I was more in love with the temporary shit that I didn't see anything else. We had a small gathering Jay invited his cousin and his three sisters and a co worker. Jay worked at the post office he delivered mail as well as his co worker. We had all been drinking with the exception of the two minor sisters. I remember Jay's co worker Sonja she had kissed me on my lips completely caught me off guard but to be honest I didn't stop her. Jay walked away and went into the house and then I went into ur bedroom where he was at. His exact words to me were "Britt that was some file shit you did". I told him whatever and I was about to walk out the room and he grabbed me. I literally was like what so now you're going to hit me like you hit your bitch ass ugly wife. Next thing I know he slapped the fuck out of me and was over top of me so I couldn't move. I was screaming and crying. The bedroom door was also locked and his oldest sister Bev broke down the door and cousin pulled him off of me. Next thing I know I grabbed the biggest knife I could find in the kitchen and his oldest sister was screaming no and I acted as if I was going to stab him and I dropped the knife the two younger sisters were there. Then Bev kinda in a hurry shoved the girls out the door, Their mother was there to pick them up. I then grabbed a chair and threw at him and he stood there and I said this motherfucker real bad today. I told Bev fuck her and I asked " you think its okay he hit me"? She then said I don't think anything is okay. I then said I should call the cops on your brother and she told me do what I have to do. I then began to pack my shit and I called Candace after all we had gotten very close and I know it was late but she was a stay at home mom anyways.Her and I could relate to so much especially when it came to men problems. Both of our men were sneaky as fuck and full of shit at times.

She was mad as hell when she arrived and she had spoke to everyone and had helped me grab some bags and we threw everything in the trunk. We then left to go to her town house. she lived in Orange Park I felt kinda bad for calling her in the middle of the night she was a stay at home mom and I know how important getting sleep is. We sat in the living room on the couch and talked. Next thing I know my phone starts ringing off the the hook and it's Jay.Candace tells me don't answer the phone, It was Jay he called so many times.Then his cousin Jerry called and I didn't answer then Jay start leaving voicemails and sending emails to me. I put my phone on do not disturb, Candace and I continued to talk more and she told me she'd take me home the next day back to my dad's house. She even told me she thinks I should go back home to my dad's home which I had kept wanting too but like Ashanti I was being "foolish". Literally every timeI had my bags packed I would go back to Jay. Candace even told me she was telling Jacobi that Jay wasn't welcome in their house anymore because he hit me and she really liked me and respected me. The thought of returning home I couldn't imagine what my dad would say.We had always been closer and he was the parent with more money and we'd often watch scary movies together and lifetime movies. But he also had a boundary issue even with my mom when they were together he had a boundary issue and was very controlling. He was even controlling to me at times which is why I moved at in the first place. Candace goes to sleep and leaves me downstairs I slept on the couch. then the next day I woke up eager to check my phone. I had seen many missed calls and texts messages and emails. One email which I still have saved to this day said "Britt you know that shit was just terrible and Im sorry and I understand if you don't want to be with me anymore but I'm wide open waiting for you". My dumbass called him and he asked where I was, next thing I knowI told him and he came to get me. We literally had sex in the downstairs bathroom and he grabbed all my stuff and put it back in the trunk of his car and we went back home to our house. I had no words to even say to him so literally show him not face and he said it would be alright and he was sorry.

Next time I talked to CandaceI remember her saying she couldn't help me anymore becauseI chose to go back to him after he hit me. Which I guess she had a point but we all have been a fool for love. Plus she had gone back to her boyfriend/baby daddy a few times even after some stories she told me. Jerry was in the kitchen area when I came back home and he had fist bumped me and asked me if I was okay and I said I'm good thanks. But you know I didn't judge at all, to each is own. There I was again going back to him because I loved the temporary happiness we would have together. We did everything together we went everywhere together and had fun. He did everything for me. I left burger king after being there for months that fast crazy lifestyle got old fast. I got tired of going to work hungover and I got tired of making minimum wage. I used to go to work tipsy and hungover almost everyday. One of the manager's that worked there Shelly she would be too with her ghetto ass so she never said anything to me. One time Jay came through the drive thru and she said she was like damn who is that talking with the deep voice I said no mam off limits thats mine. She stayed trying to smack me on my ass Iwasn't gay and I had experiences with girls but I didn't want her or any other girl for that matter. Me,Jay and Jerry who was his cousin who lived with us in our house who was also a fucking drug dealer all decided to drive to Georgia to go to Jekyll Island. I had never been there before it was many water parks and small theme parks there. Georgia is very close to Florida. that city was only one hour away from us. It was my first real "baecation". On the way there we were drinking and smoking weed including Jay who was the driver. Jay and I were matching something we did a lot I had a gray crop top and some booty shorts and he had on a gray tank top and some shorts. When we were smoking and driving and speeding at that it was a cop on top of the bridge that was trying to catch people speeding and he had a speed radar the crazy thing was I wasn't even scared or phased I was really living my best life. Jay and I did have a bad experience one time with the cops when we first started dating and i know he said bae take my debit card and you know the pin and I'll go to jail for both of us at least I can get out faster and quicker. it was crazy because we saw a police van and they weren't behind us at first but then they get over behind us and pull us over and Jay was driving but not drinking I had a mikes hard I was drinking and underage. I took that shit to the head you could definitely smell it on my breath but I didn't want my man to get in trouble because Iwas drinking while he was driving and we had four locos too tall as cans and you could definitely smell the liquor on my breathe. Hell I could smell the liquor on my breath too when i was talking to Jay. I knew my dad would kill me if I went to jail and I would be grounded as fuck too. I was scared but was sticking by my man. I even posted on snap-chat. Iremember Candace seeing it and asking what the fuck happened. Two cops walk up one on Jay's side and one on my side of the car. One asked Jay if anyone smokes in the car and he said yea my cousin and they ask us to step out the car I was shitting bricks inside. The cops searched our whole car and I was saying in my head fuck I'm going to jail. They ask for both of our driver's licenses and ask us what are we doing in Orange Park if we live in Jacksonville in my mind I'm like what type of stupid ass ques-tion is that. I said damn they didn't even say anything about our open canned four Loko drink which contained alcohol. I was so glad I had for-gotI had opened one to try it. The cops then told us that the K-9 unit dogs smelled weed from our car. They then asked how we knew each other and I did the talking and said we're a couple they were asking how long we had been together and everything I said well damn the fucking FBI. I then thought about if my dad knew the cops or sent them because he did work for the federal government.My dad was the damn feds little did a lot of people know because no one was supposed to know. I would often think to myself damn my dad has that high end type of job and w out here smoking weed and riding around with guns, weed and liquor like I can't go to jail or anything. I didn't put anything past my dad, I was so relieved when the cops lets us go and I said damn thats a real man, Jay really gave me his debit card and said you know the pin and said I'm not going to let you get in trouble and fuck your life up. He told me I could just bail him out some-thingI would'vedefinitely did if needed. I loved him and I would do any-thing for him and hell I pretty much did. I was sneaking out the window for him and I did a lot more for him. When they let us off the hook I put a update on Snapchat saying they let us go. I then text Candace saying they let us go and explained to her what had happened. Im glad we didn't have our guns in the car because neither of us had gun licenses.I played Beyonce featuring Jay-Z on the run, that was my song and it was the perfect time to play that song. When we got home Jay told Jerry no more smoking in his car while driving or having weed in his car at all for that matter. We could've both went to jail on the account of Jerry. One Jay and I had been drinking but we weren't drunk and we both had to pee really really bad and Jay was driving all fast and shit and hit his driver side mirror and it flew off. We both peed in the bushes the crazy thing was there was a gas station right in front of us. Looking back it was stupid to do but I loved that rush I would get being with him and I had never had that before or with any other manI was only nineteen. Jay and I loved listening to nineties and early two thou-sands hip hop and R&B music. When we finally get to JekyllIsland it was so packed and hot as hell. Jay paid for all three of our admission tickets and we go into. Jerry left us so he wasn't a third wheel and we got on a lot of water rides that required two people to sit in the tube together. We took pictures and got food. We were kissing and this little boy swam over by us and said "kissy kissy". it was annoying but funny as hell. Jay then brings up that topic about us having kids again. I know couples plan marriages and families all the time but I hated getting my hopes up. I wanted us to get married and make it work i was so happy with him even though we had our ups and downs. We were at Jekyll Island for hours my feet were burning and my skin looked like raisins from being in the water for so long. We left to go back to Florida jamming to the song twenty one questions by fifty cent and Nate Dogg while making snapchats.It is now September I left burger king due to wanting a better job opportunity and I was tired of getting treated like shit. So I landed a call center job for Wells Fargo but training didn't start yet. So the month is now September and at this time hurricane irma was getting close to Florida. while I waited to start training at Wells Fargo Ilanded a job in Jacksonville called dial america which was a sales call center for Sirius xm. Jay had been taking time off lately from work to stay at home with me anyways. I had two training classes Iwas waiting for to start there. So Jay made the decision that he and I go to Alabama where his childhood friend lived at with his wife and children. I also had family that lived there as well. We went to Alabama to stay at his friend's house we stayed all week. Jay only wanted to go because he was scared haha even though he hated to admit it. I really enjoyed car trips with him, he took me everywhere. I met his childhood friend Skervins and his wife Trina along with their children, They were all cool and down to earth. Jay and I were outside uploading our bags when I heard a familiar voice from a group of young boys playing basketball in the street. As I pay close attention I notice one boy by the name of Mari who is in fact my cousin. Him and his family did last live at some apartments close by last summer when I had visited them. I remember last time my cousin Mari and his parents were in Floridavisiting us and they had met Jay they didn'tin fact like him.Only because they thought he was controlling me because he was older. I didn't think our age gap was that bad at all considering I was turning twenty the next year and he was in this thirties. twenties and thirtiesisn't that much of a age gap. So I was no longer talking to my cousin. Mari goes to get his mom and dad who invite us over later for dinner once we get settled in. Jay told me that was my family and it was up to me if I wanted us to go or not. We were in the city Phoenix city,Alabama. After the five hour drive and being in the house Jay and I freshened up and went to search for a restaurant to eat at by ourselves. At dinner we took many optics together and of our food. Wed always take optics of our food and snapchats together.

I told Jay I wanted to go to my cousin's house so after dinner we went. Jay and her husband instantly bonded because they were both in the military for ten years. So the men were drinking in the garage and talking about their military experiences. I'm in the house talking to my cousin Santana with her son Mari. We were eating dessert and playing monopoly. I had taken a few shots of liquor and beginning to feel very nauseous. Liquor has never made me feel that way as Jay and I both had high alcohol tolerances. As we began to play monopoly it said I would have a family and be expecting a baby. Later during the night when I get out of bed to go pee I noticed I was spotting. I knew it wasn't my period because I had already had a period. I went to spend time with my cousins everyday while we were in Alabama and I kept telling Santana something with my body felt off but I didn't know what it was and I just kept feeling nauseous. I didn't want to say possible pregnancy because I also had acid reflux which I still do to this day so I didn't think of anything by it. Days later Jay and I are headed back home to Jacksonville,Florida. On that car ride home I started to get nauseous again and dehydrated feeling as if I would pass out. Jay stopped at a nearby gas station where I got some food and something to drink. I also did have microcytic anemia and sickle cell trait which I still in fact have today. I would often get dizzy and cold daily due to my lack of oxygen only because my body doesn't get have enough red blood cells. My red blood cell count was also very low as well which very much sucked. That temporary happiness went away once again when we get back home and Jay's phone rings and as I glanced at it when he reaches in his pocket to answer the phone it says wifey and his last name. I slam the gallon of milk down and go into the room. Jay follows me and we have sex I just lay there thinking how dumb I am. When I say I was pissed the fuck off it was to point where i wanted to call my dad and beg to come home. I texted my dad very often and even asked to come back home even though I was embarrassed and my dad said I could come back home anytime I wanted to. My dad would even ask me whats wrong at times whenever I asked him to come back home. Lord knows I wanted to move back home but I didn't want to hear my dad say I told you so or I was right. That's the one thing most parents say to you when you refused to listen to them.

CHAPTER

2

But for some reason I wanted to leave but I couldn't so I walk away to go into our bedroom and cried as I laid in the bed. Next thing I hear is my cell phone ringing. It was my friend Z, her and I were very close especially since we had to grow up kinda fast. Jay comes into the bedroom while I'm on the phone with Z, and he starts having sex with me. I didn't want to have sex with him but I just took it. I knew I loved him and I wanted us to work out but I was being young and dumb. Or as my mother would say young, dumb and full of cum. The next morning when Jay went to work I packed all my shit nice and neat then called my friend Veronica from college we were always close. She came to pick me up from our house and I stayed with her at her house for two days. I didn't call or text Jay when I was gone with Veronica and he didn't text or call me either. Veronica and I decided to get with some mutual friends and went to one of our spots in Jacksonville. It was a hookah lounge called Sahara. We had tequila shots and I began to feel sick again like I wanted to throw up I didn't know what was going on. Veronica takes me to Walmart the next day because once again when I went to pee and wipe myself I seen brown discharge. I brought three pregnancy test but I procrastinated to take any because I was scared. I get a text from Jay saying to give Jerry my key and that my bags are waiting for me. When Veronica dropped me back off home I took all three pregnancytests I also felt like shit. I saw the results of all three test shocked at the fact they were all positive. I slid down the wall in the bathroom thinking about what to do. I loved this man but we kept having arguments and it was probably best to just got back home to my dad I thought. But I had a bigger problem on my hands a pregnancy that I didn't want but I couldn't be so mad I had unprotected sex. But lets be real Jay wanted a baby and rushed me to have one. The sex between us was passionate and we always made love and never wore a condom since we first had met, I always would tell myself things we do have consequences. I just sat there in silence and I started not to tell Jay and move back home and get my shit together and never tell him and after that me and my baby move away. After all my father would still put money in my bank account and Jay would give me money every week so I was always good. I decided to text Jay and I sent him one pregnancy test optic and he asked if I had taken anymore tests and I told him yes I did. then I sent him the next two tests and he asked what was I going to do!!! When he said that shit Icouldn't tell him he was serious or playing because he played too damn much at times which everyone knew. Which I loved how he could enjoy himself and gave joy to others but at time it was annoying. He then said he was happy and on his way home. I started unpacking my bags because it was like why would I leave and have my father taking care of me and a baby in my belly thats not his responsibility. I kept thinking and wondering if Jay would discard me I mean after all he did want a baby really bad and honestly more than me. I wanted kids but I didn't want to get pregnant at nineteen. Before the pregnancy we would smoke and drink every night and I made Jay make a promise to slow down on the drinking I mean he was thirty three thats slowly but surely pushing forty. Jay took me to get some work clothes I had to prepare for my training at my Wells Fargo job. Next thing I know he was holding my left hand in his hand saying how he love me and he was going to die before me. I was like why would you say something like that its not funny at all. I didn't want to argue at all with him so I told him its not true and don't say that. Im the one that has a lot of health problems so if anything I would be the one who would die first before him. I knew he had high blood pressure but i mean after all he was Haitian he loved spicy foods and salty foods, I would remind him to take his high blood pressure medicine. I remember him telling me how the medicine made his dick hard to get hard. So he made the decision to stop taking the medication. We told everyone about the pregnancyI made the announcement on all my social media platforms. I don't know what it was but it seemed like every time Jay and I would have movie night which would be every night we would watch horror movies. We loved horror movies and it seemed like once I found out I was pregnant every scary movie that we watched was always with a couple and the man would always get killed or die protecting his wife or girlfriend. Then the girlfriend and or wife would find out that shes pregnant. And she would be alone pregnant, it seemed so real and I would have these dreams about those situations too. It really freaked me out I would just wake up from the dreams and share my head and then go back to sleep when I felt it had been long enough and the dream should be gone out my mind.

I pick up the phone and call my mother's best friend at the time Phaedra that same day who was like a aunt to me at that time. She would talk to me and allow me to vent to her about things I didn't feel comfortable venting to my own mother about sad but true. She didn't judge me either but I told her I was pregnant and scared to tell my mother so she offered to stay on the phone with me on mute while I called my mother on three way but she said she wasn't going to tell her for me it was too big. So my mother answers to phone and I tell her quickly about my pregnancy. Next thing I knew my mother asks me what is Jay saying about it and is he happy about it and basically how she didn't want that for me. I knew my mother wouldn't be mad she was always way more supportive about my decisions than my dad was. I asked my mom if she could tell my dad. I'll never forget that phone call from my dad I received. when he called me, I already knew why he was calling me, he was telling me that he was making a appointment for me to have a abortion. He told me I was going to ruin my life and body and he was disappointed in me. I was so saddened when my mom said my dad was disappointed in me I had felt like all my life I could never please my dad. I began to build up an amount of depression. I couldn't believe I was pregnant but at least one of us got what we wanted in the scenario. I didn't want a baby that was all Jay but I guess I'm to blame too. After getting off the phone with Phaedra, My mother called me back and asked why did I tell her friend and how she doesn't deal with her like that. I posted the pregnancyannouncement on instagram and snapchat which at the time were the only social medias i had at that time. My pregnancy announcement was a shocker to everyone. I started feeling like a disappointment. I thought about not telling Jay at first when i took the test and getting a abortion but babies don't ask to be here so I didn't think that would be fair at all. Hell I even thought about going home to my dad while pregnant and never telling Jay i was pregnant but it wasn't my dad's job to take care of me and my unborn could. I also don't like needing people. When Jay came home he took me to the emergency room to confirm the pregnancy they said I was three to four week pregnant and our due date was May twenty seventh twenty eighteen. I then had to make a doctor's appointment on the military base where my father worked and Jay also once worked at before I had met him. I had my dad's health insurance to use at the time which was a military plan. If I went off base it would be a thirty dollar co pay which I didn't want to pay at that time. The base hospitals weren't the best at all I've heard so many bad experiences. When I go to make the Doctor's appointmentI was already getting pissed off and overwhelmed because it took so many calls to get assistance to even make the appointment. I had to call back so many different days. On top of that it gets worse I was told I had to attend a class on base before I could even see a doctor I had never heard of any shit like that ever!!! So I was told that I needed to go to this pregnancy class for expecting mothers. It was three to four hours long. But I guess it being my first baby it would be very informativeI didn't really know how to take care of a baby I just knew the basics. As far as how to change diapers, how to make bottles and of course burp them. When it was time for the class Jay had me drop him off to work he worked at the post office and he gave me the car. I talked to his sister Bev she was the second oldest we were kinda close. I talked to her about a few things and she told her brother Jay to make sure he goes to my appointments with me. He then told Bev he would try to make it ti each one but of course he has to work. I never had morning sickness.I never had morning sickness but that heart burn especially with the acid reflux was no freaking joke. I used to get severe cramps and pains at the lower part of my stomach. Before I knew it I had to go to work for training the upcoming week so Jay took me to some stores on a shopping spree and even picked out some work clothes for me. Because of his work schedule he would take the car and drop me off and pick me up from work everyday which was fine. Sitting in the training room at a place called (ERC) Enhanced Resource Centers which was a call center in Orange Park for Wells Fargo. It was so many people there and I overheard some conversations on how some co workers were going to Hooters for lunch for happy hour drinks. I was like okay i can get down with this but I remembered I was pregnant and in the early stage in my pregnancy at that. We had received a tour of the call center and they take roll call and we walk in two groups so we can get our work badges made up. This job was definitely better than burger king and I knew I needed to also work I didn't want Jay to do everything like he already was. I wanted to have my own money which I think every married woman or girlfriend needs to have their own money its never good to depend on a man they can leave at any given time. I knew this job was mine when I went to the two interviews and I sent Jay a picture of me and he was so happy and said look at my motherfuckingwoman. He said to me in the text congratulations bae I already knew you had the job. I was so happy and if felt nice being encouraged and having that type of support in my life I've never had that before but then again that was my first real relationship. So after they give us our work badges we go back to the training room where I pick a seat in the back of the classroom and I sat by this man by the name of Kai he was cool and we would sneak snacks to eat and be texting even though we were told not to do both. I couldn't believe Heather our trainer told us day one we couldn't eat in training hell I was pregnant and her being a mother I thought shed be more understanding. It was cold as hell in training and I kept having to pee because I was pregnant which was starting to get annoying as fuck. One time on lunch break John a guy from training saw me eating with Kai and i had so many snacks and said to me I was going to be big because I eat too much. I'm like I'm pregnant what do you expect but Ididn't even take offense to it. One day I had to take a day off at training which typically you weren't allowed to miss training but I had already had my appointment made up before I even started and it was for my pregnancy so they had to let me take that day off. I would get bored in training all day anyways it was always cold and even though it was paid training just sitting there from eight in the morning to five in the afternoon it went by slow as hell and I was bored listening to someone talk all day and writing. So Jay and I are at home and when I go to our closet in the bathroom I'm wondering why he has his wife's clothes in the closet whose name is Carol. When I asked him about it he says he doesn't want to have to replace any of her clothes and I'm like we moved in this new house together her clothes weren't there so why are they there now? I told him to move the clothes to the guest bed-room and he doesn't do anything. That's when I text my dad again asking if I could come home. I did everything but took my ass back home. I get upset and push Jay and walk away, I shower then put my clothes on. I go outside to feed our cats that we somehow claimed as pets we had them since we moved in the house they were always on our patio meowing. So wed just feed them cat food and give them water and they kept coming back. They were two pretty ugly cats they had scratches or their noses that just kept showing up outside outside me and Jay's house. Or really I should say his house in which his wife took away even but,

When I feed the cats I spit up a little in the grass and I wanted to cry the stomach pains were unbelievable and unbearable. I kept thinking about the first time I met Bev and she told me to play her brother just like the others did and to get all I could from her brother. I thought about it more and more but that wasn't me or the type of person I was. She told me her brother takes care of women and will pay and give money but he was a hoe. I also thought about her telling me that so much. It was already bad I was with a married man even though they were legally separated. Then I find myself pregnant by a married man. Damn I was actually considered a mistress and it wasn't cute. Jay and I go to the military base we see the dr early because I kept having cramps and stomach pains. Typically at the military base when you'repregnant you cannot be seen by a doctor until you're nine weeks pregnant and or more weeks pregnant. The doctor told me I was going to have a miscarriage based on the bleeding they had seen from the ultrasound. They also told me I had bleeding in my cervix area which was crazy. I cried the whole way home from the hospital and Jay of course told people. The doctor also told me that I was going to need to be put on bed rest and out of work. I'm like fuck!! I just got this job at Wells Fargo and to think that I was going to be right back to sitting in the house bored as hell and miserable like I was when I stayed with my dad up until I got the job at burger king. I hated sitting in the house for long periods or times doing nothing and everyday at that. Jay rubbed my belly on the car ride home telling me it was going to be alright but it wasn't alright. I'm like why is he taking this so light but thenagain I guess men don't like to show emotion as much as women do. I hated that shit certain things need to just stay between you and your significant other. His sister Bev was starting to piss me off because she thought she knew everything because she was older than me. I hated older people like that she didn't even have kids and I had no knowledge of her ever being pregnant. Jay had pissed me off too he literally said to me later that night that he went on google to look up my symptoms to see if I was lying about them. Which i don't know who out there right mind lies about shit like that like if I'm hurting and in pain crying then I'm hurting and in pain. Who the fuck lies about being in pain?? After weeks of being at Wells Fargo I just didn't go back but I kept in contact with Kai from time to time. I was starting to get depressed from sitting at home all day and Jay worked at the post office so there was no telling at times when he'd get home from work. He actually delivered the mail in Jacksonville and Orange Park which are both huge cities in Florida. You cant even see all of both cities in one day, I would try to have the house clean and dinner ready whenever I had some strength to do so but for the most part I was just trying to stay in bed as much as I could. I was even frightened to get up and go pee without thinking about my baby falling out of my vagina into the toilet. I received a phone call one day when I was laying in bed from another job i had an interview at and I had got the job I was told which was great it was DialAmerica a call center in Jacksonville they were calling me to make sure I was still attending their training class but I had informed them that I was on bed rest due to pregnancy complications. I was already sad I had to leave Wells Fargo I was cool with everyone in my training class and I was comfortable there and for once I thought I would've made my dad proud. The only thing that would've sucked with staying at Wells Fargo is that my actual hours would've been noon to nine at night. Thats a long ass time to be sitting down on the phone at work. I had never had those hours before. Jay was a homebody we would have cookouts at home all the time and every time we invited Candace and Jacobi they never came over but we went to all of their cookouts and out to eat with them when they asked. So we just stayed to ourselves for awhile after talking about them acting like that. One of my friend's at the time whose name is Alma invited us to her cousin's house for a cookout and I thought to myself I mine as well get out the house and hangout.I didn't go anywhere or do anything and I had to get out of that house sitting there was making me so fucking depressed. It was already bad enough I didn't want to be pregnant but I didn't want to lose the baby either. Jay stayed home with Jerry while I took the car and went to the cookout they had drinks and weed and food. Alma's cousin didn't live that far away.Alma was also older than me she was in her late thirties. Everyone I hangout with was always older than me. Jay and I always texted each other when we made it to our destinations, So when I get to Alma's cousin's house who I had never met before but he was fine as hell and older like I liked them. There were a whole bunch of people around and everyone was drinking and smoking weed but unfortunately for me my pregnant ass couldn't do either. I heard from a lot of women and girls I knew who were pregnant and smoked weed and drunk wine but Ididn't want to be that woman who did that. I mean after all at some point Ididn't drink at all in my life so I was sure I could go without smoking wand drinking while pregnant. It wasn't that serious to me. Everyone was in the man cave getting ready to watch the Floyd Mayweather fight. I didn't care about boxing nor watched it. I didn't give a damn about any sport for that matter. There was hella food inside the house on the counters, I normally don't eat everyone's cooking because a lot of people are nasty in the kitchen. People lick their hands while cooking others food, don't wash their hands, Have animals in the kitchen and more. But I was pregnant and hungry after all so I ate the food. My phone rung it was Jay he was asking me how the cookout was and I told him it was alright, I then asked him if he wanted me to pick him up and he said yes. So I told Alma I'm going to get Jay, When I picked him up I asked his cousin Jerry if he wanted to come and he said nah. I looked at his cousin Jerry as a big brother to me whenever Jay was gone before I got pregnant. Jerry and I would often smoke weed and have deep ass conversations about life and ourselves plus Jerry would give me free weed but I mean after all he was staying in our house rent free. Jerry also taught me how to cook I didn't know anything about cooking which was funny and I remember growing up hearing if you want your man to stay you better learn how to cook. I would also hear the way to a man's heart is his stomach. Jerry and Jay both taught me how to cook because they could both very much eat a lot of food. Jay used to eat food by himself out of pots and pans and big ass mixing bowls with his greedy ass. Whenever Jay cooked any type of meats he would clean the meats with lemons and limes and he also would squeeze real lemon and lime juice on the meats which gave them extra flavoring I hated when black people put a bunch of salt and seasonings like I was to taste other ingredients as well. Jay would squeeze real lemons and lime juice on different types of meats and cut up lots on veggies as well. The first time I ever cooked in our new house I had to get my mom to help me cook. I would call my mom on the phone and ask her what to do and what seasonings to use and how to clean the meats it was very much funny. Especially because my mom could cook and my dad could kinda cook but then there was me I didn't know what the fuck to do in the kitchen. The first time I ever cooked in the new house though I had made some baked chicken breast and I cut up some bell peppers and placed around the chicken breasts. I had got Jerry to help me with the rice because we didn't have a rice cooker so therefore we had to cook the rice in a pot on the stove and I didn't want to burn the rice or the pot. Jay used to joke me and Jerry he said I undercook the food and he said jerry overcooks the food. I told him that he knows I'm not a house wife I knew how to clean up good though and please him in the bedroom quite well. I told Jay he didn't get with me because of my cooking he got with me because we could relate to a lot and had a connection. Even though I was way younger than Jay I felt like I was his age I've always had a old soul. I matured off pain and experience not age, We were both logical thinkers and we were both smart and good with money. His family liked me and hell I felt like we had been dating for years we had so many memories and trips and I knew most of his friends. Hell I even had helped his second oldest sister Manew drive my pregnant ass helped her drive I was scared as fuck his sister Manew was fifteen or sixteen she was very close I age to me but her and her other sister who was the youngest didn't know my real age I had never told them I didn't think it was important to tell them at all. Plus they had never asked my age so it was whatever. I helped Manew drive she has just gotten her permit she had took the test online which in the state of Florida they allow us to take our permit test online. I took my permit test online too in Florida because at home with my mom back in Virginia that permit test was hard as fuck hell even the driving test in Virginia was hard too and they require you to parallel park in Virginia something I couldn't do. It would be Manew, Nicey and I each time in the car when Manew would drive. Manew wouldn'tdrive the best but we all are like that starting out so it was okay. I taught her the right and legal way to drive meanwhile while scared for my life because I had a baby baking in my belly. I took Manew to empty parking lots and neighborhoods to drive.I even made her drive on the highway in the slow late over time. I did a lot with Jay's two younger sisters. One time I even had taken the girls to military base to the Navy exchange to get some more school shoes. The youngest sister Nicey had told me how she liked me and how I was prettier than Carol. I took the girls home and picked them up as well they didn't live that far from us they lived in Jacksonville as well. Even the parents liked me too especially Jay's mom she would remind me to eat and she would touch my belly and we gave her copies of the ultrasound optics. His mom even sometimes had cooked for me. Jay and I are on our way to the cookout and I was driving and we had a long conversation on the way there about telling Jerry he's going to have to leave in April because of baby was due in May. We didn't want that type of influence around our baby and after all Jerry didn't only smoke weed but he sold weed too. On top of that he also sold weed and would bring his clients in our home where we all lay our heads which is a no no. Jerry called Jay asking how far away from the house we were and he told him not that far and asked why. Jerry then said he wanted to come with us which was fine so I turn back around and we go back to our house to pick him up. Jerry had smoked and looked fried by the redness of his eyes and how low his eyes were. We head back over to Alma's cousin's house where we find Alma drunk and tipsy when we get out the car. She was definitely fucked up. Talking reckless and she even began to ask Jay about the military and his bad experiences which is something you don't ask people at all who've been in the service. Jay got upset and said nah we don't need to talk about it.Then Alma replies and says someone needs to. I was leaning on Jay and he said he was going to go in the house to get some food. Alma then ask me how was our relationship and for the most part I was private so I lied and said good it was actually going okay but we just had some issues like other people do. I told her I had to go to the bathroom but really I was going to see Jay and he was piling his plate and Alma's cousin comes in and says to Jay damn you taking all the food I mean Jay was thick and bulky he could definitely eat. His ass would eat out of a whole pot and or pan if you let him. But we also had money and we could've replaced the food it was no need for Alma's cousin to be loud and cause a seen. So Jay had put the plate down and said he didn't want a trouble and my eyes were on a bottle that was close by just in case he tried to hit my man who I knew could handle himself. Some lady comes in and apologizes to us and Jay said we could replace the food and she said not to worry about it and Jay said that he also delivers mail to their house from time to time. Jay and I go outside where loud music is my sound wild thoughts was playing so we go outside to dance and after while I told Jay I was ready to go that whole situation had really blew me. Like my mom always told me you cant have too many niggas around each other nothing but trouble and unwanted problems which was true, she never lied about that.

Before we had left Alma told Jay how she always sees my snapchat stories of us together. We posted videos and pictures everyday on snapchat every time we went out to eat and partying and Jay says I know B was which he called me at times. Kinda like B and Jay Z but he was like B never wants me to leave for work and I be telling her I gotta go. And I was holding Jay's cup of liquor when Alma's cousin came around and she was like aren't you pregnant and I said I am and she said you don't look it I said I know I'm very early it was my first trimester. She then asked if I was drinking and pregnant and said she gonna mind her business. I then said this is his cup. then she asked how old was I andI said nineteen. She said girl I got kids your age and I said okay. I said alright Alma we leaving,I cant stand people who assume and run their mouths so we say bye that time and finally leave. On the way home Jay drives and i was like bae that was crazy and we don't need to come back around them because Alma cant handle her liquor at all I was getting annoyed and pissed off. I then say I thought dude was going to try to hit you I was going to grab that liquor bottle and bust his ass in the head. Thats why we were really homebodies. A few weeks went by and I'm nine weeks pregnant which meant it was time for my doctor's appointment on base I went to pick Jay up from work i sat in the parking lot until he came out and my cousin Rell had called me we were on the phone talking and he asked if I was still smoking weed and my response to him was I can't do it anymore. I didn't really tell everyone in my family that I was pregnant and he took a long pause when I said that and then Rell asked if I was pregnant then i took a long pause and I said yes cousin I am. He then said he would have to talk to my baby daddy and i said we'll be making some trips up there again sometime soon. I then told my cousin that Jay was coming out and that I had to go we were going to my appointment. When Jay comes out I drive us on base where he used to work and my dad worked at. As we approach the gate on base I get my military ID ready to show the people at the gate and then they let us through. After that we go to the hospital Jay tells me to slow down because the military police are something serious. We enter the hospital I was shitting bricks hoping we didn't run into my dad or any of my dad's co workers that knew me. Everyone at that base knows me and my dad a lot of them practically watched me grow up ,may dad was chief on that base for years. We get on the elevator to go to the area were supposed to be. The military hospital for the areas where you go to see your actual doctor they have designated sides and each have different colors. We went to the red team in the waiting area. I got so annoyed waiting it was at least an half an hour wait as time goes on and on. Jay is watching sports on his phone while he does that I go to the kiosk area and I told the woman sitting there we had an scheduled appointment and I'm nauseous,weak, dizzy and pregnant. She then says it shouldn't be much longer, I was like let me sit my pregnant skinny ass down I cant show my ass on this military base. I don't need to be getting arrested while pregnant. They finally call my last name and we both get up and walk back. This military guy escorts us back to take my height and weight and to ask about my symptoms. I told him I've been having some unbearable cramping in my lower stomach area. Then he takes us into our room and we wait for the doctor to come in, A female doctor comes in her name was Dr.Greene she was really cool and she showed us our baby moving around on the ultrasound and Jay was crying I never had seen him ever cry before since we had been together. Dr.Greene then asked if Jay was the father and I had all these thoughts and emotions and I yelled no but it was by accident. Jay then said in front of the Dr and nurse when we leave We have a lot to talk about but he said it playfully and we all started laughing. Dr.Greene then printed out our ultrasound pictures and asked if I had any health problems I told her I had acid reflux,sickle cell trait and microcytic anemia which I had dealt with since my junior year of high school. Dr. Greene tells us she'll be right back with some paperwork for us to take home when she leaves the room we started taking pics of the ultrasound and sending to every-one because thats how ecstatic we were. I tried to send the ultrasounds to everyone forgetting we were on base and the signal and service sucked!! Dr.Greene gave us a bunch of papers and told us congratulations and were good to go.

CHAPTER

3

I even text Candace I'm pregnant and she replies that I'm stuck with him now for good for eighteen years and theres no getting away from him. I didn't even reply to her I hated how she thought she was better than everyone as if she didn't have what she did because of her man and it seemed as if she was forgetting that. I didn't even respond back to her and that was my time I realized I had to stop telling people things. My best friend from middle school in Virginia Tati had messaged me on instagram after I posted our ultrasound optics and she said thats crazy because she was pregnant as well. As Tati and I catch up about life and our pregnancies I give her my cell phone number, as we text she then tells me that her and Parish live in Jacksonville I hadn't seen her in years along with other friends because I graduated early so I could move to Florida to move with my dad which was my personal choice. I wanted to have a better life and my dad made more money than my mom a and i was tired of struggling when I stayed with my mom . My mom had money too and worked for the government like my dad but was bad at managing money. So Tati and I hadn't seen each other since High School. I invite her and Parish over her boyfriend/baby daddy, I had never cared for him I thought he was a bad influence on Tati and he was a trouble maker and no good for her. She always liked thugs even thoughshe was very innocent and a good girl. I needed someone to talk to so we had been talking on the phone more and more and texting it felt nice having someone to talk to especially who lived in Jacksonville and had known me for years we grew up together same neighborhood and all. I invited Tati and Parish over one day while Jay and Jerry were home and I hugged Tati really tight and touch her belly and I had never met Parish in person but i had heard the wild crazy stories like I said a trouble maker all his life at that.I didn't hug him i just say hey nice to meet you, me and Tati are talking about how we're both due in May and how we both do mater- nity optics together. Next thing I know Parish asked if I know someone who sells weed and I said my brother in law which Isometimes to Jerry as. He then said I should ask him to give him some free weed and it was a vibe I didn't like about Parish. Tati then tells me they'll be back and her and Parish walk outside to talk. I don't know what they talked about but the vibes were just weird from both after while. I had text Jay saying I had my best friend here and her boyfriend Jay comes out the bedroom to come meet them. Jay was making jokes per usual that was something he did and Parish wasn't impressed and when Jay had went back in the room Parish asked if he was the one that hit me and I said yea I made him mad and he said so that don't make it right and he asked if I wanted him to take Jay out I said no what the hell I'm pregnant I want my child's father present. I asked Parish how did he know about Jay hitting me and Tati said because he was snooping through her phone. And Tati told Parish to stop going overboard and its not their business. I noticed Tati and Parish texting back and forth then Tati announces they have to go so we hug and they leave. Later we go to Candace and Jacobi's house to celebrate and they had cooked for us a lot of food. Of course we always split up the girls stay inside while the men go into the garage and talk and drink. I couldn't drink this time but I listened to Candace talk since before i always did a lot of venting about my relation- ship to her. She did ask me what were we going to name the baby Wyclef Jean? Which was a very popular Haitian singer,rapper, actor in the nineties and early two thousands. It was a funny and good joke because Jay was

Haitian born and raised in Haiti. She then starts telling me all the problems her and her man are having. In my mind I'm like trouble in paradise, one thing about Jay and I we didn't think we were better than anyone and we didn't act like our shit didn't stink and we actually were logical thinkers when it came to spending and we didn't try to impress people and that was one thing I loved about Jay the most. Next thing I know as I listen to Candace talk I get a text on my phone from Jay that says 'Damn bae listening to them makes me appreciate you". I then text him back and I say "forreal" He texted me back saying I love you and that we were on our way" and I reply back saying "I love you more." Candace asked me what I wanted to drink and told me how she drunk wine while pregnant, I was very scared to do that and I told her a mommy mocktail. She made me a mocktail and put it in a glass so I could act like I was still drinking and when the men come back inside Jay looks at me and I tell him I was drinking wine but i was just kidding and he says thats not eight ounces. I said bae I'm playing its a mocktail its just juice. He had a cup of liquor and told me to tongue dip it to taste it and I said hell no. Whenever we went to their house we always stayed late as fuck and on our car ride home Jay and I were talking and saying how we always went to their house and they never came to ours which was true. The next day I'm with Bev she and I go to the Regency mall in Jacksonville its a ghetto ass mall that used to be popping years ago so I've heard because I had never shopped there. The mall was dead as hell inside lots of closed stores. Before we went we make some potato skins in the oven I loved potato skins with some sour cream I could eat the whole fucking box and it took forever for them to cook in the first place. I took them out before it was time and as we bite into them Bev says that I should've left them in longer I said girl I'm pregnant and hungry I don't give a damn they were almost done wouldn't hurt me or the baby. We then go to the Regency mall since we had the Hurricane Irma happen and they were giving away food stamps to all Floridians. We didn't need it but I loved free anything and those were stamps better than using cash for food most definitely. They weren't asking for any kind of paperwork to show proof of who all lived in your household so shit I gave them hella names when we finally made it inside the mall to the stand. We started outside of the mall in a long ass line but it was worth the wait it didn't seem that long of a wait. Bev got her food stamp card and I got mine after that we had to pick her brother up from work. I let her drive the car I felt sick and those stomach cramps also came back in again. When we get her brother from work he drives and I said Bae can you please stop at CVS I needed some medicine because I hadn't shitted in weeks I was constipated due to taking my iron pills for my anemia even though they really didn't work and I was taking prenatal vitamins. I was also in a group chat with two girls named Jenna and Becca who I had met when we all had to take the pregnancy class on base we were all sitting by each other and talking up until the class had ended. So we had decided to exchange numbers they were both married to men in the Navy, Jenna was a year or two younger than me and Becca was twenty five they were both white and cool. We often texted a lot in our group chat to support each other with our pregnancies we all had health problems and had crazy stories with our lives which made us all bond faster plus I needed some pregnant friends. Jenna had just recovered from cancer and Becca had pregnancy complications. So I had texted the girls on what medicine(s)I should get or if they had any ideas on what would be safe for me to take while pregnant.Becca told me to get some medicine called colace. it definitely helped with the constipation and I had got a prescription for stool softeners. Candace and Jacobi invited us to Applebee's later that night for dinner. I was like damn we hung out with them a lot and it was fine but I told Jay we needed to take a break because it seems like they always invite us places but still have yet to have came back to our house. I hate people like that and on top of that we went to every date night and or cookout they invited us to.My ass didn't know how to play golf and when we arrived there Jay and I were already lit. My nineteen year old ass hanging out with them going out getting drinks like I'm twenty one no one ever asked for my

I.D. so if they didn't ask I wasn't telling. Jay and I had pulled out flask to drink out of and our waiter saw us but we also had beers and sangrias anyways at the table he looked us in our eyes and were like y'all are good, he was cool as hell and we made sure we tipped him well. Stuff like that was fun because I had never had anything like that nor had I never been on a double date before. Jay and I were making snapchats and kissing and Candace was teasing us saying "eww y'all nasty".

One of Candace's gay friends who I had never met before was always at top golf when we got there and he was cool I was cool with everyone normally. The three of us said cheers with our wine glasses and I made a snapchat video to us saying cheers. Meanwhile Jacobi was trying to make a snapchat videos from his phone while trying to get Jay's attention but he was too busy with me hugged up on me. We finally play golf which we all sucked at but it was still fun as hell. It was fun hanging out with them but like Jay said and I've said they never show up to our house or get togethers. We had ordered food and everything I was living life and fine with the life I currently had. Jay also would give me money every week and it would be the same amount that I made every two weeks at work before I was placed on bed rest. Back to Applebee's that was my favorite restaurant Candace and I and her daughter were in her car and the guys were in Jay's car. We were all supposed to link up for food and I texted Jay saying we decided to go to Applebee's and he texted back saying "what"? and that was my favorite restaurant to eat at i always ordered the same thing which was the oriental salad with the chicken fried and that location was sadly closing so it was perfect timing. We get there before the guys do. Our waitress tells us she'll see if they have it available and because I was pregnantI was craving it more and I hated being disappointed especially when I have my mouth fixed for something. Candace tells the waitress that I'm pregnant and she remembers being pregnant wanting somethingespecially food wise. So the waitress said she would hook us up and go in the kitchen to see what she could find.When she comes back she comes back empty fucking handed I said oh God. She then tells us that the people in the kitchen ate the stuff and she told them that it was for her table. So I still order my oriental salad and the guys finally arrive late as fuck. The waitress comes out to takes the guys order and Jay tells me he left his wallet at home and said don't worry about it bae I have cash I pulled out a stack of cash but Jacobi said w pay for our food I said shit well lemme order some more shit but I was joking and we all started laughing. The waitress asked Candace how old their daughter was then ask how far along I am with my pregnancy. When were in Applebees before we left I tell Jay since he's been drinking I'd drive us home. We all pack up to go and I tell Jay we need to go to my dad's house to visit him and so he could introduce himself the proper way. On the car ride home Jay and I talked about getting married and I asked him how can we get married when he's married. He said he had the papers for the divorce and he was waiting for her to give him the papers I told him I wanted to see everything and he needs to tell me everything.I know how he would get at times when he would drink liquor he starts selling dreams. He had already put me through enough since we had been together anyways. He didn't even tell me he was in therapy until later that night he was talking on the phone in the guest room and I put my ear up to the door and I got caught when he was opening the door I didn't have enough time to run away like I planned to do but I was tired of secrets and lies because after allI was keeping a secret from my parents about his marriage. It pissed me off how my dad's side of the family always tried to talk to me and preach to me hell like their lives were any better. At least me and my child's father lived together and he wasn't a scrub. He had multiple streams of income coming in between the military benefits and the post office. We were good regardless and I hate when people try to preach to you as if their lives are perfect. I remember when I first had moved out my dad's house to move in with Jay and one of my dad's sisters had texted me saying that if something happened to her brother she would be coming for me. I had the care one day when i decide to treat myself and get a pedicure and get my french tips that was my signature look for my fingernails and my toes.Jay also loved the french tip look on me he said it was sexy. As soon as I go over to the nail salon which was right up the street from home thank God because I felt sick as a dog from the pregnancy. As soon as my sat my ass down in the chair and the hot water touched my feet Jay calls me sayin to pick him up from work. I said damn I just sat down bae and Jay tells me to tell them I have to pick my man up from work. So I get up to put Jay up as I'm walking outside to the car it was hot as hell outside and my coochie cutter shorts were cutting my vagina and I had on a tank top next thing I know as I get in the car this fine ass man comes up to me and he said damn baby you look hungry heres some money I started to cuss his ass out that was rude as fuck like my bad I'm skinny and skinny with health problems and I was early in my pregnancyI looked the fuck good to be pregnant. I sure did take his money it was free money and I gave him my number he looked like a drug dealer I had no intention on using the number I just wanted the money so it was whatever. I went to go to get me some food from Mc.Donalds I actually was starving I was going to eat after I got my nails and stuff done anyways. That was free money who wouldn't take it? Dudes name was Polo and when he texted me I saved his number under a female name. Jay and I had each other's phone passcodes but never really went through each others's phones. He always kept his phone under his pillow at night and I had no knowledge if he had ever went through my phone. I picked him up from work and I drove home for him on the way home he told me to let him out and he'd walk home and he told me to go ahead back and get my nails done. I told him I would take him home but he insisted so I gave him a kiss and he got out. I told him I had dinner ready and I was telling him the house was clean. I hoped the food was good I wasn't that good at cooking at all. When I was at the nail salon I was talking on the phone with my cousin Daizhaalso known as D which I sometimes called her. We were always close and cool since we were kids we used to be ruff rider's as kids and tomboys. I always looked up to her because even though she was a single mom with two kids her kids never went without and every timeI went to Alabama I always stayed with her. We would smoke thick ass blunts and talk bout life and reflect on our life. I had last saw her months before I was pregnant they were going back to Alabama and her sister San, her husbandson, and our cousin BoBo were visiting us they had to go through Jacksonville to get home and I was already moved out my dad's house so I had to go to my dad's house unfortunately and I hadn't talked to my dad in a while at that point. I remember getting ready and I had smoked with Jerry before I went and why I don't know. It took me awhile to be able to get to the point of letting the weed stimulate my mind and relaxing my mind. When I smoked weed my mind would be racing and I would have lots of thoughts going through my head. The first time I ever smoked weed was when I was sixteen with my cousin Daizhaand her boyfriend Brandon. It was funny as hell because when I first smoked with them I was seeing shit that wasn't there my young ass. Me and Daizha were always close we could relate to so much in life she was my role model. Jerry and Jay ended up dropping me off to my dad's house. My cousin Daizha had brought some weed from Jerry and my dad had their weird look on his face at me probably because I was high and he was pissed that I had moved out. We all go to this place called Pollo Tropical I loved that restaurant the locations were only in Jacksonville it was Caribbean food and soo good and the prices were really affordable for me.Plus in Alabama they didn't have that restaurant so it was something new for them. I remember going back to the hotel with San and everyone else after we ate lunch. They were all asking questions about Jay and asking if he was controlling and saying he seemed controlling. I had to get him to pick me up I would've stayed the night but I didn't have my work clothes which I needed since I was working at burger king still I didn't have my work shoes and I still would've needed a ride. Plus everyone was being judging and trying to tell me what to do. I hate those who try to preach to you when their life isn't yet right and or complete so i called Jay to come pick me up and when he said he was downstairs everyone walked downstairs with me I was so embarrassed and annoyed by it. I blocked everyone in the family but D. I couldn't understand why they were coming for me so strongly. Especially when all my female cousins were all single moms the only one married was San. I didn't judge because you never know a person's situation marriage don't mean forever, marriage don't mean happiness and so many married people cheat. I don't know why society makes it seem like marriage equaled goals. You never know what people endure behind closed doors within their marriage or relationship. Like me for example keeping my man's biggest secret and that was his marriage. I even told Daizha what was going on between me and Jay and how he hit me. Me and Daizha could relate to so much like being raped and more. I couldn't really talk to her when Jay was home because I couldn't talk like I wanted to. I would also often talk to my best friend Tamia who lived in Norfolk, Virginia which is where we were both from . We met each other in middle school and we went to High school together. I once told Tamia how Jay had hit me it literally just came out on accident. She paused and said he better not do it again. I also told Tamia how Jay once told me that my mouth was going to cause him to wind up in jail.

It is now the month of November it seemed like when I got pregnant the months were going by slow as hell I guess because I was so early in my pregnancy. Jay's youngest brother stops by Sonny and his girlfriend Martina. I was cool with them too they were both in their twenties. I often talked to Martina about a lot and she talked to me about a lot. She was like an older sister to me. Her and Sonny had a son together and Sonny asked if I had a belly yet. I told him not yet but I'm ready and we all laughed. We always had cookouts at our house and invited Jay's family over and it was nice. Later that night I told Jay I was going to unblock my dad and call him up so we could bury the hatchet I mean a new year was approaching soon.

I didn't tell my dad when exactly we were coming I knew he hated when people just showed up to his house unannounced but I wasn't people I was his one and only daughter at that. We go to my dad's house one weekend and I forgot my dad always parked in his garage you rarely knew when he was home. But I saw a blue Honda CRV suv in front of my dads right garage and it belonged to his girlfriend Carmen she was asian and reminded me of the older version of Selena Gomez in the face. She was always cool towards me and like a rich mom to me. She always showered me in gifts and did a lot for me, she's been around since I was a kid. Jay and I get out the car and walk up to the front door and my dad answers the door instantly and my chest was pounding fast the whole time. I then say hi dad and this is Jay and I remember my dad saying Hi and Jay said to my dad "She's in good hands and taken care of". My dad then says he needs a drink and goes to the bar to get one and I stayed there and tell Jay my dad can bring me back home. Carmen comes out the bedroom and she gives me a hug and I talked to her for awhile and tell her I'm pregnant and show her the ultrasound. She was happy for me and asking to see pictures of Jay and asking all kinds of questions. I hadn't seen her in months because I didn't live there anymore. My dad takes me to get food later and takes me back to Jacksonville we lived on Normandy Blvd. The houses were nice in that area but the location wasn't. I asked my dad if he wanted to come but he said no and I said later. Before I left I told him for thanksgiving I wanted to go to Alabama with him and he said sure. We made not have been back on track but I was just ecstatic my dad and I were talking again. I go home and Jay told me he invited Candace and Jacobi over for thanksgiving and they said they couldn't make it so from there on we decided not to go their house anymore. Jay was a homebody and when first got together I thought he was boring but as we got more and more into our relationship I started to understand him more and more. Even my ex co workers from burger king were the same way. I had heard its not a good idea to hangout with people from work and to leave work at work. I heard not to date people you work with and befriend people you work with. But at burger king I had never had any true issues. it was four of us that hung out outside of work and had our group. It was Alma,DayDay, Naeand I. They were all older than me I was always the youngest in every group Alma was in her late thirties,Day-Day was in her mid twenties and Nae in her late forties. I would get DayDay to get me drinks from the liquor store often and I would always go to their houses but they never came to mine. It was weird I would even pick them up and take them home and never required gas money but it wasn't the same for me we all didn't live that far away from each other either. I don't know I guess I was raised differently my parents always taught me to give and help people. I wouldn't require someone to give me gas money especially if they don'trequire to from me but I guess to each is own. Jay and I always had cookouts and would invite them and they never showed up. Jay and I were always the type of people that never required anything from people if we had cookouts and were inviting people to our house we don't want anyone to bring anything and if you bring something thats because you wanted to but I guess that also made us different we may not have been perfect but we weren't bad people either we were decent human beings. We weren't christians or anything but definitely decent human beings and I know Bev used to always push the church thing on us a lot and I would have to keep reminding her and everyone else who tried to throw the bible to me that I've lived in Egyptand Jerusalem when my father was in the Navy I've been inside the red sea and dead sea and seen it. Even had seen the last standing four walls of the house where Jesus lived. In my mind it don't get no more holy than that. After all people read about it but I've actually seen it which is better than reading about it. Every time Jay and I brought up church and how we don't go Bev would have her input which was annoying. I hated bible thumpers and judging ass christians like I was always taught that you cant run to the church and ask God for help when you don't even pray or talk to God. I know back in October of twenty seventeen Jay,Bev and I had an argument. We were talking about Halloween and I said I celebrate Halloween and I asked how do christians say its the devil's holiday but yet make money from it selling pumpkins? Jay the says exactly and Bev and him start arguing because she said its about harvest not halloween and I really didn't care. "Christians" are always trying to force Christianity on others which is annoying But you cant help how everyone is and change their ways and ways of thinking and thats what I had to keep reminding myself every time when hanging aroundthese people. My girls were all cool for the most part i enjoyed being around them but I couldn't tell them personal stuff at times i feel like they played way too much and that why I don't like telling people personal information about myself. People talk too much and will throw things back up in your face,I'll never forget about the time thatNae had told the girls about my relationship problems that I was having at work when all I was doing was venting to her and then when I ask her if she told the girls she then says oh I'm sorry I didn't know I wasn'tsupposed to say anything and after that I never told my business again. Its one thing to tell someone something but when that someone tells others thats when I'll never tell you anything again about me. Like don't expect to get sugar expect to get shit when it comes to my personal life. We used to drink at work and smoke weed on lunch break and also used to come into work hungover. I used to open at burger king at five in the morning I would wake up drunk or high still and sometimes Jay and I would have morning sex and he would drop me off to work at times sometimes I would take the car. Also their would be times that I would have the car and I would have to pick Jay up from work. There was this one dude at burger king I worked with named Sharrod and we used to take lots of smoke breaks too he would sometimes chill with us after work he had always had a crush on me. But I didn't like him in that way I looked at him as more of a friend and he was my age I never dated guys my age. So that was a pact me and Jay made to spend more time together and home. We even slowed down on the eating out because we always ate out. I was happy that Jay had also slowed down on the drinking with me being pregnant as well. We always would drink and smoke from the time i met him to the time I found out that I was pregnant. The next day Jay had went to work and I just happened to go into my underwear drawer and thats when I seen a pair of underwear that don't belong to me and I decided to take a optic and send to Jay and that motherfucker left me on read so I texted and asked whose panties they were and he left me on read again so I said okay cool to myself. When he comes home he doesn't say anything to me and all day all I could do was cry I was really losing my mind in that house it was already bad enough that I was pregnant and I had to sit in the house and couldn't work and I didn't have my own car and was always depressed even though I didn't show it and those pregnancy symptoms were kicking my ass and not only was I pregnant but by a married man. As I laid in bed hurting and when I hear the room door I acted like I was sleep and I had on lingerie and Jay came over to me and pulled the blanket back to see what I had on and he put and I opened my eyes when I heard the room door close and I had opened my eyes and a tear came down. He was being sneaky the wife calling and texting. He'd no longer letting me use his laptop or touch his phone which I had the passcode to. If I touched his phone he would quickly grab it back and had a look of panic on his face. I would often think that this isn't the way to raise a baby and I was losing my mind. I stayed in bed the whole night I never really had a reason to leave the room I had my snacks on my side of the bed and later that night I wake up to pee and I said to Jay so you're not going to talk to me huh? He replied back to me and said its not working between us and hell give me and the baby the house and leave and we can just co parent. I asked him "so you'llreally leave me alone with your baby"? I told him I didn't want a baby he did and i did this for him. All the nights of not being able to actually enjoy the sex because all he could ask me is if the sperm had stayed in my pussy or not. All the yeast infections I was getting from him always nutting inside of me. All the pressure of having sex twenty four seven before my period happened. I yelled that to him and I started crying. ThenI told him I wanted us to work and give our child a two parent home and I told him I'm still trying to get myself together and establish myself better mentally and in general. I told him how I did everything for him I did his school work we were both taking up computer science and I did his english classes for him and I did all his essays for him and I even did wife duties around the house even though I wasn't a wife and I get I didn't work but between him and Jerry they were both disgusting all the dishes piled up everywhere in the kitchen all the fucking time and I vacuumed more than a household that has a toddler in it and I cooked so much food that didn't even last for two days. And he thought he was just going to put a baby in me and then leave me in that house by myself hell no. I told him I would put him on child support to get a reaction from him of course and he said he didn't care and his baby would be taken care of. I just couldn'tbelieve we had really got to that point. And yes he gave me money, He cooked for mewined and dined me and paid for anything I wanted but thats also because he had more money than me and he could do that and I greatly appreciated it and him but I also was hurt he was married and when I found out I could've left but I wouldn't leave. I did take Jay to Ruth Chris in Jacksonville he had never been there before and that was one of my favorite restaurantsI loved the location back home in Virginia but the one in Jacksonville was okay and I had wanted to treat Jay and do something nice for him for once I did buy him things here and there. But it was my turn to treat us going out to eat something I had never done the whole relationship. He was at work the day I took him to Ruth Chris and I remember how ecstatic we both were all day and he was saying he was going to try to finish work early so we could make it before Ruth Chris closed. While he was at work I was home cleaning the whole house and watching a show on Netflix called Queen of the South. that was my show and the main character of the show she was a bad bitch. He had finally called me that day when he had a for sure time he would be off work so I continued eating and cleaning the day I took him to Ruth Chris I wasn't pregnant so I was drinking while cleaning. When I finished cleaning I had decided to shower and slowly but surely take my time and get ready. Ruth Chris was a upscale restaurant plus I knew wed take optics so I wanted to look like a grown woman and prettier than I normally looked. I slipped on my robe when I had gotten out the shower I had braids in my hair so I decided to put it in a big ass side bun it was pretty and perfect and I go into on closet on my side and find an outfit to year. I pull out awhite long sleeve shirt that showed a little midriff and showed off on my shoulders a little without being too much and I grabbed some blue fitted dress pants and my black heels with lace on them sexy and of course I had my french tips on my fingernails and toes. I lay my outfit out on the bed and in the meantime decide to do my makeup which was just eyeshadow and lipstick that was the only makeup i wore and knew how to do perfectly. Just as I'm looking for eyeshadow to apply Jay comes into the room and I asked him what color should I put on and he chose the color blue for my eyeshadow and my lipstick was a soft pink to blend in with my lips and look natural with a little bit of lipgloss over the lipstick to make it shine and pop. So I help Jay look for an outfit to wear he was going to wear a suit but I didn't like the ones he was picking out so he just picks a polo shirt to wear and some nice pants to wear and he had his hair twisted so he would wear a durag that shit was sexy I swear we thought we were in the nine nine and early two thousands. We had the best music and the clothes from that era. It was something about when he wore that durag that was sexy and a turn on i really used to get wet from him having it on and I would have visions and flashbacks of us having sex. I put on some Victoria's secret perfume then I get dressed we take a bunch of optics and snpachats and he drives us there we hold hands while he drives and he kisses my hand and says how he loves me and I tell him I love him more. When we get to Ruth Chris as we walk in holding hands and looking around it was packed as hell and a bunch of white people when I saw a black couple that was dressed like us in my mind I said aye and some of the white women were smiling at me and I smiled back. I noticed the black couple in front of us the host told the man he had to take off his durag and

I looked at Jay and asked him if he heard what the host told the dude in front of us? Jay said yea B its fine I'll just take my durag off too and he did. So when we walk over the the host he greets us then walks us to our table I sit beside Jay. Someone comes over quickly and asked us what beverages did we want. Jay orders an alcoholic beverage and the guy didn't ask for his I.D. so I try to order an alcoholic beverage and he asked for my I.D. I forgothow young I looked and i said shit I left him at home and Jay says shes always forgetting something to the dude,I didn't stress I was going to try some of Jay's drink anyways. As me and Jay browse the menu we both were like damn becauseof the prices Ruth Chris was expensive and I had told him that and I also told him the proportion sizes weren't the best but he was worth spending that kind of money on. When the waiter comes back to take our order we Jay and I both ask him about the proportion sizes it was funny as hell because Jay ate a lot he was very much thick like I liked my men. But I told him don't worry about it just get what he wanted and as much as he wanted. Plus we were the type of people no matter what restaurant we went to eat at we would always go home and eat again anyways. It didn't take long for our food at all and when it comes out we ask the guy to take optics of us he takes a lot and they really came out nice. The food really proportion really was small as fuck but it was whatever. Jay and I also always recorded videos of our food and took optics of it too to post on social media. When we finished eating dinner I asked Jay if he wanted any dessert and he leans in close to me for a kiss and says he wants me for dessert looking me in my eyes. I was paying for dinner and he tells me to give him my debit card so they don't think he ain't shit and he has me paying for the meal. The tab came out to ninety dollars for the two of us which wasn't bad to be honest. I been to restaurants that costed a lot more but were also way nicer but I just wanted to treat my man and tell him thank you and show him that I appreciate him. We go home and on our way home we talk about getting married and Jay said he had a surprise for me I just had to wait a little longer. When we get home we go to our room and Jay throws me on the bed and takes my clothes off and kisses me head to toe. So I never minded doing anything for him and I never used him or abused him like his past bitches.I just wantedto be loved unconditionallyhappymarried without any extra baggage. I told him I was going to go out of town for Thanksgiving and that'll give us time apart I mean we spent a lot of time together waking up together,going to bed together,watching tv together,going out together and I told him everything even though I didn't feel like he did the same as far as telling me things. But I told him I didn't want to argue anymore or fight last time we argued Ipushed him into the wall in the living room and he put a hole in the wall and when his mother came over she asked what happened and we were both silent. I know he told me stories of him and Carol physically fighting and putting each other in jail and bailing each other out of jail a few times which I didn't want to happen to us. It was already bad enough hat we had both hit each other something that should've never happened I had always had a anger problem though. And he said he loved me and wasn't going to leave me. We kiss and I go to bed, in the morning I wake up and cook breakfast for everyone. I start packing my bags to go to AlabamaI had literally blocked and deleted everyone so I didn't know how it was going to go drama wise and in my mind I was like everyone was preaching to me and lecturing me but all my aunts their kids live at home with kids at least I lived with the man who had got me pregnant and he wasn't a dead beat even if we didn't last at least he said he would leave me the house and he even had my name on credit cards and his bank accounts and stuff. And hell he did everything for me and I didn't ask nor expect anything it was the little things for me. I didn't use him nor did I want to but I noticed myself texting Polo whenever we and argued and Jay claimed one time I changed my phone password even though I didn't. But it was nice feeling wanted by another man who I didn't argue with Polo and I used to talk on the phone and I was so lonely and really going through it with Jay at times that Polo even offered me to move in with him I couldn't do that becauseI had a baby in me and I'm sure he was going to want something in return as fine as he was. What man is doing stuff for free without wanting something in return? One time in text I told Polo I couldn't leave Jay for him and he got mad and it was what it was I don't kiss ass and I'm not kissing ass of a man who I have no tides to either. So I deleted his number and blocked him which was for the best because had Jay found out he probablywould've started accusing me of cheating on him and denying being the father of our unborn child. Plus I did love Jay and I really wanted us to work out. One time Jay accused me of cheating but told me never to ever bring it up to Jerry or anyone else. Sometimes things aren't as they seem and I always told Jay that because I know it may have seemed wrong but I would never cheat on Jay and I never did. Yes, I was texting and talking to another man because I was lonely and we were going through a rough patch but there were no feelings. But one day Jerry and I were in his room smoking weed and watching Netflix movies he was like a big brother but I considered him as my brother in law because I knew Jay and I would get married one day. Jerry and I would always smoke like two blunts and talked about life in general and when he goes out the room to go into the kitchen he comes back and says Jay wants you and I come out the room and Jay sees me and when I go into our bedroom he coms into our bedroom and asked me what the fuck was I doing in the room with Jerry and I said we just smoked and we had been watching Netflix movies and he just came back in the room to tell me you wanted me to come here. He was so upset about it and it really wasn't as it seemed but I guess we shouldn't have been in the room smoking in the first place. Later on that week we make a trip to St. Augustine just Jay and I. I hated arguing with him we would both say a lot of hurtful things to each other and it was really time to stop like that was no way to bring a baby into the world. We had to stop putting our hands on each other, Every timeI yelled or cried or was depressed my stomach had started cramping. We went to St Augustine holding hands and walking until we both found something we wanted to do and Jay was drinking a mike's hard I let him drink it because he had been doing good with not drinking a lot and I really appreciated him putting that effort in. Other couples that were older were looking at us smiling and i would smile back. We went into a place called Ripley's believe it or not it was packed per usual. I had been there as a kid but not a adult with friends or a boyfriend and it was a nice feeling. We go into the museum and Jay pays and i stop him before he pays and ask if they honor a military discount and the person at the counter says yes so I show my military I.D. and we go inside I was amazed it was so much to see and I learned a lot that I didn't know. We take videos and optics and post on snapchat. After awhile of wandering around Jay pulls out a little box and opens it. It was a gorgeous oval cut diamond ring and he asked me me to marry him. I said yes you knowI wanted to marry you and we're going to get married but after you're divorced. I told him yess and I had kissed him and hugged him but I told him I didn't want to wear it yet or announce it to anyone yet I wanted to wait until Christmas to announce it to our friends and family. Plus on top of that the ring was the wrong size it was too big and my ring finger was a size six. We stayed in St Augustine until we finished touring Ripley's and I told Jay I would drive home which I did since he had been drinking even though he wasn't drunk but still wanted to be more cautious especially since I had his baby in my belly and on the way home I asked Jay what he wants for Christmas because when I go to Alabama I'm going to go black Friday shopping especially since I knew my dad was going to pay for everything, My dad paid for anything and everything I wanted I was definitely a spoiled brat. I had already ordered Jay some t shirts from an app called AliExpress a month ago I hated how majority of their shit came from China,Shit took way too long to come in the mail and sometimes the sizes of the clothes from that website were wrong. I wore an extra small or small and that shit would be so tight you could see my ribs literally. I ordered Jay T shirts that had Game of Thrones the words on it and the show symbol on it. He loved that show I had watched it from time to time with him illegally we knew how to do all that stuff after all we were getting computer science degrees I was into computer programming and networking classes they were hella easy. Later that day I started packing to go to Alabama with my dad I packed so Jay could take me to my dad's house it was easier to spend the night at my dad's house. Alabama was only five hours away but as much as I hated road trips I had to get a break and could use a new change of scenery. Jay takes me to my dad's house and I kiss him and tell him I love him and I go into my dad's house. Its already night time I sit with my dad for awhile in the living room and watch a lifetime movie, my dad and I always watched lifetime movies and scary movies together. Before I went to bed I called Jay on FaceTime to see what he was doing and he told me he was going out with Jacobi. I looked at him and said Bae I thought we made a deal not to hangout with them when they ask us to for awhile. He said Jacobi got kicked out the house and he was gonna sleep on the couch at our house just for the night.

I said okay and I said I'm going to bed I'm tired and full and I'm tired of getting up to pee so good night love you. and Jay said good night. The next morning I wake up at five in the morning to get ready and my dad was already ready hell even on his off days and during the week he wakes up at four in the morning and has a whole routine he does everyday in the same order. So once I get ready my dad puts my duffle bag in the trunk and we head to Alabama. I had my beats headphones and listened to music on my iPod touch which I still had and it was in great condition and at least I didn't have to worry about the connection messing up because I didn't need that to listen to music. I didn't know how this trip would go I didn't really deal with all my cousins I only was close with my cousin Daizhaand we hadn't been talking because I texted one our cousin's Mercedes about Daizha and how her and her sister San were picking on me and I even said how D smoked weed and none of them were perfect and just went on a full ass rant. I don't know why I texted Mercedes I should've known she was going to go back and tell which was fine. My dad's family was always very messy and had too much drama but I guess it being a small town there isn'tshit to do but eat, drink and talk about people. I know as kids Mercedes would often ask me why did I talked the way I did and by that she meant white and proper. I was from up North first of all and I always talked proper I didn't think I was all that but hell I was a kid at least I was talking proper cant get mad about that. Wouldn't people want kids to talk proper? But I was glad I didn't live in Alabama as kids it was fun but when i got older I started to noticed lot and understand a lot that was happening and going on. Its so much that happened to me as kid that everyone is unaware of and it's just a boring small town there's nothing to do at all I hated it but I loved the food and seeing some of my cousins. The drama started between me and my Daizha was because one Mercedes told her what I said and two my mother told me that Daizhawas talking about me on Facebook I didn't have at the time. It was petty as hell and to be honest I could've just asked Daizha but Ididn't so it was whatever I was pregnant and had my own issues I wasn't about to be arguing with people nor fighting I was already a hot head. Daizha's mom told everyone that I was pregnant who didn't know and you couldn't tell anyways. I told Daizhahey when she came over but of course she was mad and she spoke but with an attitude which was fine. Daizhatold me to ride with her to get the ice and I did and I knew that the conversation was going to come up and She asked "Why the fuck would I talk about you"? I the said my mom said she has y'all on Facebook and she said my mom isn't her facebook friend and showed me her facebook and the crazy part of it all my mom also lied sometimes so I don't know why the fuck I even listened to my mom anyways what was i thinking?? And I didn't know why I sent the message to Mercedes I didn't forget when she was talking about my mom and accidentally sent the message to me but it was old. The first night of being in Alabama for Thanksgiving I went with my aunt Annie and her son Rakeem and we were shopping around at places. I wanted to surprise Jay so later I went to Walmart with my dad and I knew we needed a new Tv I called Jay on FaceTime and asked him what size tv did we currently have in the living room. I told him they had a sale on television and he said he was about to put some money in my account for the tv but my dad said not to worry about it and ended up buying the tv with his Walmart credit card. And when he check out we realize that in Alabama their taxes is high as hell the tv went up all the way to two hundred and forty when it was on sale for two hundred dollars. My dad hated spending extra money especially in taxes but he still got the tv anyways. I had to help him put the tv in the car my skinny pregnant ass i always had small skinny arms. That was his Christmas gift from me. I stayed at my aunt Annie's house the whole time I was in Alabama I loved staying at her house, I often would talk to my aunt Annie anyways I could tell her things and she wouldn't tell what I told her. I remember when I asked her if she could talk to my dad because he was tripping about the pregnancy like yes I was young but people get pregnant younger than me and its alwayssomeone in a worst situation than you which is what i always reminded myself before complaining about anything and my pregnancy was planned but forced. I went back to Walmart with my cousin Mari and his uncle Denzel I didn't get anything but Walmart was packed and people were really arguing and fighting and in that city in Alabama which was Troy they literally only one Walmart and one everything for that matter which was crazy as hell!! I had never seen nothing like that before. Nothing at all to do I was so glad I had no longer lived there everyone was just so damn messy it be your own family which makes it worse,everyone knows everyone and tells all your business just no privacy nor place I wanted to live long term.

We stayed in Alabama for a few days and I FaceTimed Jay the whole time I was in Alabama and one night he texted me saying he was horny and wanted some nudes so I sent him some nudes and some of our homemade sex tapes we had. I would watch them sometimes at night and get turned on from watching them and I used to joke around with Jay about leaking them on porn hub while we were playing about it I waslow key serious about doing it. We were heading back to Jacksonville the next day and A bitch by the name of Cameron texted me asked if Jerry could sell her some weed and I didn't even reply because she was such a bitch likeI wanted to pistol whip her. She always thought we were gonna give her free weed and Jerry wanted her but she wasn't doing shit but trying to use him anyways and the only bitch in our house that got free weed was me the woman of the house the bitch that cooked and cleaned and make sure the house was in order and bills were getting paid on time. The problem I had with Cameron was she never wanted to pay for weed that we gave her and never wanted to pitch in but all for smoking up someone's else's shit.Even Sharrod said the same thing about her smoking up his shit and trying to get over and not wanting to match. Even when Cameron took me home from work I let the bitch smoke a full blunt with me and she asked for gas money like bitch what? where's my ten dollars for smoking my blunt and she always had a attitude. I would always say these Jacksonville people different up North we aren't like this and I don't ask for gas money taking my friends home when they live up the street from me like how is that putting a damper in my gas? And if I invite someone out why the fuck would I asked someone for gas money?when I'm the one asking you to hangout thats why Ididn't really have friends. When Cameron had took me home from work that one day I invited her in and let her smoke again for free and the bitch acted like she had a attitude she asked for water and I was getting her a bottle of water because I've always been the type of person I don't let no one drink off my real cups and glass or eat off my real spoons,forks,etc. This bitch literally said I'll take a bottle of water like imagine if we didn't have a bot-tle water but bitch thats what you were getting. My patience with people but she don't be talking shit when she getting free weed. Never had lots of friends especially not females friends but when Cameron was ready to leave I walked her out and she asked me am I good and I said yea. I didn't vent to everyone and even then cant tell people everything about you.

My dad and I head back to Florida and since we have to come through Jacksonville and on the interstate the Normandy blvd. exit where Jay and I live comes up first and I called Jay up and asked if he was home and we were up the street and my dad was gonna need some help bringing the tv in the house. Jay said yea he was home and I told him we were up the street and he comes out to help and tells my dad thanks for the tv and asked how much he owed my dad and my dad said not to worry about it. My dad would also often make jokes to me saying don't know you know a Haitian man is the worst man on Earth to get with he would even make jokes about how he was going to send a bomb to the house and when he tells me to run out run but he was just joking. It is now December second who would've thought it would be the last night i saw Jay, that night everyone was at our house Bev,Manew, Nicey, Bev's boyfriend John, and I. Jay and I were mad at each other I cannot even remember why. But Him and Bev's boyfriend decide to go out and Bev and John were actually arguing too that night. So the guys decide to go out and I tell Jay no drinking and text me when they get to their destination. He said he would and It was the girls and I left. Eventually I tell them I'm going to call it a night I said I'mnauseous and feel like shit. I tried not to cuss too much in front of the two younger sisters and although they knew we smoked we never let them see us smoke at all. I didn't wake out throughout the night to pee at all but when Jay got ready for work the next morning i was sleep but moving and he covered me up with the blanket and he got ready for work. We normally would kiss every morning but I was so sleepy I didn't get up to kiss Jay because, I was still mad at him and I used to take him lunch sometimes to work. At times when I was working he would even cook dinner for me sometimes it was things like that I loved becauseI never asked him he just did it for me. Hell Jay taught me how to cook and he would go all out for me when he cooked for me. I loved that Haitian food.It is now December third twenty seven-teen I was with my father at a flea market called Pecan Park in Jacksonville. My father and I always went to flea markets together for fresh fruits and veggies every since I was a kid and it kinda reminded me for the ones we would go to together overseas as a kid. I had fun with my dad doing things like that it was the little things I enjoyed doing with my dad. Plus being on bed rest at times I really had to get out the house and Jay and I were still mad at each other well at least as far as I knew I was still mad at him. I found it funny how Jay didn't text or call me while at work but I assumed he was mad at me. When my dad goes into the gas station I get a phone call from Jerry I was thinking before I answered what he wanted. I picked up the phone and said hello. Jerry then asked me if I was driving I said no and asked whats wrong and he said Jay is in the hospital and i asked what happened. He said he couldn't tell me and to get here and i asked what hospital and he said Orange Park hospital then the phone hung up. I was saying hello over and over I even tried to call back but no answer. I was trying to prevent myself from crying and my stomach had tightenedas I was talking to God saying please don't take him because that very moment when Jerry didn't tell me what was wrong but instead told me he couldn't tell me and get here I knew it was something serious. When my dad come back I started yelling saying come on hurry up we have to go to Orange Park medical Jay is there something happened but they wouldn't tell me what happened. We were all the way at Pecan Park that was by the damn airport far as hell and we had to go all the way back to Orange Park. I was sad and my stomach was in knots it was already bad enough I was pregnant while I had knots in my stomach. I was thinking the worse the whole car ride to the hospital. When I get there the whole family was there and we were in the waiting room I was calling and texting telling them I was at the hospital. Iwaited and waited and waited and I heard this one girl on the phone crying in the waiting room with us talking about how someone had a stroke and seizure at work and they worked together my dad tapped on me to listen to her but I didn't want to assume anything. Then the family comes to get me to come in the room and in the room it was Bev,ManewNiceyJerry and their mom and dad. Everyone was crying and I stopped and looked I started crying and I had dropped my bag. I walk over to Jay and look at him and I thought he was already dead but I didn't want to say it. His mom tells me to come sit down and I did I stopped crying then start back crying. The doctors then come back in and they say that they have to move Jay to another room then we can see him again. I walked out crying to my dad but I still didn't know what happened to him. I couldn't even ask what happened to him either. My dad told me he had to run home real quick and i told him i'll stay at the hospital. I then called my mom and she always answered the phone in a rude way when she was stressed out and that moment and time wasn't time to rude I was sad,pissed,crying,shocked and I could go on and on with the emotions I was feeling inside of me. I told her Jay was in the hospital and i think he was dead he wasn't moving or breathing at all. She didn't make any comment or say anything for a while, then she what WHAT!!! and asked what happened? I told her I didn't know anything. and I started crying then more and more and I told her I would call her back. The sad part is that when I was telling her the bad news I didn't even ask her if she was driving because I needed someone to talk to. My mother was in fact driving and she told me she had to pull over when i started telling her what was going on. More of the family and some friends come up to the hospital and it was really packed and I was the main one standing beside Jay the entire time,Holding his hand and crying.They finally let us go into the room to see Jay and one of Bev's friends by the name of Bianca told me I needed to sit down. I called Candace and Jacobi to come to the hospital and I was crying on the phone telling them something happened to Jay crying loudly and badly I told them we're at Orange Park medical which they didn't live far from at all. They honestly got there fast as fuck and when they get in the room they spoke to everyone and started crying, they both knew Jay way longer than I did. The crazy part is Jay and I hadn't even been together for a full year yet and i kept thinking to myself all that had happened in the months that we were together. I got up again to stand by Jay crying and Bianca asked me where was I going and told me to sit back down. I was sitting there trying to think about what happened to Jay I knew he didn't have any serious health problems I did know that he had high blood pressure something that he had wanted to keep between him and I and I did just that but I was making sure he had taken his medicine everyday. I mean he did eat a lot of salty foods like they're food was really salty and spicy it was too much for me. Jay had once told me he was going to stop taking the high blood pressure medicine because it made it hard for his dick to get hard and we were trying for a baby. He was supposed to go back on the medicine once he got me pregnant but he said he didn't want to, especially because we were still having sex while I was pregnant. I then had a flashback while sitting there crying and in the flashback it was Jay and I in the car talking bout our health problems and he said to me he was going to die before me and I asked him why would he say that and I told him you don't know that because I have more health problems than you. I had told him about my microcytic anemia which is due to the lack of normal red blood cells I have, the symptoms I experienced were fatigue,weak,tired,cold,loss of appetite, weight losscold all the time, my bones even felt cold it alreadywasn't cute my ribs showed and you could kinda see them through my shirts a little which wasn't cute or attractive at all the time sometimes even everyday. My dad would even say I was so skinny I looked like a crack head which I didn't find funny especially considering being on crack isn't cute nor funny and I also had severe health problems but I was perfectly happy being skinny. My dad was always tying to tell me that I needed to eat more food. It pissed me off when people tell a skinny person to eat like what the fuck y'all think i do? starve myself? I ate a lot of food but I was literally six feet fall and with health problems so food wasn't the answer to my problems. it wasn't the food's fault i wasn't gaining weight it was the health problems not to mention I also had a high metabolism. My dad also had acid reflux so why he made that joke about me being skinny like a crack head I'm not sure. Literally the anemia and acid reflux made me not have a appetite. Hell that acid reflux made the food sometimes. My mom would even joke me saying i looked like a crack whore or malnourished. Hell she's the reason I have anemia problems. I would get so many iron infusions for it which would work for the moment then months later I would have to get more iron infusions. The medicines didn't seem to work for me I took lots of vitamins and watched what I ate I would try to avoid the foods that also weren't good for my type of anemia but it didn't seem to help me at all. It was even a struggle for me to workout everyday all I did as far as workouts were crunches and I jogged a mile. But it was hard to even workout because my blood was already iron deficient and carried less oxygen. I also had sickle cell trait and acid reflux that heart burn and acid coming up from stomach making me throw up was no joke. The acid reflux and anemia were both something that ran in the family. I know you can die from anything but I assumed I would've died first because of the severe health problems I had.

When I'm done having my flashback as I stare into space Candace whispers me to me and ask if Jay was dead. I just shrugged my shoulders and turn away from her I knew he was dead though all the praying and crying I did wasn't going to bring him back. My mom always told me if its your time to go its your time to go and there's nothing you can do because as much as it sucks we're all going to die. Jay also had a weird smell on him it kinda smelled bad it was like the smell of death on him. There were tubes on him and he was on life support that was the only thing keeping him alive even though I think he was already dead. I just couldn't believe this shit the man I was pregnant by the man that asked me to marry him the man that I was supposed to marry and be with was dead. the messed up part we had a argument hours before I saw him in this hospital I never got a chance to say I was sorry or even tell him that I loved him, I never got a chance to get one last hug or kiss from him when he was alive. At that very moment I just found out what it meant to never go to bed mad at your significant other or anyone for that matter. You never know when someone is going to die. I then started to telling my best and closet friends in Florida what happened to Jay and my friends back home in Virginia. Candace and Jacobi hug me and say they are going to leave, they were still crying when they left. Bev and Bianca take me to Mc.Donald's to get food I had no appetite. I felt sick to my stomach I wanted to throw up I thought I was dreaming I couldn't believe it I just kept telling myself this isn't real. I told them I wasn't hungry but they got me food anyways I had to feed the baby. They told me I had to eat and the half of Jay was baking in me which was true. I kept thinking in my mind like Damn I had a baby for someone who wanted a baby I never wanted to be pregnant at nineteen and he dies. I asked Bev what happened to Jay she said someone found his body and took him to the hospital he had a stroke and a seizure while delivering mail and collapsed. At that very moment I knew he was dead because we don't know how long he was out there until that person found his body it could've been hours. I've seen miracles happen but when I smelt that smell of death on him I knew he was dead. I still kept telling myself this wasn't happening. At the hospital a bitch by the named of Jamea came up there she hugged me why I don't know as if I forgot when she texted Jay saying how he had got me pregnant and it was supposed to be her that was pregnant by him not me.

Like bitch you've clearly known Jay longer than me which means nothing I always told people you can know someone for years and still not know everything about someone and you never will know everything about a person. Like how he known her for years and had no idea she was in love with him so he told me. She wasn't cute and had nothing going for herself just another woman wanting to be someone's wife to say they got married and those would be the bitches to actually make it with the wife title. But I wasn't fake nor did I do fake shit but I didn't want to cause a scene like the man was already dead. I did have so many thoughts in my head i actually had deja vu a few times when Jamea hugged me. I saw myself snatching her wig off and pushing her into the wall then slapping her hell I even saw me hitting her with a chair. I was strong and powerful to be so skinny I often felt like Left Eye from the group TLC. But nonetheless my thoughts were a powerful thing and every time I had deja vu and seen myself do something I would shake my head to snap out of it because I knew me I also knew what I was capable of. It was just funny how someone who was always around us then at our house had a crush on my man something I never knew. Even when she would come over I would tell her she had to go home it was getting late. I was never jealous of any woman especially not a Haitian woman. I noticed some Haitians would identify their race as Haitian and not black. My mother was Puerto Rican and Black with fair skin if she was still identified as a Black woman why do some Haitians always say their race is Haitian and not black? its so annoying likewhat? I noticedHaitians,-Jamaicans,Africans all did that and I know everyone from those countries aren't all Black but I'm talking about the Black community. I wander around and walk around by myself throughout the hospital every time I got myself to stop crying I started back crying all over again because I couldn't believe what happened. I met some random lady who asked what was wrong with me she worked in the hospital and honestly talking to people helped me get it out but it didn't make me feel better but I didn't want to be rude to someone trying to help however there's a difference between being helpful and nosy. She asked me what was wrong and I told her without talking too much I never volunteered anymore than when people needed to know about me. Even if they assumed something I go with the flow no correction needed or explanation. But I had just told her my fiancé died and I'm pregnant and she walked with me back to the room where everyone was and she had asked how old was I because I looked young I told her I was nineteen and when we make it back to the room with everyone else she asked everyone if they could all step out and give me some time alone with Jay. when they all left out and closed the door I didn't even know what to say to him because I was so sad and in shock i just looked and started crying again i grabbed Jay's hand and I said "Babe I love you and I'm so sorry and

I love and please don't leave us". I said you cant leave me and Junior which is the name he gave the baby because he thought we were having a boy. I starting crying and begging Jay to wake up. I screamed don't leave us and I was jumping up and down. Then everyone came back in the room ad was trying to calm me down and the black lady I had been walking with the whole time and talking to asks us if we wanted to pray and if we wanted her to pray over Jay, we said sure and she did. Bianca even told Jay to wake up and stop playing he did play so much and everyone knew that about him he loved to play and joke around. Even Martina told Jay to stop playing she then said Jean which was his real name if you can hear me wake up. He didn't wake up or move next thing i know the doctor comes in and says that Jay's wife Carol wanted to take him off life support i was so pissed off and yes I knew we weren't married but so what she was trying to kill him like damn that was only day one of him being in the hospital hadn't even been a full day and I was pregnant by him. I wanted all smoke with Carol I had another deja vu moment my thoughts were again always powerful i couldn't control what I was thinking and what I wanted to do to her. I had a vision that I shot Carol all these visions kept coming to my mind I had to get out of there. I knew she was legally and technically the wife but the bitch made a decision like that all the way from Texas like damn. Jay had me on his bank accounts and an authorized user on his credit cards and debit cards. i had the pins to them and the passcode to his phone. I know he was going to put my name on the house and I kept procrastinating he literally asked for my social security number everyday almost, I don't know why I didn't give it to him. Even Jay's brother Sonny was mad as fuck he was asking why did they tell Carol about Jay. She never loved him anyways and was always unhappy with him too. It's about eight o'clock at night at this point and the nurse tells Bev she has to leave as we're walking out anyways and Bev said "fuck y'all". My dad was in the lobby waiting for me he had lived right around the corner from the hospital anyways. I decided to stay with my dad overnight and the next day i would go get my items from the house I would no longer have any control of or be able to stay in. I knew it was going to be hard to walk into that house knowing Jay was dead. The only man i've dated that I ever loved and had a real relationship with was gone. And I was going to be single parent something I didn't want to be. I got that married with kids or not you could still be a single mom but that wasn't supposed to be the case for me I didn't want him to die even if I was going to be a single mom. Even if Jay had got to meet our baby in person I would've felt better than if he didn't at all. One of Bev's cousin or whoever the fuck she was literally said to me that her baby daddy is in prison and how she's sad and embarrassed her kids have to see him in prison. Like bitch at least he isn't dead and I told her well that's good he's alive and you're kids can always visit him. I never wanted to bury my child's father while pregnant. My child didn't get to meet him and for some reason this random ass bitch whose opinionI didn't ask for still continues to tell me she'd rather her baby daddy be in the grave than jail like what??? Sometimes people need to learn to shut the fuck up and keep their comments to themselves because I was having another deja vu moment and that time i was actually in the home where guns are and I saw me pistol whooping her with that nine millimeter. Like I hated how she tried to tell me I'm young and can find love again like yes thats true but thats something you find overtime and I was trying to understand what age had to do with it. Whether I was younger or older it didn't mean I had to find someone else again at all. Clearly age don't have a limit at all with it comes to death so I don't know what being young has to do with finding love again. When you're in my predicament and you lose a loved one while pregnant who wants different men around them let alone in their home. It's never that serious to me and I hate when people also said to me how I was too pretty to be that sad and depressed and I could find love again. I would tell them love don't live here no more and I'm pregnant why the fuck would I be looking for love when Jay hadn't even been buried in the ground we hadn't even had his wake yet like i needed everyone to shut the fuck up because I almost spazzed out. I hate ignorant ass people especially black people the ones making our race look a fucking mess. It's crazy how I told Nae,DayDay,Alma bout what happened they were barely there for me I'm like damn I need to grieve but I didn't want to be lonely. I couldn't even talk on the phone without crying, I was four months pregnant and I had to get my shit together and fast I knew I couldn't be depressed trying to raise a baby I had a lot of shit I had to get in line before the baby came along. I didn't want to eatsleep, go to my appointments or anywhere. I was so lost without Jay.

The next day at my dad's house when I woke up crying and i asked myself I was dreaming I even picked up my phone to call and text Jay to see if he would answer but he didn't answer my calls or text me back. I had to face it that it wasn't a dream and I couldn't do anything about it he was gone and wasn't coming back. As I sit at the end of my bed just staring into space I see Jay appear beside me and he put his hand on my back and rubbed it. As I turn my head he was really beside me, but when I lean in for a hug he disappeared.That had never ever happened to me before when a person died then they appear sitting beside me or maybe it happened I just didn't know they were there I started crying and screaming and my dad comes knocking on my door asking if I'm okay and i said no I'm not why did you ask that dumb question. My child is going to grow up with no dad,He was jus taken away from us.When it comes to death i hate when people ask me if I'm okay or tell me its going to be okay. Like no one could make me feel better after this situation has happened to me and I knew of no one who could relate to the situation. Icouldn't even get out of bed I kept thinking in my head I have no purpose or reason to be here. Bev comes to my dad's house to come pick me up so I can go get my stuff from the house i'll no longer be staying at and I gave her gas money. I kept thinking in my mind damn I left my dad's house just move back months later I was thinking damn i cant get away from my dad. I loved my dad to death but I felt like Britney Spears when it comes to having a controlling dad and him trying to control money andeverything you do in life. Who wants to be controlled like you're a animal?? I hate in the Black community how when you talk up andstand up for yourself you're called disrespectful or everyone is like "oh your dad loves you and he doesn't want to see you make any mistakes". I hate that shit like everyone makes mistakes thats life no matter what age you are you'll aways make mistakes. No one wants their parents or parent in my case controlling their life and everything they do within their life. I would often hear so many people say how I have a good and I mean I did have a good dad but there were some inner issues within himself he needed to work on. He had a boundary issue which is why I left in the first place. I got offended as fuck because Bev's friend Bianca really asked me if I needed her help getting section eight like what?? I hated bitches like her welfare recipients.Nothing is wrong with governmentassistanceyou gotta get all you can when you can especially those who really needed it. There was nothing wrong with getting government its a problem when those benefits have you. I hate people who don't want to try to work or better themselves like its okay to get things but why aren't you trying to work or do anything. She was cool in the beginning but thats the vibe I got from her. and I was absolutely right about her. I couldn't stand those who let the government benefits consume their life. I was so offended when Bianca asked me if I needed her help applying for government benefits like my dad didn't make one hundred thousand dollars yearly. My dad had it like that and my child wasn't growing up on government benefits.Nothing against it but i was all for working hard to get where I needed for my child and I. I definitely was going to do what needed to be done as well, Me and Jay always talked when I first got pregnant how our kid will never going to need or want anything in life and we were going to work hard to fulfill that type of life for our baby I had a little money too. I left home for a few months and lived the best life ever just for me to have to move back home and with nothing but what I left with and some items I grabbed for the baby. I posted about what happened on my snapchat I posted some optics of Jay and I and everyone was sending messages asking what happened. I even made a post on my snapchat that said "why God"? and Jay's youngest sister Nicey responded to the post and said "Don't do that". Which why she told me that I was older than her and on top of that while they talk about God this and that and get forced to go to church my parents never forced me to go to church thank God.However I feel as if church is more bigger down south. I've lived in Jerusalem seen the Red sea and Dead sea been in them too so has my father. I'm like I may never read in the Bible but I've been to the places swam in both and all thank you. So there was nothing they could tell me about God and Jerusalem

I may not have went to church often but I know that Bible. I just cannot stand bible thumpers and being corrected especially by a child. I really loved Jay with all my heart but he died with so many skeletons in his closet all those lies and secrets he had. I was hiding one the biggest secrets from my parents that was about to unravel soon I already knew it was but I wasn't the wife so what could I do about it? As I'm packing up all my stuff I just throw things in black trash bags I didn't even care. Next I started getting some of Jay's things to get for our child and show our child eventually. Next thing I know Bev says to me"You're taking everything". Like um yea I'm taking his favorite hats and some of his Navy stuff and anything else that I want to take for our child that didn't get to meet his or her dad. They were getting on my fucking nerves I already knew how people get especially when people die they get money hungry, start claiming property, fighting over stuff and Ididn't time for that shit they were like family to me but there was nothing I could do. My name was on the bank accounts I was an authorize user on the credit cards and I had the pins to the debit/ credit cards. I let the family deal with all that I'm not fighting over money when I'm going home and my dad had it like that. They could have all that shit I don't fight over money and anything else that's not mine and I'm not

69

entitled to. Before Jay died he told me he was giving me his car and going to buy himself another one and his was paid for anyways.

Once he died I knew his bitch ass wife was coming back to take everything he had which she could have too. I don't fight over things that I can get myself and on my own. I get texts all day on my phone and phone calls but I don't reply to anyone really at all and Candace texted me saying she felt bad she didn't come over when we would invite them over ur house for cook-outs and events they literally never came to any of them they only came over to our house to get a house tour in person then when I called Candace to pick me up that one time when Jay and I fought and Jacobi stayed at our house that one time when Candace threw him out. I wanted to tell her that she should've felt bad but who was I to tell her that when I had a argument with Jay the day before he died so I felt just as bad. Sometimes life really has a way of showing you how you took someone and or something for granted. Later on the day I went to get all of my stuff from the house after we finished clearing stuff out of the house we go to Jay's parent's house and it was packed as hell and I was getting to the point where I wanted to check out of life for a moment so I could grieve for a moment and slowly but surely get my life together. Jay's mother saw me crying and forced me to try to eat something I told her I'm okay and Martina told me to eat the soup I always hated soup it was just gross to me but I ate it so they could stop telling m to eat it. Jay's mom fed me the soup meanwhile I'm sniffling and I took a few spoons full then I said I didn't want anymore. Bev drops me off home later that evening and I told my dad how Bev's friend asked if I wanted to get government assistance and my dad said I didn't need any of that and that he had me and would give me money every week plus I had my school check the military gave me monthly to live off of which was enough and I was always good at saving.Plus my dad wasn't going to let me struggle and suffer nor the baby. I was so sad Jay never even got a chance to meet my mom he was supposed to meet her they talked on the phone often but Jay was supposed to meet my mom December of twenty seventeen her and my sister were going to be coming to florida for Christmas. I remember telling Jay all the ideas I had for the baby's room whether it was a boy or girl and I was so excited. I was thinking to myself how I was going to tell my parents that the man I was with was legally married I kept trying to keep his secret even though he wasn't here anymore. I knew sooner or later my parents were going to find out about him being married and there was nothing I could do. My day my sister and mother were on there way to Florida which is a ten hour driver from Virginia. While they were on their way Bev,Nicey,Manew,Bianca and I go to the hospital for me so I could make sure the baby was okay especially since I hadn't really been eating and with my anemia problems and low iron because I wasn't scheduled for my next doctor's appointment on base until January which is when i find out the gender of the baby,I was due in May which was coming up fast. We went to the Emergency room at Baptist hospital in Jacksonville. When the doctor comes in he asks us whats going on. I start crying saying I want to make sure my baby is okay, then the doctor asked me if something happened for me to want to make sure the baby is okay. I try to tell him whats going on but i bust out crying. Then Bev and everyone else starts crying so Bev and Bianca start talking for me. Then the doctor asked me if I had any health problems I then tell him I have sickle cell trait, microcytic anemia, acid reflux and he says wow okay lets run some test to make sure everything is okay with you're pregnancy and these anemias. He said lets make sure your anemia isn't too severe with you being pregnancy. A nurse comes in and takes my blood a few times the doctor also tells us he's sorry for our loss and says he'll be back to check out us. When the nurse comes back in she also does a few ultrasounds and shows us the baby who has a big head and is moving all around sucking his or her thumb. Bev started crying saying " Awww my brother's baby and started crying badly and we all take optics and videos. Everyone kept asking me if I were okay which I hated no I wasn't okay I'm pregnant and have to bury my child's dad. I don't know how many more times I could say it over and over again. I honestly had been getting to the point where i just wanted to be alone and sit at home all day by myself being around the family I knew I'd never come out that shell because we're always crying which is normal but people grieve in their own way. One day Bev and Bianca came to my dad's house I wasn't expecting them and my dad was at work. I literally peeped out the window in my bedroom without moving it to see who it was and I went to go to the door and as i was walking to the door I got a huge stomach cramp and I couldn't move so I slid down the wall on the floor crying and laying on the ground crying, Meanwhile the doorbell kept ringing then it stopped ringing. The wake and the funeral were taking too long to get here and I wasn't prepared but I was ready to see that bitch Carol. I had some words for her and I was ready to tag her ass. One day we had a candle light at Bev's duplex for Jay it was packed she cooked a lot of food which she could cook but I had no appetite still and we saw some man walk in dressed like Jay I really said in my mind he isn't dead and I got up but it wasn't him when he took his hood off. Dude was dressed just like Jay all red and Jay loved the color red. We all thought it was Jay I hated being disappointed I sat back down really fast tears started falling down my face. My anemia was killing me that day I was weak,dizzy,cold and hot, I was sweating bullets from crying and the candles that were lit. We were all standing up saying things we liked/loved about Jay. When it was my turn I was just saying we have lots of memories and I cant wait for our baby to get here. Everyone was talking i started losing my balance and swaying side to side and I fell back on the couch and I was hot and sweating. Martina was beside me and I was using my hand as a fan and she looked at me and asked if I was okay and I said no. So eventually everyone stopped and blew the candles out I was over there suffering from the candles. Bev asked if I had any optics of her brother by himself I told her we always took optics together but I would check so her and Martina are sitting beside me and as I check a bra and panty optic of me pops up and I said oh lord and locked my phone then

.Martina then said thats why she tells people to hold on why she's looking for pictures and I started laughing. I send Bev the optics i had of her
brother by himself to her phone. I gave Bev money since she took me home
and picked me up i gave her a fifty dollar bill I knew she got tired of taking
me home and picking me up. I couldn't wait to get me a car or suv I hated
depending on others and being at the mercy of others, I know Bev didn't
mind but I just felt as if we all needed to take a break and every time I was
with Bev,Bianca,Manew,Nicey they always said they loved me and I would
say it back which I really meant it they were family but they had never said
it to me ever before they only said it because Jay died and it probably woke
their eyes up to death he wasn't even that old he was only thirty three even
though death has no age limit.

My mother and sister drive up to Florida for the wake and funeral and of
course to be my support systems. Which I really appreciated at the time at
least in the beginning I did but after awhile I regretted them being there for
me well at least my mother. When my mother and sister get to Florida they
come straight to my dad's house and it felt nice seeing them I hadn't seen
them in months. They made me feel a little better the first day my mother
wanted me to try a dress on and I said in my mind shit its going to show my
tattoo so the problem with my tattoo was that it had my ex boyfriend's
name on it which I couldn'tcover up yet not while I was pregnant. Jay often
wanted me to cover up the tattoo and even offered to get it removed for me
when he was alive, he even hated to fuck me doggy style because he said
seeing another man's name on my body made him pissed off and we would
often talk about getting each other's names on our bodies but I didn't want
to go through that shit again especially since the person I was with before
Jay lied and let me really get his name on my body and his punk ass bitched
out on me when it was time fr him to get my name of him. Im like my
skinny ass got his name on my back which hurt bad as fuck and on my back
on my damn bones. Prime example of why men ain't shit and make me

sick. The point was I didn't want my mother to see that I had a man's name on my body it was bad enough she had my little sister's father's name on her back and then she once got a man's name on her wrist which she got covered but she never covered my sister's father's name up on her back. At times I often felt like I was becoming my mother at times which scared me my mother was beautiful,intelligent and had it all but when it came to men wasn't the smartest. My mother had obtained four degrees and I wanted to be just like her with the exception of the choices she made with the men she dated. I just didn't want my mother to see that I had a man's name on my body like she had did not once but twice and I didn't want my little sister to see that either especially since she looked up to me all her life and I did a lot for my little sister. I definitely wouldn't want my little sister to get any man's name on her body,whether she was married to them or not. My mother had given me this gorgeous dress and it did show a lot of my back but thank God it didn't show my tattoo off I didn't want my parents to see that I was already embarrassedI did some shit like that in the first place. My mother and sister stayed with me at my father's house, We watched movies all day and ate all day which felt nice to get a distraction from everything and everyone I had placed my phone on do not disturb I needed a break from everyone and Bev even had me in a group chat with the family and a bunch of other I didn't know which was annoying I hated being placed in group chats so I definitely placed that one on do not disturb. Later that day we go to the wake something I wasn't quite ready for but I had to get it over with and I was kinda ready to get the wake over with and the funeral. We go to the wake later that day which was far and deep into Jacksonville and it was so packed I didn't even see the family but I did call them to see where they were but they weren't there so I went for awhile and Icouldn't stand to be there I became depressed and I cried the whole time silently. I told my parents i was ready to leave it didn't seem real at all I wanted to scream and have a breakdown the whole time sitting there every time I got depressed, stressed,or cried my stomach would tighten really bad. I was in disbelief I kept asking God why this happened to me. The craziest thing about my story is that I didn't want a baby at all at nineteen let alone to be pregnant that young at all. I had a baby for my man because thats what he wanted and it was to please him and he died. I couldn't believe he was gone, how was it that the parent who didn't want the baby was the parent that was stuck with the baby. I know I was had unprotected sex but lot of girls and women have unprotected sex and never get pregnant at all. I had to realize I had to prepare a lot in my life to be a single mom. A few days later I tried to prepare myself for the funeral which Icouldn't prepare myself my cousin Mercedes texted me saying she was sorry for my loss we were never close but I needed support from everyone and anyone at the time. But she was married and had her baby daddy while she was pregnant no one could relate to me or how I was feeling. People can never relate until they go through things, my father had gotten my mom and sister a hotel room at days inn and I had stayed with them. I cried all night and before the funeral I had gotten a heart shaped necklace with a optic of Jay and I kissing in it, I wore it everyday until i had our baby. The funeral it is time I had wore a black jumpsuit my mother,father,sister,cousin Roy were with me at the funeral it was packed as hell with a bunch of black folks and some dressed like they going to the grammy's. I had Jay's and I baby's ultrasound which we didn't even know the gender. I thought of putting the ultrasound optic in his casket on top of him but I couldn't do it. People in the family who I had never met before were coming up to me asking if I was the one pregnant and the secret I tried to keep for Jay had just unraveled I tried to keep his secret about being married but my parents found out that day anyways. When those wedding optics of Jay and Carol popped up in the church on the screen and the obituary stated Jay left behind a wife and no kids. My father was siting there reading everything word from word and he looked pissed and confused while reading. I got my sister Bri to get up and take optics of Jay in the casket for me because I couldn't do it. Bri had took a few optics for me and some of Jay's family who i had never met before was coming up to me asking if i was the one pregnant by him and hugging me. I went to sit back down and I told my mom and dad I was ready to go, the service hadn't even started yet but I couldn't sit there through a lie I was embarrassed and Jay's secret was out, His secret I had tried to keep for him the secret I had tried to tell myself was a lie. The craziest thing of it is that Jay had no life insurance I couldn't believe it his family was stuck paying for everything that they didn't have. Meanwhile Carol was able to take the house and car because she was his wife and n top of that the family couldn't do shit either. In the group chat I said I hated Carol then Bianca's fat ass really told me I reap what I sow. The same bitch living life off of welfare and section eight the same bitch who acted as she couldn't work nor was trying to work to provide a better life for her children and I couldn't believe Candace was talking at all trying to throw shade saying how I chose to be with a married man like bitch had you not opened your mouth Iwould've never known to began with. She was the main bitch saying how everyone liked me and how I had nothing to worry about meanwhile she had what she had because of Jacobi and his military benefits even though they weren't married and she still acted as if they didn't cheat and have situations going on in their relationship i hate bitches like that. I hate bitches who let a man define them who let a man control their life and let a man provide every-thing for them,some some forget a man can come and go and there ain't nothing you can do bout it. Lets not forget Candace is the one who told me Jay was married granted I needed to know but sometimes people wont always want to know and sometimes best to allow others to look down on their own then that person gets mad at you for talking too much. Candace only had what she had because of her man and the military if it wasn't fr that she would've still been staying home with her parents. She acted as if she didn't tell me about Jacobi cheating and all his dirt. Don't come for a person after you've told them shit about you because people remember and will always bring it up against you something my mother once told me and she had never lied about it. It was just funny as hell to me how people talk shit when a person dies but when Jay was alive was all in his face and at our house. As for Bianca she had what she had because of the government if it wasn't for that her and her children would be broke and struggling more than what they were. It's funny how everyone was talking shit but failed to realize if it wasn't for me Jay's baby and legacy wouldn't have been born and I didn't owe them shit nor did I have to do shit for them. My toxic mother literally was telling everyone how I was with a married man which wasn't as it seemed.After all my mother wasn't the one to judge she had bad experiences with men including married men then always seemed to be so judging I couldn't believe it. My father looked very disappointed and I didn't want to be there anymore. I literally told my mom,dad,sister,and cousin Roy who was older than my dad. Roy went with us that I was ready to leave the funeral I didn't want to be there anymore and it was packed and some of the black people were dressed like they were going to the grammy's and shit like it was a funeral not award show just ghetto. Before we left I got my sister Bri to go to the casket to take optics of Jay she took a bunch for me it seemed like that's all everyone else was doing as well. As we get up to walk out I locked eyes with the wife a fat ass mess she looked and she had let herself go compared to when she was in the military she couldn't hold a candle to me. I looked the fuck good and I was pregnant and what belly didI have? I wanted to ask her what was her excuse so bad as we get closer to the exit I coughed on Carol I didn't cover my mouth or anything and what the fuck was she going to do? I had a forty five bullet with her name on it let alone I wanted to slap the shit out of him but he was dead what more can I do to a dead person? It wasn't like Jay fucked me then fucked hiss wife that wasn't the case at all and I got so tired of explaining myself to everyone. As we finally make it outside due to the amount of people walking in Bev literally ask us if we were leaving already and I kept walking while crying. My mom did all the talking for me and said yes because its a lot going on and Brittany is going through a lot and didn't want to be there. I had never been to a funeral before where the main family members come into the funeral last thats not how my family had did that ever but to each is own. I couldn't sit there through a lie and accept that. I hate being fake and thats just not me I'm not with that shit. It was crazy to me how Jay's parents paid for the funeral but they let the wife actually put up them wedding optics and put that bullshit in the obituary they better than me. When we all get back to my father's home our cousin Roy didn't join he lived in Jacksonville anyways so he decided to just go home meanwhile me,my dadmomand sister watched the movie bad moms Christmas and ate Chinese food for lunch, I loved that movie it was funny as hell and I needed a god laugh anything to take my mind off what just happened. It is now January twenty eighteen my mom and sister stayed in Florida for a few more weeks and they go on base with me to the doctor which is when I find out the gender of the baby. I always said if I got pregnantI wanted girl first so I literally had two girl name picked out which were Alanis and or Leilani. I cried the whole appointment my doctor had only met Jay once and that was the first appointment when we received out first ultrasound, I was about nine weeks pregnant then.

My mom tells the doctor how Jay had died and I couldn't stop crying then the doctor puts that cold ass jelly on my belly then as she presses the device on my belly we listen to the baby's heartbeat then soon we find out I'm having a girl and I cried even more I couldn't even be happy, The doctor asked me how did I feel I responded back telling her I was saddepressed,upset and I didn't know what I was going to do. In the car my mother was driving and I began ordering things on Walmart online for the baby since I knew I was having a girl I was so happy but I didn't tell the family I started to fall back from them. It's like the moment I started telling my feelings they didn't want to har the shit which I didn't give a fuck they were going to listen to me that day. I even had called T mobile and got my phone number changed especially after Martina threatened me one sending a text message saying after the baby drops no talking just throwing hands. I'm just like these people don't know me I can do something and get off easily my dad was a fed like I wont set her ass up and off then her family would be walking slowly behind her next, How are they going to get mad because I'm saying whats on my mind? Ghetto people don't scare nor loud people that's why white people think the black community is ignorant now. When I called T mobile they asked why I needed to change my phone number next thing I know I start bursting into tears crying telling this lady whats going on not like she cared I'm sure but she said they would change my number free of charge and I was pregnant and couldn't be stressed out. After seeing the ultrasound optics on the ride to my dad's home Bri made a comment that made me feel better saying at least i got what I wanted but after allI didn't want a baby Jay did now I was the parent stuck with the baby life really is a bitch at times and like my mom said once to me all good things come to a end she never lied about that either. Later that night I stayed with my mom and Bri at days inn and my dad was taking bri and I back to the hotel after getting subway for dinner, my mom was partially drunk Ii was sure but when we get out the car we see the cops and they asked my father if he was Joe Jackson then the lady at the front desk says we have to leave the crazy thing was the room was in my dad's name, I was mad as fuck my stomach was in knots I was sad as fuck and depressed and I had Mayo on my sub which eventually got soggy. When we go to the room my mom sounded drunk as hell and said the white sheets had blood on them which is highly disgusting and I lost my appetite I didn't even want my sub anymore after seeing it. thats why I always check sheets and inspect hotel rooms I don't even know why they use white sheets and white towels and wash cloths.

My dad had to get us another hotel room and tells me to driver because my mom was drunk i loved driving my mom's car she had a Chrysler three hundred which looked like a baby Benz I would call it. My mom was fucking tripping telling her friends on the phone how I was with a married man like without knowing the details and if I remember she had some encounters with married men thats why I was so fucked up with men and I loved older men it was because growing up thats what I watched my mother do.Kids often mimic what they see their parents do growing up becoming accustomed to a certain lifestyle. My mom had a attitude the whole car ride to the next hotel she didn't know how to handle her liquor well when she drunk too much and she got reckless with her mouth that shit pissed me off to the max. I was tired of the judgement from everyone coming for me for being with a married man something that people do all the fucking time. something that wasn't what it seemed and I didn't know how many times I could say that. People always talk shit about people when they're dead but never when they're alive. I hated those types of peopleI was so sad and depressed I wanted to die so bad!!! Later that day we went to Jay's parents house and his father asked where were we and said they didn't see us there my dad cut me off as I startedtalking then said I got sick and didn't feel well. My dad always was lying to people like what the fuck I left becauseI didn't like what I saw and who the fuck was going to check em about it?? Jay was dead and I was getting all the heat for being with a married man like damn everyone is so quick to jump down a woman's throat for being with a married man. I remember even telling Martina I wanted to die when we were getting all of my items from the house Jay and I once had shared together and Martina told me not to say that. I broke down crying telling her I had no life without him and I would now be a single parent with a baby I didn't want to have at all. After all I was the reason Jay had a baby and a legacy it was because of me and God, he got what he wanted but not how he thought he would which after awhile I started to hate him even though he was dead and it was pointless.

I couldn't wait for my mother to leave she was pissing me the fuck off she talked so bad about me and had so much negativity to say about me, I think every woman gets caught up with a married man at some point or even men that ain't shit in their life. One day I went through my phone and through my contacts list I literally deleted and blocked Jay's family's numbers and I took them off my instagram and snapchat. I decided to take a break off of social mediaI didn't care about it and I needed time to get my shit together for me and the baby who we decided to call Leilani i let my mom pick out the name even though she was pissing me off and judging me trying to tear me down every chance she got. My mom and sister finally got back to Virginia and I had planned to go to Virginia for my baby shower and Alabama for another baby shower I just needed support from my friends and family I couldn't stand to be alone. I literally couldn't believe how nice my dad was being towards me after all he was mad I was nineteen with a thirty three year old let alone knocked up by one and when Jay died my dad didn't seem sad for me at all and told everyone in Alabama which was where his family was about it before I could tell them. After all the last time my dad actually hugged me and told me he loved me was probably when I was a child my dad never seemed proud of me nor any of my accomplishments and I'm just saying when Jay died my dad had no emotion and it was as if he were happy I was moving back home with him, when I left home I thought I would never have to return home againthat was just my fucking luck.

It it now the month of FebruaryI decided to fly home to Virginia to see my mother and sister I had to get away and out of Florida i was losing my mind so bad every time I passed by a place in Orange Park or Jacksonville that Jay and I went together i would cry, as I'm going home with my dad we passed a place in Jacksonville called burrito gallery that was our first date we had went on together when I was eighteen and he was thirty two the first date and time i skipped class for Jay we went to the location in the area where the beach is and I had never been there to be honest the food was trash but the drinks were it for me.Jay had introduced me to a drink called "Blue Motherfucker" he told me when he was in the Navy stationed in California he would always go to bars and get that drink. It was strong as hell just the way I liked it and he would order the drinks for us they never asked for my I.D. at all. That was in my era when I would wear braids all the time with crop tops and hats and i was a sneaker head. All i could do was silently cry sometimes it was hard to cry in front of my dad for some reason. I go back to my dad's house to pack and get prepared for the next morning for the flight home to Virginia which was only a hour flight which wasn't bad at all. Later that day I had went to a store called Burlington coat factory to go shopping I still didn't have a big belly at all so I didn't care for maternity clothes I just wanted some winter clothes it was cold as hell back home and always was snowing around that time. I had to also get my nails done as well to treat myself and I didn't want to look how I felt I had to get my shit together only three more months until Leilani was going to be arrivingI had a lot to still take care of within myself and my life in general.

I decide to get my nails painted pink at this nail salon on wells road around the corner from where my dad lived they were very affordable but had attitude problems so I told myself I wouldn't go back there anymore, spending good money to go somewhere where they had attitude problems i always had deja vu moments every time I had some powerful ass thoughts which is why I had to control my thoughts I knew what I could and would do. I had got a pedicure and manicure I chose the color pink for my fingernails and toenails. On my fingernails I got the letter L on one nail and for my thumbs I got a footprint on each. When I was going back to my dad's house after I finished doing what I wanted to I decided to stop at Mc.Donald's and got some food when i go to the window to pay the manager looked about my age then asked me who was having a baby as she noticed my nails I told her I was and she asked if I wanted a free ice cream said sure all happily I loved food especially free food and when she gave me the ice cream I told her thank you and I drove off happily listening to my nineties r&b music. I could never just remain happy on the way home they played songs on the radio I had knew and liked before had met Jay which made me change the radio station because some of the songs we had liked together and memories. Every timeI found a way to be happy and try to forget about Jay I couldn't and thats why I had to leave to go back home fro awhile I couldn't do it. As I finished eating my ice cream and food I drove around for a minute and I stopped and parked where there was nothing but trees I was in the middle of no where and I started crying while rubbing on my stomach. Next thing I know I took my seatbelt off then turned the car on then I closed my eyes as I went to mash my food on the gas and as I go to mash my foot on the gas someone pulls up beside me and get out their car then knocks on the window to ask if I was okay. As I roll the window down then I wipe my face I tell this tall,black,buff,older man who was fine and he asked me why I was crying I told him i was pregnant and just had lost my fiancéI wanted to be alone and some space then he tells me how he can relate and he gives me his phone number for some reason I had taken it even though I wasn't interested because the man i loved had died and the way he died and I was pregnant and alone something I wanted and I told him I would text or call him sometime lying my ass off. I didn't want any other man but Jay and he was gone and not coming back I couldn't stop thinking about. If it wasn't for the man by the name of Garett coming over to see what was going on I was going to fly through the woods and kill myself until his ass intervened. He literally had even sat there until I left maybe he seen what I was going to do or thought about what I tried to do not that it was his problem.

CHAPTER

4

As I drive back to my dad's house I began crying and talking to myself about what I need to do in my life and have completed before baby Leilani arrives which I only had three months then I think about what I tried to do to myself to my baby and it wasn't right. Babies don't ask t be here or born and that wouldn't be right because I also thought about if I didn't get killed but severely hurt and my baby would be hurt too and feeling what her mommy was feeling as well. I started feeling like the world's worst mom ever and I hadn't even delivered my baby yet. I was so tired of sitting in the house everyday and despite my mother was such a bitch when she was here visiting me for the funeral I righteously didn't want to go to Virginia to be with her for a few weeks but I thought he would be good for awhile I was running out of time and options. I was at least happy that I was going to get to see my friends. My dad takes me to the Jacksonville airport the next morning and he actually hugged me I couldn't believe it my father had never done that before since I had been an "adult". When I was about to board the plane go to Virginia I heard on the intercom they said military and pregnant women could board first so I took my happy ass up there. I didn't have a belly but I was still pregnant.I even had on my maternity shirt that said baby on board so people could see. It was only a one hour flight as everyone else started to board when it was time to I asked this lady beside me if she would let me sit on the aisle seat because I was pregnant and was going to keep getting up to pee and she acted like she had an attitude i hated Karens which is what she was. It wasn't that serious but if she didn't mind getting up for me multiple times than oh well I tried help her fat ass out thats thy she kept getting bumped inside the aisle seats are the worst anyways everyone walks past and bumps into you anyways so thats what she get.Bitch told me she paid for her seat like girl its not that damn serious I was six months pregnant I tried to help her out. I couldn't wait to go home to have some privacy after all it was going to be all females in the house so I could actually walk around a certain way and becomfortable something I couldn't do when I was at my dad's house. My mother had a six bedroom two-story house in FredericksburgVirginia. There was even one room downstairs called a "sun" room with all yellow and orange decor and the sun always shined in the room it was so nice. The house even had three bedrooms on one wing of the house and two bedrooms on the other wing of the house two separate staircases and everything. Last time I went back home to visit my mother and sister lived in Virginia Beach. There was even a bedroom in the garage I called my happy place and I was going to cry myself a river the whole time once I got there. When the pilot made a announcement that the plane was about to land I had to get up to pee and i got up to go pee and the flight attendant told me to go back to my seat I said "Excuse me I'm six months pregnant andI'm about to piss on myself" I said you don't have to do all that so excuse me I'm going to go pee. I said don't let the baby face fool you I'm not the one. They already think we're black and angry as is which I don't care. Once I get off the airplane walking to go get my checked in bag this older man that had to be in his forties maybe older came up to me to talk and ask for my number I really wasn't in the mood and he was definitely my type older,buff,black and sexy as hell but I was grieving the loss of my ex fiancé and I couldn't talk to anyone when he had just been buried. The man told me that he was a greyhound bus driver regardless I wasn't interested and he gave me his card I took it and kept walking to get my duffle bag I throw his card away in the first trash can,because I also told him I was engaged so the fact he gave me his card with his phone numberanyways like sir did you hear me? I hate men who have no respect for others. My mother and Bri were outside waiting for me when I finally get my bag and walk outside the Southwest airlines door, They both get our the car to greet me and my mother put my bag in the trunk. I plug in my earbuds and sit in the front seat sad and I started crying.We go to the closet Applebee's I loved that restaurant and Jay and I always went there that was my favorite restaurantespecially when i was a kid my mother was the one who put me on to that salad. I would always get the oriental salad it was so good with the oriental dressing with fried chicken. I told my mom this was our favorite restaurant and she literally said to me"Oh Lord I hope you don't start crying" Like how insensitive of her like I hate those who cannot relate to a situation but have so much to say to someone. Like why wouldn'tI cry its still fresh we had just buried him and my child won't her have father in her life.

As we sit there to waiting to order our food and our beverages I had ordered a sweet tea with plasticware I had OCD so bad I even requested the sweet tea in a plastic cup. We were there for awhile eating lunch which I had paid for I couldn't stop having flashbacks about everything and I had my earbuds in listening to nineties r&b music and a tear had rolled down my face. I was so miserable I didn't know what to do. I had one flashback about Bianca's fat ass telling me how I cant get upset at that woman which she was referring to Carol and she also told me that was woman's husband. I wanted to pistol whip her ass so bad. She pulled him off of life support out of spite anyways and I wasn't jealous of Carol anyways Ididn't know her nor did I care to but the issues I had wasn't just with her but Jay as well. Im like damn the nigga is dead and here I am taking all the heat for him once again. I should've took the advice of his sister Bev and played him to be honest the whole situationI was in wasn't good at all. As we sit at Applebee'sI decided to text Carol. I sent her optics of Jay and I with Leilani's ultrasound optics. I had also sent Carol a message saying "I have what you never will and that's Jean's baby. All you have of him are memories and optics I have half of him baking inside of me but be blessed and don't act like you solely love him now because he dead". Carol had a iPhone at the time as well as I did all the messages said delivered but she never responded. Carol even took the house that Jay and I and his car which he was going to give me, but it was just material items and I could get my own everything soon granted my father had money I wanted to do things on my own. My father did a lot for me but at the same time I always say "Our parents wont be here forever"."People wont always be here forever to help either". Another saying I would say is that "Life isn't that hard Life is what you make of it". I didn't need my dad to do shit for me except get me in a government job and security clearance. After all my father knew everyone that worked for the government and feds. It would upset me how much my dad would help family all the time in Alabama especially when it came to giving them money I had a few other aunts and uncles who had money as well but for some reason they'd always ask my dad for money maybe because they knew he would give them money. One time my father and I talked he said he would pay half of my apartment rent if I wanted to get a apartment but I didn't want my dad to help me with shit I wanted to get away from him and his "feds" world. I loved my father to death but he was annoying,criticizing,cared what others thought of me or him, and very manipulating. When I had turned sixteen my mother let me get my belly pierced I got a belly ring and my father had to go with me to get it done he was acting all scared and weird as if he was the one getting the belly ring. As I was getting my belly pierced while looking at my dad's facial expressions in my mind I'm like he was a chief,sniper and fed scared of a body piercing. My second flashback was of when i was at Jay's parent's house and Niecy hugged me then kissed me on my cheek I was going to miss the girls I did so much for them and with them. Then Niecy had told me she loved me and I said it back while holding back my tears it was so hard not to cry around them so I had to take a break from them to get myself together mentally ,physically,emotionally. Which I knew I couldn't do being around them while they're always crying. As i pay the bill at Applebee's while Bri and our mother go to the car. I knew this was going to be a eventful trip that I wasn't prepared for. We had to hurry up because my mother's friend was waiting for us outside the car at the house. When we get there I speak then we go into the house the name of my mom's friend was Eva Ididn't appreciate how I went to one of the living rooms to watch the television show called "star". Then for some fucking reason Eva comes in there to ask how I was holding up which was a stupid fucking question like when people die who the fuck wants to hear? I'm sorry for your loss. Who wants to hear: Are you okay? like hell nah I'm not okay I just buried my ex fiancé like shut up. Then Eva asking me if I was okay made me cry and think about it like damn I just want to sit around doing nothing and not thinking about Jay which will never happen if people kept asking about it like damn let me grieve in peace. I told Eva Ididn't want to talk about the topic then the bitch had the audacity to ask me why was I with a married man I turned the television off then got up and stood in front of her then I asked her why the fuck is she in my business and how dare you talk about what you don't know. Then she said to me its little girls like you who think that its cute to sex another woman's man,that taking a man from another woman isn't cute. I then said to her as i got closer to her that statistically men cheat because their so called wife is lacking in the bedroom and or is just boring which causes men to go out and stray,I said y'all so quick to attack the woman but don'tconfront your man. I told Eva she was a grown woman in my face talking out of her neck about my situation like she knew me that was our first time meeting at that which made me funny. I told her don't let the petite full you this "grown woman" rides monsters only ten inches and up but thank you then I walked away. I really couldn't believe my mother like I didn't want to be there in the first place but my mom has her bum ass old ass friends trying to lecture and do all that preaching shit to me like how dare her too. I was at that very point tired of everyone trying to preach to me I wanted to throw my phone in the pool in the backyard and leave it there and I wanted to scream. And I almost hurt Eva's feelings I wanted to tell her so bad her pussy stinks and thats why her husband cheated she literally had an odor down there like bitch there's too many products in the world for your pussy to be stank you too grown for that shit. Her husband is dirty if he was sticking his dick inside of her because I almost passed the fuck out talking to her because that smell was so bad. She had the audacity to be trying to school someone girl take a shower then soak that big ass of yours in a bleach bath thats not sexy then she wonders why her husband was cheating. I almost told her her stank pussy is why her husband fell out of bed and died it really did happen to him not once but twice he fell out the bed then the second time she had noticed that he wasn't breathing when she called her son to put his dad back in bed. As wrong as she was I couldn't get to her level every timeI yelled,argued,cried, got upset my stomach would start tightening it hurt so bad. Like I couldn't believe her pussy smelt like that like damn that should be a crime,hell my pussy didn't even smell like that when I was on my period or had a yeast infection. Its way too many products in the world to be walking around smelling bad like there's no fucking excuse then she had the nerve to be out here trying to preach to people bitch please.

Man I couldn't fucking believe my mother she needed her fucking ass beat did she really tell my business to her friends. I was a firm believer that people don't need to know everything about you or your family like the fact she was telling everyone my businesses. It was very funny how her friend and who I had never met before were talking and bickering the whole time while shes no where to be found. I literally went to the garage bedroom and I cried I was tired of everyone attacking me when they didn't know my truth I was tired of explaining myself and correcting people. My mother couldn't possibly be talking shit about me she was the reason I would soon get worse with my dating decisions. Very intelligent woman my mother was but when it came to men and red flags she wasn't the brightest crayon in the box at all. She had two men's name tattooed on her body on her back and wrist which one was married his name was on her wrist and she had to get it covered and it wasn't like he had gotten her name on his body. I was in the same boat as her with not knowing Jay was married, So i was so confused with the shade hell one time Jay sent my mother money for me and she had the nerve to be talking shit but wasn't talking shit when he was alive. I went to pee and while sitting on the toilet I had a breakdown I really wanted to die and not be here anymore. I got up to wash my hands and I looked at myself in the mirror while self reflecting on my life and I picked up my phone to text and call Carol which she didn't answer of course and I even downloaded texting apps to text and call her she wouldn't reply back to me. I was threatening to shoot Carol and fly to Texas to beat her ass one thing about me I was never scared of any man or woman,Anything I said I could back it all the way up.I had only talked to Carol once on the phone I had purposely called her but I told Bev once when we were in her truck it was on accident and Carol had called me back and I was silent for a moment I just told her I had the wrong number I wanted to say so many things but I was trying to avoid the drama. As I look at myself in the mirror again I couldn't help but think i was used for a baby I mean that was all Jay wanted I started to honestly hate him not that it would help he was dead and wasn't coming back,But it still hurt I didn't want to be a single mom plus I was always the one who said I would never have kids and I couldn't stand kids all that crying and whining they do now I was pregnant damn. I lay on the bathroom floor crying and holding my stomach when I hear a knock at the bathroom door I said out loud as i keep crying and sniffling. I hear a voice at the door which was Bri she asked if she could come into the bathroom when she asked that I didn't say anything. Then Bri knocks on the door again and says Britt let me in please I want to talk so I get up and open the door and let her in the bathroom. She comes in and we both sit on the floor she asked if I was kay then asked if I wanted help planning my baby shower I told her sure but give me a moment to get myself together then I'll come to her room. Before Bri walked out the bathroom I told her don't be like me i told her this situation I'm going through don't ever allow it or go through it its not good like look at me I'm a mess, Bri hugged me then goes to her room. As I'm getting ready to come out of the bathroom I hear my mom scream my name and her stank ass friend Eva told her what I said. I didn't give a fuck because she was wrong like people have to learn to stay in their place I'm not a pushover. I didn't even say yes ma'am or anything to my mother I was getting to the point of being sick and tired of her ass, I took my pregnant ass time walking down the stairs and all. Then she gets a whole attitude saying how I was wrong for saying what I said to her friend who she claims to had been trying to do some type of business with her and that when I leave she still has to deal with her and do business with her.Im like same ole mom I see nothing has change with you when it comes to money, I asked my mom how could she let that bitch talk to me like that. I told my mom that at the rate she was going they wouldn't have any clients because Eva's pussy smelled so bad it would kill the clients. My mom raised her hand as if she were going to slap me and I stood there with my chin up and without blinking as a tear rolled down my face then my mother told me to just get out of her sight. I walked away thinking to myself wow she would actually hit her pregnant daughter some mom she was. I literally called my dad crying telling him I was ready to come back home, He then told me that he would see what flights he could fine so I could come back home.

Bri comes to my room which was on the opposite wing from her room and we start thinking of where to have the baby shower then I tell her the name of one of my favorite restaurants in Virginia Beach which was called Kelly's Tavern I loved that place they had cheap food and it was a hole in the wall type of restaurantI also knew some people that worked there. Unlikemy bougie mother when I came to picking restaurants to invite others to I actually cared about other's pockets and not breaking their pockets. I had made cute thank bags to give out to everyone with Brihelping. I also used an app called punchbowl to make some invitations to send out to everyone I had about twenty invitations to send out via text message. When Bri and I talked to my mother about my baby shower she said that she didn't want the baby shower to be at Kelly's Tavern like first of all my baby shower I was the one pregnant she had already had her chances in the past with being pregnant and having her own baby showers. So I ask her where is she trying to have the baby shower at like she was so extra it was about me not her I was the pregnant one. Like damn I guess it wasn't just my dad that had control issues and would try to gaslight me it was my mother as well. Growing up they never were the parents they needed to be and they thought money helped with everything a fucking mess they were. I'll never forget getting raped a kid a few times due to their lack of attention. I remember having to stay with my dad's family in Alabama a few times as a kid which wasn't the best I hated it there I had no type of stability and at night I would talk to myself and tell myself i had to be better than my parentsI had to give myself and daughter stability. So I then ask my mom where is she trying to have the baby shower with a fucking attitude she then says a place called cinema cafe which was a movie theater that had an arcadebar and served alcohol they had tables in the theaters. It was nice we knew everyone there and that was our spot even people I went to high school with. Worked there as well that I was cool with and would often hook me up with the bill or the food proportions not that they had to but I really appreciated it. I didn't want to have a baby shower at a fucking movie theater though like how ghetto and I mean yes kids have birthday parties there but they're actually going to watch the movie and they rent out the whole theater or certain sections like I actually wanted the talk to my friends and catch up I hadn't seen them in years since I had moved to Florida. My mom even had already made invitations like I was just pissed off me and Bri had took the other car to go into town to even get baby shower decorations for the tables and chairs. Ididn't want my baby shower at a movie theater I knew that much. My mom then said we could have the baby shower in the lobby area where the bar is and all the tables and that someone we knew there could put a rope over in the area I told my mom whatever then walked away, I hated how she made everything about her and always tried to take over.

I then told her whatever and let her do what she wanted I then began to think to myself like damn I'm miserable in Virginia and Florida like I couldn't win at all. I told my mom I needed to get my hair done before my baby shower she knew two people who did hair one was her friend another welfare bitch the welfare clothes her, feeds her and fucked her. Her name was Monica she and her family were all from New York they had the accents. They were hood rats and I was trying to understand why my mother was associating herself with them. I was honestly shocked only since as long as I knew my mother she only would be around those on her level in life especially financially. Monica and her sister Nicole were both cool for the most part they had nice big ass houses only because of section eight housing and they were scammers very much. They too had too much drama which I didn't want to be around I had my own problems, I got Nicole to do my hair for me since she did her kid's hair and seemed to have did decent work. One night i was dropped off over there and it was late as hell I was annoyed by that part but she also fed me which i appreciated, I typically don't eat everyone's cooking but they seemed to be clean and their house was spotless. I literally just wanted five to six feed in braids pulled to the back with hair added in of course pulled into a bun. It took her hours to do that like she didn't know what the fuck she was doing and she made me cry also when she asked about my father's dad Jay. She asked if he was happy about the baby and I said well he was happy then she asked if he wasn't happy anymore and trying to hold my tears back I cried and said he died after that it was a silence in the room for awhile as I wiped my face with my hands. She then apologizes to me I said to her it was fine you didn't know. Her sister Monica comes over to see if she was almost done with my hair which I was dropped off at nine at night and it was fucking midnight. Im like in my mind at this point she didn't know what the fuck she was doing I was highly upset and annoyed, my belly was also tightening I just wanted to go lay in my bed and cry. She finally finished so went I went into the bathroom to look at it I was pissed the fuck off that wasn't even close to what I asked for but I said fuck it and i'd get it redone elsewhere that was a waste of my night and time. Some bitches just don't need to do hair at all. I tell Nicole thanks then I leave because I wanted to go off and scream but I didn't feel well, so I ask Monica on the way to my mother's house if she could redo the hairstyle because I didn't feel like it at all not even close to what I asked for.

Monica tells me she can do my hair later because at that point of her taking me home it was damn near one in the morning it was already bad enough I didn't get much sleep at all due to getting up ten times at night to go pee. When Monica dropped me off i gave her some gas money and told her thank you. She then told me call her around lunch time and she would do my hair over and not charge me anything. I had to call bri because i dint have the code to the front door and we didn't have keys the front door had a code on it you had to punch in and you only get three chances to get the code wrong before you have to wait awhile before trying the code again. I don't know why my mom had that shit anyways if the power went out we all looking crazy as hell unless we unlocked the garage and pulled up the door to get in the house that way. Bri even said my hair was ugly too one thing about my little sister she could dress and didn't lie. I go to my room to look for a outfit to wear for my baby shower just in case I wanted to go shopping which I wasn't in the mood for at all, I really didn't want a baby shower but I wanted to see my friends it had been years since I've seen them. I literallycouldn't sleep at all I tossed and turned half the morning had I not been pregnant I would've smoked a fat ass blunt or got a glass of wine to help me go to sleep. When I finally went to sleep my mom came in the room to wake me up to get ready and everything to get my hair redone i had to take the hair out and wash my hair again which I was annoyed by like some bitches really do need to go to hair school and get a cosmetology license I'm like hell for all of that I could've went to the professionals and paid regularprice,sometimes you truly get what you pay for. Growing up I always had long ass hair but in the black community some of our mothers would tell us not to allow anyone to play in our hair but then they allow these hair stylists to do our hair who in reality fuck up our hair with the over processing of the relaxers and other chemicals that they use.

I eat and get my ass ready to go to Monica's house which I low keydidn't want her to do my hair but I needed it done and she supposedly does a good job with doing hair according to my mom and Bri. At this point i had just needed my hair done in general I just wanted some feed in braids pulled back into a bun which I could do on my own I just needed the braids to be done. I get dropped off to Monica's house and I instantly get annoyed a house full of kids which were in fact hers all them damn kids she had then it was loud and her house was nice but a mess. I began to get annoyed even more she literally had took forever to start my damn hair like it don't take that long for feed in braids. She literally had to smoke cigarettes and talk on the phone to some man in prison, When she finally decided to do my hair she had the phone on speaker but put the phone on mute and told me not to say anything not that I gave a fuck like lady I just wanted my damn hair done like I have my own crisis going on I don't give a fuck about anyone else's problems. As she started doing my hair I listen to their conversation of course not by choice her damn phone was on speaker. She tells the guy in prison which was her brother how her sister's husband ran over some man Monica was fucking. Even though Monica had a fiancé who she often would consider her husband to every damn person. Her and her sister Nicole's husband seemed very close they would even be hanging out until midnight which to me is very suspect. Why would you be hanging out with your sister's husband until midnight and longer? Unless you're fucking him thats what it seemed like to me. I couldn't believe what I was hearing though I said damn ran the man over with their range rover and had him pinned into two vehicles then left him for dead. I said in my mind what in the fatal attraction, this seemed like some lifetime movie type of shit that they had going on and I wanted to get the fuck out of her house before the cops came knocking. Monica had six kids with her husband and he had six kids before her no wonder why they were scheming and scamming with that government assistance I'm not saying its right but to each is own. Monica also told her brother that Nicole's husband may be going to jail and looking at some serious time i mean yea that was attempted murder and they said the man who they ran over that Monica was fucking only got ran over because he talked too fucking much saying how he would tell her fiancé so basically him talking too much is why his ass got ran over its not right but sometimes you have to plot and plan to destroy someone without telling them what your going to do to them. Monica said he was in the hospital with a broken leg and rib he also didn't show up to court I guess because he was so scared. Hell if someone ran me over I'd be scared to but a snitch I would be they could've killed that man and they were so damn stupid just listening to her story she said they didn't know there were cameras at the grocery store like well duh!!! Worlds dumbest criminals I've seen. They really should've been on that show. I was also trying to figure out why she was discussing the situation on the phone just dumb as hell. Wasn't my problem at all, she finally had finished my hair then she tells me she has to leave and doesn't have time to drop me off and my mother was also at work. I couldn't do uber or Lyft that was the country area they lived in which would've costed a lot of money I was ready to go home I was tiredhungry and hurting. Monica also needed to beat her kids ass I hated disrespectful ass kids. One of her daughter's NayNay literally took her slow time getting ready for school but purposely missed the school bus then Monica had told her she mine as well stay home and then NayNay told her that she knows, I would've beat her ass I don't believe in beating children but her kids were all out of control not cute at all. Monica seemed to not care what her kids did at all they never seemed to listen to her that day I was there getting my hair done at all I couldn't deal with that shit. Some kids need to get they ass tagged with that belt to act better, when i was growing up I couldn't act like that or do that shit but Monica didn't seem to care about her kids much. Even once Bri told me the kids always miss school and are late. The school counselors even told Monica if her kids kept missing school that she was going to contact a social worker then would also have her kids repeat the grades they were in at the time. In my mind I told myselfI couldn't be a parent like that you have to do better than parents like that. It's parents like Monica you have to make a example out of I swear like thats pitiful as fuck. A sorry ass excuse for a mother and to think its so many women who cant have kids but want them then thats how she treats hers and allow them to act. I was just ecstatic my hair was done it was just the way that I had wanted it too and it was cute I had some cute hair accessories for the braids as well.

Monica left me and I noticed her daughter Kiana was getting ready to go to work so I asked her if she could take me to my mom's house and I would give her some gas money and she said she was running late which sounded like a personal problem but she still took me to my mom's house. I was glad she agreed to do so because there was no telling when her so called mother would return home i hated waiting for others as well as being on other people's time. When Kiana drops me off i give her a twenty dollar bill she ddi have to go far to drop me off while also being late for work i call Bri to open the door for me I didn't have the code it was cold as fuck with snow and ice on the ground. We are just a few days away from my baby shower which was on a Saturday. I let Bri help me pick out a outfit for the baby shower I pick out a short sleeve maternity shirt that said arriving soon with baby footprints and some skinny jeans with a scarf,with some black ugg boots with a black coat. Then Bri and I go over makeup for me to wear I wasn't big on makeup at that time nor did I really know how to apply it all I really wore was eyeshadow and lipstick. I was bored out of mind so I decided to go downstairs to get Bri to take some optics of me all dressed up in the sunroom and after that I cooked us some lunch we both go into one of the living rooms to watch the tv show "star" on this app called Hulu. I was starting to feel a little better to be honest I wasn't crying anymore I had to keep it up, when I didn't talk about Jay or think about him I didn't cry anymore which is what I wanted I kept telling myself I couldn't keep being depressed and sad it wasn't good for me or the baby. It is finally Saturday morning we get up to get ready early we were in Fredericksburg we had to go to Norfolk for my baby shower. The baby shower was at two lunch time I knew the movie theater would be packed it was a new movie in theater too. We go to dollar tree before we go to Norfolk to get some decorations for the tables i was still annoyed how my mom made the plan for me to have "my" baby shower at a fucking movie theater like she pissed me off how she was always doing shit stupid shit at that. Like that wasn't what i wanted at all she got on my nerves with that shit I had my own money I didn't need her help for anything at all. Bri,my mom and I all go into dollar tree together my mom once again grabbing the balloons,table cloths,baby shower decor even though Bri and I had already went to get stuff my mom stayed taking over then she bitches how my dad has a control issue like bitch you do too I was so sick of my mom I really regretted even being there anymore,I was ready to return back to Florida. Once we all go back to the house to get ready I get Bri to help me apply my eyeshadow we take optics at the house before we leave. Then we load up the car to head to Norfolk which was about a hour and some change away. I was so ecstatic to see my friends it had been so long I had butterflies in my tummy.

I plug in my earbuds listening to nineties r&b music the whole car ride when we get there the movie theater was packed as fuck, a new movie had came out which is what everyone was there to see. When we get out the car with the balloons and other stuff we walk up the the front it was cold as hell I didn't miss the cold weather in Virginia along with the snow and ice. When we walk into the movie theater to the right side there was a seating area with a bunch of tables which had said revered with ropes there which was for my baby shower event. All the attention was on me which was fineI loved getting all of the attention and all eyes being on me. As we start setting up some of my guest start to arrive and some of my mom and sister's friends. It felt nice to get out to be around positive friends and family around me. I hated sitting in the house for as long as I did. My friends who were there were Asia,Asiah,ZuriTamia,Kailey,Ayanna,Amani,Nay ,it was a small gathering if anything then of course my mother's friends and sister's made it seem like a lot of people were there. I get Asia to fix my eyeshadow and make it all dramatic like her makeup was. She was very dramatic person and her makeup was always over the top which I loved. She was the last person to show up and was empty handed which Tamia brought up to me how Asia wad empty handed. Tamia even said how Asia could've brought a gift from dollar tree which they do sell a bunch of baby stuff and I mean she really could've came with a gift its one thing to be late but another thing to be late ad empty handed. It was whatever though it was my day and I wasn't letting anyone ruin it. We all take group pics and I take pics with my friends touching my belly while we wait for our food. I posted the optics on the app snapchat which when I upload the optics I noticed Jay's younger two sisters Manew and Neicy saw the optics and even screenshot that I was having a girl named Leilani. I thought I had blocked them off my snapchat as well as the rest of their family and friends but it was whatever I had already made the choice to not allow them to see Leilani when I first had her until I was ready. All that crying and shit they did was making me depressed and I had to stay away from them pus they weren't going to talk shit to me and treat me like shit it was my baby and I had told Bev in a text that I'm the reason her brother has a legacy not God me. I told them if it weren't for me there would be no baby something we all need to remember.I didn't have to be obligated to do shit for anyone I was grown and I damn sure didn't need them for shit I had money and my dad did too. I knew the girls would go back to report that i was having a girl but oh well that didn't mean I had to let them see her hell I wasn't even home in Florida. I had even got a cake made and the cake said "baby Leilani arriving soon" with two baby shoes on the cake and a pink bow on the bottom of the cake, the cake was in the freezer in the kitchen at cinema cafe. I had ordered some potato skins and a pina colada virgin daiquiri, when I had ordered drink my mom's friend Dani kept telling me no and Iwasn't drinking that I didn't think she realized I got a virgin one, like of course I wouldn't drink a real one while pregnant hell I didn't drink wine or anything while pregnant I've heard of people drinking wine or smoking weed while pregnant but i couldn't do that I mean at one point in my life I didn'tdrink or know about liquor so I mean it wasn't a big deal to me in the first place. I don't see how people act as if they cant wait to have their babies to drink and do whatever else it is that they do. I looked at it as detoxifying my body and taking a break but to each is own I didn't care or worry about what others did to each is own as i would say. As everyone started talking about the men they were talking to Zuri took over the conversation to say that she doesn't fuck with black men at all only white and latino men, I wasn't even mad at her we all have preferences cant get mad at her for feeling how she feels at all. She then showed us the man she was talking to who was latino and fine as hell I was glad to see Zuri got out of that pretty boy phase she was in I know we like what and who we like but me personallyI cannot date no man prettier than me or whose hair is longer than mine no thank you!! My friends at the timesI hung out with were all different which was fine my friend groups were always different I was always popular and cool with everyone. Zuri was a intelligent nerd who loved anime and singing when we were in middle school together we literally even had a girl singing group with one of our friends named Erica at that time in middle school we were obsessed with a boy singing group called "Mindless Behavior" we always talked about being their girlfriends and how we were obsessed with them it was fun and cute. We would make youtube videos all the time also videos of us singing and dancing to post on our twitter pages and hope to be discovered to get a record deal, those were the good times I swear I missed being that young and having all that fun. Erica,Zuri and I all literally lived in the same neighborhood we lived on our own different streets though we would meet up every weekend outside but we would always go inside of my house or Zuri's house but typically would practice outside,Zuri and I had knew each other first every since seventh grade then Erica moved to our neighborhood eight grade year we all went to the same middle school where we had to wear uniforms and shit the school was ghetto as hell in the hood. But Zuri and I had always been close even our mothers were close to each other, I knew a lot of personal stuff about her and vice versa. i was even cool with Zuri's step sister Tiara she was way older than us but was even like a big sister to me, our families did a lot of event together and cookouts. Next is Nay we go way back to elementary days she literally is two years older than me but when I say we were close as kids she was literally my uncover girlfriend we did a lot together and with each other. But it was one of those things we could still be friends like nothing between us ever happenedI always loved her but i never imagined us actually being together as a couple because she was definitely a friend I needed to always keep around me closely she knew a lot of my business and family's business and personal stuff. We went to a elementary school together in Virginia Beach together and lived in the same neighborhood diagonal from each other. As kids we would play house which I think every kid played to be honest we would kiss and finger each other. We almost got caught a few times by her mom we always almost got caught by her mom but she lived at my house in Virginia Beach we lived in townhouses she would always come over to my house and spend the night at my house she had family out there in our neighborhood too her cousin Avayance was a trouble maker and after school sometimes I would have to go to his grandmother's house she would babysit me which sucked he would always try to touch me inappropriately. I hated going over there and he would terrorize me with this Chucky doll he had literally the ugly ass killer doll from the movies from the nineties and early two thousands,But Avayance also liked me why the fuck he did I don't know. Nay's grandmother would always cook for us and let us eat a bunch of junk food and also walk to the store by ourselves all the time something our moms knew nothing about. That was literally the first friend I had that I stole with and everything. We basically ran the neighborhood we lived in hell one time I told Nay what Avayance tried to do to me so we literally through barbecue sauce all on his grandmother's townhouse everywhere,I got my ass beat by my mother but he shouldn't have tried to touch me sexually, every since I was a kid I've always had this thing where I don't allow people to do things to me and get away with it. I was literally in elementary school too but fuck it I knew I couldn't beat him up even though i was a tomboy at the time I was wild as fuck. In elementary school Nay and I would always have arguments and be able to come back to being friends. We would both get jealous if we felt as if one of us was trying to replace the others with new friends it was wild. Crazy thing is her and I are still friends. Our mothers became the best of friends thanks to us being friends.

Nay,her mother,brother and grandparents lived in that neighborhood longer than us but we all lived out in that neighborhood for years. One time Nay and I were dancing and had our shirts tied up in the front and were acting as if we were strippers and her mom walked in on us doing. I even had a crush on her brother for years we used to sneak his games grand theft auto and midnight club for the playstation two and when Nay would come to my house we would play it we had to sneak grand theft auto because whenever we would ask her brother to play it he would say no or we weren't old enough to play it. Hell when i started hanging out with NayI tried my first cream soda and donut sticks its the memories for me. We used to go to this one gas station and steal beef jerky sticks and put them in the baggy you get for them then put them in our pants shit was crazy, we never got caught doing the shit but of course we stopped doing it those who keep doing what they shouldn't are the ones who get caught I mean greedy people always get caught. We would always tell people we were cousins that was my first childhood friend and only childhood friend that I had. Nay became a LPN she's on her journey to become a RN slowly but surely. I also tried to hangout with friends who were doing well in life but i also try not to judge because people will always have a story and some sort of obstacle in life. Next is Tamia we had met in middle school i was in seventh grade and she was in eight grade we literally lived in the same neighborhood too and even rode the same bus her,Zuri,Erica and I had all lived in the same neighborhood and went to the same ghetto ass school. I didn't become closer with Tamia till we went to a worse school than our middle school in Norfolk called Lake Taylor High School all them schools were ghetto and near the projects which i think is what projected the schools to being as bad as they were with the projects near those who lived in that type of element were coming into the schools making them bad. Tamia and I didn't start hanging out and talking on the phone everyday until we went to High School we had english class together which we both loved english class. I had stains on my two front teeth which I always got joked for it was crazy because all those dentist I would go to and no one could get them stains off my teeth just fucking pitiful. Those stains didn't get removed off my teeth until I moved with my dad my sophomore year of high school when I was attending a christian academy in Orange Park. All those years it took to get those stains off my teeth because I wasn't even ugly. I had a nice body and my hair went down my back that was my only flaw so after them stains got off you couldn't tell me shit after that. Even when I moved to Florida Tamia and I talked on the phone everyday all day she was even there for me when my cousins got shot by my uncle and one had died I found that news out while on the phone with her. She was always there for me and I was always there for her. We would mail each other birthday and Christmas gifts every year and when I would come home to Virginia I would make it mandatory to see Tamia. My mother and or father would always pick up Tamia for me and we would pay for everything for her because she didn't have it like that but those are the types of people my my parents were. They would pay for other people's kid's food and drinks when we go out and sometimes if we were to go shopping a shirt of something for them. Tamia lived with her aunt and they didn't have kit like that so my parents would pay for her not that they minded and at least with Tamia she was the type of person who didn't try to get the most expensive item on the menu she actually cared when she wasn't paying especially. Tamia's aunt was cool too she would sometimes let us drink wine or buy it for us when we were nineteen and twenty years old. I would invite Tamia to my family functions and everything we always had to pick her up from home but my parents never asked her for gas money or anything my parents aren't those types of peoplenever had been and thats definitely a trait I got from both of my parents that I loved. Even though my parents were toxic at times they did raise me right at least I thought they did. Tamia and I would go shopping at the MacArthur mall it was always booming in downtown Norfolk. I even met a lot of her friends they were cool all except one by the name of Shani she was a fat bitch that made me sick ghetto as fuck. You can take the girl out the hood but cant take the hood out the girl. Tamia once told me her, Shani and few others had went to Applebee's and Shani didn't like some wings and didn't want to pay for them so they lady took them off the check but didn't grab them from the table yet so literally when they were all getting ready to walk out Tamia told me the bitch grabbed the whole fucking plate instead of putting them in her to go container with the rest of her food like a normal person would've done and took the whole plate of wings out the door with them. Tamia even told me that two older women in their fifties saw her and had their mouths open the whole time even said Shani was pushing Tamia out the door with the plate of wings and Tamia had on white pants. That's why I didn't like Shani.Hell even when Tamia invited us to Max and Erma's once for her birthday dinner Shani told the waiter she wanted to swing on his dreads and almost started a fight with my friend Amani who Tamia met through me and invited too.But me and Tamia knew everyone in Norfolk and one day my girl is going to be a Dermatologist and too be honest the more I started hanging out with Tamia I started to forget about Zuri for awhile because Zuri was such a kid all the time and had childish ways we were getting older and she was older than me by a year and just childish. But I loved Zuri like I said my friends and groups were always interesting I hung out with everyone. Tamia even said Zuri was childish as fuck it took Zuri a while to come out of that childish mentality.Zuri was always smart as hell even in middle school she was in honors classes and my girl eventually got herself two degrees and she's going to become a federal agent one day. My girl Kailey she was a few years older than me I met her in Virginia Beach at the Beach house during a modeling event and we've been friends every since we both started to eventually do modeling gigs together and we would hook each other up with them she was in school to be a Esthetician and skincare specialist which she eventually had become.

My next friend who was at my baby shower was my girl Amani she was a little hood but bougie and cool we went to the same High School our junior year in Virginia Beach Tallwood hell me and my girl even went to summer school together I was in Summer school taking English twelve the last class I had to take so I could graduate early my junior year and my girl had to retake her SOL which were state test in the state of Virginia you take at the end of the year from Elementary to High School why they made us take that shit i don't know but they shouldn't. We even lived in the same neighborhood too right around the corner from each other. I always hung out with Amani and her cousin Bree and we would always go to MacArthur mall we lived there!! One Halloween my mom dropped Amani,Bree and I off tot the mall and we decided to go to Sephora to get free mini make-overs we then went shopping then of course took lots of optics. I stayed at Amani's house I would always get her to do my hair and makeup she did aa good ass job.Asiah even went to Tallwood high school with Amani and I. The three of us used to always hangout with each other at school and talk about what guys we talked to at the time. My parents would even pick up Amani and take her home too. Everyone already knew each other for the most part I always had the same people around me. At my baby shower I kept telling myself I hoped that Asiah and Amani don't fight because they didn't like each other but I was like we too old that shit and I would hope they didn't start a fight at my baby shower I would've been pissed the fuck off. I even had text Tamia was sitting beside me telling her those two didn't like each other anymore and almost fought when we were all in Summer school the summer of our Junior year I don't even remember what they almost fought over and she even said that she hopes that they don't fight that'll be ghetto then she said if they were to fight she would kindly escort them outside because thats ghetto and I was already sad and grievingI didn't need the extra drama, I hated drama and I already had my own drama happening back in Florida which is why I had came home to Virginia even though I had drama going on there too with my mother I didn't need any extra drama. Next is Ayanna now that was my girl we used to smoke weed together Ayanna, Amani,Asiah and I already knew each other we all went to Tallwood together. Ayanna was a senior I was a junior but we did have Government class together we sat by each other everyday we had that class. She would always tell me about her boo she messed around with for years and we always smoked weed we even lived in the same neighborhood. We would go to the mall together and I would hangout with some of her and her friends,We stayed taking optics in Government class and Ayanna is a RN now and doing very well I'm proud of her.

My friend Asia we go back to middle school her and Zuri had been friends before us for years they go back to elementary school days.She had showed up late to my baby shower and Tamia said that was rude and ghetto of her which is was let alone empty handed. I remember in middle school when Zuri had a hotel birthday party and Asia,Zuri and I had to sneak out the room when Zuri's mom was sleeping while the others kept lookout. I miss those days and being a kid no worries or responsibility shit like that was fun!! Asia was always very intelligent she was in all honors classes middle school.Her and Zuri were always more closer but they had known each other for years and longer than I did. But Asia knew how to do some hair and makeup too which she went to cosmology school for and later had a baby we didn't even know she was pregnant because she was so tiny hell she was skinnier than I was but she always looked on point. Last is my girl Asiah we went to Tallwood together we stayed hanging out the thing I loved about her the most that we seemed to have in common is we both loved older men I swear we did. I always dated guys older than me and all my friends were typically older than me which theres nothing wrong with that we all have preferences when it comes to age gaps and friends. I could talk to Asiah about my men problems that I couldn't with Tamia or Zuri because I may get judged especially with Tamia her problem was she judged people. Tamia's problem was she definitely judged too much and I loved my girl to death i did but she needed to get her shit together and it was the fact she was always judging that got on my nerves, she could check everyone else but her life Like if i like older men so what that shouldn't affect her or her life. So it was cool you'll always have a friend or a few you tell certain things to that you may not with the others. Most importantly Asiah and I both got raped as kids so it felt nice talking to someone who could relate to me also Zuri got raped as a kid too so it felt nice meeting people who I can talk to who wont judge me also Tamia too. Its crazy how many of my friends can relate to being raped as a kid. Now it is time to for me to open my baby shower gifts when I get to Ayanna's gift she gave me a toys r us gift card and she gave me a card as I start reading the card I get all sad and I tried my hardest to hold back my tears. Her card reads "You're going to be a great mom I love you and Leilani I wish you two nothing but the best and you're going to kill motherhood. I then closed the card then Nay says "Awwww thats so nice". And everyone else smiles and says "its okay Britt let those tears out". I open the rest of the baby shower gifts my girl Tamia was working at a baby and toddler store in MacArthur mall called Gymboree they were closing for good so sis had bags and bags full of brand new baby girl onesies ,shoes and hair accessories. My mom then says dang Tamia you brought the whole damn store,Tamia laughs and says "they're closing anyways so i had to go all out of for my girl", I tell Tamia thank you and I love her. Next i open the bag that Zuri gave me it had hella baby clothes in it and she left the price tags on the stuff I get told her that she didn't have to spendthat much money on those clothes and told her she spent too much,Zuri then tells me that its for her niece and to hush because shes going to spoil her niece. I said alright then and thank you so much big sis. I open the gifts that Kailey gave me she gave me some babygirl Nike sets and ballerina sets it was so cute!!! I told her I loved it and that the Nike outfit would be the hospital outfit it was a new-born size too so I told her I would send her optics of baby Leilani wearing it. I skipped Asia because she was empty handed which was inappropriate but it was whatever and I knew she couldn't have been broke she ordered more food than we all did,Baby gifts don't cost that much dollar tree has a bunch of baby stuff. Hell she had even ordered way more food than me and I was the pregnant one.Nay and her mother gave me a whole bunch of gift cards to baby stores which was greatly appreciated I couldn't wait to use them. Amani gave me baby shoes and hair accessories I lovedthe hair accessories. I couldn't wait to do baby Leilani's hair at all, Last my girl Asiah she had gave me some baby girl clothes. Even Bri's friend Casey and her mom had gave me babygirl clothes and shoes andI had gifts from people who couldn't make it one boutique we go to in Fredericksburg the lady always hooked us up with clothes and accessories. My mom's friend Leslie even had hoked me up with some babygirl onesies sets and hair accessories which I greatly appreciated. By that time I get a phone call its my dad he tells me he's almost here I had no idea he was coming which was another surprise. When Asiah and I go to use the restroom all of a sudden some cops bust into the restroom which scared the fuck out of us, Asiah always had an attitude problem and didn't take shit off no one, the cops had guns and everything pointed too I had never seen no shit like that in person let alone towards me i was pregnant and pissed off thinking what if they had shot us or me or my belly. When we leave out the restroom the cops all go in there and ask us if anyone was in there we say yes then eave quickly,I was kinda embarrassed everyone was looking at us and Nay's mom asked if we were okay. I told her yes I just feel a little dizzy, the cops were looking for someone who they were chasing and had got loose lucky for them that movie theater was very packed that day. When the cops go in the restroom and come out they looked pissed and out of breath no one was in handcuffs or custody. That shit was crazy but I couldn't let it kill my mood I mean after all it was my day and it was about me and I was around positive people who loved and cared about me. My dad paid for my meal and my mother's and sister's so as everyone starts clearing out after they pay for their meals the waitress Kimey who we've known for years comes to us and tells us one person didn't pay which appeared to bee Casey's mother,she purposely did that shit too she knew damn well she didn't pay which would explain why she left so quickly in a hurry, I hated people like that especially black people manI swear it be your own damn race of people to do some shit like that that makes it worse. My dad said it was fine and he ended up paying for it he hated confrontation and everything was always fine to him like thatwasn't fine it was trifling who the fuck does that? How can you possibly forget to pay when the waitress had gave everyone their checks, I wanted to grab her ass by the hair but bitch was bald headed she had that Halle Berry hair cut Icouldn't lie it was cute but that shit she pulled wasn't cute at all like she was a grown ass adult in her damn forties.

It is now March seventeenth twenty eighteen, I wanted to go to Alabama for my next baby shower my cousin Cedes and I are both pregnant at the same time she was due in April and i was due in May. Hell even our cousin Tori was pregnant but we had no idea because she was always thick body wise and had a bell so we didn't know at that time. I think her mother knew they were good at keeping their family secrets but yet would talk about everyone else's not that I gave a fuck I didn't live there, Tori's due date was the day before I had Leilani. Before my dad and I get there a few days before my baby shower and I asked my aunt Annie if i could have the baby shower at her house it was big, nice and clean and she said yes then she asked me what types of foods did I want at the baby shower and I tell her: Baked beans, ham sandwiches, Fruits, chicken, rice and ham. She said to me I was definitely pregnant but that was fine next I text Cedes and San to ask them if they could plan the baby shower and invited everyone for me which they said yes. They were going to plan the games and get the decorations and everything else for me I really appreciated it. I called up Raeshun to do my hair for me she was affordable and lived in Alabama one thing about it she could do some fucking hair and slay it hell she even knew how to design clothes, sewdo makeup, make diy things and more. She was in her early thirties at the time and we always talked and were cool hell I thought I was in my damn thirties. Raeshun put some small feed in braids in my hair and I loved the braids they were all black and she did a good damn job and you're not sitting in her chair all damn day. I also had got a manicure and a pedicure too while I was there in Alabama hours before my baby shower even though it was cold as hell I still have to get my pedicures. When we all get to my aunt Annie's house I was sad and depressed again but when I was talking I felt pee coming down my leg and i stand up and say lord I peed on myself ,then my cousin Tori stands up and asked me if I was sure my waterdidn't break and I told her I'm sure then I go into Cedes old room at her mom and dad's house to change clothes and I say to myself so much for trying to be cute but we were in the house anyways so I just change and put on some sweatpants and a short sleeve shirt I often would get very hot and overheated in long sleeved shirts anyways and my whole pregnancyI was always hot and having hot flashes.

Cedes and San had kinda annoyed me by saying I couldn't play any of my baby shower games I had never heard of that one before who isn't allowed to play their own baby shower games? Thats why I don't like people taking over things and planning things for me. That made n sense to me all the baby showers i seen on social media people definitely are allowed to partic-ipate hell its your baby shower,People are weird. I opened my baby shower gifts as I do when I get to one gift D says that's from her and her mom which was cool and D and I were bad to being cool again. I was very much hurt-ing and sad again but I kept faking my smiles and some of the family was there but not as much as I wanted to be there but it was all good. My aunt Annie gave me a beautiful pink blanket with Leilani's name on it I loved it and out of all baby shower gifts I had gotten that was the best to me. Cedes and I both take optics touching each other's bellies. Later that day my Aunt Tricia Ann who is D's mom tells us that Tori is pregnant and she says "This is some funny shit" I had already found out though and my dad busted out laughing. My dad and I head back home within two more days of being in Alabama. The main thing i loved about going there was that good southern food it was the real deal and my aunts never disappointed when it came to food everything was already made from scratch. I remember my friend Melonie I had met her at this universitywe went to in Jacksonville,Florida we were both freshman's she was also in the military in the Army reserves but she was Puerto Rican so one Thanksgiving I was eighteen and Melonie had never been to Alabama or had real made from scratch soul food made by black people. My aunt Tricia Ann had told Melonie and I to shuck the corn it was funny as hell watching Melonie struggle and my aunt then told us that we were taking way too long for her and told us let her takeover. It was funny as hell but fun at the same time even my Melonie had never knew how to shuck so that was another thing about going to Alabama my dad's family had great southern hospitality they were just messy as hell and thats the thing I couldn't deal with I hated messy people especially when it comes to adults like y'all are too grown to be messy, I was told that after awhile being messy is a sign of misery and I couldn't agree anymore.

CHAPTER

5

It is now the day that its time to return to Florida I couldn't wait to be honest I was tired of traveling and two months away from giving birth, one thing about babies they come whenever they want to and not when we want them to. I knew one thing I wasn't having Leilani on base them base hospitals and doctors sucked. The Navy hospitals in Jacksonville were always on the news especially in their labor and delivery sections, one time at the base my dad worked at this one nurse was dangling the babies around and the dumb bitch recorded it and posted it.It was literally on the news and everything a fucking mess she was fired and whole career over like what the fuck is wrong with people? Like if you do some shit like that you need your ass beat and she should've went to jail for that its already bad enough bringing kids into this world its a mess nowadays. Hell one time I was in the lab waiting room on base waiting for my results and some random older lady told me not to have my baby on base i then had told her trust me I'm not I barely want to come here for doctor appointments then she told me use my Tricare which is the military insurance until I cant anymore,I told her I am my dad earned the benefits and I'm using all my benefits that I possibly can before they run out them benefits are nice especially when your sponsor is retired who would be my dad he's my sponsor. Even my dad had told me so many times I wasn't having Leilani on base either, it was crazy how he was mad when he found out that I was pregnant and how he told me that he was mad then wanted me to get a abortion but he was definitely coming around he even had brought Leilani some baby booties that said roll tide when we were heading back to Florida and when we were in the store getting them he told the cashier he was going to be a granddad and she then told him congratulations he seemed all happy which was a good thing. When I posted the optics of Cedes and I on my Snapchat along with the cake that said "Baby Leilani mommy cant wait to hold you" with some white baby shoes on the cake and I even posted the food on snapchat and once again Manew and Nicey saw the videos and optics then screenshot so they knew once again confirmed I was having a girl. Apart of me did it on purpose with the posting the pics and videos that indicated that I was having a girl. Because I knew that Jay's family had me on Snapchat and would see it.

My dad had told me on the car ride that he would go to work to the ID lab to get someone he knows to see what benefits Jay had I mean he was only in the military for ten years and his rank was a E-five. I knew we would be good regardless if Leilani got her dad's military benefits or not and I'm sure Carol's fat ass had already snatched them up anyways with her lazy money hungry ass. I hated bitches that don't work or want to but want to be quick to reap some fucking benefits from someone. I was a bitch that don't mind working and will work like a dog so my child has and with my dad i never had to work as hard as the next I had already had a few thousands stacked up anyways so I wasn't worried. Since I had a name picked out and knew the gender of the baby I was going to get life insurance for Leilani but my dad said he was could her a forty thousand dollar life insurance policy one thing about my dad he didn't lie at all so see I was always going to be good I didn't even ask my dad to help me out or expect him to help me out but I greatly appreciated it. My child was always going to be set regardless but that life insurance policy was a must folks never have life insurance then when a loved one dies they so quick to make go fund me and asking people for money like people are supposed to be obligated to help out and a lot of times stuff like that is scams. I had been making moves anyways in silent to make sure we were good and all we needed and by we I really mean Leilani, I had two months to really get my shit together time was going by very fast because it's now the month of April my mother's birthday was in April the twenty six to be exact I had to figure out what to get her and mail to her even though I wasn't a big fan of her nor had I had been because of what had transpired but I had to get my shit in order I couldn't worry about the drama I was bringing life into the world. I knew I eventually had to reach out to Jay's family but I wasn't going to until I needed them for the DNA testing so Leilani could get her father's social security something she was entitled to and deserved, I knew how to deal with them and handle them I wasn't worried about them either i had what they needed and who they needed so I wasn't worried. Those little threats their family had made didn't mean shit to me I had money and my dad was a fed so I don't think they wanted me to press charges. I'm the nicest,coolest,sweetest person ever until you piss me off I can turn into a bitch quickly and fuck up someone's life.

I call Bri up to ask her what our mother liked gift wise because she was so damn ungrateful when it came to gifts and picky, i typically try to gift people with what they like and lets see my mother loved wine,moneydesigner bags,Olive Garden,Longhorn Steakhouse,Ruth Chris and shit that costed money. I decided to just cash app Bri one hundred dollars and told her spend the money on a gift for our mom or take her out to eat and if there's money leftover to pocket the money for herself I didn't care at all, I then told Bri to tell our mother the gift came from her and not me. Since the first time I had found out that I was pregnant I was already preparing early for stuff to buy from Walmart overtime to have everything I would need, for the longest time I would just buy boxes of pull ups and wipes then I started getting into bottles and baby swings and bouncers that were unisex. When I found out I was having a girl I went back to Walmart to buy a bunch of girl decor and girl bath tub and bassinet and to be honest everything in sight that was pink and or purple. Later this day which is April tenth twenty eighteen my dad and I received a phone call that Cedes is in labor her baby came a week early I was happy for her she was having a boy its crazy because Jenna had also texted in the group chat saying she was having her baby boy. Everyone was having their baby hell I was ready to have mine too i really was. This was also the day I stopped fucking with Jenna and Becca because Jenna literally said to us to have fun "Bed Sharing" with ur babies because Becca and her husband were struggling badly so they had to move into her mother's home so of course the three of them Becca,her baby boy and husband were going to have to share a room. Then there's me Ihad to share a room with my baby I knew but it wouldn't be long we were going to be moving out soon from my dad's house but I didn't appreciate the bitch saying that shit especially when she knew my child's dad died. So I wrote a long ass page to them in the group chat something I do best before I cut people off and block them after every message says delivered. I don't play that shit bitches hd to be humbled a bit and I had to remind them both why they had what they had,I sent another message saying y'all only have what y'all have because of your husbands who are in fact rookies and broke I said y'all are the type of bitches to brag about being military wives but don't have shit to show for it meanwhile y'all husband's fighting to stay in and y'all all struggling in real life I said I have thousands saved up and a single mother don't mean I'm a poor or struggling one so lets not insinuate that all single moms are struggling at least e do it all by ourselves withoutdepending a man or men to take care of us. I have my own money my child wasn't even born yet and she already had a forty thousand dollar life insurance policy and I was getting my shit together. When all the messages I had typed up said delivered I blocked them hoes I sure did I hate married women that think their better than the next like did y'all forget you only have what you have because of yourhusbands so lets not forget that detail please and thank you . I'm a bad bitch I know the struggle due to losing my child's father and that situation mad me a badder bitch than I already was. thats why its so hard I think having married friend with kids when your a single mom its not all of them that act that way but hell its enough of them that act as if their better than the next some of y'alldon't work and never have. I had already been a Prada of letting a man take care of me and then one day he fucking dies and Iwasn't about to let that shit happen again to me, my child and I were definitely going to be good but I hate bitches that act as if they're better than the next when withoutyour husbands you still don't have a pot to piss in or a window to throw the piss out of. Granted it wasn't Becca it was Jenna who made that ignorant ass comment but I got that vibe from the both of them since day one and I didn't like it. I knew I should've been mixing and mingling with my own people I thought in my head jokingly. But at the end of the day I hated being around bitches who thought they were better because they had a ring on their finger like y'all do know marriage don't mean forever or equal happiness which is what most fail to realize but more power to them. I was about to be a single mom and somehow someway I still was doing better than those bitches,Their husbands were fresh meat in the Navy meanwhile they bragging and talking like their husbands were in for ten to twenty years so fuck out of here. I kept them on my snapchat so they could see how great my life was about to get. Honestly whenever I blocked people's phone numbers I would always keep them on my social media so they can see how I'm living and looking to feel dumb about themselves like damn I cant believe i said that to Brittany or did that to her. Hell after all single moms are the boss bitches of mom's ,doing it all alone no help either. My situation was living proof to make sure you have your shit together because a spouse,boyfriend/girlfriend could die at anytime thank God I had a few thousands saved up and I had my father who lived in Florida who i could go back home to. I also wanted to cry because of that comment Jenna made only because I'm like damn the bitch knew

117

my story and still made that comment but I couldn'tallow myself to cry I couldn't feel story for myself nor allow myself to. I mean behind her and her comments were going to be a bunch of other people who would say worse because I was a single mom unfortunately people are just ignorant and there's nothing you can do about it.

My dad and I go car shopping for me he gives me check for ten thousand dollars I broke down crying then I hugged my dad I really appreciated one thing about my dad and I we are going to save out money and we are both logical thinkers we always have been and always will be. Which is why we always had money we were the type of people we never freely and loosely spent out money we always thought about how much we could get of something before just spending. My dad had also taught me that just because you have money don't mean you always have to spend money my dad was always cheap as fuck kind like Jason Pitts from the television show "The Game" had money and was still acting broke but I understood why. I just wanted a used car for about forty five hundred to fifty five hundred so I could possibly pocket the rest of the money, my dad knew I was a logical and smart thinker. I was surprised it took him so long to get me a car I thought I would've gotten a car when I had graduated high school early but that didn't happen or when I went to college but that didn't happen either but I couldn't dwell in the past I had to worry abut the present at that moment.My dad and I go to car shops all around in Jacksonville area and Orange Park to all the used car dealerships no luck April was still also tax time. My dad was very smart and he knew about cars he even showed me how I could tell that some cars had been in water. I tried to sometimes outsmart my dad I was really hoping he would let me keep the rest of the money that was leftover. We finally go to this place in Jacksonville on one hundred and third area which is the hood, they had nice houses ,apartments and townhouses but the area was a high crime area kids always getting shot through windows while sleeping that was in fact the same area where Jay's parents lived they had a decent house but that area was a no for me. All the car dealerships we went to on one hundred and third street were right up the street from Jay's parents house. I was seeking for a nice used suv but at the rate we were going and with it being tax time we found a bunch of nice SUV. But for the years and the cheap prices my dad told me something was off which he was right you could smell that some of the vehicles had been in water but they were so nice but my dad told me that he wasn't going to just put me in any type of vehicle just to have me in something then something happens to it but one thing about my dad I trusted him he always knew what he was doing especially when it came to spending money. We finally go to this one shop he had a bunch of nice vehicles inside and out I wanted a suv but the ones he had were used which wasn't even the issue but they were scratched and ripped all up on the inside which would cost money to get fixed I didn't just want any type of vehicle to say I had one. The guy who owned the sho was African and not even to be racist but I guess its whoever it offends but oh well cant please everyone and help how others will feel with what you say but I really didn't like doing business with black people because our own people are sometimes crabs in a barrel and they always trying to pull a fast one especially them people from overseas. His ass looked crooked I mean game recognized game,I saw a Nissan Altima that i wanted my dad and I test drive it he lets me drive it whileI drive he tests everything to make sure everything works in the car, When we get back the man who owned the shop whose name was "Fancy" asked how did I like the car I tell him I loved it the Nissan had leather seats,bluetoothsunroof,key fob, and everything else Iwanted in a vehicle the one thing it didn't have was a touchscreen which I knew I could get added into it eventually no big deal. After all the car was going to paid for that was a real treat when you pay cash for a vehicle the same day and I loved it. I asked Fancy how much for the Nissan he tells me five thousand which wasn't bad it was a two thousand and nine. My dad talks him down to forty five hundred and the guy agrees to it which I was surprised its literally April and I only had one more month to go before it was time for Leilani to get here. The guy Fancy gives me a hug and I gave him a look like "ummmm" then he tells me congratulations asking when was my due date and what was I told him May twenty eighth is the due date and i was having a girl. We go into his office and my father filled out all the forms and paperwork for me and gives him forty five hundred in a check so I didn't even have to touch the check he had given me thank God, hell I didn't want to touch the check I just wanted to pocket it when we finish up the paperwork I was all emotional trying to hold back tears I was like my dad brought me a car not that i expected him to but I greatly appreciated it and best thing of all no car note hell thats a true blessing. My dad and I walk outside and Fancy does as well and gives me the key and I told him Thank you very much. Then my dad tells me that I can keep the check for ten thousand dollars and told to go ahead and drive my car home he'll be there soon. I was crying and driving because I didn't believe my dad actually let me keep the check he's never done anything like that before so I told myself the next day I would go to Navy Federal credit Union to add Leilani onto my bank account and get her a bank account card with Navy Federal you can get your child if they're under the age of eighteen a bank card called a "Cucard" it wasn't a debit or credit car the thing I hated about that card from when I had one is it can be money in the account but you have to withdraw the money out at the ATM, it wont let you use the card anywhere I remembered my " Cucard" kept declining when I went to use it when I was like sixteen and I had to call Navy Federal and when I did and explained to them what happened they told me it was because it wasn't a debit or credit card which on the card it doesn't say debit or credit. Nothing more embarrassing than when your card declines with money on the card. but its just until Leilani turns eighteen.

But the next day I was planning on putting five thousand dollars in a account for Leilani my child was going to be set for life I had to get her health insurance as well I was going to add her onto mine with the help of my dad that military insurance is lit and I was a prime member too. My child was never going to have to work as hard as the next person's child I might've been preparing to be a single mom but I was going to be the best single mom ever hell single don't mean struggling even though thats how society sees it but you cant help everyone people will think and or feel how they do and there's nothing you can do to make them agree with you. Later that day I text Shelby my friend who was in her twenties her and I had met when we were at the private college in Jacksonville together. I asked her what was she up to she then told me she was at the Walmart on Blanding which was in Orange Park so I told her I would meet her there to get some more baby stuff and I told her I was on the way as she was walking out the store I saw her walking out and rolled down the window to tell her to get in and I'd take her to her car. She told me that my car was nice it felt nice having my own car too no more waiting for people to pick you up and giving gas money even though I didn't mind at all. I took her to her car I was parked beside her car she sat in mine for awhile we were just talking a lot she asked me were things getting better with Leilani's dad's family and I told her how I blocked them to be honest. It started to rain a bit so I didn't go into the store and I told Shelby to text me sometime this week and we could go grab some food and shop around at the Orange Park mall she gave me a hug then said hang in there mama you got this. I told her thanks and that I loved her she said I love you too. Shelby was like my nerdy friend she loved Anime and she could paint and draw her ass off. I even asked her once if she could draw a canvas of me and Leilani she agreed to it I told her I would pay her I just wanted to hang it up when we moved into our townhouse and or house. I could've took the apartment my dad said he would pay for if I wanted but I didn't want my dad to do shit else for me he was one of those parents that bring up what they do for you and my biggest thing was if you're going to help someone thats fine but you don't have to talk about what you do fro people either I hated that about parents especially in the black community it was annoying if you're going to help and do for others thats fine but you don't have to talk about what you do. I had more than enough saved up to even pay the apartment or townhouse up for a year if I wanted to but I didn't want to touch my money yet I wanted to keep stacking up my money,I wanted to save up a additional ten thousand then I would move out of my dad's house. He didn'tpressure me to move out of anything but I'm sure he would be ready soon to have his house back and plus I was going to need space because a mom and baby sharing a room wasn't going to be it for me for long.

I decided to text Alma,Nae,DayDay in our group chat to see if they wanted to grab some dinner. They picked me up in Alma's car she had a nice used two thousand and nine lincoln. Nae was driving her car for her Alma was only in her late thirties and used to act so damn old it was funny as hell she would be already driving like she was an old ass lady. My dad had waved at them through the screen door he was standing there as I walked outside to get into the car when they text me saying they were outside. The crazy thing is we all lived around the corner from each other and everyone still worked at Burger King except for me. I get into the back seat and we go to crafty crab on Blanding Blvd in Orange Park I had never been there before I loved seafood but a lot of the seafood places around in Orange Park and Jacksonville were all overpriced and they would be stingy with the crab legs. When we get there they seat us right away then they give us bibs that said crafty crab with gloves which I was glad. The waitress comes over to take our drink orders and because I was pregnant as fuck and showing they no one ordered liquorI was glad because I definitely wanted a drink but I couldn't drink which sucked but soon I would be able to drink once I had the baby and weeks went by.When the waitress comes back to get our orders we all get crab bags whichhas shrimp,eggs,potatoes, crab legs. It didn't take long for our food to come out at all before we all started eating we all take optics and we didn't really talk much about thing out of everyone I was close to Nae the most she was in her forties older than my mom she was like a mom to me but I didn't forget when she told the girls something I told her in private so I just learn not to make the same mistake twice. it felt nice to just get out the house and to not cry and be depressed. When we finish eating at crafty crab we go to the Walmart up the street I grabbed some candy out of there since we were in there thats when I see my old teacher "minister Smalls" from the christian academy I attended when i was in tenth grade but she also watched me grow up I would attend the summer school she had at one of the churches for years I had been going there since I was in Middle school. She was very close to my dad and Iknew her nieces and granddaughters. I used to attend church with them and hangout with them sometimes. One time I smoked weed with her two granddaughters who were way older than me they didn't care when they would watch me they were cool and once again I aways would hangout with the older crew. But I had seen Ms.Smalls she had noticed I was pregnantI cannot remember exactly what she asked but I know she made a smart comment about me being pregnant thats when I told her that my child's dad died as a tear came down my face and I quickly wiped my face. See how eager people are to judge without knowing the full story but then again she was a "christian" I expected it. I told her it was nice to see her and I left out the Walmart. I could tell she felt bad for what she said to me by her facial expressions, that's why you don't judge people you never know one's story.

Nae drives Alma's car and they take me home on the way home I tell them thank you for getting me out the house it was much needed because its the end of April and y'all know a bitch is almost due at any moment. In May I told them I wouldn't be moving around too much and going all around like that because I was due at any moment. When they drop me off home its dark and they wait for me to get into the house before they drive off. My dad asked how was the crafty crab because he had never been and I told him the proportion size sucked and they charge all that money then he said he don't know why black people always want to get seafood I said Forreal because it adds up and you'll never get the amount that you want without paying money. Then I tell him that I saw Ms.Smalls at Walmartand spoke with her for a moment she still lived in the same house and worked at the same Christian academy which was on the street from us on Kingsley Ave in Orange Park. I tell my dad I'll be in my room I didn't ever tell my dad everything that I was planning he could be very negative at times and act as if he knew everything it would be annoying. I was writing a list on things needed to be done tomorrowI knew I had to open that bank account for Leilani and add in five thousand dollars then get her "cucard". I also later that night packed my hospital bag I wanted to be very prepared. I receive a text on my phone from Garett the man that had stopped me from taking my own life without knowing that. he asked how was I doing and if he could take me out for breakfast,lunch,or dinner. He was very attractive but I didn't want to date anyone I didn't want to really be bothered by any man either, I was annoyed that he even had texted me I always got approach by older men it was what I liked but was also annoying. I was alone and very lonely but I was also still grieving. When I had first met Garrett he told me his wife had died and I guess that's all we had in common only we could relate to losing a significant other. Then another text comes in that says "I thought you'd use my number months had went by and I never heard from you I hope you'r doing much better I know you'll never get over him but it still feels nice talking to someone who can relate and you can grieve for as long as you need to I hope to see you soon. I didn't respond back to him instantly at all because I really had to think about if his intentions were pure and what he wantedafter allmenain't shit. I thought about what if he wanted sex or something back in return like most men because I was pregnant and I wasn't having sex with any man with another man's baby inside of me I couldn't even imagine doing that shit.

I went back to what I was doing as far as making to do lists and to get lists for Leilani, He had a iPhone just like I did and I left him on read I couldn't think about going on a date with any man while being pregnant by a man I loved who was gone and never coming back. I showered and got ready for bed while thinking about if I was going to go out with this man I mean it was just food then I texted him back and asked him what is it that he's seeking from me and or in return if I agree t go out to eat with him. I also asked him if he remembered that I was pregnant.Garett responded with laughing emojis saying he just wants company he said and he also wanted to invite me to this group he goes to for grief the group is for adults who've lost their boyfriendgirlfriend,spouses and haven't been able to get over it.He said the support group helped him tremendously.He said I'm more than welcome to attend it and its adults from the age groups twenty to fifty its only about fifteen people in the group they sit in a circle and everyone goes around in a circle and talks in the group is every Tuesday at six at night. As i talked to myself I told myself it sounded interesting not like I was working anyways I had nothing but time it seemed beneficial its nice being around others who can relate to you thats what makes you feel better as a person. It reminded me of a AA meeting when he said you sit in a circle and everyone goes around talking abut their experience. I then texted him asking if he wanted to grab lunch tomorrow or dinner I could meet him somewhere, I told him it sounded interesting and we could discuss it more in person instead of text. He said yes we can meet for lunch he asked what types of foods I liked then said he's not trying to get sex from me or anything else from me.He just feels as if he could help someone with a problem he could once relate to he promises. I responded back saying I'm eight months pregnant and I'm not picky I eatlike a grown man with laughing emojis to follow what I said. Then he asked what side of town did I live and I responded saying Orange Park wells road area. He said that he lived in that area too then asked if I wanted to go to LongHorn or Red lobster. I picked red lobster then he asked if one would work for the time I said yes thats fine. Then asked if

I wanted him to pick me up I responded saying I can meet you there its fine plus i have errands to run which I did. He then said alright I'll see you tomorrow at red lobster and lets see if you can eat a lot like you say with laughing emojis. I saidI sure can lol but then I told him i'll see him tomorrow for lunch. I was feeling so guilty for some reason going on a "date" while being pregnant but really it wasn't a date though or at least thats what I kept telling myself. I get up out of bed to see what I wanted to wear I mean after all we lived in Florida it was always hot as hell it was summer and I was going to be having a summer baby soon. I definitelydidn't care about being cute just comfortable but I had no idea what to wear for this so called "Not a date". I had never really had male friends before unless they were gay because other than that they always wanted to fuck. Plus as a kid I was always getting raped by my mother's male friends or fuck buddies I should say, I was raped by one of her male friends by the name of "Ale"I'm guessing that's what they called him I'm not sure nor do I care but he had a daughter who was younger than me and she had a sister who was the same age as me Terri and Tia. I would sometimes go over to Ale's house with them sometimes after school. Sometimes he'd even watch Bri and I for my mother. He and my mother would also fuck and he would also touch me inappropriately whichI felt happened lots in the black community it was always a close uncle or friend of the family who was raping the children meanwhile our parents left unaware because they're too fucking trusting.

I had bed wetting problems up to the age of twelve I think part of the issue was I was scared of the dark to get up and go pee would often have dreams that someone would grab me in the dark when I would get up to go pee. Lots of my friends especially Zuri, Nay and Tamia were very unaware, Icouldn't ever let them know that because bitches get mad or you piss them off when mad day comes up they will definitely ell your business I've learned that from my mother and in general from a few situations. My mother would also say I was lazy and I'd have to wear pull ups. That was very fucking embarrassingly but my friends didn't know ever. But at times Bri and I would stay over at Ale's house I would be wearing pull ups and in the bed or on the couch he would literally sit on the couch beside me then start fingering me or he would take off my pull up and start to eat my pussy often he even would stick his big,thick,long dick inside of me which almost killed me I would be crying and begging him to stop which seemed to be more of a turn on for him. How does a grown ass man's dick even get hard from touching a minor? like thats some sick ass shit, He even told me not to tell anyone or there would be consequences, it would be times I would be bleeding in my vagina and on my vagina I didn't know how to tell my mother and I didn't want her to be upset with me so I decided not to tell her I would then use vaseline on my vagina which clogged the pores of my vagina I finally learned later in life as I got older but I didn't know that then as a little girl, my innocence was gone and my virginity was gone. I tried to do everything I could to prevent my mother from seeing how open my vagina was and from seeing I had lots of bleeding and scaring on my vagina. I felt so dirty and icky this grown ass of a man was telling me how he was going to marry me he even said I was his girlfriend and tried to gas-light me and manipulate me into saying it and making myself believe it. I had a odor I could smell coming from the inside of my vagina between the blood and the vaseline and it even hurt to pee I didn't want my mom to get into trouble I didn't want to got taken away from her either and I knew my dad wouldn't take care of me either he literally sent me to Alabama a few times as a kid while he was in the Navy which I fucking hated. When Bri and I stayed over at Ale's house he even said he wanted my sister but I told him I was who he wanted and he could do whatever he wanted to me and I wouldn't tell on him, just don't touch my sister we were six years apart I would literally allow someone to kill me if it meant she could go on and be free even as a adult I would risk my life for Bri. It was already bad enough it was happening to me this grown ass man who was in his thirties was fucking me without my consent. I even tried to fight him off and I would be begging and pleading him he was literally buff and thick like all he did was work out or as if he was fresh out of jail. He would even finger me when we were in the car and he was driving he would even make my sister sit on the side where she couldn't see him do it and as he fingered me I would silently cry tears falling down my face. Then when he finished fingering me he would look me in my eyes and suck the cum off his fingers it made me sick. I couldn't imagine what my mother would say telling her that shit considering the man raping me was the same man that was fucking her and raw at that then he grabbed my hand and put it on his dick and made me stroke his dick with the cum still on all his dick.

This was the same man whose daughter and her sister went to the same elementary school and daycare with Bri and I. This was the same man who was a grown ass man infatuated with a little girl, he would rape me every chance that he could and then try to bribe me.One night he was really fucking bold after he fucked my mother he came into the bedroom at his house where my sister and I were both laying in sleeping he literally tapped on me to wake me up and looked at me and beat his dick until he came. I couldn't even believe my mother had took Bri and I with her whenever she would have dick appointments. What kind of mother did that and little did she know i as the one being raped a young ass innocent ass little girl and she didn't even know. Shit like this happens so much in the black community our parents being naive and trusting of men and boys they've known for years which meant absolutely nothing. Whenever we stayed at Ale's house Brimom,and I he would come into the guest room and he would take off my pull up and start eating my pussy and finger me at the same time while he gave me head. He would put tape over my mouth.One time he had a house full it was Tia, Terri,Bri,Elijah and I and Ale did the same thing he made me go into his bedroom when the kids and I were all playin hide and seek and put me on the bathroom sink then started kissing on me and having his way with me. I ran to the hallway bathroom and threw up aa few times then i sat down on the floor holding my stomach crying and asking God to help me. I was silently saying "Why me God" and asking "what did i do God?" After he was done he told me to get out so later that night I went rambling through his downstairs drawers to see what kind of weapons I could find then I started to take a butcher knife from one of his knife sets but I didn't want him to notice it was gone so I grabbed a old rusted pocket knife in his mail drawer I putin my pants and I decided to hide it somewhere no one would ever find it considering it was a house full of kids.

I then made a plan in my mind to stab him when he came into the room to try to rape me again I told myself i was going to stab him in his stomach I didn't want to kill him and go to jail but I wanted to get him down so Bri and I could escape from his house. It went on long enough and I had got to my breaking point i was sick of it. I was so scared I wondering what if I had gotten pregnant and everything one time he asked me if I was on birth control I didn't even know what the fuck that was. See how he was taking away my innocence the first time he introduced me to sex or i should say unwanted sex. I had even called one of my mom's friend's Mary I was very close to her I had wished she were my mother instead of the one I had and I asked her if she could meet us and gave her a location which was the next neighborhood over. I had always knew the name of it because it was nicer and had a better playground. I had called Mary she then answered on the third ring she lied and told her my mother told m to ask her if she could pick us up from Ale's house at six in the morning and she said that was very early but she would and she asked me to send her the address. I told her Ididn't know the address but i could get it off the mail I told her I would send the address when we had gotten off the phone but I had lied and told her the name of the neighborhood next to Ale's neighborhood she then said okay and see you guys then before I hung up I said okay auntie she then asked if i was okay. I told her no but i would be eventually for good.

She then asked what did I mean and I had told her nothing just talking. I knew I couldn't tell her I was planning on harming the man who had raped me she wouldn't have allowed me to. Ale had ordered us pizzas for dinner while we waited for the pizzas Tia,Terri,,Elijah and I were all in the living room watching movies and drinking juice thats when Ale called my name to come upstairs and told everyone else to stay downstairs he needed me to get something for him.Elijah was Tia's brother and from the looks of it Ale had hella kids he was a big time hoe he was only in his thirties with seven kids, He was definitely a rolling stone as the song goes. There's nothing cute about having all them damn kids especially when you're not even taking care of all of them the way that you should be that's trifling and you're a sorry ass excuse of a father and man. I never understood why men go out there having unprotected sex with all these different women making all these babies and shit. That's why society always would say that black kids grow up without daddies granted that all races had men that aren't shit but i kinda agreed with what society said.

I tell Ale I didn't want to help him at all and I was watching the movie with the kids and Tia then asked why didn't I want to help her dad i said because m watching the movie then Ale says my mom is on the phone and says I'm in trouble so I get up to go upstairs i was scared as fuck I couldn't help but think that Mary had called my mom to ask her why we needed to be picked up early as I walkedupstairs my face was turning red and the palms of my hands are getting sweaty as fuck. Little did Tia know her daddy was a rapist and had a fetish for fucking little girls. When I get upstairs and walk to Ale's room which was the first door on the right hand side and open the door and walk in he's laying naked on his bed and tells me to sit on his face and as I walk over to him he tries to help me take off my clothes I tell him that I can do it because all I could think of was the pocket knife I had in my pants closed up sitting in my underwear. As i take off my pants and shirt I grab the pocket knife and keep if close beside the side of the bed where I was standing at then Ale tells me to touch his dick and grabs my hand and puts on his dick as he moans and I grab the pocket knife and open the pocket knife right when I go to stab him there's a knock on the door I throw the pocket knife on the floor on top of my clothes scared. Then Ale jumps up and puts his clothes back and whispers to me go to the bathroom and put your clothes back on and pushes me. Im in the bathroom silently yelling fuck fuck fuck!!! time was going by and at this point it was ten at night I noticed on wrist watch on Ale's sink in the bathroom in his bedroom.

He told Elijah he was coming down and to go downstairs and get the pizzas then when he tells me to come out the bathroom I do and as he goes back to make up the bed he notices the pocket knife which i realized I didn't have I left it on the side of the bed in between the bed and the nightstand I didn't think he would've noticed it. When i go downstairs he tells all of us to wash his hands and get to the table as he goes to get the pizzas and pay for everything. When he preps everything for us to eat he had ordered two pizzas, different flavors of wings, sodas and bread sticks. He calls me us all to get our plate of food and he asked us all if we had a pocket knife that was in his mail drawer I was screaming in my mind. Then he said someone-could've gotten hurt had it got in the wrong hands and he said out loud that was a weapon and someonecould've went to jail if they used it on someone while looking me dead in the face. I was trying to think of a new strategy of how to hurt Ale before Bri and I had gotten hurt but I had to wait until we all had went to bed to do so and i had to be careful that time to ensure I didn't get caught again. After we all finish eating Ale tells us all to take turns showering so we could get ready for bed. He had a three bedroom house so the other two rooms were guest rooms he made Elijah sleep on the couch. Terri and Tia slept in the same room and Bri and I slept in the other room. Ale had also told the kids not to tell their mom that Bri and I were over there. The craziest shit ever was that Bri and I weren'tsupposed to be there because my mother used to be cool with Terri and Tia's mom Crystal but they had a fall out and my mom was then fucking Ale that's pretty fucked up and nasty like how can you fuck your ex best friend's baby daddy/man. Terri then asked why they couldn't tell their mom about us staying the night there with them and Ale said he didn't need no drama. I don't know why he even said that because kids talk and they will tell.

Ale then tells me I can use his bathroom to shower I told him I was good and I was just going to wait my turn. I didn't go in his bathroom and I told Bri when Elijah finishes showering to let me shower after him and she said okay. I shower next after Elijah gets out and gets dressed which took him forever to do so like I was trying to not get raped again and again. When I get out and I get dressed I get a phone call on my phone from my aunt Mary which was my mom's best friend she asked if I had gotten that address yet I tell them her no I haven't forgot about her I told we just finished eating dinner and we all just are getting settled down for bed but I told her the name of the neighborhood next to us, we were in Virginia Beach at the time so it shouldn't have been that many neighborhoods with that name in that city. I then tell her as soon as I finish getting ready for bed I would text it to her then she says okay pumpkin then hangs up the phone. As we all part ways to go to our designated sleeping areas I'm holding my stomach and hurting still bleeding and my vagina hurts and it stings when I went to pee. I couldn't help but think of how much trouble I was going to be in and I kept thinking to myself that I was going to have to tell on him. Bri is laying in bed watching tv and she notices I'm holding my stomach and she asked me what was wrong with me and I told her that I couldn't poop and I hurt when I tried to go as I get in bed wit her. I get out of bed she asked me where was I going then I told her to the closet in the room we were in to be nosey to see what he had in his closet but before I do so I locked the bedroom door. I told Bri she better not tell or open her mouth I loved my sister to death but she was definitely a little fucking snitch and I would often have to bribe her with my allowance money and with candy in order for her not to tell sometimes she would want me to do her chores or something else that she didn't want to do. As I open both sides of the brown wooden closet doors it was lots of shit in there and I had seen clothes,boxes with papers, there was even a safe in there that I tried to quickly open that had the keys inside of it. Ale wasn't going to get away with raping me for as long as he did I had to get some type of revenge on him I wanted him dead to be honest but I didn't want to go to jail so as I keep rambling through the closet I see old bats, old shoes, trophies and awards, I had even found anther pocket knife which I grabbed and put in my pants without Bri seeing me do so then I hear a knock at the door so I hurry and close the closet door quietly and I yell "I'm changing clothes just a minute" then I opened the door it was Ale I was for sure I was going to stab his ass this time I mean after all he was raping me I was a kid which was a crime I was sure and it was wrong,If anything he would be the one going to jail he asked me to come here so i say sure and then i say one second please then I go back to the bedroom Bri and I were sleeping in and I throw all our shit in our overnight bag then tell her make sure she has everything and told her we were leaving and put her jacket on then get back in bed and don't leave anything behind, Bri asked where were we going I then tell her don't ask me anymore questions right now just do it we have to go. When i come back into the room to get you we're leaving. I told her don't say bye to Terri or Tia either they're sleeping so just wait for me and I told her quietly get up and make sure she packed everything we came with.

I back into Ale's bedroom and I asked him what did he want then he says he knows you what I want then he starts kissing on my neck and grabbing the breasts that I didn't have. Before I knew it I had slowly reached into my night pants to grab the pocket knife and I touched on his dick on the outside of his pants something he had showed me and taught me what to do. Then i grabbed the pocket knife and I stabbed him in his stomach hard and I pushed it in his stomach as deep as I could and fast before he pushes me and he drops to the floor yelling fuck and holding his stomach with blood being visible on his white tank top he was wearing then I grab the flashlight off his dresser before using it to hit him he asked what was I doing with that and says way as I hit him as hard as I could in the face with it. I grab the house phone on the way out to call the police then run into the room with Bri i grabbed our overnight back I tell her to come on. I grabbed the duffle bag throwing it over my head. I asked her if she got everything and tell her come on and i hoped Elijah was sleep we had to go downstairs and I peeped through the rail to see if he's sleeps thats when I noticed he wasn't there at all but I saw the bathroom light was on I tell Bri come on run lets go be quick I told her we grab our shoes and run outside to the next neighborhood I had already called the cops and dropped the house phone. We fly down the stairs making our way to the front door before Elijah came out the bathroom I didn't even put my shoes on I just grabbed them thank God I had socks on but I let Bri put her shoes on then I tell Bri hold my hand and run. My belly hurt really bad and I had to pee but we had to go to the next neighborhood first couldn't get caught by the cops.

Thats when I take my phone out the duffle bag then I check my phone it was only one in the morning thats when I decided to call my aunt we were stuck and the cops would be there soon. Bastard better be lucky I called the cops for him but I call my aunt Mary I break down crying saying auntie please come get us from that neighborhood I told you to pick us up and I said he kept raping me so I stabbed him. My aunt Mary said what loudly then told me be quiet and stay put she's on the way to come get us. She said she was about twenty minutes away from us i said please hurry auntie the cops are coming and she says dear God I'm on the way I'll go as fast as I can. Bri asked me what were we doing outside in the cold I told her we were leaving and I then told her I cannot tel her what happened right now but when she gets older I promised to tell her what happened to me and occurred. I had a lot to worry about as is I had to make sure I wasn't pregnant. All I could think about is if I had killed Ale or not, I really didn't care before I left out his bedroom he was bleeding out but he deserved it he had been raping me which was wrong I was a fucking child after all!!! The fact he had daughters and he was a damn rapist. I wanted to yell,scream and cry but I had to be very strong for my sister I didn't want her to tell on me or see me upset it was so much that was going on in my mind at that moment I just wanted my aunt to hurry up and get us the fuck outta there. After all I had to explain to her what I had done I had to go to the hospital and my vagina was burning. I was holding onto to Bri cuddling with her I even gave her my jacket even thought she had one and we sat on the playground set and waited for my aunt. I didn't know if she was going to tell my mom or what but after all I trusted her more than my mom hell she was even like a damn mom to me, she was like the mother I didn't have that I needed in my life. My mother would often have different sexual partners she would often take us with her to these partner's homes and hell she was the reason I had gotten raped!!! I also told myself when I had kids I would be way better than my mother. You give her a drink and some money and she's good. I then start hearing sirens which were getting closer and closer and still no sign of my aunt Mary who was my mother's best friend at the time. That's when I see a black Buick SUV arrive which was my aunt Mary's SUV she had at the time and I tell Bri to come on and she was driving so fast the tires made a loud noise when she stopped. I said in my mind thank God because the ambulance And police were getting close and I also had to explain to my aunt Mary what I did and why I was so scared but not as scared as I was in the beginning because I had a good enough reasoning I knew I wouldn't go to jail for what I did it was self defense after all I was a little girl who was getting raped by a grown ass man who had daughters which makes it 10 times worse and disgusting. He made me feel disgusting about myself for so long he made me feel as if it was my fault he made me feel guilty about it all but in reality he himself should have felt guilty dirty and disgusting. How does a man's dick even get hard enough to rape a little girl? That's very sick and you have to be a sick fucking human being to do some shit like that. Bree and I hop in the back seat I put her seat belt on her

135

and I asked Mary if we could please just go to her house and I would explain everything to her I didn't want my little sister to hear what happened to me because it should have never happened to me in the first place and I put my jacket over Bri and my arm around her. Mary then says yes that's fine I'll take you girls to my home get you situated and then says Brittany you and I have some talking to do, I tell her yes ma'am and I say please don't tell my mother with a tear rolling down my face I said I'll tell you everything you want to know and need to know just don't tell my mother she's not going to believe me if she's going to be upset she might even send me away I said the situation is that bad I just don't want to tell you in front of my little sister she doesn't need to hear this or know this I shouldn't even have been going through that and as my aunt Mary and I make eye contact I think she already had an idea of what I was going to tell her she then drives off and says she'll take us to her home and get us situated and together. On the way to her home she asked us if we're hungry I told her no but Bri said yes ma'am and she wanted McDonald's we stop at the nearest McDonald's on the way back to at Marys home breathe in orders a bacon egg and cheese biscuit with a hash brown and an orange juice. When we finally reach at Mary's house Bri said that she was sleepy she had already ate her food in the truck along the way so let Mary puts her in the guest room to go to sleep and her and I then go downstairs where she asked me what happened before I can even get out would happen I burst into tears crying and screaming asking her for help I knew she would help me and I knew she wouldn't tell my mother. I told her how owl had raped me and that wasn't the first second or third time he has done it and how our mother always leaves us over there. I then say I feel disgusting icky it burns below it hurts I'm bleeding I'm scared I don't know what to do and my aunt just grabs my hand and gives me a Kleenex. She then says to me while holding my hand we're going to get through this and we're going to get some help for you and see what all we can do I told her I didn't want to be taken away from my mom it was as if I was protecting my mother even though she was one of the people who needed to answer for what happened to me because had she never left me with that man he would have never been touching me inappropriately in the first place and we wouldn't have been through this and I wouldn't have stabbed him In the first place I then ask my auntie if she thinks that I'm pregnant and if she could look at my vagina for me because it was red and sore itchy and it burned I also had tons of Vaseline caked up below on it . She then tells me to grab a towel out of the closet and tells me to lay down on the towel on the floor and open my legs so she can see what's going on she was also a nurse which is better for me because no hospital visit was needed at least I thought . She shines a light on my vagina so she can clearly see but of course she goes to wash her hands before touching anything and she puts on some gloves she then tells me is red and hurting and I'm sore because he was a grown ass man who had no business touching me down there and trying to fit inside of me in the first place she also had spare pregnancy tests and she makes me pee on the stick in front of her so she can see if I was pregnant or not and turned out I was not pregnant thank God. I then ask her what are we going to do about the whole situation and I tell her I'm scared and I began crying again she told me it was a difficult situation because if she would have taken me to the hospital I could have gotten in a DCF case Department of Children and families case which would mean my mother would be under investigation and I could have possibly got taken away from my mother and placed into temporary foster care until the investigation was over so it was a very difficult situation my uneven said I could stay with her and if that were to happen that she would be there because she wanted me to get tested to see if I had any sexual transmitted diseases which at the time I had no idea what that even meant I didn't even know that much about sex I just knew enough to know what it was only but I wasn't having sex it was getting taken away from me more so. My father lived all the way in Florida so telling him I was scared to do so and I felt that my father would have been in jail or prison I didn't know what to do because I had had this happen before but this was my first time speaking up telling someone who believed me who saw it and saw that proof and evidence that I had been raped. At that time I was more so scared to tell my mother because this man was also having sex with her while fucking me who was a minor I didn't know if she would believe me or not after all she wasn't the best parent nor was she the worst but maybe that's me taking up for her people always thought that my parents were the best parents ever because they both had a little bit of money and we always had nice things and everything handed to us growing up but The thing is we don't ask to be here we don't ask to be born so I felt as if when you have children you're supposed to want to do better for your children you're supposed to provide for your children the material things were never asked for they were just given to us . We always had packed houses with a bunch of neighborhood kids our parents always pay for other people's kids and bought a bunch of snacks and would take other peoples kids with us to all these fun and cool places and everyone loved coming to my mother's home my mom always had the big nice houses and furniture and all types of games and more material things in her home and our home is considered the fun neighborhood house no one wanted to leave in every neighbor-hood we lived in growing up but The thing is they don't actually get to see those other sides of my parents that I had to see they don't get to endure what I had to endure they don't know what I've been through what I've seen was happened to me. The thing is I tried to protect myself and my innocence I try to protect my mother But the truth was who was going to protect me when that story came out? My aunt Mary pulled some strings for a few hours later where she worked at so that she could make sure I did not have any sexual transmitted diseases because legally my legal guardian would be the one who would have to take me but because she worked at this specific CareSpot and knew everyone there was cool with people it was one of those things that was swept up under the rug out of sight and out of mind she made an appointment for a few hours later before she would have to call my mother to come get us or take us home. I really appreciate it the help it felt nice having someone on my team my side and having someone there to believe me I had to tell my aunt everything that I had did to this man because of what he did to me I even asked my aunt if I was going to go to jail and she told me no she would not let that happen ever and I did what I had to do to defend myself and I wasn't wrong as she's going to do all she can to protect me at all costs after all she knew everyone as far as the medical field lawyers and more. I just didn't want my mother to find out I was so scared of what she would think of me what she would do to me if she would resent me or send me away. Considering this wasn't the first time in my life that I have been raped as a child I wanted to tell someone and it felt nice to tell someone I even told my aunt that I stabbed him and hit him in the face with a flashlight but I was nice enough to have called emergency services,I could've simply let himdie. My aunt then told me I should've allowed him to die there because if you do something like that to a child innocent child at that you deserve those consequences of death which she wasn't wrong at all. As more tears come down my face I couldn't even believe that me I was going through that I had to endure that pain and suffering I didn't feel like one of God's favorites. For quite some time that he was raping me I felt as if I wanted to die I felt suicidal and I didn't want to be around anymore in life because I was suffering so much and for so long. My aunt Mary then tells me to go upstairs in the guest room and try to get some sleep with my sister and to check on her and she'll take me to CareSpot in a few hours we all needed rest and to recharge, I told her yes ma'am and I went to go rest which was the hardest thing to try to do for me I kept thinking about if I killed him and how I stood there watching him bleed out and did nothing even though I shouldn't have done anything at all. I kept thinking why don't keep stabbing him all the pain and suffering he calls me it was time for him to suffer and endure some pain he did that to me for so long I was so miserable and sad to go over there I was so embarrassed to tell anyone, since was when is it OK for a little girl to be sexually abused? I kept having nightmares and flashbacks about the times when he write me then I had a dream about how I had stabbed him and he died before the police got there then I had a dream about Nay's cousin Avyance raping me too and always trying to touch me sexually. I didn't know why it always happened to me you just can't trust "men". Hours later my aunt wakes Bri and I up to start getting ready so that she could take me to the doctor to get tested for any sexually transmitted diseases and or infections. I let Bri get ready first since I was hurting and still bleeding. That's when my aunt Mary pulls me aside asking me had he touched my sister I told her while looking her in her eyes crying no he never did but-wanted to and I told him that I was who he wanted instead and begged him not to touch my sister but he could do whatever he wants it to me that's when my aunt began to start silently crying and she tells me go get ready while she does and that she would be out in a moment. I told her yes ma'am then I said I couldn't allow him to do that to my sister because I've been really would've had to kill him and she was silent then I walked away. Once Bri is all dressed and ready and comes out the bathroom I then go in there so I could shower and I kept thinking to myself if the water was going to burn when it touched my vagina because it was so sore and I was bleeding and I had all that Vaseline caked up on it I was really hurting it was even hurting me to walk a little bit then I began thinking that I actually had to go home like that. I knew my mother would know something was wrong with me and asked me what was wrong with me and why I was walking like that I was so freaking scared I was shaking and nervous and I just couldn't stop crying when I actually got in the shower I turned the hot water knob making it lukewarm it surprisingly didn't burn like I thought it would. Once I get dressed and ready to walk out the bathroom that's what my aunt Mary asked Bri and I again if we were hungry I actually told her I was my appetite was coming back she then said that she would grab me McDonald's and or Burger King on the way to the doctors appointment she really just wanted me to eat because I had an eight from being scared which I still was but my stomach just wouldn't stop growling. I told her I would take

McDonald's and I would like a bacon egg and cheese biscuit and a sweet tea and Bri gets the same exact thing as me that was my sister's favorite thing to get from McDonald's every time we went there she always got the same things she never like to try new things she was also a very picky eater I was always greedy and ate more than her. we finally arrive at care spot I was so nervous But luckily my aunt was a nurse there and thank God for the people who look the other way and she was able to be my legal guardian so that I could get the sexual transmitted disease and infections check without having to call my mother and or father. I knew the results would take a few days because my aunt had already told me that before we even went there but some results they were able to tell my aunt the same day which were infections thank God I didn't have any. When the doctor took a look at my vagina I grabbed my aunts hand and the doctor asked what happened I couldn't even tell him or talk I was so embarrassed and scared and nervous that my aunt did all the talking for me and she knew the doctor anyways. She never talked in front of me or my sister she told the doctor she would speak to him outside in the hallway. I was so nervous I didn't know what she told him what she was going to tell him and if I was going to be sent away by my mom. A few minutes later my aunt comes back into the room with Bri and I she grabbed my hand and grins at me saying you're going to be OK baby. I just had one more issue my sister she was a snitch and she talked too much I couldn't help but think what if she had told my mother I had to go to the care spot well my mother asked her think. But my aunt said she would take care of everything and she wouldn't tell my mother what happened because she promised me she would not and she even told me she would deal with Ale and I trusted her again she was like a mother and I could tell her things and she wouldn't tell my mother or my father she also never doubted me always believe me if she was there for me when I needed her the most especially in this situation and I really appreciated it. My aunt also got some creams for me for my vagina to help out with the redness the itchiness and the burning I knew how to hide things at home without my mother finding out so I had no problems with that. We got the cream the same day after the appointment then I sit in the front seat my aunt grabbed my hand and whispers you're going to be ok we're going to get him and I believed her on our way, back to my aunts house to get our bag my aunt calls my mother to tell her she got us and she made up a lie saying that she called me and asked what were we up to and wanted to spend some time with us before she went out of town which my mother was completely fine with. As I listen to the conversation between my aunt and mother because my mother was connected to the Bluetooth my mom told my aunt that she could keep us for as long as she wants it to him I said all right that's fine I'll bring them home later will give you a courtesy call before we do so.I've been told my aunt when I get older I want to be just like her saving people and helping people I couldn't imagine how many other girls my age were going through the same thing that I had to go through an indoor I also told my aunt that I wanted to start an organization for those who can relate to what I've been through when I get older. on the way back to my aunts house she takes Bri and I to Dollar General so that I could get some panty liners which I didn't even know what that was I had never used those before I knew what a period was as well as pads. I told her she didn't have to pay for it I had money but she insisted and she told me what not to use down there anymore she even told me don't use Vaseline because it takes up your vagina I will put it on my wall area of my vagina and where the redness was on the outside, After all I was a kid I had no idea.Later that night she takes us back home on the way home she asked if we wanted anything to eat one thing about it she always fed us and took great care of us we always had fun going to her house. I let Bri pick what we got for dinner I didn't want my aunt to be running all around town and of course Bri chose McDonald's she was a very picky eater again and also We always ate at McDonald's I was kind of getting tired of it to be honest. But I would often let my little sister have her way I mean she was six years younger than me it was whatever as long as my little sister was good and taking care of that's I cared about

Especially when she was with me and we weren't home I knew I was solely responsible for her. I knew if anything happened to her my mom would literally kill me like the one time when I accidentally made my sister bust her head open literally her forehead was busted and blood was gushing out when we were kids Bree our cousin Caleb and I we're running around in this townhouse we lived in in Virginia Beach VA and we were hiding from our cousin Caleb in our mothers bedroom I heard him coming running upstairs and I told Bri to get down and I pushed her head down and it hit the bed So loud and hard she screamed and when I turned to look at her blood was gushing out of her forehead so fast it was everywhere I was so scared I picked her up and ran downstairs with her and my mother was mad so mad like she almost hit me I thought she was screaming and yelling and crying my aunt had to hold her back we literally were rushing to get to the patient first that was the closest place they had next to a care spot that will be able to help her out with her injury. My mom was literally yelling screaming cussing and my aunt who was Caleb's mother had to hold her back and take me away so that my mother wouldn't attack me or hit me or something I was so scared because I really thought I had killed my little sister it was such an accident I didn't mean for ahead to hit that I was just so excited and we were playing a game that I didn't know her head would hit the part on the bed that it hit. My sister had to get five stitches on her forehead and ask my mother leaves me to go into the room with my sister while they prepped her for the stitches this random man was sitting next to me telling me don't feel bad he's gotten stitches before and they don't hurt and he said my sister will be fine he told me it was ok I was scared for my fucking life. After that I felt bad too so I told my sister we were no longer allowed to run around in the house ever again she could have really died with them out of blood that she lost it even took years for that scar to go away off of her head after the stitches were removed. When that man was talking to me everything that he said went in one ear and came out the other I didn't want to hear what he had to say like that was you like this is my little sister was talking about two different people and you're not making me feel better he really was not he made the situation sound much worse I was a kid I didn't know what stitches were I didn't know anything about surgeries or anything all I knew was I was responsible for what happened to my sister and every since that day I made a vow to myself that I would never allow anyone or anything to hurt my sister ever again even though it was my fault that she got hurt and I blame myself for so long and it took me a long time so forgive myself and get over that hell my sister still brings it up to this day how I made her hit her head. So we get McDonald's my sister gets so happy meal she loves chicken nuggets and fries she could eat it every day if you let her. I would always get some type of burger with fries and a sweet tea. We eat on the way home somewhere I really didn't want to go I also couldn't stop thinking about how it would be at school with Tia and Terri I'm sure they knew I stabbed Ale. I didn't know how everything would be next time we went to school and after school but I was starting not to care I had a good reason for what I did. when we pull up to our house my aunt gets out with us and gives Bri and I hugs and tells her she'll see you soon and she pulls me to the side and tells me don't worry she'll take care of everything and everything will be taken care of in due time.I guess it's true what goes around comes around because a few weeks later I over heard my mother on the phone with someone telling them how I'll went to jail because some girls said he raped her it felt nice knowing that he got his actually what he deserved and he was actually found guilty so kudos to whoever those girls were who had the proof that he did that to them because he also did it to me so by them turning him in they also helped me. When we went back to school and the daycare after school programs I never saw Tia and Terry again,I wonder what they thought of me what they think I did but I didn't even care anymore because everything happens for a reason and he got his I don't care whether they liked me or not I didn't care whether I would hear from them again we're not all that matter is that evil person I did what he did to me was finally getting exactly what he deserved and I finally earned by Justice which felt so nice in The year of 2020 my mother tells Bree and I that Ale had died. Which I didn't care nor have sympathy after all he was the man that was raping me. I even asked my mom if he had died in jail then I asked her didn't he rape another girl in my mother got very offended and upset about it right then and there i really should have told her that he had raped me For so long But she probably would have gotten upset with me she also probably wouldn't believe me. Just like when I got sexually assaulted in college and before I could tell her about it she had turned my phone off luckily I had an iPhone so even when your phone is off you can still text other people who have iPhones in FaceTime them even get them to call you using Wi-Fi little did a lot of people know that. My mother was one of those people that you couldn't talk to about stuff like that the sad part about it she claimed that she was raped as a kid to me. I didn't care that the man had died he got exactly what he deserved when you do people wrong bad things always happen to come back on you even though we're all going to die but still at least he's no longer here anymore to hurt anyone else. It happened again to me my eight grade year by someone who I thought was my cousin by the name of Marquel he wasn't my real cousin but for some reason black folks always considered someone they were very close to their family. I once trusted him when I was a kid I was very much a tomboy a cute looking one. We considered his grandmother our grandmother and all. We always hung out with Marquel and his two younger cousins Ariel and Aliyah, Ariel was my age and Aliyah was Bri's age we were all very close with each other. We stayed going to grandma Rose's house, even though at times she was a old bitch lets be real. She was all about what someone had to give her which was very annoying she would talk shit about my mom but she wasn't talking shit when my mom was giving her money and whining and dining her grandchildren. Hell one of Grandma Rose's sons went to prison fucking with some white girl and she said he raped her I've been raped so I never am one to call someone a liar when it comes to that they had to have had enough proof he went to prison the apple doesn't fall far from the tree I guess. Hell we knew Marquelwhole family and we stayed at Grandma Rose's house. So again she was all about what people had to give her and every time she did someone wrong karma ate that ass up. Once my mom had Bri and I's birthday party at Cinema Cafe again we had so many memories at that movie theater it was very popular and nice. My mom had rented out half the theater&grandma Rose,Marquel,Ariel,Aliyah,JayJay which were the grandkids and lots of Bri and I friends were all there it was fun and cool we saw some kid friendly movie. When the movie was over there was lots of pizzacakeice cream leftovers grandma Rose took all the ice cream home without asking my mother which is trifling and her deep freezer went out which is wha the fuck she got. I don't know why people always feel so fucking entitled like all you have to do is ask people when you want something and the worse a person can say is no I mean it wasn't that serious. My mother had did a lot for her and her dirty grandchildren whose parents were all pieces of crap's worse than my mom and literally grandma rose would talk about my mother to others and everything one time I even over heard her talking about my mother to her sister who had a mustache which is not cute and I'm not even sure how she had a husband that's not attractive or sexy at all women with mustaches looks a damn mess I wouldn't even want to kiss someone like that if I was a man. But I was so close to MarquelI knew all of his friends I knew the whole family I was a tomboy I hung out with all the boys always we would always raise our bikes or dirt bikes and play video games together he even knew some of my friends and had a crush on my childhood friend Nay. Hell even growing up Bri and I always had the best of the best birthday parties and even though Marquel and my other cousins weren't my age except for one my mother would still invite all of them so none of them felt singled out like when I was turning twelve and I had a limousine pick my friends and I all up from our house and then my mother also had got a game bus which was so fun and the limousine took us to the restaurant we were eating at called Max and erma's at MacArthur mall that was our favorite restaurant ever until they finally closed down help my mother even paid for everyone's meals and stuff just just the type of person she was and I always said if I ever had kids I would be the same exact way as far as paying for everyone chill child and whatnot however I know some people aren't fortunate enough to always give their children money to go places and etc which is fine. And grandma rose will still have so much shit to talk about my mother which I did not appreciate because she's not talking trash about my mother when my mother was doing things for her so why do you think that you're going to do it now and when she talks about my mother hell I went back and told my mother then my mother confronted her I sure did you're not going to get money and free things for my mother and talk about her that's not how we roll. One time my mother caught Marquelon top of me trying to stick his dick in my vagina but it was jabbing me in my ass which hurt really bad and I was trying to get him off of me and it just so happens when I pushed him off of me my mother just happened to be coming around to the side of the bed where we were at on the floor she was putting things away in my dresser when she saw us she then tells me to go downstairs and she slaps the hell out of me then tells me that I'm not to be trying to have sex and do anything like that and she also told me she was going to tell his dad on him and I know it looked like I was trying to have sex with him but I was not he was in fact on top of me and I was in fact trying to push him off and telling him to get off of me but you see that's the thing with us right victims people never believe are so quick to judge and assume I mean she's the one that walked in after the fact so I get it may have looked like I wanted it or some-thing I was trying to take it but that was not the case at all and that is why rape victims do not come forward when they have been sexually assaulted because people are so quick and eager to judge them instead of trying to help them that's also why I was so afraid to tell my mother what happened with the man who was having sex with her but then raping me when she would leave me with him. What hurt me the most about the situation was the simple fact that one night I was in the car with my mother and she told me that if I keep saying I got raped people aren't going to believe me and they're going to ask me why does it keep happening to me. I thought that was the most craziest thing I've ever heard in my life because granted at that time frame in my life I had a belly ring which my mother allowed me to get when I was age sixteen,because I graduated high school early my junior year and that was the graduation gift I wanted so I will often wear crop tops and or tube tops to show off my belly ring and the abs I love working out and I only cared about my abs and my six pack that would come in time to time that was my sex appeal and the only part of my body that I cared about and of course my long hair that I had at the time that I had. I just couldn't believe my own mother would tell me that I needed to stop dressing the way that I did and saying that I got raped when I didn't even tell her about the situations with Avyance and Ale raping me. It was crazier to me because once upon a time ago my mother told me that she was raped as a little girl by some man who was supposedly a friend of the family so that just goes to show you is always the man in the family and or the friends of the family that are the ones raping little girls or girls in general. But it really hurt me that my own mother made that statement towards me that is why I was so scared to come forward the first two times that it ever happened in my life and tell her if she said that to me then I can't imagine what she would've said to me the first two times with Avyance and Ale. That statement she made towards me is exactly why women and girls do not come forward when they have been raped and or sexually assaulting people don't believe you when they get you yes I was wearing crop tops and two tops at sixteen or seventeen years of age but my mother was allowing it she had never said anything before about my wardrobe she allowed me to get that belly ring piercing at sixteen so I was very confused. It's also very ignorant I think to judge someone and to tell someone that they got raped because of what they had on it doesn't matter if I was completely naked that does not give the right to rape someone especially when they didn't get consent to even touch you in the first place and I hate people who think like that basically it's like those people who think that we are taking up for rapist which is not ok and it makes me wonder if they rape people too.I don't even know why my mother was judging my clothing preference after all crop tops and tube tops have been out for years hell even in the fifties they dressed like that. These thirteen year olds and the trends were coming back into style even in the nineties wearing tube tops and crop tops hell just saw midriff in general was what everyone was doing it was a trend a popular trend I was coming back and I was obsessed with that trend I mean I had the body I was comfortable in my own skin even though I always had a weight problem thanks to my mother who is putting me into modeling I got my first modeling contract when I was in the ninth grade but when I tried again the older I got it was so hard. The Modeling game is definitely something serious the people who own the agencies are cruel and mean and rude and they want you to look a certain type of way which at that time when I had gotten to Modeling plus size models weren't it yet unless you were already a very famous popular celebrity. I always struggled with my weight it went up and down as a kid I was always skinny but the thing is I love to eat granted I was always tall for my age I also had a high metabolism but when my mother decided to put me on birth control my junior year of high school that's what my weight really started to go up . But through it all all I cared about appearance wise with my long beautiful hair and my abs I love showing my belly ring I love wearing my natural hair out all my life I had grew my hair out I went from getting relaxers to being natural and I loved it. But the modeling game definitely made me gain a complex about my body and my inner self it made me feel as if I wasn't skinny enough or pretty enough I couldn't even get the part for this one commercial my mother have forced me to do all of this modeling stuff something I didn't even want to do I think she mainly put me in it because of the money the money is always good and Modeling especially when you're young starting out and getting paid just to get pictures taken of you. My junior year of high school is when I developed acid reflux which is a family trait unfortunately on my dad side of the family we all had acid reflects it very much sucked every time you eat something or even before you eat you get heartburn and chest pains and food feels like a stuck in your throat really sucked it made me feel as if I was having many heart attacks at times that I didn't even know what that's supposed to feel like. That's really when I start losing weight on top of that I found out that I had sickle cell traits and microcytic anemia my red blood cells were smaller than a person who does not have that in a blood count was very low. Which would cause me to get dizzy, weak , loss of appetite, weight loss , fatigue, icky, sleepy. I would always have to get iron fusions and I stayed in and out the hospital . I had wanted to be skinny skinny so bad that my ribs would begin to show and more I guess you really do have to be careful what you ask for I definitely got what I asked for just not in the way that I wanted it to be. That night I cried in my room when my mother told me that because my own mother who could actually relate to the situation said that to her own daughter since when is it ok to touch someone without their consent? That was exactly why I decided I wanted to live with my dad and go to school in Florida to be closer to my dad I was always closer to my dad and my mother my mother always beat me and yelled and use profanity towards me and that's not the type of parenting skills I would recommend or I would do to my own child. Growing up in the black community when you get an ass whooping black parents use any damn thing they can get which is normally the first thing in sight they used to whoop you I do not think that beating your child is the answer but to each his own. I hated that soon I would have to go to Florida with my dad I really wanted to but I was yet leaving behind my sister I always try to give my sister money when I couldn't when I had it and I will always save up and put money aside for her I would buy her things and mail them I try to do so much for my sister because I knew that once I left she would really be miserable living with our mother and it sucked because there was nothing I can do about it I knew until I got my life and self together I always said that when I was old enough and have myself together that my sister could come live with me and I would always tell her that and the difference between me and my mother I never lie to my sister she did hell she lied to me too about so much.

CHAPTER

6

There were so many times when my sister and I would be left at grandma rose house to hang out with all her grandchildren and we will all play together go outside and play hang around their friends and more. But every time I went over there it seemed like Marquel didn't learn his lesson from the first time of being caught and I'm sure his father did not care considering it was accusations from women of his father doing the same thing so like father like son I guess they would say. My mother even had to step up and once tell Mark Wells mother that he tried to rape me my mother had his mothers phone number and called her up to tell her so then his mother asked my mother what is your daughter saying he did. For someone who had cancer she was such a bitch she really was I hate women that are so quick to act as if their sons don't do any wrong let alone their children don't do any wrong not the way to raise your kids specially when someone is accusing your child of rape and they actually did it that's very messed up and the fact that she's a woman even more messed up. But I've noticed it tends to be the women that judge other women and girls who've been sexually assaulted and or raped which is so messed up. My mother then told me that she told his mother she would fresh charges against them and she made sure she came down and got her son immediately after my mother telling her that people do anything to protect their kids even when they're in the wrong. But with this boy there was just no learning his lessons for him ever before I left to go to Florida for college he literally tries to do it again and we almost got caught by one of his uncles who was also in jail because he liked white women and they always accused him of rape I guess it just ran in their family because that's not weird at all first his father then his uncle then him damn I wonder who would have been next. And granted I was talking to this guy when I was seventeen he was in his twenties but so at the end of the day if I tell you don't touch me or if I don't want to have sex with you then keep your hands and body parts to yourself and mark wells dad found out about the guy that I was talking to because he over heard my conversation on the phone once and he didn't tell me but when my mother kept trying to talk to him about his son putting his hands on me sexually mark wells dad literally claps back saying well you know she's fucking some man in his twenties even though the guy and I hadn't even had sex yet.I hated how the whole thing got flipped to make me seem like I was the bad person in this scenario it was as if Marquel'sfather was shielding his son and making it as if it's okay to sexually assault and rape people. I couldn't believe it so at that moment my depression and anxiety came back in and I mean I was definitely going to college within the next month or two so it had me scared once again. So before I went to college we stopped dealing with them overall and stop going over to grandma Rose's house they were all in fact about what you had to give them she never really did anything for us anyways I mean cooked a few meals a few times to feed us that's it my mother would go over the top with the gifts that she would buy her grandchildren and everything. We never got any gifts or anything in return not that I'm saying they had to give things because I mean you don't always have to return the favor of course but I always thought it was a nice friendly gesture and it was just something that you did gifts don't cost that much I mean I think it's the thought that counts but to each his own I'm guessing. Felt nice not having to go to their house anymore and possibly be raped I have to protect my body parts from someone who kept trying to touch me inappropriately over and over again even one of mark wells friends who lived next door to grandma rose liked me but I was not into him at all it was not my type this whole situation was why I never had guy friends at all because they always end up liking you or want to have sex which is a no for me. I had never even had a gay male friend ever and I just didn't wanna be around any guys for a long time they were not to be trusted.

is the next day, it's six in the morning I make me a nice big breakfast and i tell my dad goodbye he left home every morning at six and would get up every morning about three in the morning. He had a morning routine that he did every morning from watching the news at three to cooking himself breakfast to chilling then ironing his clothes then he'd shower and whatever else he did. I typically didn't tell my dad my business or what I had planned I never believed in telling a person everything about yourself including those close to you. No matter how long you've known someone you'll never know everything there is to know about a person which is what i tell myself and have Learned and expected I even tried to tell other people this but to each his own those who get it get it . I throw on a maternity shirt that says arriving soon and has baby footprints on it and I throw on some workout shorts with some mommy slides that were so comfortable on my feet it had extra padding in them because my feet and back always hurt so bad because of my pregnancy I was so glad I was almost close to going into labor. I grabbed one of my Chanel bags my mother had given me she always gave me gifts just like my father and or money to try to guilt trip me and gaslight me and for some reason I will always accept the gifts and money instead of saying no but I rather take their money and gifts then spend my own money on gifts and purses after all my parents always had money . I go outside to my car put the key fob in start the car up turn on the AC and crack the windows a bit I take the key fob out and go back in the house to grab my stuff and made sure I had everything before running all my errands. I always crack the windows when turning on the air conditioning and the car to let all the hot heat out it was summertime after all we lived in Florida it was always hot . I grab a soda and some snacks then I lock the house up and get in my car putting the key fob back in the slot open my sunroof put on my Chanel glasses plug the aux cord into my phone play some nineties R&B music and I start to drive. As I'm taking the shortcuts to go to Navy Federal Credit Union I pass by the same spot where I met Garrett who once again basically saved my life and my child's life and I begin thinking about how I wasn't ready to date and I didn't want a relationship I know he said he didn't want sex from me or anything at all for that matter just to help me and talk about what he also could relate two from losing his wife but men lie and men always eventually get what they want some type of way after all Jay did. He got a baby from me something that he always wanted and talked about from the first time we even had met so he definitely got what he wants at mission accomplished and every time I would try to leave him I would have all my bags packed he always got me to stay every time so a man definitely can get what he wants whenever he wants especially if he finds a woman who's desperate enough and doesn't know what she wants a woman that's fragile a woman that's never been loved before or had certain things in life before from a man he figures he can then treat her any type of way and do whatever he wants to her and she'll accept it and take it. After all when I was with Jay I had actually become that type of woman and it's crazy growing up I always said I would never allow a man to put their hands on me I would never allow a man to treat me like crap and make me feel bad about myself but then I did it and that's the thing people don't realize we all say things but is actually different when you're really placed into that situation.

I kept telling myself I wasn't going on a date with Garrett we both could just relate to the same situation on losing a loved one and I was going to hear him out about this program he was telling me about for people who can relate to what him and I had been through. I mean after all I was pregnant and I was not going to have sex with a man with another man's baby in my belly and after all I knew what I wanted and didn't want and he told me what he wasn't trying to get from me so as long as we were both on the same page everything should have been good. I kept thinking of what to wear to go to lunch with him I mean after all it was not a date but he was much older than me and also I had such a baby face like I always looked so young Even though I was mature in my mind and so was mature I matured off of pain not age but he was fine and in his 40s and look just like I like him even had a dad body, which was a whole turn on for me but I just couldn't get turned on enough because I wasn't interested in dating him indoor seeing where it could lead. I was still grieving and trying to prep myself to be this perfect single mother that I was soon about to be I was not prepared or ready I was also still grieving and I didn't know how to deal with it or what to do. I arrive at Navy Federal across the street from the base where my father worked at the time to open my daughter who is soon going to be born a bank account adding in five thousand dollars to that bank account then she would soon be getting her father's Social Security check monthly once she was born and we did the DNA testing with Jay's parents and I. Even though Carol was back and taking everything she couldn't get everything just because she was the wife Jay had left some things and my name as well and for his military benefits which we were soon going to find out he had put to leave them behind to his child. Which my dad soon found out when he got someone he knew personally and was close with who worked in the ID lab to search up Jay's name to see if he had benefits and he had benefits for if he ever had a kid(s) to give to his kid(s). Not that I was ever worried because I had thousands of dollars saved up anyways and I was going to be working for the government pretty soon thanks to my father once the baby was here and I was healed up my father always taught me to never depend on a man not even him which I took Heath of especially once Jay die. A man can come and go also like in my situation die unexpectedly one day so you have to be prepared for anything or not.

Growing up watching some of my female cousins become teen mothers not saying that it was cute but also I didn't judge things happen we all made mistakes to each his own again. I remember my father telling me not to be like them he also told me not to let a Man sweet talk me into having a baby and or doing things that I don't want to do if only I had listened to my father and you know we look at our parents sometimes when they try to tell us things for our own good and we don't want to listen but we forget that our parents to have been our ages once and had been through the same things we've been through if not worse it's OK to listen to people and take advice from people it's not what people say is how people say it and present it to you when trying to help you. When my dad was telling me that advice that day he was talking about one of my cousins who resided in Alabama who I was very close with growing up again I don't judge people to each his own we all make mistakes but when you make a mistake you're supposed to learn from the mistake and not do it again. But I told my father I would never allow that to happen to myself granted I got pregnant at nineteen years old I was going on twenty. Anyways and I also had myself together grant said I didn't work anymore at that time but I had thousands and thousands saved up my child wasn't even here yet and I was already setting up accounts getting health insurance picked out getting life insurance policies and so much more I was definitely prepared but when it comes to being a parent or parents you'll never be prepared. Babies don't come with instructions and manuals you just have to go with the flow of things granted I got pregnant at nineteen years old. I don't consider that a teen pregnancy even though some would because the word nineteen has the word teen at the end. After leaving Navy Federal Credit Union I decided to wash my car and vacuum it out at one of my spots on wells Rd. I loved that car wash it was always booming and packed and very affordable. After leaving that car wash I decided to go to Walmart I wanted to finish getting Leilani who was going to be arriving into this world within a few more weeks more things whether I thought she needed it or not.

That day I even bought a cute car magnet that said baby on board I was definitely going to be prepared for my baby when she got here. Then I go home unpack my car and trunk take everything in the house, As I'm doing so our next door neighbor Billy who practically watched me grow up she lived next door to us with her husband and her mother and her mother husband lived across the street from us they had been in that neighborhood for so many years they've literally known me since I was a kid I talked to her for quite some time every time I talk to her I conversations lasted for so long that you would literally forget what you were doing or have to tell them like it's time to go they definitely meant well I had been inside their house when I was a kid I used to swim in their pool as a child they were definitely like family to us they did a lot for us my father did a lot for them over the years and helped out with a lot. She told me she was sorry about my baby dad dying and she asked me if she could tell me a story similar to what happened to me I thought in my mind I don't want to start crying right now because I'm finally at this state where I can talk about him and the situation without crying and I don't want to go back to that point it took me so long to get there. I sit on the porch with Billy Joe because my legs got tired from standing and she told me to sit down which I'm glad she did because I don't know how much longer I could take standing up and it was so hot outside but she tells me about this time when she was about seventeen years old mind you when she was telling me the story she was forty eight year I remember giving her a birthday gift when she turned forty eight old that year. But in her story she was seventeen years old and she was marrying her high school sweetheart who asked her mother if they could get married that was also the same guy that she lost her virginity to So her fiancé was going to be going into the military and they literally were planning out their wedding She told me she was all happy and excited telling everyone she was going to be getting married to a marine and she told me A few days later when her fiancé was in the car with his father she gets a phone call that they were in a terrible car accident and he died when she told me that a tear rolled down my face because it was so similar to my story whenever you're happy and in a great place in life you just can't be fully happy without something happening that ruins for you. She grabs my hand holding it Squeezing it very tight telling me that I'm lucky to have my father who let me move back home after everything and then she tells me that she wanted to get married to her ex fiancé but he died and she really loved him granted she granted she has a husband had a husband when telling me the story who she very much loved but she told me no man or guy could ever replace your first love which I definitely agreed with. She also told me in life when you're happy and good things come your way there's always going to be an obstacle or challenge that prevents you from being with who you thought you wanted to be with or should have been with or preventing you from doing what you felt you needed to do in life she said it sucks but that's just life and there's nothing that we can do about it she said when your number gets called you have to go and she said there was nothing she could have done about it. She said and her mother was hurt and sad for her but also wanted her to marry the man she had lost her virginity to especially in that time frame. She then told me she knows it's going to suck being a single mom and all she ever wanted was to be a mom and have her own child and or adopt but she said I'm smart pretty and intelligent and I have a father who has money and really loves me and lets him help out as much as I can. I told her thank you as I wipe my face and I told her I had to get ready to go I had somewhere to be as I get up to walk away she grabs a cigarette to smoke.I decided to take a shower to freshen up of course because all that ripping and running had me sweating hot and out of breath and again it was summer already. When I get out the shower I decide to turn on my Bluetooth speaker something I haven't used in quite some time because when I moved out to move in with Jay I had decided to leave that at home. I open my closet doors looking for something to wear I was again now nine months pregnant and it was at least ninety degrees outside. The more and more I think about what Billy told me it made me not want to go out once again with Garrett but I figured that what could be the worst that could happen on top of that I was taking my own vehicle in meeting him at a restaurant a public restaurant at that.

I decide to wear a Long pink dress and some sandals as far as my hair I had box braids small ones which I loved braids at that time and I decided to do my makeup the only type of makeup that I could do as far as I knew and ever tried to do was mascara Apply some mascara eye shadow and lipstick which is all I decided to do because I mean it was summer time and it was very hot and I was for sure the makeup was going to come off anyways due to the heat. I get a text on my phone as I'm getting ready it was Garrett asking me if I was still going to meet him for lunch I waited a few minutes to reply because I didn't want to seem desperate granted it wasn't a date but still I never answered the phone either on the first two to three rings that's just me. I replied back to Garrett saying that's the plan lol, I grab a Chanel bag that matches the pink dress I was wearing my eyeshadow was blue and my lipstick was pink to match my dress as well I picked a dark blue Chanel bag and grabbed a pair of Chanel glasses looked at myself in the mirror with my big belly and I get ready to head out. Thank God red lobster was up the street from my fathers house truth be told because I was due within a few weeks but babies come whenever they feel like it I really didn't want to be going out a lot and doing too much because I was so scared that my water would break and I would be alone and not know what to do plus red lobster was my favorite restaurant I couldn't resist it let alone seafood. On the way over there I'm listening to Aaliyah rock the boat that's always been my favorite singer since I was a kid I literally had all her CDs all her movies and magazines I even tried to grow my hair to her length. It's funny because growing up I used to literally do all the dances to her music videos with her I knew every dance I literally even wore Tommy Hilfiger boxers and the Tommy Hilfiger tube tops just because she slayed that look that was definitely a trend from the nineties. When I pull up to red lobster this big truck pulls up beside me and it was Garrett funny how we pulled up at the same time but we both did live on Wells Rd. When I get out the car he gives me a hug and I hugged him back then we walk up to the door he opens it for me already was a gentleman but I wasn't impressed Nor did I want a relationship with him and I had to keep reminding myself that because I knew me and how I could get and The thing is a man always seems to be my biggest downfall the older I got that's also how it was with my mother I definitely did not want to become my mother with the drinking excessively which I had already been a alcoholic when I was with Jay. But I definitely did not want to become my mother at all I want it to be better than her I want it to be a better mother and woman than her and she ever was. When we walk in and go up to the Hostess we instantly get seated at a booth Then our waiter comes over to us asking us what do we want to drink I got a Peach tea and Garrett ordered a bud light beer. I jokingly asked him if he was really going to drink in front of me knowing I can't drink and he smiled and laughed and said my time was coming. He then asked me what was I getting and I told him I was getting my usual which was the coconut shrimp I love the dipping sauce that you get with the shrimp he then asked me was I going to get anything else because he said if I don't recall you told me you eat like a grown man laughing while saying that and I told him I do eat like a grown man normally he told me he was getting crab legs before I could ask him what he wanted. He said he was getting two orders of crab legs at that and he also told me to get whatever I wanted I was like don't tell me that and I said in that case playfully let me get Everything on the menu and he says go ahead with a straight face. In my mind I was like oh he must got some money but I do too so that don't work on me Sir but I ended up deciding to get the coconut shrimp with fries and some crab legs. When the weights are comes back with our beverages Garrett lets me order first and then he orders his food then when the waiter leaves we start talking he tells me that I look very nice and I say to him damn did I look ugly the first time you saw me but of course I was just joking and he laughs and said of course not you just look really damn good today. I smell nervously and say thank you then I quickly changed the subject and I asked him more about the program he was telling me about in text. Then he says straight down to business I see I like that.

When he tells me about the program he again tells me how the program is like a class that you attend once a week is for those who've lost a boyfriend girlfriend and or spouse it's basically a support group to help others who've been in the same shoes as you who can relate. Garrett told me he lost his wife she was in a car accident and died instantly and he's been going to the support group for a few months and he loves it it's nice being around others who can relate to what you've experienced and endured in life and it makes him feel better and it makes the days go by easier than it did before he started attending the support group. I then tell him I'm sorry for his loss and I said it sounds very interesting and I think I do want to attend the support group definitely one or two sessions before I have the baby. I then ask Garrett what type of work does he do he literally tells me he's retired military and he works on the base the same damn base where my dad also worked. My heart start beating ten times faster because I couldn't help but think what if this man knows my dad or works with my dad after all everyone on that base knew me from when I was a kid to how I looked at that time and also everyone on that base knew my father we used to get the hookups on everything. I couldn't imagine hanging out with a man that knows my father let alone works with my father it would be so weird and awkward and if my father were to find out if he knew this guy the first thing he would think is that we were having sex. I wanted to ask him if he knew my father I mean after all it wasn't like we're dating or together we're just hanging out as friends at least. I just didn't ask him if he knew my father and I said oh wow I'll be working on that base after I have my daughter and you know recover might run into you I said playfully. Garrett asked me words was I going to name my daughter and I tell him Leilani. He then says that's a very beautiful and different name how did I come up with it I told him I was watching a show call my wife and kids and it was the episode when they were in Hawaii because the name Leilani is Hawaiian And the girl who the sun had met in Hawaii that was her name and I thought it was beautiful and different so I always said whenever I have a daughter I'm going to name her that at the time it wasn't a common name like it is now unfortunately I'm like man I can't never be different. I then asked Garrett if he had any children which killed me to ask him that I could have helped but thank what if he did and they were older than me but he said he did not have any children but he always wanted a kid or two. He said to me he often thinks about had his wife not died if they would have had any kids or not. I asked him if he ever thought about adopting there are so many kids that get mistreated and so many parents who don't want their kids but yet there's people out there who want kids they can't have them or never got a to. He said he never thought to look into it but he's also always down to dating a woman that has a kid or two already and possibly being a stepdad I couldn't help but think what if he was talking about me after all hell I was fine and looked good and he did too and we were on the same level in life financially mentally and physically we were at the Same places in our lives and I loved older men and men who had their shit already together I don't take care of a man and I'm not trying to build a man either but then again I wasn't supposed to be looking for A man either I was still slowly but surely grieving.

Our food is finally coming out all of it and I take out the hand sanitizer I've always had OCD and I've always been a neat freak whenever I touch doors and use public restrooms or touch anything that's in public I have to put on hand sanitizer I feel so disgusting if I don't and that's how people get sick by not being by not being clean. And Garrett had put some of my hand sanitizer on too in my mind I was like yess A man who's actually clean and has good hygiene I love to see it. I playfully told Garrett don't expect me to look cute while eating because I don't and I'm not going to be looking cute while eating. He then said I would hope not while laughing as we eat our food he asked what I had planned later on tonight I then asked him if

163

he was asking me on a date and he said it could be whatever I wanted it to be but he just wants to hang out later especially since we lived up the street from each other. I then asked him what did he have in mind and I would think about it that's when he asked if I liked jazz music because a place in Jacksonville had great food and nice jazz music if I was into jazz and I told him I love jazz music I was in fact into all different types of music and he asked if I'd be down to go with him later date or not to date. I smelled and told him sure I just felt so guilty because the man I loved and had buried months ago was still on my mind and the love I had for him was still there it wasn't going away no matter how hard I tried for it to go away I even had hatred towards Jay because he lied to me about a lot and he kept me in the dark about a lot he literally die with all those skeletons and bones in his closet that is not the way I want to go out of the world when I die I'm not taking anything to the grave or anybody go to your grave with your own sins and leave other people out of it. But I knew the love I had for him would never go away from me and leave me after all we had a daughter on the way together. You can't ever replace someone or the love you had for someone just because you find someone new what I've learned and taught myself. Finding someone was never the issue for me it was finding someone and having to make sure that I'm not treating them as if they're Jay. I kept thinking I was moving too fast and I kept asking myself in my mind if he really would've wanted me to move on people always say that but I mean how do we really know that's what that person wants it when they're no longer even here anymore? But it felt nice to get out the house and actually do things it felt nice knowing that I wasn't crying anymore and couldn't cry anymore even if I tried because I had to make myself hate Jay because of everything he put me through with my parents and his family and all those lies and secrets I always will love him but the heat was starting to be so real towards him which wouldn't change anything I mean after all he was dead and not coming back so didn't really matter anyways. As I sit at red lobster talking to Garrett another thought that goes in my mind is if I actually wanted to tell him that he prevented me from killing myself I kept wanting to but I just didn't tell him I just didn't want to think about being sad or depressed anymore I didn't want to think about why I was trying to kill myself and how I could've killed not only me but my unborn child to or even if I didn't kill myself my unborn child because I was trying to kill myself I didn't want to think about it or talk about it either I just wanted to be happy and in a happy place in my life.

I was glad that Garrett save me from killing myself in the thing was he didn't even know that he did that but I greatly appreciated it also I appreciated him telling me about the support group and getting me out the house it really helped me not go back into a depression stage in my life. I wasn't sure if I liked him in a dating Wade but I liked his company it felt nice being around people I mean The people who were supposed to be my friends were never really around like that. He then asked if I wanted him to pick me up or meet him at his place. I told him that I would meet him at his place I loved jazz music but I had never been to a restaurant that had live jazz music before ever. I knew my dad would ask me where was I going I was just going to tell him the truth besides the going on a date part of chorus but I was going out to a jazz restaurant with my three girlfriends Alma, DayDay and Renee. I was too grown and pregnant to be lying though to be honest and after all I was literally grown my father's problem is I never had curfews or anything but I hated how much he tried to treat me like a kid that's exactly why I was moving out of his house pretty soon I was planning and I was going to move my little sister in with me and Leilani once I got everything else situated that I needed to get done first. My mother and my little sister and father had no idea that I was moving Bri in with me and Leilani but I thought it would be nice and it was time for Bri to have a change of scenery and I have to do it all that bullshit that she had to endure and deal with our mother. It wasn't fair to her that is exactly why I move far away to Florida to get away from my mother as kids like we don't ask to be here none of us do for that matter but that doesn't mean you have to take out your anger and frustrations on us it's not fair I already had everything mapped out I found the townhouse that I was going to get which was not too far away at all from my father I actually in fact found three because you never know have to keep your options open and be prepared just in case is full by the time I'm ready to move in and everything. So Garrett and I ate all of our food and our waiter bought us out Another peach tea for me and another beer for Garrett. Out of nowhere I asked Garrett why was he still single because after all you're very nice looking and you have a lot going on for yourself and you seem to be very successful he then responds and says he has yet to find a woman who meets the same criteria as him he said he's been through them all the users and gold diggers. The lazy ones who don't have anything going for themselves nor trying to do anything in life for themselves. The ones who just wants sex no commitment or relation-ship and he said after a while it took him a minute to realize that he could never replace his wife He also said it took him a while to figure out that no woman can ever replace his wife no matter how hard he tried he couldn't find a replacement and he had to really allow himself to heal the proper way because jumping back into a relationship after being married for so long wasn't good for him. I told him that I understood him completely I also told him I appreciate him getting me out the house and telling me about the support group makes me feel a lot better when I can actually get out the house and I'm busy and active and I'm not thinking about my ex fiancé. I told him it will always be hard for us because we lost are sig-nificant others and of course you can never replace them or replace those memories which is the thing you can't replace someone. I told him I'm not looking for someone either but if someone comes along who I feel would be great around my daughter and want to be a potential stepdad and they have themselves together and they know what they want then great but if not it's ok. I didn't want any and everyone around my daughter and my time is pretty much soon going to be going towards my daughter and time is precious and valuable and I don't want to be wasting time either. He told me I was smart and makes sense he then told me I see him as if I have my head on right because a lot of young women bring their children around all different types of men which is not good that's how things happen bad things at that. I then tell him that I've been townhouse shopping and he asked me if I needed help and I said well I have three places these are set places that I want to move into on one hundred and third street area which still wasn't that far from my father Or Garrett at all. He then told me at least the base will be right there From those three townhouses I told him about.

The waiter comes back and asks us was it one check or two checks and Garrett says one check and gave the waiter his card. I then tell him thank you for lunch and I look forward to seeing you later. He asked me what time worked best for me that's when I told him 8:00 o'clock And he said that sounds good I then asked him what was he going to wear he said a suit the place is very upscale. I said Thank you for the details and I will definitely meet you at your place he gave me the name of the apartment complex where he lived they were very nice apartments. when it's time to leave Garrett pulls my chair back and grabs my hand so I can get up I then tell him thank you and don't let the belly fool you I still do a lot by myself while I laugh. I really appreciated it because no one has ever done that part for me not even Jay it was just the little things for me that made me happy I mean I didn't want his money we had just met plus I had my own money. Money doesn't impress me especially when it's not my money to spend I had my own I was great at saving and I knew how to make my money accumulate very quickly without touching it that's key. When we get to our vehicles he opens my car door for me in my mind I'm like thank god I vacuum my car out and had it good can't be walking around looking good with a dirty car that is not attractive. If I saw something like that it would be a major off. He kissed me on the cheek and told me that he would see me later and I said sounds like a plan he then said he would text me the number then he tells me to drive safe and I said same to you thanks for a great lunch He then says anytime and closes my car door. I felt like I was definitely starting to fall for him way too fast something I did not want to happen something I tried to prevent but that was me I always Fell in love too fast after all I love the temporary things the temporary happiness.

When I finally go home I talked to my dad for quite some time asking him how his day was and telling him that I have my hospital bag all packed up and ready just in case the baby comes at anytime then I tell him that I'm going to hang out with alma Renee and day day we were going to a jazz restaurant well club I Should say but not that he needed to know. The thing that annoyed me about my dad the fucking most every time you tell him something he'll literally say Oh yeah and I'm like I get annoyed because I'm like yeah I just literally told you or said that it pissed me off for some reason like he'd try to be a asshole. that was exactly why I was moving out of his house after all I had a baby on the way anyways can't stay at home forever parents won't be here forever to help support and take care of you nor did I need or expect that anyways I chose to get pregnant by someone so it wasn't my father's responsibility to take care of me and my child I could do that anyways I didn't need his help although people say it takes a village to raise a child I agree but at the same time people aren't always going to be around to help you people have their own lives and own problems. I don't depend on no one to take care of me not my parents not a man not anyone else to help me either I never asked for help I was always too proud to ask people for help and that was with anything I would always figure out a way on my own and that was one thing about me that I loved I was independent and intelligent and always found a way to not need people that's how I was going to raise my sister and teach my sister once she moved in with me when I got one of those townhouses I was getting to not need and depend on people my mother had definitely spoiled my sister Brie way more than she ever spoiled me that's why my sister was so stuck up and always depended on our mother and asking for stuff and my mother would do it not a good way to be granted I was my dad only child I still knew how to do things for myself without the help of others I always did my own research and I always knew what to do and moves to make that were fit for me. After all my father told me never to depend on a man he was also a man so I definitely couldn't depend on him you never know when someone is going to die and after losing Jay that definitely changed my perspective of thinking of life I didn't want to need anybody I always would tell myself I didn't need anybody and I was too proud to need anybody. I loved being an independent young woman granted my father would still give me money at least I had that right mindset to not splurge and spend the money but in fact save and let the money stack up and accumulate overtime hell I was even putting the money my father would give me which would be a few thousands into a bank account for Leilani my child was sent regardless and was always going to be. I didn't need a man nor did I want a man granted Garrett was around and did feel nice having that male attention around me, but I didn't need him either we were both very much on the same caliber and life. When I finished talking to my father I decided to go in my room and close the door I often will stay in my room to be honest and just think And cry. So I watched this movie called till death do us part basically in the movie this woman is married to this controlling and abusive ass man behind closed doors but in the public eyes he's a perfect loving caring successful husband. It was a brand new movie on a TV station called BET, which stood for black entertainment television I love that channel they had all the black movies and shows up there and it was nice for us to have our own channel again and movies. In the movie The woman basically fakes her death after finding out she's pregnant by her husband who didn't want a baby at all even though she did so she could get away from him and she finally did get away from him and basically they found a homeless man and paid him a few homeless man and paid him a few thousands To act as if he was a real doctor in the hospital where the woman went to once she actually got into a car accident while pregnant and her best friend was in on it with her to help her get away from her husband. When people die you get life insurance money from them and her husband put the best friend in charge of everything so at the time he had no idea because he grieving so then the main character whose name was Madison Gets her one and only best friend Chelsea to get her life insurance money and she gives it to her and she helps her friend Madison move away to a different city in California where she then buys a house for her and her unborn child and she starts a new life and then she gets a job at a local diner where she of course works so that she can allow that Life insurance money to accumulate more and she won't have to touch it as much. Then she meets a man who's a single dad who lives next door to her and they begin to date and everything while then she meets a man who's a single dad who lives next door to her and they begin to date and everything while she's pregnant Madison is pregnant and he helps her out and it's just a perfect story and it's slightly was starting to describe Garrett and I. as I rub my belly while laying on the bed watching this movie I tell Leilani that we're going to have a house as well I'm going to buy us a house And we're going to move away to a different city in Florida and get a fresh start moving to a city where no one knows us and I don't know anyone and just live our lives. I definitely needed a fresh start almost everywhere in Jacksonville reminded me of Jay and I and all the memories we had we did everything together we went a lot of places together we traveled a lot together even in Orange Park I just really needed to get away from there and that is why I love that movie so much because if I were in her shoes I would do the same exact thing except the life insurance scam but I get why she had to do it she had to do what was best for her as a mother who was expecting a baby trying to get away from her abusive husband and I salute her so much for that. I just love the whole idea of having a fresh start with my child somewhere else there were so many cities in Florida too many cities in Florida for everyone to be up underneath each other and yet people say Jacksonville is boring I'm like so why do you guys live there all these cities in Florida we have and People complain about being bored they aren't traveling enough As I'm on the bed watching the movie till death do us part I decide to get up and find a nice dress to where and some heels. I pick a nice black dress that had the that had slits on both sides And I picked some black high heels with lace on them with lace on them I decided to put my braids up in a nice bun with a swoop. Then I picked some gold dangling earrings and a gold bracelet to wear to match the earrings With a gold necklace and for my make up black Mascara with red lipstick and black eyeshadow. I was starting to really fall for this man and I didn't want to be I was even taking my slow time preparing for the outfit that I wanted to wear for some thing that I knew was a date but I just didn't want to admit that it was a date. Around seven at night I get a text from Garrett asking am I getting ready I'll reply back to him telling him of course. I had a belly at nine months but it wasn't a huge belly like most would have after all I was still skinny that dress really had me glowing as well as my make up and the happiness I hadn't felt in awhile had me glowing as well as my pregnancy . I was literally six feet tall without heels and had a long ass legs you can tell me I wasn't the shit. I tell my dad I was going out when he comes out of his room because he told me to hold on a minute which I knew he wanted to see what I had on he was just one of those parents even though I was grown and he said I'm pretty dressed up I said well yes upscale restaurant jazz restaurant at that you have to dress up it's just like going to Ruth Chris hey have a dress code and dress policy. I also grabbed a shawl to wear with my dress I had all these dresses and outfits for my mother to wear and it felt nice I'm wearing one of them getting all dressed up like a Barbie doll and going out some thing I hadn't done in a while. I'll tell my dad bye and don't wait up for me I'll be back when I get back I've been told him I hope my water don't break I said playfully but I was very much serious due date was May twenty seventh and it was already the month of May. Hell my birthday was in May and Bri's birthday was in May lots going on in the month of May so I had to be prepared if my water would break at all times I even kept my hospital bag in the trunk of my car I even kept one in the trunk of my father's car as well. My father walks me outside which was still hot as hell and I get in the car I text Garrett telling him that I'm on my way to the apartment complex where he lives at that's when he texts me the apartment number and building number and tells me that I can come up to his apartment and tells me that he still getting ready for our date I look at the message in my mind I'm like umm but I knew I liked him and I was starting to get feelings for him couldn't hide that either. I finally pull up to building five he lived at apartment Five hundred and two. When I walked to the door thank God he was on the first floor because I had on high heels I hear a little bit of nineties R&B music playing in the background I text him telling him I'm outside of his door. He instantly opens the door And tells me to come inside he gives me a hug and kisses me on the cheek and tells me to sit down and make myself comfortable I take my high heels off considering he had a really nice apartment and I was too pregnant for that I had to let my feet breathe. He sits down beside me on the couch And he puts my legs on his lap and starts massaging my feet and talking to me telling me how I have pretty feet then I say to him thank you I guess and I said aren't women supposed to care about their appearance especially their feet lol I said what kind of women did you have in the past who had ugly feet and then get pedicures? We both look at each other and laugh then he says he better get up and start getting ready and I could make myself comfy and get something to drink if I want it I told him the water sounds nice and he told me I can go to the kitchen and get a bottle of water as I get up to go to the kitchen I see a picture in a frame of him and I'm guessing his ex-wife she was very gorgeous she was fair skinned with long hair and absolutely stunning. When he comes out of his room after getting dressed I tell him that his wife was gorgeous and he thank you.

He asked me if I was ready to go and I said yes I'm very ecstatic this is my first time going to a jazz club and he passes me my High Heels helping me put them both on and strap them up. He then puts his hand out so I could grab it and get up and we both walk out the door on the way out one of his neighbors who is an older guy spoke to him and I and I said hello and we kept walking he grabs my hand. He opens the passenger door to his truck and I get in then he closes the door once I'm in the truck. On the way there he asked what kind of music did I want to listen to I said nineties R&B that was my era of music. He then joked me asking what I knew about that type of music and I laughed then said play with me. Then he makes a comeback saying he would never play with me in my mind I took that so sexually mainly because I was pregnant and horny but again there was no way I was going to be having sex with a man while pregnant with another man's baby in me I did not think that was cute at all. He grabbed my hand and kissed it and he began telling me about the different options I had to try at dinner he said we might as well get everything I said sounds good to me with a straight face. Everything was moving so freaking fast indeed I liked it but I also like temporary things which is where I always went wrong with dating and being in relationships even though I really didn't have my first true relationship until I was with Jay. When we arrive he's turns the truck off and Opens his door just when I took my seat belt off to open my door he told me don't even do it let him I definitely was not used to that at all nor did I really expect it. He opens the passenger door then grab my hands so I can get out the truck I kept thinking in my mind we were moving so fast that's why I said I didn't want to date or see anyone but everything that was going on between us and the chemistry felt like we were dating. As we hold hands walking up to the restaurant I could hear the jazz music which I loved jazz music so much we get inside the restaurant it was very nice and upscale everyone in there seemed to be older. When the Hostess takes us to a table it had a white tablecloth on it with a lit candle on the table they bring out two glasses of wine instantly it sucked because I wasn't one of those who drank wine while pregnant nor did I judge those who drank wine while pregnant to each his own but clearly they could see I was pregnant so I just asked for a glass of water Then I request it for sparkling wine so I could fill as if I were drinking too since I'm pregnant and we all laughed and they said no problem and the Hostess said I looked gorgeous and I told her thank you. Garrett asked the Hostess if she'd be willing to take a optic of him and I together and she took a few of us they came out very nice He then told me he would send the optics to my phone. Then the Hostess tells us our waiter will be right with us and I tell her thank you. Garrett then tells me that I look very gorgeous and he loves my hair up in a bun I couldn't stop smiling and blushing I was blushing so much like I was on a date for the first time. We both look over the menu and he told me there was a lot of things he wanted me to try he said I could definitely help myself to whatever I wanted but he was going to order a bunch of food so I told him just order everything he was going to get for us that's completely fine I'm going to eat it regardless. I tell Garrett excuse me I have to go to the restroom I asked him where it was and he showed me and told me he would order the food and drinks if the waiter came back before I did I said ok sounds good. When I go into the restroom I take my phone out of my wristlet Then decide to take some optics of myself I started to tell Renee,DayDay and Alma about Garrett about telling people stuff ruins things so I've learned before Plus I felt as if they were very judging at times and I didn't judge them so sometimes it's best to keep all good things to yourself. I didn't consider Garrett and I dating I was honestly just living in the moment and joined the temporary moment because I knew it was only temporary and it would only be temporary. I also didn't want to mess up anything by asking him what we were doing.

Renee once told me that I was too secretive but I mean after I told her something and confident she went back to the other two and opened her mouth sometimes if someone tells you something you don't have to tell everybody else so the other two friends to fill everyone in because if that were the case I would have told everyone at one time together but I didn't want to so after that lesson learned I never told them anything else again. It was slightly questionable as well because why was my name coming up in conversation when I wasn't even around that's why it's very tricky having female friends especially when there's a group of you. I wasn't big on post-ing who you date and talked to on social media either I only did that with

Jay so I definitely wasn't prepared to do that again and after all I told myself I didn't want us to date or consider ourselves dating. When I walk back out the restroom towards the table I noticed Garret was staring at me and smiling making me nervous when I get to the table I asked him if he liked what he saw and he said definitely did I have some beautiful long legs and I'm just beautiful in general. I start blushing again saying thank you he gets up to pull my chair out so I can sit down and push under the table. Then I asked him if he wanted to dance and he said yes he then playfully tells me he hopes I can keep up I said don't let the age fool you Because in my mind we're both the same age baby I say playfully. As we dance this older couple beside us was dancing as well and said we were a beautiful couple and I smiled and said thank you it definitely caught me off guard I didn't mean to say that but who's actually going to explain to someone oh we're not a couple and explain what it is we're doing? Nobody. Then Garrett looks at me in my eyes and ask me if that's what we were now and I tell him I don't know it just slipped out but I would like to know you more and not rush anything and he said that's fine he definitely wants to know more about me especially if we're going to be a couple I just smiled at him and kept enjoying the moment I love the temporary happiness.

Garrett asked me while we were dancing if Sunday Which was the very next day if I wanted to come over to his apartment and have lunch by the pool and I told him sure why not it felt nice just staying out of the house being active doing things that made me ecstatic. I then tell him I hope you can cook and he says what I definitely can then I say I can't wait to try that cooking. He then says it sounds like you want me to grill out tomorrow I said I mean I'm free all day I have no plans and I said show off them grilling skills while laughing and he asked what did I want I said anything that you cook is fine you know I'm not picky I told you I eat like a grown man and he said sounds good but he'll still need me to go to the store with him and picked out some things and I can help him cook then we'll have lunch by the pool they have cabanas. We stopped dancing when we notice our food is at the table which he had ordered for me when I was in the restroom. He ordered us crab cakes, bacon wrapped pork tenderloins, creamy spinach stuffed salmon, bourbon pecan chicken. When we go back to the table once again he pulls my chair back so I could sit in it and pushes me up to the table I told him I could get used to that and he said I should get used to being with him because he always does stuff like that. He picks up his fork and feeds me some bourbon pecan chicken which never had before But it was so yummy. We talk about tomorrow with having our cookout and I asked if I needed to bring anything or buy anything then Garrett said no just bring yourself. I still felt so guilty because it seemed as if we were moving fast and as if I was moving on with my life with another man already. But I really was catching feelings for Garrett but I didn't want to tell him that because once again men lie they also deceive and they always disappoint. After all he said he didn't want anything from me but yet here we were walking around as if we were a couple but I guess we were just both living in the moment. Garrett even asked me what did I have planned for my birthday which was May fifteenth but I told him I was unsure and I wanted to take it easy as my due date got closer he then told me that he understood completely. Out of nowhere I told him how much I love being around him and how I enjoyed his company then I asked him what did he want from me and I told him I know I've asked this before but that was before we started hanging out and talking as much. He then tells me that he wanted a relationship with me and that he could see himself with me I told him I would have to think about it long and hard.

We actually surprisingly did not finish everything that we had on the table at all which is funny considering we both eat a lot When the Wade tour comes back to check on us at our table he asked us if we needed any boxes I responded yes please and he asked if we were ready for the check and Garrett said yesand hands over his Navy Federal credit Union debit card. When we get our boxes for our food before I can even box anything up Garrett decides to do it all for me that was a thing he did everything for me it seemed I didn't have to do anything around him nor did I have to ask of anything of him but I also didn't expect anything from him. When we go back to his truck he once again opens the passenger door for me so that I can get in and he closes the door for me. On the ride Back to his apartment he asked me why was I so quiet and I told him I was just deeply thinking about him us and everything he then says he hopes it's all good thinking and I told him it is as one tear falls down my face and I tried to play it off I told him I really liked him I just didn't want to rush or ruin anything.I told him we were talking and seeing each other almost every day and talking all throughout the day and things always seem perfect in the beginning and then after that that's when everything starts to go downhill from there and it's never the same. He then tells me he doesn't know what my ex fiancé did to me but that he's not him and he would never hurt me he then told me he'd be lying if he said he never got upset or angry but he would never do me wrong or dirty that's not the type of man that he is and he knows that he's older than me But he's not a older man that's seeking a younger woman for sex lies and bullshit. That sounded so familiar though sounds like some shit that a older man would say I told him.

Then I told him I'm sure he could have any woman that he wants it what is it about me that makes him want me. I told him after all I was about to be turning twenty very soon and he was forty at that moment in time he was the oldest man that I've ever dated or talked to after Jay at least at that time. When we finally pull up to his apartment complex he asked if I wanted to come in his apartment but I told him I think I was going to go home I was pretty tired they needed to think about a lot when I take my seatbelt off And he takes his off he gives me a hug for a long time then when he lets go I'll look him in his eyes and I'll lean in to kiss him but I knew I couldn't allow it to go any further than that. He opens the door for me and I walk to my car to get in he kisses me on my cheek closes my door and I drive off. I was so in shock I had to drive home in silence I was around the corner anyways it killed me I had no one to tell this to well I didn't want to tell anyone about it telling people things ruin the moments Some things just don't need to be told to people at all some people hate to see others happy and of course misery loves company. I really wanted him and I knew I had to have him but I kept telling myself I had to wait a little while longer I have self control especially which seemed to be working for me.

When I get home in the driveway I text Garrett telling him I made it home safe in that I will see him tomorrow he responded back saying ok gorgeous. I go shower then I lay in bed rubbing my stomach feeling Leilani kick like crazy in my belly. I was so ready for her to come out at least it was the month of May I have my hospital bag packed and all you couldn't tell me anything however I really didn't know how to care for a baby I only knew the basics grants it before Jay had died on the military base they offered classes the first time moms they had classes for breast-feeding and so much more. I had never attended any of the classes because I was grieving so much that I didn't even want to go anywhere it got that bad which was expected I had lost a love of my life not only did I lose the love of my life I had a life growing inside of me that was going to be his legacy. I set my alarm on my phone for eight in the morning Before I knew it I was finally able to fall asleep when I woke up at about four in the morning to go pee I had a few messages on my phone from Garrett.

He said how he enjoys my company and time he Appreciated me giving him some of my time and he really wants to give us a try But of course whenever I was ready or felt like I wanted the same thing which I definitely wanted the same thing but first I just wanted to have my baby I had enough or me as is I just wanted to enjoy the moment I didn't even respond to his messages and I read them on the screen instead of actually opening the messages and leaving him on red because we both had iPhones I even begin thinking if I should tell him how he saved me from killing myself but I didn't know what his reaction would be so I just never told him about it.

It is now the day before my birthday and Garrett asked me over the phone when he called me what did I want to do for my birthday and I told him I had no idea I really wasn't big on birthdays I was just always grateful to be alive for all the years I had been

It is now May twenty first twenty eight teen, I have the worst Braxton Hicks contractions ever the pain was crucial and very unbearable my father had even taking me to one of the best hospitals in clay county where I went to labor and delivery and they put a van over my belly to monitor my contractions which hurt very bad I was crying and I didn't know what to do hell my father didn't even know what to do. I had decided to text Garrett letting him I was in the emergency room but I was ok just hurting and in a lot of pain and crying the pain was very crucial and unbearable I told him he then responded back to me asking if I needed him to come to the hospital to keep me company and be there with me because he felt as if he should but I responded back to him telling him I would let him know I was trying to wait and see if they were going to keep me or send me home first before I had him drive all that way for absolutely nothing blessed my father was there and I didn't know once again if they had knew each other considering the simple fact that Garrett and my father worked at the same Naval air station base and could've possibly knew each other so I was trying to keep the peace just in case I was going to labor. The craziest thing ever my cousin Tori literally had her baby the same day that I was in the hospital thinking it was time for me to have my baby. When I say I was so pissed off that the hospital sent me home it didn't make any damn sense I had all those health problems those contractions were out of control. I couldn't even think or wonder what would happen had I invited Garrett to the emergency room to be there with me and if him and my father knew each other I had bigger problems to worry about.

I couldn't believe the hospital sent me home Just for me to go into labor hours later the next morning early that morning. When I got home I told

Garrett over the phone that I was hurting in a lot of pain then I told him if I were to go to another hospital I would definitely let him know so he could be there with me definitely needed more support other than my father plus I didn't think my father will want to be in the same room with his daughter while she's in labor that would've been very weird.Garrett told me to try to lay down and get some rest and then he would check on me within a few hours then I told him okay babe then hang up. I laid down so go to bed when I hear a knock at my room door which is my father he was on the phone with everyone in Alabama telling them what happened at the emergency room telling me how one of my aunts so they should have let me stay because I'll be having a baby soon even though my due date wasn't until May twenty seventh. I tell my father goodnight and tell him I'm going to bed I didn't feel very well and I was hurting so I figured by going to bed I wouldn't have to feel and deal with the pain so much because I would be sleep but I guess I was definitely wrong about that I literally kept waking up out of my sleep to go to the bathroom on top of that it felt like I had to poop every time I would get up to go to the bathroom and I kept pushing and pushing and pushing but nothing was coming out or happening so then I would just go back to my room to lay back down and try to get more rest I did that for hours all throughout the night of morning it is now two in the morning when I go to pee Then get up I notice a lot of blood and I heard a gushing noise which was my mucus plug so ice cream thinking that I had a miscarriage and my dad runs to the bathroom door knocking on it I tell him we have to go to the hospital I said I'm bleeding really bad I said I think I'm losing the baby I then say dad please help me as I start crying I kind of felt bad for my dad because he was new at this I mean after all when my mother had me my dad was out at sea mouths away so he wasn't there when my mother was in labor he came to visit us after she had already had me so he was very new to this plus my dad freaked out a lot he didn't like blood especially other peoples blood and he even freaked out when he took me to get my belly piercing. The hospital bag was already in the trunk of his car so me barely being able to walk I grab my phone and charger I get into the passenger seat and my dad's car power off we go to the nearest hospital which was around the corner from where my father lived and unfortunately the same hospital where Leilani's father was pronounced dead which definitely sucked I hated that hospital everyone in fact hated that hospital that hospital was considered the killer hospital I definitely didn't want to go there but I had no choice I was bleeding really bad I had a lot of health problems and I was pregnant so I definitely had to move fast if I wanted to save my baby because I had no idea what was happening to me or going on with my body. When we get to Orange Park medical my father leaves me in the car by myself while he runs inside to go get some help from someone literally when he leaves me I hear a gushing noise which was my water breaking which was very crazy it was crazy or because that would happen to me when I'm left by myself I didn't even know what to do I couldn't even react I was in shock to be honest everything was happening so fast when my water broke I had on sweatpants but The thing is it seemed as if my sweatpants were wet for a short amount of time and then it dried up. When my father and a nurse comes outside to get me with a wheelchair I tell them my water broke and no one was reacting the way I thought they would they probably thought that because my water had just broke that I had a long ways to go before it was time for me to push out the baby they were definitely wrong. I guess it was just normal to the people though which is why they really didn't react I was even more upset at the fact that these people were making me fill out paperwork when I just said my water broke I have been to that hospital so many times before so the thing was I should have already been in their system on top of that I already didn't want to be there and they had a pregnant woman whose water broke filling out paperwork I literally flung my military ID and insurance card at them when they told me that I had to fill out paperwork I could not believe that bitch I was livid I've never heard of that before that is why no one likes to go into that hospital. My father who hated confrontation was looking crazy at me but I didn't care I was trying to understand why I had to fill out paperwork at a hospital where I've literally been at more than ten times in my life.

When this male nurse pushes me while I'm in the wheelchair towards the elevator and my father follows us I swear I had the worst luck that morning the elevator door acted as if it didn't want to close those contractions were killing me and I accidentally went off on the nurse he was talking and I felt bad because he was all nice and whatnot and I was like can you please just come on please just hurry up I'm hurting because those Braxton Hicks contractions were kicking my ass but surprisingly I didn't cry as much as I wanted to. Finally they take me to labor and delivery these people made me put on a damn nightgown it was hard for me to even get up out of the wheelchair because of the contractions and I had to go to the restroom when I go to the restroom I locked the door because that's just what you do but the contractions were so bad I literally was on the ground crying I had to pull the help button then one of the nurses starts talking to me once I pulled the help button telling me that they can't help me until I get up to unlock the door meanwhile I'm telling the bitch I can't get up so I don't know what part she didn't understand. I heard my father's voice around in the area meanwhile I'm still on the ground crying struggling to get up when I'm finally able to get up off the dirty ground I don't even know what I was thinking to sit on the ground where so many shoes have probably been. When I finally get some strength to get up off the floor and open the door crying still I go get in the Bay where the nurse was at my father then tells me he would be right back because of course he didn't want to see that the nurse had to check me to see how dilated I was before my father left he said the nurse acts like she scared to touch you and I tell him yeah I've notice. When the nurse finally has me lay down after her and I have a slight argument because she's telling me to open my legs and I'm telling her I cannot open them because it hurts so bad I can't do anything and she says she can't help me as well I open my legs like it took the life of me not to jump on her ass while being in pain when I finally am able to open my legs she says Oh my gosh the baby's head is there in my mind I'm like damn that was quick because normally I've heard stories about people being in labor for twenty hours or longer. Next thing I know they're running with Me on the bed which had wheels on it taking me so I can have the baby we waited a while then they tell me we're waiting for the doctor I said and where the hell is the doctor I asked. I then asked you mean to tell me the damn doctor don't stay at the hospital and wait they're on call I asked what type of shit this? When the doctor finally arrives it's a male at that point I didn't even care like Sir get this baby out of me it hurts and she's hurting me. I asked where my father was and I was told he went to go move the car because when we first arrived to the hospital he pulled up in the area where the ambulance would typically pull up at so he definitely had to move the car. The nurse that was on the right hand side of me ask me if I had anyone there with me at the hospital I told her no just my father then she asked me where was my baby dad at and I told her he died and in this hospital it took the life of me to hold those tears back. When I responded to her she looked very sad. The doctor he tried to open up my vagina I don't know what happened and what was wrong with me but I simply just freaked out on him and I screamed no and I guess he got annoyed by it which I did not care and he literally threw his hands up and he was sitting on a stool that had wheels and he rolled back which was completely fine I delivered my own baby and I was very proud no help no medicine no anything even when I asked for medicine I was told it was too late hell I couldn't even get a cup of water. I was literally in labor for less than twenty minutes. Considering that I didn't have the epidural or any types of medication natural birth didn't hurt me at all like people said it would and the ones who said it would hurt to have a natural birth they didn't even have a natural birth the contractions is what hurts you the most pushing the baby out without medicine was easy for me granted we all have pain tolerances. But natural birth didn't hurt me my baby girl was only six and seven ounces she was very tiny also a pound away from being a preemie. I held my baby and cried I still couldn't believe that I would now be considered a mother I still couldn't believe that I had a baby. I asked one of the nurses to pass me my phone and I texted Garrett To let him know that I had the baby even though it was very early but I'm sure he was up I also took some optics of Leilani and I I was so ecstatic I really didn't know how to feel she was so tiny I didn't even want to hold my own baby because I didn't want to drop her after all I was always very clumsy growing up. Surprisingly he responded back instantly and asked if he could call me everything between him and I was just moving so fast like it would be nice to have had a man but I didn't want a man and I swear I kept telling myself that and telling him that I really didn't want to catch feelings but I already had caught feelings for him in the first place it was a little things that he did for me and to me that made me feel better about myself and to think we didn't even have sex yet. I was still very unclear about his intentions because I mean after all I couldn't tell if there were still any good men around that actually did things like what Garrett did without requiring or wanting anything in return. One of the nurses comes over to me telling me my father is in the hallway but she said she would allow him to come into the room once they moved me to another room I told her ok that's fine. The doctor then asked me if I wanted to see the placenta I told him yes I was very curious to see what that looked like when he showed me I said eww it looks like an alien and everyone laughed at me then he asked if I wanted to keep it I said definitely not that looks like the appetite from SpongeBob.

I responded back to Garrett telling him they were about to move us to another room so once I was moved then I would call him I promise he said ok babe. When they moved me into the next room before my father comes in since he followed us to that room I asked them if they could allow me a few minutes to get myself somewhat together I felt icky I just gave birth. They give you your baby fresh out of your womb so Leilani was slightly dirty. but I didn't care it was the fact that I created life I brought a baby into this world The lady said she would tell him I then told her tell him about two minutes I just kept looking at Leilani and crying I couldn't even allow myself to get up because now I was a single mother with a baby I didn't really know how to care for a baby I just knew the basics of caring for a baby which was the how to make a bottle, how to change a diaper, burping a baby after they drink their milk. But I had a few books and I had my mother to ask for help and cousins who were mothers although everyone parents differently I wasn't prepared to be judged for how I choose to parent my baby I really hate it when people tell others how to parent like we are all different we all have different mindsets which is completely fine to each is own. My father knocks on the door I could see him through the window I tell him to come in and signal him with my hand to come in he literally asked how was it I told him quick and it didn't hurt I feel like a trooper then he tells me that he moved the car then he realized I didn't have the hospital bag and the trunk so he had to go back to the house and get it and when he came back asking about me the nurse said I already had the baby and he said already and I started laughing at him.

My dad told me that he called his girlfriend whose name is Carmen she was Filipino and like the mother I wish I had she had money and she always took care of me she even bought me gifts and things when I didn't even ask for anything I could also tell her a lot of things that I couldn't tell my mother or father and she would never repeat anything she always took up for me plus she had money and I loved how she stood up to my dad because again he was always very controlling, manipulative, annoying. One time they argued she literally told my father she wasn't going to keep taking shit off of him because she has money and she doesn't need him in my mind I was like I know that right girl. That's the problem with men when they feel like you're hopeless and you have nothing that they can treat you any kind of way not her she was not going for that and that's what I loved about her.

Plus she always took us to these nice restaurants and cool restaurants whenever she came around we always went out to eat and I loved how every time we went out to eat it was always a new restaurant. She never cared about money or how much something cost it and my father was always trying to correct her and tell her what to do with her own money which would be very annoying at times I would even have to jump into the conversation and tell him it's her money let her spend it on what she wants then my father would tell me that she's paying too much for getting ripped off I said not your problem can't help everybody hell at those times I was only seventeen to eighteen years old. Carmen lived literally in the same city as my father about ten to fifteen minutes away from him he called her so that she could come up to the hospital and see us when the nurse comes back in I get her to hand Leilani to my father and he holds her then I take a few pictures of them together then my father takes all these pictures of me which I looked a damn mess while I was holding my baby he was so excited and it's so funny looking at how it's static he was to see his first and only granddaughter when I was pregnant though he told me I needed to get an abortion but everything always changes when the baby actually comes into the world changes everyones minds I wasn't getting an abortion in the first place though I don't believe in that it just depends on the situation and what happened to each is own but I was not killing a baby Just because my father didn't want me to have one that's crazy my body my choice.

When Carmen gets there she washes her hands then she holds the baby she was all happy for me and she had gave us some money a few hundreds she always gave me money even when I did it there ask for it But I greatly appreciated it I was never ungrateful. She then makes jokes calling my dad Papa Joe and we all laughed after all I was his only daughter. The nurses then come in telling me that they had to take Leilani so the room where they take all the babies which I didn't like at all because I already had that Emotional attachment to my baby and I didn't trust hospitals We seen things on the news every day about people killing babies and hospitals and swapping babies and more. I send optics of baby Leilani to my mother and sister who were both in Virginia next thing I know my mother tells me that they are on their way to come to Florida which was a ten hour drive she always drove to florida very fast she made a ten hour drive not seem so bad. I had begin to feel guilty about not calling jay's family to the hospital but I was at that moment in my life where I was very healed up and it took months to get to where I was mentally and I didn't want them around me crying because then it would make me get back into that depression mode ok course it was ok for them to cry he was a Brother, son, friend, and now father who was absent because he was deceased. Plus when jay's brother sonny's girlfriend who is also the mother of his child decided to threaten me I made the decision I don't have to allow my child to see anyone at all who I don't want to especially when they don't have respect for me as the mother we can't do things to people and expect to be rewarded when we do things to people that's not how life works. When she threatened me I should have in fact filed an injunction against her it definitely would have gotten granted. I mean after all my father also had those credentials to make stuff like that possible and happen so I was never worried or concerned or was I scared I was just trying to actually stay out of jail because I knew me and I knew I had anger problem and I was not someone to play with I might have had a baby face and been all young and nice but I also had another side to me and when that other side comes out nobody can stop me.

I had three missed calls from Garrett so when the nurse comes back in I whispered to her if she could have everyone leave the room for a moment I needed to make a personal phone call and I didn't want anyone around to hear and she whispered back yes ma'am so she tells my father and his girlfriend that they had to leave the room for a moment she needed to check me to make sure everything was ok with My body since I had just given birth naturally. They both say ok and they exit the room I then tell the nurse thank you and I then called Garret back telling him sorry I was very tired and in pain and that my father and his girlfriend were there and a lot was going on He then said it's ok baby and asked if I needed anything at all I told him I definitely needed to see him but of course I would let him know when they kept changing our rooms and everything was very chaotic. I told him in the mean time I would just text him and I asked him if he wanted a optic of me and Leilani and he said of course he wanted a optic of his girls. Before I hang up the phone I told him I would talk to him later and I accidentally said I love you and surprisingly he set it back it was definitely an accident I was just so used to being in that relationship that I was in with Jay and I got so accustomed used to saying certain things to him that I forgot he was gone and I didn't have a relationship well I did but I had No title that I put on it yet. When Garrett said it back I didn't even hang up the phone I just took it away from my ear and was staring at it for a while then I hung up.

The nurse who was in there with us while I made my personal call sad to me he sounds like a lucky guy and I then told her with a smile you have no idea when I asked her if she could please tell everyone they could come back in the room and she said of course then I told her thank you and she said no Problem. I was actually kind of excited my mother and sister were coming to Florida to visit us because I definitely needed family and support around more so I was excited to see my little sister even though my mother had no idea that soon I would be taking her away from her within a few months of me getting myself back together mentally physically and emotionally. My sister always would ask me before I had Leilani if she could come stay with me if I ever decide to move out of my father's house I told her yes little did she know I was already making moves so that she could come stay with me I was going to get a three bedroom townhouse. But I didn't want to announce anything at all until I actually had the keys to the place I knew I had the income that wasn't an issue at all I just wanted to make sure I had the furniture and everything so that when it's time to move in I have everything that's needed for my girls. Plus I would soon be working on the same basis as Garrett so we would definitely possibly see each other every day at work somehow someway whether it was going to lunch together meeting up after we got off work him coming into my building me going into his building we were just moving so fast and I loved it but

I also didn't want to ruin everything I've realized that sometimes I feel as if I was the reason as to why a lot of my relationships didn't workout because I would be so in love with the moment and caught up in the moment that I'm too blinded to see red flags and to do things that I should have done in the very beginning and sometimes you have to pay a price for ignorance and not knowing things.

My mother and sister would call us every once in a while to keep us updated with how far they were florida and I had told them that they could stay at the hospital with Leilani and I. One of the nurses comes into the room asking if we were hungry I told her I was starving she gave my father Carmen and I the cafeteria menus I ordered so much stuff like it was as if I had a tapeworm in me I literally could not stop eating. I even told them to get whatever they wanted not that I had to pay for my stay at the hospital anyways my military insurance covered it all I just had to pay a thirty dollar copay which was nothing. It very much irritated me because every time my baby was laying on my chest and we were just relaxing that's when the nurses would come in to do checks on her and people will come in asking if we wanted to take professional pictures I'm like do you see my hair it looks a mess and my baby is sleeping very much annoying hell they were doing more than the baby was. Next time Bri calls us she tells me that they won't arrive until nine at night. After my father, Carmen and I eat lunch that's when she tells us she's going to leave she gives us a hug and kiss and I tell her thank you so much for coming to see us and spend time with us for the hours that you were here I really appreciated it and it felt nice being around people. Then my father told me he was going to go back home granted he went home and showered and changed and was dressed up when Carmen was there with me but after all we had been up since about Two in the morning. My dad is the baby then left us I told him we were just going to get some rest. When my father finally left I called Garrett back and asked him if he could come spend some time with us at the hospital he then told me of course it was so crazy meeting him at the time frame that I met him because we both could relate to losing Significant other And it was just so crazy bonding with him the way that I did I never thought that I would meet someone again or find love again we literally spent so much time together and I was really falling for him. What had me interested in him the most was the fact that we could relate on that mental level because anyone can find someone and meet someone but not everyone can relate to someone on a mental level especially when you lose the love of your life so he doesn't realize how much he actually helped me overcome that.

He lived around the corner so I knew he would be there in no time which I was right when he arrives I told him he arrived fast and he said he was speeding to get to us and it was thinking about us all night and morning he couldn't sleep. Leilani was in her own personal bad that had wheels on it next to me for babies In a clear crate next to my hospital bed where I was laying she was sound asleep. I definitely had taken a lot of optics of her while she was sleeping and with me holding her and kissing her I made so many videos for Snapchat I posted on Instagram I was sending to family members and friends my phone was blowing up the whole time. Garrett then kisses me on my forehead then he walks over to look at Leilani and I asked him if he wanted to hold her but he said he could wait because she was sleeping so peacefully but he did touch her hair. He told me to stay right there in bed he had some things in the hallway for us that he had gotten earlier that morning when he figured I would have gone into labor soon he came back in with flowers balloons a huge card and some stuff for Leilani. I was already emotional and I started crying and Garrett sat at the foot of the bed rubbing my legs telling me that with him around we had nothing to worry about and he wasn't like the other men that I have been with in the past even though I really didn't tell him about my past I just filled him in bits and pieces of Jay because again that was my first true real relationship that I had. As he wipes my face wiping my tears away for me he asked me what am I thinking about and what's on my mind and I told him I'm just living in the moment I don't want my heart to be broken I don't want to be lied to or hurt he then says he would never do that and he knows how hard it is to have trust and a man especially when you've been treated a certain type of way. Then I kissed him on his lips he took a picture of him and I together and I told him I looked a damn mess and he said you just had a baby and he doesn't want to always see me perfect he wants to see how I look not dressed up at times with my hair messy because then that would mean that our relationship would have to be based on us both being perfect which made perfect sense to me at that time. The thing was everything was perfect I was nothing but happy.

I then asked him if he wanted anything to eat and to order what he wanted and I gave him the menu he then tells me he's never had hospital food before and asked me what was good I said well I just had a lot because I was starving so you know when you're hungry everything is good and I told him I guess we'll have to figure out what all is good here so order as much as you want you know how we roll we order everything I said laughing. Then I turn on the television giving him the remote controller telling him to watch whatever he wants it and he said he's watching me and I told him he always has a slickest comebacks ever as I laugh at him. Then the doctor and nurse come in to tell me that they need to check my iron levels to make sure I didn't need any infusions and or a blood transfusion which I had never told Garrett about I didn't really think it was important and the Nurse told me that she would check my blood levels to make sure I was good and I told her ok then she asked me if I was afraid of needles and I said no she stuck the needle in my vein to draw some blood from me and once she was done she put a band aid on it then she left the room saying she would be back with the results and I tell her sounds good thank you.

Garrett asked me why would I need a blood transfusion and or aren't infusion so I finally decided to tell him that I have sickle cell trait and microcytic anemia but I always felt fine of course I have those good and bad days when the bad days come in I feel weak, Icky, dizzy ,sleepy ,loss of appetite, fatigue but I always know how to prepare myself for those days and I never let those days keep me down I've been used to it for so long that I new it do. He then told me to let him know if I needed help with anything and he meant anything even if it meant that he had to take off of work then I told him I didn't want him to have to do all of that for me but I greatly appreciate it I've Had those two health problems for years.

Garrett then asked me if I wanted to get some fast food instead of the hospital food then I tell him babe is whatever and he said no babe it's up to you because you're the one that just had a baby I want to make sure you're comfortable and I asked him what did he have a taste for and he said anything I said so again you know how we do you can just bring back anything for us to eat and he said ok he would be right back I said I'll be here waiting for you he then kisses me on my lips and leaves. When I post on Snapchat that I had the baby my college friend Veronica which we had been friends for years I knew her mother her father her brother and her whole family and some of her friends. We used to go to the hookah lounge together and mudding and racing other cars I had the time of my life when I met her and we could both relate to being Raped. Because she had a Dodge Challenger I would often call her Letty from fast and furious which she kind of looked like her plus they were both Puerto Rican With long black hair and a nice body. She then told me on snapchat that she was going to come see Leilani and I later at the hospital and I told her that was fine we were at orange park medical. It was a damn shame I had texted my girls from Burger King Renee, Alma and DayDay To tell them that I had the baby and see if they wanted to come visit me especially since they knew I really didn't have a lot of family and support they all said they would wait until we got out the hospital which I was slightly in my feelings because I mean I was always there for them I would give them rides home no matter where we were coming from I would never require gas money from any of them even though they would require me to give them gas money but I'm like whatever I guess they just didn't have it Like that but I was always there for them more so than they were for me when I would invite them to our cookouts and or events they never showed up but I always went to their events and cookouts. Every time I went around them all they ever wanted to do was drink smoke and chill which gets very old very fast. That's why I really wasn't going to be dealing with people especially now that I was actually considered a mother as I sat in that hospital bed and waited for Garrett to get back with our food I had so much more thinking to do so I went through my contacts list in my phone and I started to delete phone numbers out of my phone after all if you don't talk to certain people why I have their number saved to your phone in the first place they are just taking up space in your phone which was true plus since I was a mother it was time that I made mom friends and hung out with those who were moms no one will understand a parent better than a parent.I told myself it was time for a change within myself also I wanted to be More conservative I wanted to go back to school and after all I was going to have a government security clearance and a government job so I need it to be on my a game. I wasn't big on telling people big plans that I had and or life changing decisions I was making for myself the only time someone would hear about my accomplishments is when it's time to say checkmate I think that's the best way to tell people things.

It definitely killed me to not tell my closest three friends the man that I was with but I just didn't want to ruin things at all people don't want to see other people happy and doing better than them they get jealous and envious. Especially those that are close to you that are considered your friends they're the main ones that hate to see you strive and doing better than they are. I didn't even tell my mother about Garrett because first of all he was forty years old and she was in her forties. Ididn't know how awkward they would feel about that I hated how people Were so quick to judge younger women like myself who chose to date older men it was literally only a twenty year age gap which isn't bad at all hell I've seen worse I don't judge people I don't care people don't pay my bills to each his own you like who you like and what you like that's your business not mine. Also another reason I chose not to tell my mother it's because she's the type of woman you piss her off she's telling all your business we already had that incident occur before when my mother was telling everyone how Jay was still legally married and all of that like certain things people just don't need to know I was already embarrassed enough about the situation and she made it no better for me.

Nonetheless I was now twenty years of age I wasn't trying to use this man for money because I had my own money I had my own car and pretty soon I was going to have my own place So what could I possibly use him for hell I was even in process of obtaining my government security clearance which was the same damn thing he had I just genuinely adored older men and I would only get the with the older men who were on my level financially and physically and I would only get with the older men who were on my level financially and physically so that I don't feel as if they're trying to use me on those two aspects. All my friends that I hung out with her typically always older than me which was completely fine every since I was a jit I always preferred hanging with the big kids I always obtained so much knowledge from being around older kids and or friends that the older I got when it came to the workplace I would always be around the older adults. I've always had a old soul and felt as if I was always older than I truly was.

When Garrett finally came back with our food which I was so glad because I was starving all over again he had Zaxby's which was right up the street from the hospital I love that place he had bought back different flavors of boneless wings chicken sandwiches fries and sweet teas for him and I he knew I love sweet tea it was my favorite beverage whenever I would go to any restaurants. He even told me he thought of me when he went to Zaxby's because every time we would go to a fast food restaurant especially I would always ask them if they provided a military discount I mean after all he was in the military for twenty years so you might as well use your benefits plus I had a military ID thanks to my father and I was definitely using my benefits my father earned that and work for that. Once I told him we can't be letting those benefits go unused then I told him he worked hard for those benefits might as well use the military discount as much as you can where you can. He said that's why I like being with you you even help me save money as he sets the food down to wash his hands.

He asked me what did I want to eat first I told him it didn't matter just give me whatever I was just starving again he even had the sauces that I like see he was a good listener and I love that about him he looked at every detail on my body from head to toe, he knew my dislikes, he knew what I liked, He paid attention to the way I walked our thoughts like it was that simple to read me but the main thing that got me about him he actually paid attention he knew that I had a beauty mark on my left cheek Hell he even knew I had a mole On my right hand on my middle finger on the right hand side it was definitely the little things that made me fall in love with this man who was 20 years older than me but age is nothing but a number granted sometimes that age really does matter because people never think about when you get older but he looked good to be forty. And he was all mine the crazy thing is we still Didn't have sex it would be a lot of times when I was pregnant that he would give me neck massages, foot massages, Back massages and I would get so horny and turned on from it but I knew I couldn't have sex with him while I was pregnant. He would even give me kisses on my neck which was definitely a turn on for me that was definitely One of my spots. When he gives me my container of food he kisses me on my lips telling me that my lips taste good and he loves how big and full they are then I tell him thank you with a slight smile and he asked me what was wrong or on my mind so I decided to tell him about how my girls didn't want to come see me until after I got out the hospital with the baby and I told him I appreciated my father and his girlfriend being there for me as much as I appreciate it Garrett being there for me but I really just needed a lot of love and support around and granted I had that it just wanted my girls to be there too I've known them for so long I then begin to tell Garrett how I've done a lot for them and what I've done for them and I don't like stuff like that so while he was out getting our food I had been deleting a lot of phone numbers that I felt I didn't need in my phone because it was just taking up space and why have someone number in your phone if you're not going to have intentions on talking to them he then said he understands me completely and that's why he's really an introvert and he don't deal with people like that at all not even the people at work he speaks and keeps it moving he said people are never there for you when it counts just when they need you that's when they're there which I definitely agree with completely I was just upset by it and I told him these Jacksonville people are definitely different. He told me to do what I felt like I needed to do and he told me if I needed to delete their numbers then do so he said after all it wasn't like I didn't have family and people who loved me at all in Florida and I told him he was definitely right I told him I really appreciated him the most for being here. Then I tell him how my friend from college she was about two years older than me Veronica she worked in insurance and she had at home in Jacksonville she bought when she was twenty one I told him she was definitely a big and Inspiration in my life I definitely wanted to buy a home at twenty one just like her.we could relate to a lot and we slightly have been through a lot growing up in life in general I told him that she wanted to come see Leilani and I grant said I had known her longer than Renee alma and day-day But it was crazy how I hadn't even talked to her in a long time and she was willing to come see me in my newborn baby in the hospital knowingly knowing that I lost my child dad and he died and how hard it had been on me for months and she was literally there for me but not them when they personally knew him she didn't even know Jay. That's when Garrett just told me to let Veronica come visit us catch up with her enjoy her time and company and just allow her to be there for me he then told me that I couldn't worry about those who weren't there for me because they wouldn't be missing from our lives we will be missing from their lives then I told him that's why I would always fall back from them anyways I hate drama and messiness and Renee was already in her forties and she was so messy like when people tell you things in confidence you don't have to go confide with our group of friends like it's ok not to.If I wanted them to know I would have told them that's why it's so hard having female friends they too damn much. Plus my mother always told me you can never have a lot of female friends which she never lied I watched her go through a lot with females.

I told Garrett thank you he then gets in the bed beside me as we eat and watch Television then he asked if I had checked on the baby and I told him of course I did I really wanted to hold her but she's resting and he told me that sometimes when she's resting I need to be getting my rest as well I said I know but you know I'm an early bird and it's hard for me to take naps. I get a text on my phone which I really hadn't been checking my phone as much because I've been chilling And admiring my newborn baby but my father told me that he would come back up to the hospital once my mother got there and sister. I responded back to him OK then I put my phone back down the nurse finally came back in the room who drew my blood and she told me my arm was a little low and that she would give me some iron infusions While I was there once I finished eating. I hate it getting iron infusions you could literally taste the iron in your mouth it was disgusting But I told her she could go ahead and do it now and Garrett asked me if I was sure I said yes mine as well do it now before the baby wakes up so he gets up removes all the containers of food we had and puts them on the table by the sitting area and window then the nurse said to me your husband sure is helpful that must be nice and I said yes definitely nice and appreciated. She starts giving me the infusions She walks to the door telling us she would be back then Garrett asked me if he could see us getting married I told him you never know what the future holds then I told him if he was going to act like this when we get married then of course I also tell him all I've ever wanted was to get married and have a family

Then I asked Garrett if he could see us being married and he said yes I'm definitely the type of woman that he would want to marry let alone have children with and he told me you never know what the future holds then I said that would be a nice future. Everything that we were both talking seemed so nice and sounded nice the problem was getting to that point which concerned me things always are perfect at the beginning and I didn't want to ruin anything I just didn't want us to rush anything I wanted us to take our time and get to really understand and know each other more even though we knew a lot about each other and that's what I told Garrett and he told me we can do whatever I wanted which in my mind I took that the wrong way in sexual way when he said anything I wanted all I could think about was how horny I had been but I just kept telling myself I have to wait a little while longer. But at least he actually had respect for me I know too many women who've had sex with men while pregnant who weren't their baby daddies. Not judging them or saying is wrong but me personally I could never do that or imagine myself doing that. It is now about eight at night when I get a phone call from Bri She was telling me that they were almost there and they needed the name of the hospital I told her the name of the hospital was Orange Park medical. She said OK and that they would be there soon then I hang up the phone on her When I look over Garrett was sleeping on the couch meanwhile I'm watching TV still trying to process everything next thing I know I hear Leilani crying she was waking up so I get up out of the bed slowly and carefully to go pick up my baby then I bring her over to the bed I was in to breast feed her she was so tiny and fragile she literally looked just like her father in the face. That's when Garrett wakes up asking me if I got the baby and I told him of course I then told him my mother and sister were almost here at the hospital and that he could definitely leave if he wanted to he asked me if that's what I wanted and I told him of course not but we could always see each other later on that night even tomorrow which is when we were being released from the hospital anyways. I told him I wanted him to go home and get some rest

I didn't want him to lose out on sleep because I was losing I don't sleep plus little did he know I was definitely thinking about a lot in my mind I had so much to process and think about with me and him being together and him possibly being a stepfather to my daughter it was a lot to take in I didn't know what to do at that point but once again I was just living in the moment I didn't want to overthink anything at all that's when things really get ruined. I told him that my mother and sister were almost to the hospital they had drove all the way from Virginia I definitely wanted him to meet them just not now of course I know that my mother would be tired from that long drive and my sister from sitting in the car for that long.

But lying to him for whatever reason I told him he could definitely meet my family and by my family I meant my mother and sister I know my father was not going to be going for that shit, plus I was still unsure if he had knew my father or not. He gets up and grabs his backpack that he had brought with him that had his charger and some toiletries. Before he leaves he kisses Leilani on her Head then kisses me on the lips and I tell him thank you for everything and that we would see each other tomorrow I also told him to call or shoot me a text once he makes it home and get some rest for me. He said of course he would let me know when he made it home already knew that though as he opens the door to our hospital room he tells me that he loves me and I look him in his eyes and I say it back to him not knowing if I truly really meant it or it was just the moment.

CHAPTER

7

Next thing I know I received a Snapchat notification it was from Veronica who said that she was on her way I opened the message responding back to her telling her great can't wait to see her also my father mother and Bri were pulling up all at the same time outside so they all ended up walking up together to the room that I was in meanwhile I'm still feeding baby Leilani seeing if she would fall back asleep or not. When my mom and Bri and father come into the room my mom has some bears in her hand that were for Leilani and they see me feeding her of course my father made everything awkward I was literally just breastfeeding and my breasts were not out but because of how uncomfortable he gets very fast I put my breasts away when I do so he was unable to see anyways which he turned around when I did that I didn't see the big deal about a woman just breastfeeding her baby nor did I understand why out in public people made such a big deal about it like if you're uncomfortable simply just don't look some people just can't mind their own business I hate it people like that like you're eating so clearly the baby has to also eat as well if you're so uncomfortable then don't look. My mom and bri walk over to the sink to wash their hands because they definitely weren't holding my baby until they washed their hands i already had OCD as is. My mom holds the baby first kissing all over her which I hated when people did that like I don't know where your mouth has been my mom was already starting to get on my nerves she kissed my baby in the mouth like literally my baby came out of my vagina and I hadn't even kissed her in the mouth that's disgusting.

Bree was acting all shy and scared so I told her if she was going to be acting like that don't even hold my damn baby because I didn't want her dropping her she was even taking pictures of Leilani and she accidentally had the flash on trying to blind my damn baby already and she said sorry out loud and everyone laughed at her. I told my mom and Brie they could sleep on the couch and I believed that it was a pull out couch as well and I could get them some extra pillows and blankets from one of the nurses. Soon I receive a Snapchat notification from Veronica asking what was the room number so then I respond back to her with the room number before I knew it she walked in with one of her friends I had never met before but Veronica was also very popular she knew everyone and normally friends of hers that I would meet we would always friends of hers that I would meet we would always become cool anyways. Veronica was holding Leilani and my father asked her was she still speeding around town in her challenger and she said you know it then we all laughed. Veronica was by far the coolest friend that I had ever met in Jacksonville not only her car but her actual personality she was from up north just like I was she was also a real friend I know when I first met her she told me how her her mother and brother had gotten into a really bad car accident they were hit by a gas truck when she was just a baby and it cost her only out of everyone else to be severely hurt to the point where one of her hands was smaller than the other and she would also limp when she walked but she was still absolutely gorgeous and stunning she was definitely a true friend granted I had new her longer than the three friends who should have been there for me I really appreciated that she was there for me and I told her that as a tear came down my face. Veronica was also into modeling for many years just as I was so we would often let each other know when there was casting calls for modeling in Jacksonville I even gave her my cell number because I forgot that I had changed my cell number because I didn't want jay's family to get in contact with me anymore. I told Veronica to text or call me anytime she put me on to a lot of good restaurants a lot of nights I would hang out with her and some of her friends who soon became friends with me at some hookah lounges in Jacksonville that were Mediterranean and all we had this one spot we would always go to called Istanbul They had belly dancers and everything even the drinks were cheap and good because we knew almost everyone that worked there They never really asked for ID.

When I first met Veronica her family would always pay for me and my meals not that they had to but I greatly appreciated it so I would definitely return the favor for her a lot of times and take her out as well and treat her Some of her friends in fact used her because she had came into all that money from that car accident she was set for life and she didn't even have to work granted she wanted to and I definitely saluted her for that. Her mother even told me when I spoke to her over the phone when she called her mother so I could talk to her that a lot of her friends abandoned her and loved her and told me to make sure that I don't do the same and I told her mother of course not granted the phone wasn't on speaker so Veronica didn't hear what her mother had told me but I told her that I adored her and I really appreciated her coming to visit me in the hospital because I was having the same situation with my friends and I told veronica's mother how my daughters dad had died which veronica had already filled her mother in anyways I couldn't really talk the way I wanted because my parents were there and I didn't want Veronica to know what her mother had told me. Veronica had even asked if she could take the optic with Leilani and I told her yes that was fine She gets her friend who she brought with her to take the optic of her holding Leilani and I told her to send it to me so I could save it She said that she would then I told my mother that she was the one I used to talk about When talking about our crazy college days and my mother said to her nice to meet you and Veronica said you too then she told me that she was going to head out and give us some privacy and I told her thank you for coming to see us she said anytime and I told her friend nice meeting you and she said it back.

A nurse walked into the room telling us that between tonight and tomorrow morning someone would be in the room To get all the information for the birth certificate I didn't even have a middle name picked out for Leilani yet so I allowed my mother to pick out the middle name which she should have been very lucky and grateful that I allowed her to judging by her actions every since I didn't even have a middle name picked out for Leilani yet so I allowed my mother to pick out the middle name which she should have been very lucky and grateful that I allowed her to judging by her actions every since her dad had died Leilani dad had died. My mother picked the name rose for Leilani's middle name which was honestly completely fine and made sense especially since her first name was Hawaiian so you want the name to actually make sense. My mother then asked me if I was going to put Leilani's ads name on her birth certificate I told her no because she's dead then she made this face saying I'm wrong and I shouldn't have said it like that. After all it was true and with how I have been feeling lately I started having hate towards him because he did a lot of wrong to me too and I started having those flashbacks about what he did to me and it started to make me hate him but I still loved him and then this great guy comes along and it's like I wanted to be with Garrett but I had love for Leilani's dad that's not something that you can get over overnight it takes time.

Then my mother asked me if I was going to give Leilani her dad's last name and I told her no when she asked me why I said well I have two last names and he had two last names on top of that his wife still has his two last names so hell no. Then once again my mother calls me out again saying that I'm wrong I'm like how the hell is that wrong just because he's dead doesn't mean I have to give our kid his last name is he really going to know his wife has his last name never changed her last name back even years later so why would I want our kids to share the last name of him and his wife that's a no no in my books. My mother was always calling me out when I was wrong but do we really need to bring up the past and backtrack to all the times when she was wrong? Then my mother starts asking me when was I going to call Leilani other grandparents for the DNA testing I said literally I just had her today I can't do anything yet I said on top of that I have to find their phone numbers and or pop up at their house if I don't have their phone numbers. My father jumps in the conversation saying how he would pay for the DNA testing and I told him it didn't matter who paid for it I'm sure most likely I was going to pay for it or my parents of course but we still had to wait sometime I just had my baby today and my mother is already talking about money like damn.

I ended up posting the optic of Veronica holding Leilani on my Instagram and my Snapchat I said it's crazy how all my supposedly friends know that my child's father died while I was pregnant and no one seemed to care except for my college friend who I met in twenty sixteen was very sad I guess like the great saying goes choose your friends wisely I hadn't even talked to Veronica in a long time and she literally was speeding even though that's something she would always do anyways but was speeding to come see us at the hospital a for effort for her that really made me feel appreciated. I then said at least someone thought of me and on my post I also said it's sad that my supposedly friends literally live right around the corner from the hospital where I had my baby at and not one of them came to see me when they know that I'm going my supposedly friends literally live right around the corner from the hospital where I had my baby at and not one of them came to see me when they know that I'm going through grief through a tough time grieving over the loss of my child father who died when I was pregnant but I guess when you can't relate you don't care but one thing people need to remember is don't ever think a situation cannot happen to you or to someone close to you because it can I'm definitely going to kill motherhood and being a single mother I was definitely built for this and at least I'm financially stable to be a single mom then I uploaded the post on my Snapchat and Instagram couldn't wait to see what people had to say underneath my post. Not that they owed me anything but I just felt like it was the principle I was always giving them money and bringing things to their functions and events and I did a lot for them so in a way yeah what I expected in return was loyalty I've never asked anyone for anything and I don't because I'm too proud too if I really need something that bad I'm a type of person I'm going to get it and by myself no matter what's needed of me but I guess we're all just raised differently.

Bri kept telling me over and over again she cannot believe that I'm a mother I said I can't either but I guess we better get believe in because it's baby girl is here now. When I finally actually get the chance to check my phone I had several messages from Garrett he had told me that he made it home safe he then told me he was missing us and thinking about us he also sent all the optics that we took together at the hospital. He then told me if I needed anything to let him know he knows that I'm going to be busy and I have family in town so I finally decided to respond back to him I really wasn't paying attention to my phone as much I was paying attention to my baby girl who was now here and I was so happy I waited nine months for her she literally came a week early. I responded back to him telling him I'm glad he made it home safe then I told him we miss him more I also said thank you for the optics I love them. I wanted to post the optics on my Instagram and Snapchat so bad but like I told myself just live in the moment don't rush and or ruin anything people don't need to see and know everything that you have going on some hate to see others happy because they're not happy. I also had to send optics of baby Leilani to my friend who was like a friend who was like a sister Tati. We literally talked on the phone every day she was the main person before I met Garret calling me to make sure that I got up and I was eating drinking a lot of water and keeping my sanity together it wasn't easy at first but I greatly appreciated her we go way back to middle school been friends every since.

Later that night I tell my mother and sister to order whatever they wanted from the cafeteria because it will be taken care of anyways. I let them both look over the menu then tell them when they decide what they want to eat for dinner let me know so that I could hit the call button on the remote next to me on the bed. I wanted to shower so bad then I discovered my shower shoes weren't in my freaking hospital bag so I just didn't worry about it I took a wash up in the sink and told myself I would take a nice hot shower when I got home the next day. When they both finally decide what they wanted to eat for dinner I hit the call button then the nurse responds talking on it and I tell her we would like to order dinner she then tells me the cafeteria is closed I said ok thank you so I then tell my mom that I can get my dad to bring us something to eat there were so many restaurants in that area and my dad lived literally around the corner so I knew couldn't be a issue. When I called my father to even see if he was filling up to grabbing us some food to bring to the hospital after telling him that the cafeteria was closed he then asked what did we want to eat for dinner and when I asked Bri and my mother they said Zaxby's in my mind I'm like I already had that but it was whatever. My dad asked what we wanted from Zaxby's I literally just told him that I would send him a text message of what we wanted I really hated him getting food for us in the first place because he always messes up the order if they don't have something instead of him calling to tell us that or ask us what we like he gets whatever and I hate that he always messed the orders up even when you send him a text message of what you want to eat it was so annoying crazy thing is I wasn't even hungry until they said Zaxby's. while I'm on the phone talking to my father I get Bree to type up the orders on her phone to send over to him and my mother even told him don't fuck up the orders and we started laughing. When my dad finally comes into the room with the food and drinks hey my mom start bickering like they always do so I just pay them no mind sometimes it's funny to Bri and I. We say thank you to my father except for my mother. Then my father says yup and asked me if I was being discharged tomorrow and I told him yes I just didn't know what time yet no one told me yet because they still had to do the birth certificate paperwork and some other paperwork that I had to fill out my father then asked my mother what hotel did she want to stay at one thing about my father even though him and my mother had never been married and even when my mother came into town he would always pay for everything for her even though she always seemed to go overboard or if she asked my father for money or pretty much anything he would do it for her not that he had to do it for her and she was always ungrateful. It was crazy my mother and I had both lost our fiancés, Jay died first then in 2019 my mother's fiancé died he was an ex marine I swear my mother loved those military men maybe that's where I got it from and older men but he was really cool and he was like a father figure to me when my father wasn't around because he lived in Florida. My mother's ex fiancé definitely did a lot for Bree she called him dad and everything because she was slightly embarrassed of her own father. My mother always felt like she had to stay at the Marriott whenever she went out of town me person-ally I didn't see the hype staying at the Marriott it was very overpriced for absolutely no reason to be honest that's the thing with people with money like my mother they always feel like they have to spend more and do more that's how you lose out more money like it's not that serious a hotel as long as it's nice looking affordable and you have a clean place to lay your head like you don't have to do all of that that's my mother for you. It was the fact my father was paying for it for me she always tried to get over on him when he would give her money and or do nice things for her that he didn't have to do because I was grown now after all what my mother forgot about.

then my mother turns the TV on and the volume up and she watches one of her favorite TV shows love and hip hop Atlanta I too watched that show but had a lot of catching up to do. All I told my mother was to please turn the volume down on the TV and she was already complaining it was like when things didn't go her way she started bitching and throwing fits as if she was a child it was So annoying she was way too grown for that after all she was in her forties like this isn't about you it's about my baby I asked her to turn the TV volume down because Leilani was sleeping then she responds back saying we're not used to having the TV down this low like my mother's problem was she didn't know how to accommodate herself whenever she went elsewhere without the complaining I would even joke with her at times even though I was dead as serious telling her don't ever go into the military because you wouldn't make it. I eventually fell asleep quit Leilani on top of me the bed railings on the hospital bed were in fact up and when one of the nurses came in there to check on us she told me that I shouldn't have the baby on top of me like that while sleeping because she could roll over or something granted the bed rails were up and I also hated already day one of having my baby when people tell you how to parent but I didn't even have the strength or energy to go off on anyone I also hated how they kept coming into the room to wake my baby up it was me off because I myself was also trying to rest when she was sleeping. Even my mother was getting annoyed because they kept waking us up every time they came into the room. I then said OK and I placed my baby the one I had come out of me back into her sleeping arrangement they had made up for her it was like a container placed on top of something that had wheels on it at the bottom and I rode her beside me I did not want to take my eyes off of her because I didn't trust hospitals at all I didn't want them switching my baby.

I decided to send Garrett a text message saying we could possibly see each other tomorrow I had some errands to run I definitely needed a pedicure and a manicure also those braids that were in my hair definitely had to come out so I needed to go by new wig I decided to send Garrett a text message saying we could possibly see each other tomorrow I had some errands to run I definitely needed a pedicure and a manicure also those braids that were in my hair definitely had to come out so I needed to go buy a new wig to put on for after I take my braids out I knew those box braids were going to take forever to take out so while Bri was around that was the perfect time to do everything I had to do as well as my mother being there. When I texted Garrett he said he would drive me around if I wanted to meet him at his apartment and park my car there because he didn't want me driving it was crazy because I just couldn't believe this man comes out of nowhere and he's so perfect like everything is perfect it seems so unreal to me. I told him that was fine and that would work I just first had to see what time we were being discharged from the hospital and when we're getting home and everything and when we're getting home and everything then once I get everything situated of course I would let him know and he said ok babe..

It was so crazy the next day we were already released from the hospital which I was kind of glad because there's nothing like sleeping in your own bed and I was literally back driving and everything granted I had a natural birth with no medicines but it really didn't hurt I didn't have any pains at all. A nurse came into the room with someone who was wanting me to fill out paperwork and also get the information for the birth certificate she even asked if I wanted Leilani's dad's name on the birth certificate I told her no because he was deceased anyways then she tells me she's sorry for my loss As my mother and Bri goes to my mom's car so she could put the car seat in properly and pull up to the front since I was in a wheelchair Holding Leilani as I am with my father and a nurse a lot of strangers walk past us congratulating me and saying how I had a beautiful baby and I was smiling and all ecstatic telling them thank you. The nurse was coming with us to ensure that the baby would be in a car seat which was completely fine I had already had everything I needed for Leilani. We load up everything and my mother's Chrysler three hundred which we referred to as the baby Benz. The next day I had to go to a grocery store around the corner from my fathers house called save a lot I had to get some baby formula just in case it was needed. I was breast-feeding but I had come to conclusion that Leilani wasn't getting enough milk from my breastmilk but I still want it to keep trying until a week later when that week later came around she was still acting the same always wanting more milk and she was hurting my breast and nipples plus I was tired of leaking milk out everywhere. So I told my mother who told me that I could get cabbage leaves to draw up the breast milk which I had never heard of before but I'm all down for home remedies and natural ways of preventing and or stopping things. Later that day I made Britry some of my breast milk which technically she was curious about trying it anyways and she said it was disgusting when I tried some of my breast milk it tasted sweet then my mother comes around talking about I should have taken the placenta from the doctor we could have made placenta smoothies I looked at her and said that's fucking disgusting.My parents and I always had the type of relationship where I could use profanity Around them but to them I wasn't being disrespectful hell I could even call my father a asshole which he really was and he would laugh he wouldn't even get upset about it because he knew it was true and sometimes he would call me one back. I then told my mom that was some white people shit and she was definitely on her own with that one because that's nasty that came out of my vagina I was good on that.

I told my mother I would get the cabbage leaves after I go on base to the first checkup appointment for Leilani and I. My mother drives us to the base with Bri When we get there the doctor literally said to me whoa your breasts are huge I looked at Bree she looked at me I looked at my mom she looked at both of us I'm like well yeah I have breast milk in them which was spilling all over the place you could see the breast milk through my sports bra just leaking out I wasn't even embarrassed but I felt so nasty I was like this is not being a sexy mom at all I feel like a nasty mom but who was I trying to impress? Hell I just had a baby few ago, she was so freaking tiny and one day when we Were going around to find my mother and Bri a hotel to stay at and of course Leilani and I were going to stay with them as well Bri was being grown as hell and almost made me drop my damn baby which pissed me off. I thought in my mind that when she comes to stay with me we can't have that grown stuff I was already going to have enough on my plate as is so that was the last thing I needed because if she was going to be acting like that she could stay with our mom. At times my sister was also all about what you had to give her as long as you're whining and dining her she's fine she was definitely becoming a typical teenager. there's nothing worse that I hate the a grown ass child. Before we leave from the base my father had gave me a whole bunch of Similac baby bottles that already had the milk in it you just have to put a new bottle nipple on each one everyone knew us at that hospital said they would always hook us up with certain things. Which was greatly appreciated because formula was very much expensive I could definitely afford it but I would look at those prices and say damn. On the way back to my father's house I asked my mother if she could stop at a store so that I could buy some cabbage leaves and she said sure I go inside of the store called Winn-Dixie to buy one cabbage head. Then we head to my dad's house So I could grab a overnight bag since Leilani And I were going to stay at the hotel with my mom and Bri. When we get to my dad's house my mom and Bri both shower and get dressed and my bedroom we all felt icky after all staying at the hospital.

I then text Garrett telling him I would be about an hour or two before I was ready to see him then I tell him I was going to be coming alone without then I tell him I was going to be coming alone without Leilani.

Leilani is now four months that's when I decide to reach out to her other grandparents I really didn't want to but I was getting my child where she was entitled to from her father and earned which was his Social Security. Plus my dad kept bugging me about it so I figured it was time to do it and my father told me that no one was going to touch me or they were going to be in jail and having junctions all against them we don't play that we go to the police very quickly after all my father was above the police. Nonetheless I texted. Jay's mother Sending her a long message telling her that I had Leilani and sending some optics along the way also asking her if her and her husband could do the DNA testing with Leilani and I that was what was required according to the people at the Social Security office the woman told me that if the DNA matched then we would get the Social Security which I wasn't worried about the DNA not matching we all knew that Leilani was Jay's daughter that was definitely his twin. I had also already found a few companies that did DNA testings, I was basically just trying to do price comparisons to see which would be more affordable I was also looking at the hours of operation so I could see which company would best fit everyone's schedule.I then told jay's mother that they could see Leilani if they liked. Jay's mother had an iPhone so I saw when she read the messages and she put heart emojis for the optics of Leilani. When Jay's mother responded back to me through text she asked me if it was ok if they all came to my father's house to see Leilani the next day. I had to ask my father but I told her yes I'm sure my father wouldn't have minded whether I asked him or not plus I was more than sure he wanted to be around to make sure that I didn't catch a case. I definitely wasn't a punk and I wasn't going to let anyone put their hands on me my father was a sniper in the Navy so he definitely had lots of weapons around and I knew how to use each and every one of them I hate the type of people that say they dislike those who have to use guns to fight it's not even a matter of using a gun to fight it's a matter of me using this gun to teach you a lesson if you don't die to keep your hands to yourself and stop threatening people. After all what's the point in buying a gun if you're not going to use it to protect yourself when you feel threatened for your life?

In my mind I kept telling myself I hope they don't bring Martina because she definitely was not allowed to be at my father's house she was in fact the only one that had threatened me to things that I didn't appreciate from everyone else was the simple fact that they were gapping running their mouths like don't wait for this man to be dead to say what you have to say about him and I you should have said all of that when he was alive I hate when people have things on their minds but they always want to wait until this too late to say something I guess death has that effect on people for whatever reason. It was very crazy to me how Martina actually was threatening me when I was pregnant saying after I dropped the baby that her and I were going to fight like I Didn't know all of her dirty laundry after all when her and I used to smoke blunts together in her SUV she would tell me a lot of problems in the past that she herself had with jay's family while she's trying to threaten someone. She would often upset me at times because once we had an event and I said damn black people always late then she called herself correcting me saying no Haitians are always late. I wanted to tell her so bad sweetheart you're still black. I didn't know why a lot of them thought they were better or that they weren't black but they in fact were. I knew my father wouldn't allow anything to happen anyways he definitely hates it confrontation and he didn't argue with I knew my father wouldn't allow anything to happen anyways he definitely hates it confrontation and he didn't argue With anyone I've never seen my dad get into any type of confrontation with anyone other than my mother and of course Carmen.

It is now the next morning my father and I always got up very early whenever Leilani was sleeping I myself tried to sleep as well as much as I could but at times I would have two decisions to make do I want to get rest while she's sleeping or do I want to do what I need to do while she's sleeping. Depending on how tired I was sometimes I really would sleep in but other times I would tell myself while she sleeping I need to get everything done that needs to be done before she wakes up when it comes to babies their sleep schedules are all thrown off so you never know how long they're going to stay for. My father had already cooked breakfast for him and I which I really appreciated we typically both ate the same thing for breakfast whenever he would cook or I would cook we would always eat fried bacon and fried well done eggs.

I went ahead and did my fifty crunches which I did every day I would do 100 crunches a day. Fifty in the morning and fifty at night before bed to keep my abs tightened and toned after I had Leilani my stomachwent back to being flat But I had discoloration on my stomach which took a few weeks too go back to his normal skin tone, which I was so glad. I went ahead and showered, brush my teeth,washed my face then I Grabbed my robe to put on that was always in my bathroom at all times then I go back in my room and find some workout attire to throw on. When I first became a mother workout clothes we're definitely my best friends They were so comfortable plus having a newborn baby who's going to spit up on you all the time there is no need in trying to look cute anyways.

I received a text message from Jay's mother she was asking if she could give my cell phone number to Bev who was the oldest sister I responded back to her saying sure, She then responded back telling me to text Bev and I said OK. So I text Bev like her mother asked me to to see what time they were trying to come over to see Leilani. She then responded and asked if they could come over around noon I responded yes that's fine. Then she left me on red so I go to my father and asked him if they could come over at noon he said it was fine not like we had anything to do anyways plus it was weekend. Leilani finally wakes up crying that's when I go make her a bottle of milk and feed it to her. I say out loud to my father I'm glad I got myself together before she woke up I also said I can't always choose to get sleep things have to be done at times,I made a joke and had said I'll when I'm dead.As Leilani is drinking her bottle I take some optics of her and I talked to her as she drinks her milk.

It says now noon and jay's family arrives parking in front of one of my father's garage doors. My father tells me that they were there he had cameras outside of his home plus he never seemed to miss a beep or sound but I guess that was expected coming from him he had been in the military way too long he even had these fucking traps in the house you could never see them at night unless you turned on the hallway light stuff was in the way when you're walking in the hallway I would literally always trip over stuff and I asked him why did he always have that crap there he would then tell me in case someone tries to break in they'll trip and fall over stuff one time I told him while laughing the person tripping and falling over stuff is me. I was slightly nervous and I go into the room to get Leilani she was in her bassinet my father didn't open the front door until they rang the doorbell. They all speak to my father it was Jay's mother and his three sisters. My father shows them which living room to sit in while they waited for me to come out and they were making small talk with my father asking how he was doing and everything I could kind of over here from my bedroom as I grab Leilani out of her bassinet and grab one of her burp cloths.

When I went into the living room I was acting very shady towards everyone I said hi to everyone. The hi that I said was very dry, Bev the oldest sister tried making small talk to me by saying that I gained weight which was very ignorant to say especially since I was already insecure about my weight little did she know but I also did just have a baby granted my weight went from one hundred and twenty to one hundred and sixty but I was also six feet tall so it didn't look that bad to me because as soon as I had Leilani my weight was starting to go back down anyways. When she told me that I didn't say absolutely anything at all I just slightly smiled. Then I passed over Leilani to them and Jay's mother asked how old Leilani was I then told them she was four months old. Next thing I know everyone starts crying I couldn't even allow myself to cry or feel bad for them because of everything that transpired when I was pregnant I never forgot anything. A tear almost fell down but I acted as if I didn't notice they were crying I just looked at the television and glanced at my phone from time time.

They cried loudly and for quite some time they were even saying how she looked just like Jay which she definitely did and I could tell she was going to have his skin tone he was dark skinned and I was brown skinned but her ears were very dark which my mother told me that that indicated she would be dark skin Which I didn't care about the color of the skin. Bev had asked me how I had been I told her good.

It is now time to start planning the day so that we can all meet up either at my father's house or Jay's parents house for the DNA testing to be done. I had discussed everything with my father about the company that I wanted to choose to go with that was remote and would drive from Jacksonville to Orange Park I decided to just have Jays parents come to my father's house and the price was two hundred and fifty dollars. I then told my father I just needed to discuss times with Jay's parents I knew my father could get off of work early with no problem even take the day off if he wanted to but as for Jay's parents their schedules always changed and I want to say at that time his mother had two jobs meanwhile his father I don't ever recall him working I knew he was just a pastor and he would get odd jobs at times. The funniest thing ever about them they were rich in Haiti but poor in the states. When Jay and I would get into arguments I remember I would tell him if his country is so perfect maybe they should all go back I would even tell him they don't even have police control over there whenever we would get into arguments about him taking the baby who wasn't even born yet over there I didn't lie though their country sucks meanwhile people complain about living in the states at least we have put these control they don't you go over there and you get robbed instantly fresh off the airplane.

I had to text Jay's mom to see when they would be willing to come to my father's house so that we could all do the DNA testing. She responded back to me telling me to just pick a date and time and we would go from there.I was honestly trying to get it done as soon as possible though Leilani was four months old with the Navy Federal Credit Union account with a few thousands so once we got everything established with her father Social Security I figured I would have that money go into her checking account. I didn't need her money that was her money from her father and I was going to stack it up for her. Later that day I called the DNA testing company in Jacksonville that I was choosing to go with with the date for two days later and the time at nine in the morning I always preferred morning with everything that I was doing. Then I text Jay's mother with the date and time I also told her that her husband would have to be there too for the DNA test she responded back saying ok.

The two days come up and Jay's parents got to my dad's house around eight in the morning. We all were talking while we waited for the DNA tester to arrive who then gave a Courtesy call so let us know that she was in traffic after all she was coming from downtown Jacksonville I then tell her that's completely fine I understand. When she arrives she rings the doorbell my dad goes to open the door meanwhile jay's father has Leilani we were all in the living room by the kitchen. When the DNA tester walks in she then says she needs mom baby and dad's parents to come around as she puts gloves on so we could all get tested she then uses cotton swabs To swab our mouths holding the cotton swabs in our jaws one by one. She then tells me that the DNA test results would be in three to five days three to five business days I tell her ok thank you she then prints out a receipt and asked how Were we paying I was going to pay cash but my father said debit card and he paid. Then we say thank you to the woman and she leaves Jay's parents whole Leilani and play with her a little while longer before they have to leave to go to work then soon my father has to also leave to go back to work. My father walks Jay's parents to the door and Before they walk out jay's father tells my father that we should all get together sometime to go out to eat and my father said that'll be nice then they leave.

When I called my mother to tell her that the DNA test was complete she asked how much it costs and I told her she then asked if Leilani grandparents gave any money or offered to pay and I told her no she then said they should have offered to pay and called them broke. I then told my mother I was the one who needed the DNA test so it was whatever I was going to pay but my father chose to pay. The DNA results came back in in the mail to my father's house which was what I needed to show the people at the social security office in Jacksonville so they lonnie could start getting her father social security check monthly they also had to back pay her. For some apparent reason Bev had sent me a text message asking if it was possible that I could send her as well as her mother a copy of the DNA results why I didn't know we already knew that Leilani was Jay's daughter I also didn't cheat on him even though I definitely could've I had so many opportunities but I send it to them anyways. When the results finally come in the mail the same day they came in I decided to call the Social Security office in Jacksonville so I could go ahead and make us an appointment so that we can go back up there in person with the results as well as the bank information for Leilani bank account I also had to take her birth certificate and Social Security card as well.

The more and more I try to be mature adult and allow myself to grow I started letting Jay's family get Leilani and allowing her to go over there more and more often one time I didn't appreciate how when I picked her up she had poop debris all in her clit area on her vagina. That's why I didn't want her to go over there the thing I hated the most is when Bev would try to tell me she used to work in a daycare we would sometimes have slight disagreements I literally told her working in a daycare taking care of other people's kids isn't the same as having your own kids I then told her she gets paid it's not like she was doing it for free I also told her you may know how to take care of those kids in a daycare but that doesn't mean you know how to take care of my child I said that since you think you know everything don't bother asking me if she has any allergies or anything you know just do what you do because you know how to raise kids and the first time my child ends up in the hospital we're going to have an issue. I hated those especially her who tried to correct my parenting skills or tell me that they knew what they were doing working with kids isn't the same as having your own kid. I also didn't like how Jay's mother would often try to rush me out of their house because again like I once told them I don't have to bring my child around you I'm doing this to be nice and try to be a mature adult. I also didn't want to be angry and have anger always built up in me whenever I go around these people because that's not healthy and if that were the case there was no need to go around them at all if I was going to keep that anger there because then it's like they're getting the best of me and they're winning.

The thing with Bev and I we would always bump heads then come back from it I even started letting her braid my hair back in cornrows then do sew ins since I was trying to get more into wearing wigs since I had always wore braids for quite sometime my real hair was so long,It used to go down my back touching the bra latch that is until the relaxers I used to get broke my hair off because the woman who I trusted to do my hair was over processing my hair with the relaxers. I had to also keep cutting my hair to get all the relaxer out of my hair so that I could go natural which was definitely a lot of work being natural I was actually starting to miss getting the relaxers. Being natural required a lot of products and time and attention to your hair as a black woman way too much was needed to be done to get my hair the way I wanted it to be which would be slightly annoying at times. But as crazy as it sounded I actually trusted Jay's sister to start doing my hair and installing my wigs she seems to do fine to me that is until I started getting her to cut out my wigs and every time I would look at the length of my hair I was feeling as if she was cutting some of my hair only because the amount of hair that would be on the ground when I would get up after she was done installing my wig I couldn't help but think she was cutting my Her after all my mother always told me never let a bald headed person touch your hair and Play in your hair but then again I think that in the black community all black moms told their daughters that.

But Bev and I would often take the girls out to eat which was her two younger sisters,Leilani and I. she would even invite her best friendShavonneand her two daughters. One time Bev even told me that the youngest sister Nicey Was slightly upset when I had left them alone for quite some time because she always seemed too attached to anyone who came around in their lives grant said I did everything for those younger sisters a lot of things for them as if they were my sisters. One night Bev Shavonne and I were going to this place to get some fish and fries I was driving my car and out of nowhere Bev starts talking about how she didn't appreciate how I told her mother how her brother hit me even though he actually in fact did hit me so I didn't know that we were going to normalize things like that being ok whether a person is dead or not right is right and wrong is wrong when she said that I told her your brother did hit me and I'll never forget that just because he's dead what I'm going to do is teach our daughter not to allow a man to do some shit like that to her. Because if my daughter told me that her boyfriend and or husband hit her I'm going to kill him my damn self you can bet that. Then she asked me why Leilani didn't have her brothers last names and I responded back that's my child that came out of my pussy and your brother didn't even have his own last names he has a whole wife who still has his last names that's not cute. I didn't know what made her all of a sudden start asking all these crazy questions about the baby that came out of my pussybut we were about to have a problem especially when she thought that she was going to threaten me like dear I literally had a gun in my glove box and I was the driver I could have took all of our lives. Bev had even been watching my Snapchat stories from both her younger sister's accounts since I had her blocked. The bitch brings up how I was engaged to Garrett.I then kindly remind her how her ignorant ass cousin told me I was young and beautiful literally when Jay had first died he hadn't even had been buried in the ground we hadn't even had the funeral yet. I then said remember your cousin told me all of that and how I could move on and find someone I definitely have found someone and I've been engaged she's been there every since I was pregnant it was such nice feeling being with a man who isn't married and has yet to put his hands on me even when he was upset. I then told her life goes on I can't sit around forever sad and miserable it sucked what happened but unfortunately that's life and we have to sometimes expect the unexpected.

She then responded back while sitting in the passenger seat beside me while I'm driving how she never took up for her brother when he put his hands on me she was the one who broke the door down and helped me then she said that wasn't right. I then tell her it wasn't right but you're normalizing it because your brother is dead we literally have a daughter I would never want someone to do that to my daughter at all because they would definitely be six feet under.

Bev then told me how her friend Bianca said she wanted to slap the hell out of me for allowing Carol to take everything and I told her I'm not glad that your brother died or happy about it of course not but let me tell you something I have thousands of dollars in my bank account and it isn't because of your brother I made it in life I'm doing what I need to do for my child and myself a man don't define me because a man can come and go and see what happened with your brother one day he unexpectedly died which unfortunately sucked but I'm doing 10 times better for myself. I then said all that Carol took I can get myself as well I rather have things in my name not a man's name or not a man doing or getting things for me that's where women go wrong at they need men to get them things and help them get where they need to be in life not I. then the bitch literally said to me they were going to file for grandparents rights. I then told her I have a government security clearance and in the state of Florida that is not a thing if you're going to be threatening people with things at least do the research I told her because that's not a thing instead of Florida I then told her try that on someone with a GED just don't try with me.

She also told me how they were trying to help me even got a lawyer for me to get things instead of Carol getting everything but the lawyer told them they couldn't do anything without me being present there which I didn't care about I had money and me and my child were going to be alright and pretty soon we were going to be living the golden life in my Jill Scott voice. It amazed me how she had to be around her friend to talk like this but man I was so proud of myself I had really been maturing because I had a handgun in my glovebox and I was driving it was already bad enough that I had a déjà vu moment of me turning that damn car over and climbing out and leaving they fat asses in the car. It just amazes me how a lot of times Bev and I had actually been alone together and she never brought up any of that stuff at the moment she gets around her friend she wants to show out I'm not scared of anybody bigger than me or older than me I'm not. It pissed me off the most that Bev was really coming for me like that I really started to ask her if she talked to Carol like that.

Bev even told me that Jays childhood friend who we went to visit in Alabama took up for me saying how if he was me he would be mad at them as well and not want to deal with them I was glad someone was on my side and understood I wasn't doing any of this to be petty or out of spite I was hurt, bewailed, in pain And I didn't appreciate how they treated me when Carol came around I mean Jay was already dead like what more could she do to a dead person? I was the one who was pregnant after all talking about they didn't want to make her mad I remember when they told me that pissed me off I literally thought in my mind make her mad I'm the pregnant one of you're making me mad.

I don't know what made me tell Bev this but I literally told her that I had thought about killing myself when I was pregnant and I almost did it until my fiancéGarrett who wasn't my fiancé at the time stopped me from doing so she literally said bitch i would've fought you. Man when I see visions of me having déjà vu moments the mine is definitely a powerful thing I literally was having visions of me shooting her pistol whipping her stabbing her and more she was really pushing her limit especially when she chose to call me a bitch I might have a baby face and had been younger than her. But I literally told her her luck was very much running out in her words she needed to choose wisely I then said to her and her friend I just want you to know I have a nine millimeter handgun in my glovebox and another one under my seat disrespect and or threaten me again and your family will be walking slowly behind you next and I'll have you buried next to your brother you and your friend I said do not disrespect me again because I don't have to do shit for you I yelled. I then asked her you think your brother was so perfect? He was not I then told her I'm going to protect "my" daughter at all costs to keep her away from men like your brother you know the ones that are married and they have to lie to women and they just want to use a woman for a baby. I said the man who has to hit on a Pretty Woman because she's given him some true knowledge and words of advice that he doesn't want to listen to. What pissed me off the most was the fact Bev was demanding that I changed Leilani's last name to her dad's last name. I told Her whether he was dead or alive my body my baby my choice. I then told her whenever you decide to become stable enough in life financially and physically maybe you can have your own baby and it can have your last name but don't tell me how to parent I don't care if you are older than me you could definitely take some notes from me.

I told her call me a bitch again and see what I can do I promise you I told her I'll be at that courthouse first thing Monday morning like a rich white woman fell in a false fucking report please don't make me go there I said you know my father is above the police right able to be a damn shame for you to never be able to see your brother's daughter again. I told her she was getting too disrespectful and above herself and I'm not the one. Man I couldn't wait to get home to call my girls and tell them what this bitch said to me let alone my father because we don't play that we don't act kindly to threats granted a threatened her but the issue was had she never said everything she said to me I would have never went there with her but I don't play shit. I've always hated the type of black women and or girls who think that you're supposed to be scared of them because they're loud bigger than you in ghetto like that's not cute looking a damn mess. I then told her that she needs to train her friend Bianca to learn how to get a job like real bitches do and get off of welfare because that was not cute. Bitch did everything but get a real job and actually try to provide for her kids it's bitches like her that make every excuse on why they can't do something when they start getting a little taste of welfare life. I then said to Bev that her friend Bianca shouldn't even be speaking on my life she's older than me and I literally started from the bottom up somewhat and somehow someway I'm still doing better than her a damn shame. Out here making us black people look bad she's the reason why society thinks that there's more black people statistically on welfare than white people even though there's actually more white people statistically on welfare than blacks. I just hated how they would rather teach their children that getting free benefits from the government and being a welfare or your life while not working or trying to as a flex and she had the nerve to be speaking on me and bringing my name up in conversation when I'm not around bitch please. I then asked Bev how many degrees did her or any of her friends have that were bringing my name up in conversation I told her it's a damn shame I'm younger than all of you and I've somehow someway surpassed you take notes. It was crazy after we both stopped bickering we finally arrived to the food place to get the fish and fries and drinks to have a potential movie night but after everything that happened and occurred in my car I wasn't even feeling it. Then bev and Shavonne Make jokes at me because the guy that worked at the place were picking up the pants of food from was trying to talk to me he was also flirting with me and they were both like oh he wanted the skinny brown girl. When we get the pans of food we go back to bev's parents' house she would often bounce back and forth between Shavonne's house and her parent's house. The saddest part was about it all she was struggling when her brother was alive and after like life isn't that hard life is what you choose to make out of it.

I don't understand or know what goes through peoples heads to where they think they can say things to people and get away with it in this day and time people nowadays will really shoot you and or kill you for the Littlest things ever in my generation. Everyone had guns especially the people that you would least expect to look like they had one even in road rage situations people will shoot you. I was definitely licensed to carry you can never be too careful. Especially with me being a single mother I had to protect my child at all costs.

Later that night when I got home and got Leilani bathe and in bed peacefully sleeping, I had to call my mother and sister to tell them about that bitch Bev. I couldn't believe she said all that shit to me like baby was holding it in but had to be around her friend to say it all I hated those types of bitches like say what you had to say without your posse being around if you are so big and bad. My mom then told me that they were all black fat and ugly and said I should have picked a better looking man with a better looking family my mother based everyone off of looks and appearances And breathe said that was crazy and Bev should be lucky she didn't lose her life I then said she definitely should be my mother then said the bitch isn't a dime at all None of them are my mother also said she was glad that Leilani was starting to look like us and by us she meant me. I then put the phone on speaker and go into my dad's room to tell him about what happened as well and he was laughing at the part when Bev said they were going to try to get grandparents rights my father then said they can't try to get anything because they aren't her only grandparents just stupid like if you're going to try to check people know the facts first. My father then said they didn't want to piss him off because he can do a lot and make a lot happen in less than twenty four hours legally Which he definitely could My father knew everyone who worked for the government the state and more.

CHAPTER

8

When Garrett and I had parted ways Which definitely sucked it sucks more because I Knew it was my fault I was definitely to blame I guess I just really wasn't ready to move on from Jay. I was back to having no one around so I downloaded a mom app called peanut I figured I needed to take that time to try to heal more and a man wasn't the answer to my problems I just needed some mom friends to hang out with. I was determined to meet some mom friends that lived locally in Orange Park in Jacksonville area so we could have play dates and just hang out and etc. Whoever made that app was a freaking genius the app was basically like mom tender you know you meet moms who are married and or single me personally I prefer to hang out with the single moms because only single moms can relate to single moms plus I felt like the ones that were married always felt as if they were better than single moms and the thing I would have to remind people about myself being a single mother being a single mother doesn't mean that you're struggling so I don't even know why society wanted peo- ple to see it that way. I was meeting so many mom friends and it felt nice to finally have friends who were moms I always felt as if it was harder to have friends around you who aren't parents because they have the freedom to come and go as they please they have the freedom to do what they want when they want for how long they want because they don't really have any responsibility of having to be a parent. I definitely loved being a mother a single mother because I worked my ass off not for me but for my child and I definitely made it my daughter may be that strong independent woman that I needed to be.

Not saying that I'm glad her father died because I will always have love for him but that situation turned me into a woman that I didn't know I could be my daughter definitely saved my life if it wasn't for her I don't think I would have had anything to look forward to or anyone to want to do well in life for. Being a single mother is definitely very challenging but every day I felt like it made me stronger. I was accomplishing things in life I finally had a great career path and I was only twenty going on twenty one.

I noticed I started hanging out with my gay Kai who I had met at the Wells Fargo call center in the training class Him and I started hanging out a lot we were very close we talked on the phone all throughout the day and hung out almost everyday considering we had nothing but time that is before I back to work. We were so close that his husband literally asked multiple times how did him and I meet and I would literally give him the same response each time his husband didn't like me at all because he thought that I wanted kai even though we all loved dick so I didn't know how to take that. Kai and I hung out so much that even his own mother thought Leilani was his daughter and accused Kai of having a affair with me.

I'm not going to lie I wasn't a big fan of kai's mother at all in fact I almost stopped dealing with him when I first met his mother she was braiding my hair I literally went to her house at six in the morning with Leilani and I didn't leave until seven at night. She braided my hair it was absolutely gorgeous it just took way too long for me sometimes cheap is not always the best I just didn't want to go to a hair salon and pay one hundred and eighty dollars granted I would've been out of there within three to four hours had I done that. But I didn't appreciate how his mother say that my child looked like she had a down syndrome knows as a baby I thought that was the most disrespectful Thing that you can tell a person especially someone that you just met for the first time I literally thought that was very ignorant because I've seen down syndrome children would regular faces I didn't appreciate that at all then had I went off on her I would have been in the wrong and I was surprised Kai didn't take up for me or say anything whether that's your mom or whomever when someone is wrong they need to be checked for it.

Even kai's aunts told his mother that she was deadass wrong for that like certain things don't need to come out of people's mouths at times and when it comes to talking about people kids that's a big ass no. They had a house full the house was big and nice and pretty much all of cash on hunts and some of their kids lived in the house which was left to them by Their mother who had passed away. For the most part the rest of Kai's family was cool everyone smoked weed and drunk. One thing about going to their households are they're clean and they're going to feed you Which they could definitely cook because typically I did not eat everyone's cooking. Kai's family would babysit Leilani for me they practically taught her how to walk and talk and when they would watch her they would feed her eggs and oatmeal and introduce her to all types of new foods hell even chis mother started braiding Leilani hair for me when she was only three months old which helped her hair grow a whole lot because I had no idea how to do hair. They were like family to be honest and it felt nice they always had get togethers and would invite us we always had events at their homes they invited us out with them a lot. It was funny because even when Kai and I would go places with Leilani people would always think that we were a couple and would offer to take pictures of us.

We literally would always go out to eat together to Saint Augustine all the time that was our spot and more he even helped me get into this one townhouse that I have wanted on one hundred and third street. He even would help out in so many other ways if needed they were genuinely good people it was just the messiness that I couldn't deal with but then again I mean he was gay So what did I expect?

It is now May of twenty eighteen I had finally turned twenty one which I had been waiting for all my life I was so tired of getting people to buy liquor and or wine for me and by people I mean Kai it was cool and all and I was all for sharing but it was like damn I didn't wanna drink it. One of my mom friends by the name of Megan Had met up with Leilani and I at this one popular park in Orange Park around the corner from my father's house that I had been going to every since I was a kid so it was very nice to take my own kid there. It was basically the memories for me but megan and her Daughter Raelyn Had met us at the park after a while of us being there we decided to go to Chili's it was very close and around the corner I was starving plus it was my birthday When we go to Chili's I finally get to order a alcoholic beverage legally because typically whenever I would go out to eat with someone for some reason they would just never ask for my ID so felt nice being legal. Megan even paid for the lunch and bought me a dessert for my birthday which I really appreciated. We always had play dates normally at her house but it was still nice having mom friends. We get our waiter to take some optics of us with our girls which came out very nice ask Megan and I talk a little more we give our girls our cell phones so they could watch some YouTube videos to stay occupied since they both chose to not color anymore which was completely fine. We had been at Chili's for quite some time so when the dessert comes out after we box up some of our food give Megan a spoon and tell her to dig in because I couldn't eat it all by myself. She and I both finished the dessert and she gives the waiter her card to pay for lunch then when we leave Out the restaurant we were both parked beside each other we were both parked beside each other considering Megan had followed us there. We give each other hugs and say our goodbyes I then told her to text me when they made it home safe.

Now that I had had my twenty first birthday lunch I then had to plan Leilani's birthday party which was the next week. My father kept telling me that we should have had her birthday party at the park the nice big one that Megan and I had had a playdate at but all I could think about was what if we had to cancel due to inclement weather. So the more and more I look around for affordable things to do I decide to have her first birthday party at a banquet hall it was very affordable and in Orange Park it was literally only fifty per hour and it was very nice they set up everything it had everything we needed as well they also did military discounts so I figured that we book it for about 3 hours that would be good enough so that's what I was sticking with the thing that pissed me off about my dad at times he always tried to persuade people to do things that he wanted them to do as if he was the one paying for it then he ended up paying for it anyways not that I asked him to or required him to but I always appreciated it because I know there's some out there whose fathers end or mothers didn't do as half as what mine did for me. Then I figured that I could get the food and beverages from Sam's Club and bulk after all I really knew a lot of people in Jacksonville and Orange Park and then I had a lot of mom friends. I found a app called punch bowl which is what I was going to decide to use to send out the invitations to everyone. For the theme since Leilani name was Hawaiian I thought about the movie called Moana that was definitely very cute and I was going to have a Hawaiian theme in the banquet hall.I had already coordinated the plans with the owner of the banquet hall and talked everything over she required a deposit my father had took care of that for me.

I have once a party city with Leilani to start buying balloons and Hawaii themed decorations so we could take pictures with everyone. I had even started making goody bags because I was so ecstatic about everything. For the food I decided to go to Sam's Club to get chicken wings and a bag of fries I also have bought some cases of sodas juices and chips it was cheaper to buy in bulk if you asked me plus I love Sam's Club.i also wanted to make small sandwiches. Granted I could have just bought some Subs already pre-made but I wanted to actually enjoy making all of that stuff for my child's first birthday party. There I was trying to be a over the top mom. As my dad and I when my dad and I go in person to meet with the woman who is in charge of the banquet hall she was a black woman and I was like ok I'm all for supporting black owned businesses but then it slowly started to go downhill especially when she tells us that you can't come in ahead of time to set up you basically have to set up at the start time that you can't come in ahead of time to set up you basically have to set up at the start time that you tell people you've told people the event would be starting which was crazy and ghetto people love getting money at all cost I didn't like that at all. My father had already paid the nonrefundable deposit for the place I wish I had known that's how it was because I would've just said let's have the party at the park but I didn't want to be hot and outside it was Florida after all. I had also discussed everything with my mother her and my sister were planning on coming for Leilani's first birthday party the day before it started. I even had the same Moana outfit ordered for Leilani to wear at her birthday party I was just hoping and praying that it arrived soon. For her cake I was going to be adding some optics of her on the cake which I was going to order from Walmart. Whenever Bree and I have birthday parties my mother would always order us cakes with colleges of photos on the cakes of us which I loved the idea so I always said that whenever I had kid(s). That I would do the same thing.

I even asked Kai if he could make some rum punch which he agreed to do. What's a kid's party in the black community without liquor? The lady literally told us that we couldn't have any alcohol but who actually listens to people it's not like she would actually know anyways because I had red cups and on top of that the rum punch was going to be in a gallon jug anyways so how would she really know? I even told myself that I was going to invite jay's family which I actually did invite them and they said they would try to show up what I would tell myself with them is if they come they come if they don't they don't they'll receive optics though of Leilani dressed up as Moana. The more and more I started going to therapy my therapist was teaching me different techniques that I definitely wish I had knew back then he also would tell me a lot of times that I cannot get upset about what I have no control over and that I cannot control people or how they think feel, act and think which he was absolutely right. The more and more I started to actually use his techniques and take his advice and actually listen the better off I actually started to become and I was loving the new me I was becoming.

I had already sent out the invitation so far I had sent out a good fifty invitations. I already knew there would be a lot of people there anyways because Kai Was going to invite his whole family which I knew the entire family they all lived in Jacksonville the problem I had with him was he didn't listen I wanted everyone to RSVP because I needed to know how many seats and tables needed to be in the banquet hall and I literally said to RSVP but he never listened. As I'm out and about minding my own business looking fine as hell with my slim body my Medium long curly black and red wig, a tube top, and some shorts with my Gucci sandals on in a store trying to gather the rest of what we needed for Leilani's birthday. This fine black man Wearing glasses who appeared to be forty kept staring at me the whole time I was in the store. Looking back I think my biggest downfall with men was the older men. I hate when people stare and don't speak I always have my mother it's the same exact way. Nonetheless he was checking out and when he finished he went to his black Audi to put all of his groceries in the car then I noticed him walking back up he came up to me giving me a card with his first last name and cell number on it. When I look at his card it says Theo It also said that he was a professor he then asked me how old was I and I told him that I was twenty one when I also looked down at the card I noticed that he had his cell number circled he also had his office number up there as well.

He was fine as hell looks like I was getting my birthday wish He had told me to text him later and I told him I could do that he also asked what my name was and I told him my name was Brittany. He then said nice to meet you and I told him nice to meet you as well and shook my hand then he left. I finally check out in line then go out to the Chrysler Loading everything up in the trunk hoping that he was around to see the whip I was driving. I roll down all the windows and open the sunroof blasting some music driving back to my dad's house I was only around the corner. Later that day when I get back home I decided to text Theo when I did text him I noticed he had an iPhone but I texted him saying hey this is Brittany the woman you met in the store earlier he didn't reply instantly it took him hours to respond which was expected I mean it was the weekend after all. When he finally text it back we were definitely being very professional through text after all he was a professor and I had a government job so I definitely want it to prove to him that I was young but on the same caliber as him. When he texted me back he asked if I was in college and I told him that I was working on my second degree and I was already enrolled at a college locally in Orange Park he then told me that he's a math professor but at the college where he teaches at they have a program that he happened to be the director of that basically helps students earned their degree a year earlier which was very popular.

He then asked me what was I studying in college and what did I previously study I told him I had previously studied business human resources and I was currently studying for computer science. He then told me that those were both very great career paths then he asked what did I do for work and I told him that I work for the government he then asked what did I do working for the government I told him I worked on the military base in material management. He then asked again how old I was I told him I was twenty one years old then I asked him what his age was and he told me to take a lucky guess I then asked if he was forty and he said yes. For some apparent reason he asked me if I could send a copy of my driver's license I guess he wanted to just make sure that I wasn't lying about my age because I look really young which is what he ended up saying anyways after I've thought about why he wanted a copy of the license which is understandable can never be too careful nowadays. When I sent a copy of my drivers license he didn't say anything back so I just gave him some time granted he was very fine and I really wanted him sexually I also didn't want to scare him away and be clingy especially right and be clingy especially right off the bat. in fact didn't hear From him anymore that day.

My mother and Bri arrived in Florida earlier than expected they did come up the day before the birthday party but they had gotten to my dad's house very early whenever my mother had to drive far distances she would always try to leave at the crack of dawn so that she could arrive at her destination early which makes perfectly good sense to me. This time they chose to stay at my dad's house with us instead of getting a hotel plus my dad had a pull out couch I even had offered to give my mom my bed granted my dad had a 3 bedroom house only two granted my dad had a three bedroom house only two rooms were being used a third room had a bed in it but that was his junk room. Plus my mother told me that she would help me make the sandwiches for the birthday party I had to get Bri to help me blow up all the balloons but I told her we will wait until the day of about an hour before the party starts to blow up the balloons I had already made all the goodie bags I had to go to Walmart the next morning to pick up the cake. I had my Bluetooth speaker that was going to be there so we could play kid friendly music. My father was going to fry the wings and the French fries for me I had already bought the plates napkins cups plastic Ware all from Sam's Club which was definitely cheaper that way to do so.

The night before Leilani's birthday party chi his husband and some of their friends invite Bri and I to go to this bowling alley that was always popping in Orange Park called Splitz. I had never been there before but I don't even change my outfit I keep on the same outfit that I met Theo in just in case I find me another man and Bri had on a crop top and skinny jeans. We were blasting Pretty Ricky all the way to the bowling alley Kai also told me that his husband coworker who was also a CDL driver like kai's husband was going to be there his name was Carlos he was light skinned a few years older than me and skinny and also not my type we both cannot be skinny that is nasty bones rubbing against each other Eww. When we get to splits I told Bri to order whatever she wanted I ended up getting this large ass drink it was definitely worth the money and they let you take the Togo as they should. Bri orders two orders of potato skins one for her and one for me we love potato skins with sour cream on them. Bri and I bowl with everyone else I sucked at bowling I really did plus I almost busted my ass twice. Kai and I Take some optics with our drinks and our hands he was in his late twenties. Then bri and I take some optics that I sent to our mom. When I sent our mom the optics of us at the bowling alley she texted back saying that when we got back she had something very important to talk to us about I started to think in my head oh boy this can't be good she always had some shit going on.

I seen Kai's aunts at the bowling alley I go up to them and give them hugs They were both very cool I loved being around them they weren't messy at either. Meanwhile Carlos gave me a hug and he's trying to be slick But I've heard it all before he tried it though. Bree gets a box from the waitress then I pay for the food and I tell Kai we're going to head out it actually felt nice when my mom came into town and had watched Leilani for me so that I could actually go out and enjoy myself not that I was ever bored or complaining that I didn't enjoy myself because even if I didn't go out without Leilani when I had her we always went on play dates and went to a lot of kid friendly places and events so we always had a good time even before I had mom friends when she was just a baby I took her to see Curious George we did a lot together that's why I hated when people say it's not like your kid(s) will remember I'm like you don't remember a lot from your childhood either but it's the memories you make and the pictures that you can take and show your kid(s). I was the kind of mom granted I took a lot of optics on my cellphone but I also would print out a lot of the optics at Walmart so I could make scrapbooks because technology definitely fails us at times.

On the car ride home back to my dad's house I was blasting Pretty Ricky nothing but a number that was my song I remember when I was a little girl at the babysitters house her daughter and I were dancing to that song and I had tide my shirt up showing midriff and I was belly dancing and grinding and she literally came out of nowhere and she grabbed the back of the shirt that I had tied up and pulled my shirt back down. Bree was being all grown like she knew that song she was a whole two thousands baby which I used to tease her about. When we finally get back to my dad's house it's about midnight I was tired and exhausted I had been having fun when my mother came into town I always got to get a break for my child not that I expected one or needed one but it was just a nice feeling.

When we pull up to my dad's house I tell Bri how our mom told me she had something to tell us one thing about it before I went out when my mom was in town and she was watching Leilani for me Leilani was already fed bathed and in bed to be one less thing that my mother had to do. When we walk into the house Leilani is sleeping but my mother was still surprisingly up which I was surprised especially after making that 10 hour drive because I could never but more power to her. I then asked her what was so important that she had to tell us that she couldn't wait and Bree said oh Lord what did you do now then our mother tells us about how we have a older sister at that point I had absolutely nothing to say to her other than just asking her about our sister and I thought we only had one sister before but you told us that she had passed away when she was a baby and her name was Ashley she then says well unfortunately I lied to you guys and Ashley is back and she's 20 3 and telling us how Ashley had a daughter named Hazel who was a year older than Leilani which was crazy and telling us how Ashley lived in North Carolina and she had to give her up to her family after she had her to take care of her because our mother couldn't take care of her at that time. In my mind I thought to myself damn my mother and father were always putting their children aside for other people to raise like damn that's not fair and I get things happen in life but do better. I then asked our mother why did she lie to us because she told us that our sister who was named Ashley died as a baby after my mother pushed her out it was things like that that was nothing to even lie about see how your past always comes back to haunt you? I try to act as if I didn't care that she lied but I really did care because we had an older sister who's literally missed out on all those years of our lives because our mother chose to lie to us. She then tells us how Ashley had texted her while we were out at the bowling alley she also tells us how she gave our phone numbers to Ashley which I hated when my parents gave out my phone number to people without asking granted she was our sister but still I hated that I'm very selective and I always have been about who I've given my phone number out to can't trust everybody. Bri then says to our mom dang been holding out on us for years. Bri asked our mother how did she even know if that was her daughter or not. Our mother then tells us how Ashley had all of her information And was the person who found her. My mother also lied a lot but when she showed us the optic of Ashley and her daughter Hazel Ashley looked exactly like our mother same skin complexion same face same face structure and features everything it was crazy. She was very much gorgeous she was just a dike and I think my mother had a slight issue with that which I did and I didn't care I don't judge people I always would tell myself if it doesn't affect me then has nothing to do with me. Hazel was definitely gorgeous as well you could tell that her father was white which he in fact was. Our mother then tells us that she would go more into detail about the whole situation later on in the day and told us that Ashley would be reaching out to us soon. I was slightly tipsy and tired and that really did it for me that was a lot to take in I mean if only Ashley had been around when I was growing up it would have been so nice to be the middle child not only that but to have a sister that's so close to me in age to actually be around who can relate to the same things I can relate to that would have been so nice. I wasn't upset with my mother because after all I didn't even know her story as to why she gave our sister Ashley away but it just sucked because all those years she missed out on our lives and we missed out on her life those are years you can never get back again.

It is now hours later we all get up at about eight in the morning. I asked Bri if she wanted to go to Walmart with me so that I could pick up the cake and make sure that I had everything else that we needed I wanted to start early because time was definitely going to fly by very fast considering that the birthday party was at three in the afternoon. I hated rushing I always liked to be prepared a few hours in advance which I think is a good thing we all should do that but to each his own. I still had to pick out an outfit to wear and everything.My father also had to fry the chicken wings and french fries Which he was already complaining about that's why sometimes I don't like when he has to do things I really don't considering the fact that no one even asked him to do so in the first place. I tell everyone I would go to McDonald's to get us all breakfast then bring it back then Bri and I were going to go ahead and go to Walmart so we could pick up Leilani's cake. I already knew the cake would be gorgeous on top of that I gave them three optics of Leilani to add onto the cake then I wanted it to say happy birthday Leilani. Whenever my mom and Bri came into town Bri always loved being around her big sister something about us blasting our favorite songs on the radio and making snapchats made her enjoy being around me more especially since I was older than her by six years.

When we go to McDonald's I buy a whole bunch of different types of breakfast sandwiches with hash Browns for each then I asked if they did military discounts which I already knew they did however certain locations didn't honor it. We make a stop back at my dad's house so I could give Leilani my mom and dad their breakfast. I told Bri to wait in the car I was trying to hurry up and running the house to put the food down somewhere so Leilani wouldn't see me leave because if she did she would have started crying saying she wanted to come with us. Any other time I definitely wouldn't have minded my own child coming with us I even had made her a DIY idea for her tablet so she doesn't have to touch I even had made her a DIY idea for her tablet so she doesn't have to touch it when we drive it when I drive basically the tablet was inside of a pencil pouch and I tied rope around the passenger seat so she could watch it without messing it up since I had to connect it to the Bluetooth Which was a life saver. When we pull up at Walmart I receive a text on my phone from Theo saying good morning and he apologized His weekend was very busy I didn't reply back to him instantly because I didn't want to seem desperate. I then told Bri about him since she was getting older in age I could now tell her certain things she never ran her mouth or told our mother either she was starting to be mature so I told her how I had met Theo at the grocery store he came up to me after he went to his car when she drove an Audi a nice one then comes back inside just to give me his card and tells me to contact him sometime I then told her he was forty years old then she makes a joke saying damn I always get the old ones and I said I love it I love it in my Fantasia voice.I park at the Walmart near the entrance that says market since the bakery was near as soon as you walked in we get the cake I'll take some optics of it it definitely met my standards because there was going to be more than fifty people at Leilani's birthday party.

What slightly irritated me was the simple fact that I told Kai to have his family RSVP I definitely didn't mind them all attending they love Leilani they were all cool they did a lot for Leilani and I and I greatly appreciated it but when someone is asking you to RSVP so that I could know how many seats and tables to get he definitely should have did it. He had a huge family so I definitely already knew his family was all going to be there when we go to self checkout so that I could pay for the cake I receive another text on my phone from Bev saying that they weren't going to be able to make it they had to take care of something very important I then responded to her saying it's all good I'll send you optics. It definitely sucked that Garrett and I were no longer together because this was actually going to be the perfect time for him to have met my family and my close close friends but it was my fault why we weren't together. He didn't even ask for the engagement ring back. So the best way to get over one man is to get under another man I really wanted Theo but like the great saying goes everything that looks good isn't good for you if only I had thought of that then.

I was never eager to look for a man because I never approached any man if they wanted to talk to me they had to come to me themselves I don't care how good looking they are. Men just always seemed to come up to me to talk to me or people would always try to set me up on dates. Hell even Billy's mother Whose name was Latrice and her husband tried to set me up on a date With this Mexican guy who had a white man name. Billy's mother husband and the Mexican guy named Kenny were both professional painters for this company. And from time to time I would see the company truck at Billy's mother's house. One day Latrice called my cell number to tell me that someone who worked with her husband thank any wanted to Take Me Out on a date in my mind when she tells me this I'm just like I hope he's not ugly I definitely had a type I didn't like skinny men I liked older men and they had to have meat on their bones race definitely didn't matter I don't discriminate. I then thought to myself they wouldn't hook me up with someone who they thought was no good for me. Lattice and her husband were very cool he would often give my father real Cuban cigars and liquor. After all these people had actually watched me grow up into a young woman they did a lot for us and vice versa. As Latrice tells me more about Kenny I then tell her she could give him my phone number she then tells me she will have him call me and I told her sounds good thank you.

Later that day after speaking with Latrice . She calls me to tell me that her husband and Kenny were working together at Orange Park medical the same place that I had Leilani and the same place where her father had died. They just happened to be there painting the outside of the building so I decide to go up there when I get off the phone with her so that I could meet him and I had texted him telling him that I was on the way she also told me when I was on the phone that she was going to let her husband know that I was on the way. When I finally get there I told him what kind of car I was in and the color of the car then I noticed someone walking over closer who was tall and skinny and Mexican. He wasn't ugly at all he was just so skinny, but I still gave him a chance because you never know until you try and it's not good to judge a book by its cover. I had Leilani in the back seat in her car seat she was watching her iPad I typically never allowed anyone around my child nor to meet my child ever I didn't do that especially until I did a full background check and I knew what we were doing.

As he gets closer to the car I get out of it I did roll the window all the way down with the air conditioning on for Leilani to keep her cool. We talked for a bit he told me how I was very gorgeous something that I always got a lot which was very annoying because that didn't make me ecstatic I already knew that I was gorgeous after all I used to be a model a paid model at that. The more we talk and get to know each other he asked how old was I I told him that I was twenty one years old I then asked him how old he was he told me that he was thirty five years old. He then asked me what's his age going to be a issue I then told him no I prefer my men older. He asked if I was going to be available later on that night and if so would I be willing to go on a date with him Two a nice restaurant on the Southside in Jacksonville. He then tells me he knows I have a daughter and my time pretty much goes to her so if I'm open to going out with him if not that's OK too we could also get to know each other more before we start going out I then told him I would let him know then I told him that we had to go we gave each other a hug we give each other a hug and I leave and he opens my driver door then closes it when I get in.

Later that night after Leilani and I had had a playdate with one of my mom friends we had took our girls to the park we even had a picnic at the park and talked about our men problems. I really enjoyed having more mom friends that were single with no husband because they could truly relate and understand how I was feeling and what I was enduring on a day to day basis ask the mom friends who had husbands not all of them but some of them thought that they were better because they had husbands but the same ones that were thinking that were also the same ones who would be complaining about how their husbands do absolutely nothing for the baby and they're always stuck home with their baby while their husbands were out living their best life. I had asked my girl Jasmine which is who we had the playdate with at the park she was a single mother who had two kids a son and a daughter If she thought that it would be a good idea for me to go on a date with Kenny now typically I wouldn't tell anyone at all what I had going on was thinking or planning but I needed some insight plus it was crazy how I could help everyone else out with their problems except for my own problems I could never help myself at times I was useless or I would never listen to the advice I was giving myself which was good damn advice. She then told me just go out with him you never know where it could lead next and so you try I then told her she's right. When Leilani and I get home I ask my father if he could watch Leilani for me while I went with Renee day day in alma for Valentine's Day because that's the holiday that it was and he said sure I told him she had already ate dinner and got in her bath then I told him I was going to start getting ready because we were going to a restaurant on the south side but I never told him which restaurant I just told him we couldn't decide.

As I start getting ready to shower I clip my wig up with a hair clip, throw a bonnet on over it Then put some face wash on my face then I hop in the shower. I grabbed my robe to put on Over my towel after I got out the shower then brush my teeth and rinse my mouth. I had no idea what I was going to be wearing but last time Kenny and I had spoke about a time to meet at the restaurant we chose the time of nine at night Because I told him that I had to put my daughter to bed before going anywhere which she was perfectly OK with and had he not been ok with that I was going to delete and block his number my child came before anyone. When I go into my room so I could get dressed I decided to wear a tube top with some skinny jeans and high heels but I put the heels in my purse and decided to wear my Gucci flip flops for the time being. I walked back into the bathroom to remove the hair clip then I brush my wig down it was a long black wig that had red tips on the ends I was so obsessed with black wigs something about that color on my skin tone was just sexy plus my natural hair was jet black and I love the color red. I spray some bath and body works perfume on my neck and my wrist called beautiful day I grab the lotion and the hand sanitizer from underneath my sink to place into my blue Jean Chanel purse and I then go to kiss my child on her forehead and make sure she didn't pee on herself and I told my father that I was leaving. He then told me to be careful and safe I told him I would text him when I got to the restaurant I then asked him if he wanted me to bring him anything back and he said no but knowing me whenever I ate out I always brought my child toys back and food and my father something back as well .As I'm on my way to the restaurant once I made it out of my dad's neighborhood I started blasting my music and being young wild and free which when I was kid free I was able to blast my music and listen to the types of music I wanted when I was around my child listening to music I always would listen to the clean versions of songs which was completely fine I just didn't want my one year old using profanity that wasn't cute to me at all.

When I get to the restaurant it look nice on the outside and inside from what I could see. The restaurant was very packed and I called Kenny to see where he was at he told me he was about to be arriving at the restaurant so then when he finally arrives he parks next to me he even had a nice car. We both get out of the car we give each other hugs then he gives me a vase with flowers that were gorgeous I had never had any man give me flowers before except for Garrett it was little things like that that made me happy temporarily of course. Then we go into the restaurant he opened the door for me also and we go to sit down He then told me to order whatever I wanted so when the waitress comes over for the drink orders I told him that I wanted a Margarita on the rocks and he got a beer but he spoke Spanish to the woman when he said the drink order. He then asked me if I knew Spanish I told him a little bit he then told me that he had to teach me some Spanish I then told him that sounded good to me. He asked me how did I know Spanish I made a joke saying Dora the Explorer and he laughed but I said on a serious note my mother is Puerto Rican. I then ask Kenny what's good here at this restaurant he then told me he normally gets steak with a fried egg and it comes with a whole bunch of different types of meat so I told him I wanted to try that he then also told me that it came with a side of white rice which was my favorite we ate white rice with everything literally everything my father had all these rice cookers and of course his girlfriend was Asian so they also ate rice with everything. When the waitress comes back with our drinks I let Kenny order our food then he spoke it in Spanish again I was just looking when the waitress walked away he asked me was I jealous I then told him there is no woman on this earth that could ever make me jealous. He tells me to put my he tells me to put my hand up Right hand up and he puts his right hand up to see whose hand was bigger I definitely had some man hands but it comes with the height I even have big feet I wore a twelve in women's for shoes. Kenny then asked me why was I single and I told him because I can't find someone but I was never really looking for anyone either I then asked him why was he single and he said all the women he gets with are gold diggers.

When the food comes out my clumsy ass was slightly making a mess and Kenny called me out saying I was making a mess like a child I didn't take offense to it but I did so I didn't even say anything. As we eat our dinner he starts speaking to me in Spanish and then I asked him what it certain words mean that he was saying and he was telling me what they meant then when the waitress came back to ask us if we wanted dessert he said he already had dessert which he was talking about me then she laughed and they both started speaking Spanish I said English please and he was being funny making jokes about me being desert he said. Once he pays for everything I get a box to take my food to go it was definitely very delicious and a great proportion. We walk out outside to our cars he told me he had a bear for my daughter and I told him thank you I appreciated the gifts and dinner out of nowhere he starts kissing me I kissed him back then I told him that I would text him once I made it home.

The more and more Kenny and I started hanging out together we would even see each other during our work lunch breaks we would go sit down at restaurants eat and have a glass of wine or two or a beer while on our lunch break. He would always take me to these restaurants I had never been to before which was great because I was the type of person I was very simple I love going to the same spots where I knew the people at and sometimes change is very nice and it's good to try new things he would always take me to a lot of Spanish restaurants which I loved there's nothing better than eating authentic Mexican food everyone can't make Mexican food the same. He was even buying my child stuff and granted he was Mexican so one thing about them they're going to have jobs and money he would always take out wads of cash from his pocket one time I joke fully asked him if he believed in having a bank account or two. Granted I was the same way but I never carried more than two thousand dollars in cash on me that was until I got with Leilani's dad who had told me to stop doing that and put my money in the bank because at least if I get robbed and they take my debit and or credit card I can get that money back but if I get robbed and they take the cash I can't get that money back which he definitely had a point I learned lot from him. Kenny told me he really didn't trust banks and he would leave his money at home and shoeboxes and his safe he even showed me his guns one time when I went to his apartment which he didn't want me over because he didn't have much furniture why I didn't understand all that money he had with rubber bands on it. The only thing that was a turn off about him was the simple fact that he had smoked cigarettes I had never been with a man before that had smoked cigarettes then again I only at the time so far been with only two men who were Jay and Garrett. To each his own I guess but that cigarette smoking is a turn off I didn't even smoke cigarettes I would only smoke weed and or black and milds even the black and milds tasted disgusting and it was so hard at times to get that taste out of my mouth no matter how many times I would brush my teeth and rinse my mouth out so I just made the decision to stop smoking black and milds since technically smoking one black and milds like smoking a pack of cigarettes it's just as equivalent and tasted disgusting.

Kenny and I had met February of twenty eighteen the first week in February at that. I really hated the month of February because that was Jay's birth month then of course I hated the month of December because that's when he died. One day Kenny and I hang out he then tells me that he had something to tell me and I'm like oh boy I wonder what it could be it was literally a two weeks before Leilani's birthday party but we met up at a restaurant and he tells me that he likes me a lot but he doesn't want to hurt me or lead me on but he's still married. When I say I sucked my drink down very quickly I did because I literally didn't understand I had told this man that I had an accountant with Jay granted he was legally married but separated or not married is still married I also had told this man I hate men that lie and mislead women. Enter to think that his ass was married to it was like I couldn't catch a break now this is my second encounter meant with a married man who would be proud to say that there with a married man or were with a married man that is not a badge of honor it's a disgrace. He then tells me he didn't want to hurt my feelings but his wife doesn't want to get the divorce he does nor does she want to sign the divorce papers he then tells me that she's been getting all his text messages because they're still both on the same accounts with Verizon and she told him that she wouldn't divorce him if he kept talking to me which I'm more than sure she wasn't trying to divorce him regardless of what he did I hated petty Women who were doing things out of spite

But I mean I couldn't judge her if my husband did me dirty I too would probably manipulate him and gaslight him into doing everything that I wanted him to do until I had no use for him anymore I didn't know what they had going on or what was going on. He also had told me how that's why he didn't have furniture in his house because he had been trying to save money aside for the divorce and to pay her off which was crazy. Me and this man literally had unprotected sex not once or twice but a few times so I had definitely caught feelings and his head game was had me head over heels. He even fucked me in his work truck. I really wanted to cry in front of him because this was now the second married man that I had been with but of course I didn't know but that was the thing I had to pay my price for being ignorant granted he did lie but I was lacking knowledge I wasn't fully thinking had I done a background check on him it would have told me that he was married but I didn't even have his last name I literally got up from the table and left him I told him don't call me again or text me anymore. He grabbed my hand telling me to sit down then he said maybe we could be friends I got up again and told him I see why you've been so single you have a serious control problem I cannot be controlled you will not try to control me either black women don't play that shit.

I also told him maybe had he been honest and upfront with me we could have actually been friends but it was seeming as if you got what you wanted now you're done with me type of thing which is what I told him I also told him that before the sex part you could have just told me that you were still legally married you saying that y'all are separated and you don't have sex is not making me feel any better about myself or this Situation. I hated looking stupid and being the last to find out about anything especially something that important I definitely had every right to know that so that I could have made the decision for myself not you making the decision for me.

I had nothing but hate for this man and he had definitely killed my mood for that day I even decided to tell Latrice about him and she apologized to me I told her it wasn't her fault she didn't know just like I didn't know people only tell you what they feel like you should know not the things that we need to know which is what sucks about some people and I actually like this man

It is now almost time for the birthday party so I allow my mother and breed to use my bathroom and tell them to get dressed in my room I was going to get Leilani dressed last because I didn't want her to mess up her outfit yet somehow someway every time you have a toddler looking all cute they end up messing up their outfits. Bri and I start using the balloon pumps to blow up the balloons and tie the ends as fast as we could to place them into trash bags to start loading up and my mother's car father's car in my car my father had already cooked up all the bags of chicken wings that I had bought as well as the fries we start loading up the party decorations and everything else that was going to be needed at the birthday partyLeilani wanted to ride with her grandma which was completely fine the place was right up the street from my father's house which was definitely perfect I still didn't like how the woman who owned the banquet hall only allows you to set up at your actual time slot like that's crazy so we get there a few minutes early just in case there's time we can start setting up a few minutes earlier I had Never heard of anything like that before. That was exactly why it was very hard for me to try to support black owned businesses the price was definitely great don't get me wrong but the lady had way too many rules and it wasn't that serious like we're paying you and we had to clean up the place ourselves so it was like lady relax but nobody was going to make me upset During my child birthday party not even my father we all knew how fucking bossy he could be that shit would piss me off I hate it when he tried to have control over everything and everybody just because he paid but it wasn't like I asked him to he chose to a personal choice so don't start acting like you run the place. When Kai shine and his mother arrived I get them to start helping us put tablecloths on each table and empty out the bags of balloons and start setting up the food to put on the tables up front then Kai's mom Told us to watch out why she did some stuff too she then told me don't freak out everything would be perfect. What also had slightly annoyed me was the simple fact I was texting Kenny over and over again to see if he was coming to Leilani's birthday party and I still hadn't heard from him in a while anyways so I said fuck it and I just deleted and blocked his phone number it was like he had disappeared anyways to me that was a red flag I couldn't even stress about it Theo look way better he was older and he was are.

I had decided to text Theo after my daughter's birthday party after all I was busy as well and when he was busy he didn't seem to respond back to me so I figured I would do him how he did me I was tired of giving my all to these men and still getting crapped on. As everyone started to walk into the banquet hall I had a box telling everyone to pick out a Hawaiian lei since the theme was Hawaiian. As everyone starts taking their seats I start table hopping talking to everyone with Leilani on hip. It was even crazy seeing one of my mom friends there who lived in the same apartment complex as Garrett her name was Jordan she was in the Navy she was stationed at the same base where my father and I worked at. Jordan her daughter Kayla Leilani and I always hung out at her apartment complex by the pool and inside of her apartment we would have play dates almost every day since we lived around the corner from each other. Every time I went to her apartment I kept hoping and thinking that I would run into Garrett But that never seemed to ever happen which very much sucked. One time I had even told Jordan about Garrett and she told me she didn't think that

I was wrong for feeling the way I felt. I had even explained to her how it didn't mean to come out the way that it did of my mouth but it just did I mean we were moving so fast too fast and as we got more serious into our relationship I literally told Garrett that I would never love him as much as I loved Jay I also told him he could never replace Jay and what we had which was very much true but it still shouldn't have came out of my mouth I was very truthful by all means sometimes a little too truthful.

It was so nice seeing all of my mom friends that I had met on the app called peanut all in one room some of them I hadn't met before at all yet but some I did so it was nice for all of us to talk about how we met each other on peanut and We all talk about our experience meeting on peanut we even decided to all take a group optic all of us mommy friends with our kids and we were going to post on social media saying we all met on peanut We were also going to tag the name of the app on the post which of course I was going to upload on my social media accounts later that night I was that one extra person that liked to edit the optics I had to make sure everyone was on point and the optics were on point.Kai's mother put on gloves with me to serve everyone but she then told me I was taking too long and being too bougie so she told me to move out the way and she would serve everyone she started grabbing the food with the gloves on with her hands putting on people's plates I was trying to have some type of etiquette using the food tongues to serve everyone. Of course Kai had all of his family there when the rest of his family came we were definitely out of seats luckily there were some extra chairs in the kitchen area thank God that is why I wanted everyone to RSVP like it's always that one person that just doesn't follow simple directions thank God I thought to buy extra food and beverages also from Sam's Club because we were close to running out but my father decided to fry some more wings at the banquet hall in the kitchen area they had cooking utensils and more. I get Kai take optics of my mother, father, Bri,Leilani and I. I also had huge pumps of hand sanitizer when you first walk in and smaller pumps on each table I was very big on good hygiene

Plus you would think after touching a door that other people have touched people would actually have the common sense to wash and or sanitize their hands but after all people are nasty I definitely have made it clear I didn't want anyone serving themselves.

The optics came out all nice I had on pink shorts with a blue halter top That you tie around your neck and some pink Gucci sandals. It was nice seeing all the kids run around it even gave me an idea for her Leilani's second birthday party I thought to myself maybe we should have it at a park that way the kids could actually enjoy themselves more and be tired out more I just like to be better prepared just in case inclement weather conditions were to happen. It was then time to sing happy birthday to Leilani and everyone in chi's family had their cell phones out recording and taking pictures of us as I stood up front with my mother brief father and Leilani to sing happy birthday and we sung it the regular traditional way that everyone else sings it then Kai's aunt who we called Cupcake Yells out that we have to sing it with some soul and everyone starts laughing. I was even drinking some rum punch and I told all the adults that there was rum punch everyone was enjoying it.I noticed my mother and father talking to some of my friends as well all I could say was I hope they aren't talking too much and telling too much they both could do that at times especially my dad talked too damn much. We put Leilani on the ground so that she could play with her smash cake which was the free cake that all one year olds got for their birthdays no matter where you went to get your cake I thought it was very adorable Tia who was Kai's cousintold Leilani to dig in the cake but she was looking all scared like she didn't want to so I decided to go over to her to help her and that's when Kai's mom said y'all let her do it as soon as she was about to do it we all start laughing and then she stopped and Kai's mom told us we were too loud then we laughed again.

My mother and father asked if I wanted Leilani to open her birthday gifts at the banquet hall but I told them no we could open them at home because we already had a lot of stuff to take back anyways with us plus I didn't want anything to get lost so I just told them we could wait. We only had the banquet hall for three hours which definitely wasn't bad at all for the price so after a while my Father told us it was about that time to start wrapping it up because we also had to clean up the place for the next event. My dad then took the cake away from Leilani because she was making such a mess and we had to clean up all messes we didn't think we didn't even think To put her underneath a tablecloth then let her play with the smash cake.

I had kid friendly music playing on the Bluetooth tower speaker that I had but of course Kai and his family who were slightly ratchet and ghetto start playing ratchet music especially when everyone left while they stayed back to help clean up. I literally saw Kai's mom Take the whole pan of the sandwiches my mother made she took what was left instead of just asking I literally didn't even get that many sandwiches I literally saw her walk out with the pan and she thought it was funny I don't like stuff like that just ghetto and no class. My mother even said the same thing I said just ghetto like it's one thing to ask people but don't just take it and then she's laughing about it as if it's funny like I said they were good people but at times they were very messy and I cannot stand to be around messy people. Once we finish cleaning up and loading up all three vehicles between my mother father and I we then go back to my father's house with everything the house was completely full and packed overtime the house was going to be even more packed with furniture and other items because my townhouse was going to be ready in the month of August but of course I still didn't open my mouth about it until I got the keys in my hands I never liked to jinx myself or tell people what I was thinking or planning pretty soon I was going to have the conversation also with my mother about my sister moving up with us so my mother could get herself together in general. Once we get situated and unload all three cars taking everything back into the house I decided to respond back to Theo I told him I apologize for the late response I have been busy it was my daughter's birthday party. He responded back we were still on a professional level then next thing I know I receive a text message from him saying that he wanted to be deep inside of me I literally had to look at the phone to make sure that I read that message right. He was definitely fine and I also wanted that as well I had been wanting that since I saw him so he was finally starting to speak my language.

Every morning he would get up at about two the morning so that he could go to the gym where he would stay at until about 3:00 in the morning then he would go back home to his condominium which wasn't far from me at all. Sometimes Jordan and I would babysit each other's daughters if we had to stay after a little while longer at work than our normal time scheduled to get off so often Leilani and I would stay the night at Jordan's house which was always fun we literally see each other every single day even at the work we would go to their apartment and sit by the poolside we would go out to eat shopping a lot and it was crazy because even though we were seeing each other we never got into any type of arguments from sing each other too much. One time Leilani and I stay the night at Jordan's apartment and Theo had asked me the night before if I was going to be able to come to his condo the next morning at three in the morning and I told him yes. I asked Jordan if she could watch Leilani while I went to Theo's condo which she also lived up the street from him so it was perfect and it was before I had to to work. I showered at Jordan's house and put on some comfortable workout clothes after all the clothes were going to be coming off of me and it was very early in the morning so there was no need to try to look cute. I would also always tease still sending him nude pictures of myself as well as bra and panty optics of myself which he would ask for All the time he even once told me that the first time we Make Love he doesn't want to use a condom because older men love the way it feels raw. I really couldn't believe I was taking all these chances and not wearing condoms with people as if I really couldn't believe I was taking all these chances and not wearing condoms with people as if sexually transmitted diseasesweren't a thing.

For some weird apparent reason I actually agreed with him when he said he didn't want to wear a condom and I just said OK daddy I wasn't even thinking straight I was just looking at how fine he was. I was very much sure he knew how fine he was.

I had set my alarm and everything for that time Jordan told me she didn't mind watching Leilani after all we both looked out for each other since we were single moms and we live so close to each other at three in the morning when I get up to go brush my teeth shower and get dressed I received a text message from Theo asking me if I was ready for daddy I responded back to him saying daddy. He then sends me his address And I texted him back letting him know I was ten minutes away and he said ok. I was slightly nervous I really was But when I pull up there was a gate but the gate was opened at that time of the morning I was guessing. I try to search for the building where he was at and once I called him to tell him that I was at his door when he sent to me the apartment number he asked where I was at and I said your door again he said no you're not so then he had to help me get to his apartment I had no idea they had the same numbers out there which was crazy. When I get there he gives me a hug and tells me to come in I told him that he had a nice place and I take my shoes off then we walked to the bedroom and I stand outside of the room while he clears off the bed he then tells me to come in and we start kissing I was so nervous and it was so cold in there.

He picks me up and puts me on the bed and kisses me on my lips some more then he tells me to take my clothes off and I do slowly and sexy I had on a black thong and a black bra. I also had on socks which thank God I had a pedicure and my feet weren't ugly because he took my socks off for me. As he starts kissing me head to toe and all over my body I start getting wet which didn't take much for me especially when I wanted that person. As soon as he slid his long ass dick inside of me Which I could feel every inch of and I knew it was very long by how deep he was going inside of me it's slightly hurt but felt good at the same time so I was taking all inches. He starts talking to me well he's inside of me and I start grabbing his back while moaning in his ear. I was playing a dangerous game with him when I allowed him to have sex with me I'm protected and then soon I was going to find out some shocking information about him That I definitely needed to know but I hate that I found out because I was already head over heels for him. When we had sex he even had came inside of me the first day we had sex then he had the nerve to ask if I was on birth control and I told him no and he said OK. I was thinking in my head was this man trying to trap me because we couldn't do that I had a lot on my plate as is and a baby I couldn't have another one right then and there I had too much I was trying to do and take care of plus I had just met him I shouldn't even have been having unprotected sex with him. When we finish having sex I lay on top of him with my head on his chest for a minute I was definitely sleepy after that he then asked me what was I about to do and I told him I was going back to my friend's apartment my daughter and I had stayed the night over there and I'm going to grab my daughter some breakfast on the way back then go get ready for work I have to drop my daughter off to daycare I didn't have to be to work until nine in the morning so I was good but I always like to be ahead of myself. He then asked me did I work out I told him I only did crunches and cared about my abs he then told me that he worked out at the gym up the street every morning and I told him maybe we can workout together sometime and he said definitely while rubbing my back and my hair.

I told him I had to go to the bathroom and he shows me in the room where it was at so I go to pee I was thinking in my mind I couldn't believe this man had this big condo and it was just him at least that's what I thought but that's all I knew right then and there so when I go back out I tell him that I'm going to go ahead and head back because that traffic on Blanding Blvd was always crucial at certain times the day. He gives me a kiss on my lips and I then told him that I would text him later and he walked me outside.

On my way back before I arrived at McDonald's I called Jordan to ask her if she wanted me to grab her any breakfast and she told me sure she wanted the bacon egg and cheese biscuit meal so I also decided to get that for myself then I asked her what drink did she want she told me a Sprite and I asked her was Leilani good she said yes she's still sleeping I said great and thank you so much she then asked me how was the sex I said it was great I'm sleepy and shocked she then laughed and said she would see me when I got back I said sounds good then I hang up.

I really didn't realize how much of my time I was giving to Theo even when I was supposed to be hanging out with my friends I was sneaking away to go have sex with this man there was another time when we were all Jordans apartment it was Stephon who was Kai's cousin who also had a crush on me but I didn't want him then of course Jordan and her daughter Kayla,Leilani, Kai and I. We all had a movie day at Jordan's apartment we all had also brought over some liquor and food and we were watching men hating movies on Netflix. I get a text on my phone from Theo asking what was I up to I then told him I was up the street from him at my friends apartment he then told me that he wanted me now and I asked him what about later he said no now because he was going to be busy later with his kids. I then asked Jordan if she could watch Leilani again for me which technically they were all there while I went to Theo's house again and she said yes I told her I really appreciated it I also didn't want to make it a habit of always asking her to watch my kid for me I knew sometimes it can get annoying granted I also watched Carla for her while she was working later hours and or going on as well. I then told everyone if anyone needed me to bring anything back just shoot me a text and I would grab it. I then texted Theo telling him I was on the way and he said ok he's waiting for his pussy.

When I go to Theo's condo this time I knew exactly where it was I told him I was outside and he comes and opens the door then I go in and take my shoes off and I told him that I wanted to suck his dick and ride it and he told me he would think about it he then throws me on the bed taking my workout shorts off and my tube top off then he starts to eat my pussy for awhile which I enjoyed every moment off while moaning and rubbing his head. Then he stops and slides his dick slowly inside of me while I moan and he takes it slowly back out then puts it partially in me slowly then slams it inside of me really hard and I moaned really loud in his ear. He then asked me if I liked when daddy does that and I replied saying yes daddy That's when he slammed his dick hard inside of me again. I was moaning really loud and he pulled but that time he came on my stomach. He then kissed me on my lips and lays down beside me out of breath then he asked me what was I going to do for the rest of the day and I told him I was going back to my friends apartment we were having a movie day drinking and eating a whole bunch of food watching men bashing movies and he shook his head when I said men Bashing movies and I laughed at him. We both get up and get dressed he was also about to go somewhere as well he told me he had to go pick up one of his sons I wanted to ask how old his son was but I didn't want him to be like his son was my age or something it's a mood killer.

When he and I both walk outside we take optics together not that I was going to post or anything just for me to keep in my phone. Before I get back to Jordan's apartment I asked her on the phone if anyone needed anything then I told her that I was on the way and everyone said they were good Jordan just asked if I could bring her back some gum I said what kind she said it didn't matter I said gum got it I'll be there shortly. When I go into the gas station that was right around the corner from Jordan's apartment I buy some gum then when I get there Leilani comes up on me I asked her if she was hungry then chi said now you know we fed her I say you right so I don't even know why I asked. I then show everyone a optic of Theo and I and Kai with his gay self was like he is fine as hell I said he's a professor at a Community College in Jacksonville then chi asked which college I said FSCJ and then he tells me that's the same college that he went to and I said

257

oh Lord. Kai then asked what did Theo teach at the college and I said math. I really didn't want to tell them and or show them in the first place but Kai already knew I had a dick appointment he always seemed to know when I one of those.

After we had sex at his condo that one time the more and more we started talking I didn't realize this was a red flag but I would always ask him if I could come over after that instead of him coming to me and he would tell me that he was busy or that he would come to me but I really tried not to make a big deal out of it or think too much into it I was just in love with the sex he was forty years old with a twelve inch dick and I was taking all of those inches every time we had sex my vagina lips were always enlarged and sore but I didn't even care I loved it, Plus I had never ever had that before but I was definitely missing out. I was playing an even more dangerous game with Theo because I was actually allowing him to come over to my father's house whenever my father would leave for work while my daughter was sleeping and it never occurred to me what if my father had to come back home to get something that he loved I didn't even care about that or think about it. Theo was literally coming over to my house every day having unprotected sex with me and he came inside of me.

It is now the month of august which It is time for Leilani and I to move into our townhouse which was on one hundred and third street which still was technically up the street from where Theo's condo was. I had the furniture brand new furniture at that that I got from a furniture store named Badcock. I had already had the talk with my father about allowing my sister to come and move up with Leilani and I which was the whole point of me rushing to really move out of his house at that point Leilani had her dad Social Security money stacked up she had twenty five thousand dollars saved so far in her account which I was very proud of myself for stacking up her money. That wasn't even all the money she had that was just in one account she had that wasn't even including the other five thousand dollars that she started out with and her other Navy federal account. I had already had the discussion with my mother to allow Bri to move in with me which she was completely fine with she definitely mentally and physically plus I wanted my sister to have a great life she could go to a great school that was near my dad because the schools in the area in Jacksonville near where our townhouse were didn't have the best schools. The crazy part about it all soon we weren't even going to be living at that townhouse for as long as I thought we were and to have thought I was going to pay up my rent for year. My father's house had so much of our junk and furniture and boxes all in his front living room he literally told me not to order anything else or buy anything else until I move out which was completely fine I understood completely considering the fact that his house was already quite junky with all the crap that he had himself so it was whatever I just wanted to make sure that we had the basic that we needed. I had even went to Sam's Club and splurged on cups, plates, Plasticware snacks beverages because it was all in bulk so it would definitely last longer I even got the paper towels and toilet paper from Sam's Club I was very much obsessed with shopping at Sam's Club to be quite honest.

My mother had told my father and I that she Bri and one of my mother's friends Leslie were planning a trip to come to Florida so they could bring Bri.I already had the keys to the townhouse and I already took care everything Bri even had a nice big room. I had got us a 3 bedroom townhouse which is exactly what we needed after sharing a room with Leilani not that I minded of course I just wanted to keep stacking up money But between her and I we had a lot of clothes and accessories my child actually had more clothes and shoes than I did which was funny I was always shopping for her which I loved to do. I even had told Theo I had a townhouse which was up the street from him he responded back to me in a text message asking when was I going to give daddy a Key. I responded back saying soon daddy it was crazy this man had me so head over heels for him really it was his good looks and the sex. Within two days later my mom Bri and Leslie drove up to Florida so bring Bri, I was very excited to have my little sister staying with me that was definitely a big responsibility nonetheless I could definitely handle it plus it would be nice to have a little more help with Leilani so I could possibly get more rest and whatever else not that she had to be the baby sitter for me.

For some reason I still was ignoring the red flags with Theo because the simple fact he was no longer allowing me to come to his condo anymore he would always have to come to me or find an excuse or way to come to me instead. When I finally had moved into the townhouse with the help of everyone after getting everything set up I told Theo I was all moved into the townhouse and he told me he would come by later but I was starting to notice with him that when he meant later that meant never. So one day Jordan, Kayla,Leilani and I had all went to Applebee's for a late lunch I love that restaurant with a passion I always order the same thing every time as well I then decided to be very petty and text Theo a message then tell him wrong message and it wasn't meant for him I even asked Jordan if I should do it and she said go for it and see what he says. I then Texted Theo asking him what was he up to then he responded back saying he was about to be leaving work he then asked what was I up to I told him I was on a lunch date then he responded back in all caps AND QUESTION MARKS A LUNCH DATE??I then said yes he responded so fast to stuff like that that I would tell him he didn't like that shit but it was ok for him to not respond to me and do me the way he was doing me so I could play the game too I figured. But I also wanted my dick from him So I decided to stop being petty and I then told him that I was Eating a late lunch with my daughter and one of my coworkers and her daughter and he said oh OK I thought you were trying to replace daddy and I responded saying of course not daddy. Sometimes I felt as if the shit I would tell him would boost his head up after all he was older and a professor wiser and smarter.

The same day they all arrive in Florida for lunch my mother requested red lobster I told everyone that I would pay for the red lobster it was just me Bri, Leilani, Leslie and my mother. One thing about it I hate it going out to eat with my mother and Leslie they were always complaining about something especially Leslie she was the queen of sending food back my father always taught me that once you complain at a restaurant about food that you have don't even reorder something because that's how people spinning your food you have to make your food and I definitely took that advice. Granted I had money I was always smart about my money and when it came to spending especially my father always taught me that just because you have doesn't mean that you always have to spend that's where so many people go wrong at in life. I went ahead and paid for the red lobster whenever my mother went out to eat with us the bill always cost it a lot because of the amount of alcoholic beverages she would get which costed a lot and made the bill go up more faster I typically would drink upon arrival but of course because I was driving and my child was in the car I would just bring a shot or two and drink it in the bathroom at the restaurant or something or even pour it in my lemonade or juice whatever I had at the restaurant. Granted I would order alcoholic beverages as well but not as many as my mother I would get one or two the most after all I had my child in the car with me I couldn't get drunk or be driving tipsy. While we were at lunch I had texted Kai to see if him and Steven would be open to helping us load up the uhaul and everything at my father's house so that we could move to the townhouse and they were down for it I told them that I would buy them lunch and some liquor and or weed after everything was complete I even asked Kai if he could ask his mother to come help decorate and help my mother out as well since she just did a ten hour drive plus I consider kai's mother a mom to me at times when my mother wasn't there she would often give me a lot of good advice at times plus kai's mother was a tourist just like I was so she knew me all too well she herself also once told me that I was too secretive but I was a tourist just like her so she understood she also told me that I had an anger problem which I definitely did so I couldn't even be upset or mad at her for telling me the truth. One thing that I loved about his family was they always helped out people no matter what and I always returned the favor.

Is finally move in day everyone was at my townhouse helping me set up everything I had bought brand new furniture from Badcock some of it I had decided to just pay cash for because I didn't like financing and or paying for stuff monthly. Plus I had a lot of credit to spend at Badcock but I didn't want to get above myself right off the bat as for people mess up at I was only twenty one with a government job and my credit score was in the seven hundred and thirties which was great And this was my first time moving out of home to be in my own which would be great my father always told me to never move into an apartment and or house with friends or a boyfriend because when everyone's name is on the lease including yours and people start messing up and not wanting to pay stuff it's a reflection on you as well which he was absolutely right plus after Jay died I always had told myself I would never move in with friends and or another man ever again especially with my name not being on a deed or lease because of what happened to Jay granted he was married but still there's nothing like being in your own shit. And I was sure my father was ready to have his house back to himself he never told me that but I was for sure there's nothing like being in your own house in space in place after a long day being able to do what you want when you want. I wasn't even that far away from my father anyways so we were all good regardless.

One day when I went to Kai's house I showed him another optic of Theo and I that's when my world came crumbling down a prime example of why you cannot tell people your business some people just hate to see others happier than they are Especially miserable people Kai and his husband were in fact very miserable they were always arguing and fist fighting and involving others into their marriage problems and I wasn't even married had never even been married I can't even count how many times I would get called to diffuse a situation between Kai and his husband it was quite annoying. I can't even count how many times other people would get called to diffuse a situation between kind his husband and after a while people get tired of that especially people who have never even been married and can't even possibly relate. They would be violent they would be fist fighting throwing things arguing with each other no one wants to be around people like that.

But Kai literally told me he bets the professor is married I then asked him why would he say something like that he then says because they're all married and I hate it to admit it but chi was actually right as he goes onto his Facebook page something I didn't have at the time the last time I had a Facebook page was in the sixth grade. Kai then asked me what was Theo's first and last name I give it to him scared as hell and he then turns his phone asking me if that was Theo and I said it was then he clicks on his profile and it says he's married to a woman by the name of CJ. Once again this is the third married man I have now found myself with so embarrassing I kept missing all the red flags him not wanting me to come back to his condo anymore after the first two or three times of going there him not responding and or answering my calls it now made sense because he had a wife I literally had been at their condo what If this woman had came home and found him and I having sex together I cannot imagine what she would have done nowadays people are crazy they literally would shoot you or try to fight you even if you had no idea that their so called man was married or in a relationship.

Kai then asked me if I wanted him to reach out to the lady so me sitting there in disbelief I just wanted the sex from him that was all at that point. I then told him to give me a moment let me text Theo and ask him about this situation to see exactly what he's going to say just in case he tries to play me then we send the messages to his wife there's nothing worse than getting caught and still lying when I texted the bastard asking him if he was married he then replied back to me telling me that he was but there was more to the story talking about they were separated and all this other stuff that I knew were lies you're separated but you just had a fresh picture posted on your Facebook page from a day ago which are supposedly wife. See it always seemed like whenever I would find a man and everything was going perfectly fine it was always too good to be true I always gave my hopes up the sad thing about it was all I wanted was some unconditional love and a stepfather for my child since her father was dead I really started to regret saying what I said to Garrett because man I have really messed things up with him and he was gone there was no way I could get him back and I was a firm believer that sometimes it's best to leave the past in the past granted we were still Instagram friends but I never wanted to search up his page because I always thought to myself what if he got into a relationship and I go stalking his Instagram page then I see him with another woman happy I'd be sad and feeling stupid and regretful More than I already did.

I then responded back to Theo asking him if they were separated and there was more to the story why does he have a current picture that he just posted yesterday on his Facebook page I told him that at this point we're too grown to be lying and he already got caught I told him the mother-fucker replied to me telling me that he likes to live a drama free life and he doesn't deal with drama especially from women I responded back to him saying so I catch you in a lie after I find out that you're married and you're mad because you got caught now you looking crazy I said yeah ok have nice life. Meanwhile I'm telling messy ask I everything that Theo is saying to me I swear this man loves drama like I feel as if him and his husband actually enjoyed others downfalls and others misery but then again misery loves company those who are already miserable hate to see others happier than they are. The crazy thing about Kai that really made me fall back from him was I hated how when his husband gets upset at him his husband literally starts calling all of us friends one by one to tell us all the negative things that Kai had ever said about us to his husband granted I had never been married one thing I didn't do in relationships was tell everything that a friend tells me because it wasn't my place and I'm sure had they wanted my significant others to know they would have told me and no matter how upset I get at my significant other why would I call someone they knew or were close with to tell that person that they had been talking about them nothing but pure messiness I hate messy ass people but there's nothing worse than a messy ass man.

Every timeKai's husband would get upset with him he would call all of us who were friends with Kai one by one to tell us everything that chi said about us good and bad but for some reason the bad always seemed to outdo the good that definitely made me fall back from both of them for a long ass time there's nothing worse than telling someone who's your closest friend something and then repeating what you told them that's why I never trusted people and I never liked being friends with those who wanted to be friends in large ass group it sounded like drama. The messed up part about it all whenever kai's husband Jamal would tell us what Kai said chi literally would be sitting right beside him as his husband Jamal is telling everyone what bad things Kai said he never apologized he never said anything about it that's because he always knew he was fucking wrong granted I needed to know that Theo was married but I needed to find that out for myself not everyone can deal with finding things out from others some people you have to let them find out for themselves because then you tell them now they're mad at you.

Yes I needed to know that the professor was married but no I didn't want to find out from a friend a friend who was already messy as hell. Since I didn't have Facebook I got chi to send a text to CJ who was this woman married to Theo who looked like the low budget version of Jada Pickett Smith she looked a damn mess but I told Kai since my day is now ruined time to ruin her day as well we can both be unhappy together so I get caught a message Theo's wife and of course I shouldn't have or I should have proof read everything he texted the lady he always had to go overboard. He literally texted Theo's wife telling her that her husband was out in the streets slinging dick. That someone who her husband was having a affair with which was me even though I didn't know wanted to talk to her over the phone which I in fact did then Kai gives my cell number to this woman it's crazy because that same day when all of this mess occurred I was actually off work I had some errands to run with chi while Leilani was in daycare. When I go to the college that I was attending in Orange Park online chi of course was with me and that's when I get a phone call on my phone from a nine zero four number which the area code was Jacksonville FL I answered the phone and it was Theo's wife so I put the phone on speaker and I told Kai to be quiet.

The woman then starts talking introducing herself I then told her that my name was Brittany and I was having unprotected sex with her husband of course I had no idea that he was married and my friend who messaged you was the one who found out for me I didn't have much social media. She started asking all these questions I've really felt bad because now I was one of those women who is leading the wife know about her cheating no good husband and it felt so bad I would never want to get that phone call in or message from another woman who was sleeping with my husband. CJ or as the nickname Kai and I gave her Jada Pickett bitch Started asking me how did her husband and I meet I told her over the phone that we met in the grocery store in Orange Park he approached me I was minding my own business he literally had went out to his vehicle and came back in to give me his business card that had his first and last name as well as his work credentials as well as his cell and office number. For some reason whenever I would talk on the phone with anyone who wasn't my family I always had a older professional work voice but she then asked if I had any proof I told her I could send her all the screenshots with her husband's phone number we even had optics that we had taken together. She then started asking me if I believed in god and was a firm believer then she started preaching which was getting on my damn nerves and kai was huffing and puffing saying shut the fuck up silently of course because she was connected to my bluetooth in the car.

She then asked me if I could provide her the screenshots I then asked her if she didn't mind if I could have her cell number so that I could send her those screenshots because again I didn't have Facebook nor was I about to make one to send screenshots I also told her that I had been to their condo a few times when she wasn't there there was absolutely nothing in the condo at all that indicated a woman even lived there it was as if her husband had moved everything which I'm guessing had to be the case I didn't see anything that showed a woman lived there. I Even told her that her husband told me he was giving me a key to their condo she then starts snapping talking about to what condo not mine I said well unfortunately I have all the screenshots with your husband again phone number I have optics of him and I standing in front of your condo I then told her this is the name of her condo this is the address and this is your building and apartment number I don't have to lie.

She didn't say anything at all for quite some time then she just asked if I could send her over the screenshots I told her I certainly could as soon as she sent me a text message. She had asked me something and I told her that I loved her husband I told her we had been together for months and we had seen each other almost every single morning and sometimes when he would get off of work I could definitely hear in her voice she was very disappointed and upset but don't be upset at the messenger I didn't know just as much as she didn't know. It had slightly pissed me off how Kai thought it was funny as if he enjoyed the whole situation after all he was the one who told me about it sometimes people don't want to find out certain things especially not from others.

I then had asked Jada Pickett bitch how old Theo was she literally told me that he was fifty three I then told her wow he told me he was forty and honestly he looked as if he could have been forty. Black don't normally crack for some of us. She then said they had a total of fifteen children combined together but of course he had more children than her that was a lot of damn kids. Kyle had did a background check on him once we went back to his house I couldn't even focus or go into my school I decided to do it another day I was so distracted and I wanted to know more about Theo that was my problem I always ignored red flags and I never did background checks on these men. Kai did his background check for me on his computer in his office Theo had a total of fifteen children and he only had one child with his wife who was in elementary school and one of his baby Mamas was in her early thirties on top of that he was very much behind in his child support and this nigga had the audacity to be driving Audi. I sent Jada Pickett bitch the screenshots between Theo and I showing his phone number with the optic of him by himself as his contact photo also I sent her the photo of him and I outside of their condo and in some of the screenshots that I sent her his contact name said daddy and had some emojis beside it. As I'm sending her everything I had which was the proof that her husband was cheating on her I even had sent her a screenshot of his hand on my vagina lips opening it up one day after we had sex he came inside of me and on my vagina he decided to take that picture then I told her that was his hand. She responded back to me in a text saying she was very saddened by the situation. She was nice at first, Then she began to start being a bitch. Her husband literally had a key to my townhouse and everything, She even started sending me screenshots between her and her husband that were current of him telling her she loved him and her saying it back to him I wasn't getting jealous but I was just upset about the situation, She had even sent me an optic of her her husband and all of the fifteen children combined which is a lot of damn kids she better than me because baby I could never marry someone with that many fucking kids but then again I see why he had so many kids he did have a big, long,dick. She then started preaching to me sending me all these long ass paragraphs through text saying that she hopes I could forgive her husband and I need to develop a relationship with God so I didn't keep getting trapped by men who didn't care about me granted I hated to admit she was right. But for some reason I strayed away from being a mature adult for a moment I told her I didn't need man To simplify my life and be happy in life. I also told her my daughter and I would be perfectly fine I may have been a single mother not by choice but I definitely wasn't struggling financially or emotionally I only brought that up because she said She hoped I could forgive her husband so that God could give my daughter and I the life we deserved. She then told me that she didn't mean any harm she was just looking out for me as if I were her single daughter dealing with this.I ended up responding back to her telling her thank you I appreciated it and I left it alone.

CHAPTER

9

Just when I thought my luck couldn't get any worse than it did I began to start feeling sick I had noticed for a couple of days but I didn't pay any attention to it days before talking to his wife. After finding out he had a wife I kept telling Myself maybe I just needed some rest After all I was a single mother I also had my little sister living with us I was working in school and taking care of two kids That's a lot for anyone to be doing by themselves. I decided to go to Walmart to get a pack of pregnancy test as I rushed home I took two of them they came back positive. I didn't want to tell her but I was going to tell her she definitely needed to know and he needed to know when I decided to finally send her a text I asked her if she would be willing to meet up with me she responded back saying she was unable to meet she was tired from her woman's retreat. I Then asked her if her husband had a vasectomy because that's what he told me once then I told her I understand and I already feel bad enough anyways I just wanted her to know something that I just found out but I told her don't worry about it I will figure it out on my own she then texted me asking if I was claiming a possible pregnancy I responded saying yes I was sending her the pregnancy test with my face in it she then said Theo and I would have to figure it out because she wasn't responsible for cleaning up this mess. I then responded to her asking her who asked her to clean up the mess I told you because

I thought you should know is what I sent her. She also started telling me how the She also started telling me how the consequences of the situation wouldn't go on dealt with with Theo and I. She then told me that you read with your so I was so confused as to why she was telling me this because it wasn't like I knew he was married I had no idea so why the fuck would God punish me? See that was exactly why I couldn't stand Bible thumpers. She also told me how Theo would have to figure out how he wanted to deal with the situation.

I then responded back to her saying" Ok but you also can't be mad at me because I didn't know your husband was once again married. He didn't wear a ring or anything and trust and believe I don't want a baby by your husband or to claim a baby by your husband this sickens me. Your husband knew he was married at the end of the day and did what he did. If I knew he was married I wouldn't have dealt with him that's not me and that's not something to be proud about. I'm just the messenger telling you about your husband and what he did. Which I didn't have to say anything at all. I'm not even proud about this which is why I said I would take care of it. I'm about to get a house in a few months and moving far away as possible from your husband trust and believe that". She then responded saying she wasn't upset with me and how there was a price to pay for ignorance. She then said because of my lack of attention to his foolishness and lies placed me in a situation that I didn't deserve to be in. She then sent another text telling me that I was a smart and articulate young lady and sleeping with a man who chooses to keep me out of his personal life wasn't a smart move at all because I found myself being pregnant. I then told her thank you for the knowledge.

The very next day I reached out to Jada Pickettbitch to let her know that I went to the military hospital on base where I worked to let her know that the pregnancy was confirmed and I was in fact three weeks pregnant. I told her that I had reached out to him to let him know with his trifling self. She then responded saying" Ok. Again, that's you and him that have to deal with this, not me. I knew you would reach out to him. Though you say you are disgusted by him, if he were to come to you, you would welcome him in. That's what happens when we give ourselves to a man sexually without requiring anything of them. We become tied to them and wrap our emotions all up in them despite what they do. This is what you asked for, remember? Because y'all had a connection, you were willing to have a baby with him. So I responded back saying" Nobody wants that headache I reached out to him because I thought he should've known. Just because I reached out don't mean I want him I wanted a baby before I knew he was married. keep that same energy for your marriage..........what are you going to get out of your marriage dealing with a connection cheating ass husband? What I didn't like about having communication with her was she was so shady I was trying to have some type of respect for her I mean after all my father was in his fifties and my mother was in her as well as Theo and Jada Pickett bitch the only difference was my mother was older than her and father older than him.

The bitch really started talking too much in text when she sent the next message saying "I'm grown dear Brittany. I'm not going to get into a back and forth situation with you. I'm not responsible for dealing with your emotions or attitude because you decided to get involved. I responded to what you told me. I didn't tell you not to tell him. You were being tough as nails saying you weren't going to reach out to him. Whether he was married or not, LOVE yourself enough to not keep having babies by men who are not committed to you. Quit being willing to have sex before you get their hearts and a ring. You deserve more and your children do. Save yourself for marriage and give your children the right to have a two parent home. It takes two... remember my dear. You're not exempt from responsibility. How I handle my marriage and my husband is how I handle it. I'm in the marriage. You're outside of a marriage. Working for the government, having friends older that you, and dating men older than you does not make

you mature. Taking care of yourself, and taking your children's best inter-
est and needs into consideration before you put them in situations they
didn't ask for, is what makes you mature. I told you dear, I've been down
all the blocks....The focus isn't on what you accomplish externally, it's about
what you accomplish internally. You have internal work to do. Not knowing Theo was married doesn't excuse your actions toward yourself. He did
not treat you like a lady, he didn't let you into his "single" life, and the
exchange between y'all was sexual in nature. Ask your older friends to help
you mature into a lady who knows the difference between love and lust.
Regardless of his cheating, he loves me and lusted after you because you
were available. It is what it is.... don't be angry about it, show up differently
in the world so you can attract what you need and deserve. She was throwing shade but at the end of the day her husband was the one with the community dick out and about making all these damn kids having unprotected
sex with every bitch in the streets. I had some Mortal Kombat finish that
bitch because she was getting a little above herself so I texted her this next

"We don't have to go back and forward. If that's the advice you would give
your kids or anyone's kids I feel sorry for you. Sis I am tough as nails because
unlike you I wouldn't stay in a marriage with someone who cheated on me
and I didn't. Even though I was twenty one I have the right sense of mind to
get out of relationships that's toxic. I've experienced a lot in life to be twenty
one you don't know me nor what I've been through. Ma'am you do know
me and child's father were engaged up until his Untimely passing. And
had he been here we would've been happily married with multiple kids.
Marriages fail just like your previous ones and his previous ones. Marriages
fail, people can grow apart. Just because your married don't mean your
happy. It don't matter if I have 1 to 8 kids at least I know my sanity is
Better than dealing with a lying and cheating man. Don't ever settle for a
no good cheating man because no matter what he does I see you not leaving. he must have a spell on you. He was just asking me to go with him on
vacation. I'm not mad about nothing , You right I did get what I wanted.

273

just because I'm having sex with a person don't mean I'm in love. It's a difference between having sex and falling in love. This is the same man who was having sex with me in your bed and on your couch and floors. You so worried about me when you need to be worried about him a cheater who would bring another woman in your home let alone in your bed. I mean I didn't understand again why she was trying to throw shots I'm more of a come to my door type of person and talk to me I don't like to argue behind phones. So next she said this "Thanks for showing your maturity... again, I'm the wife. Why are you mad at me?? Y'all did this behind my back Take care of yourself dear Brittany". and I see that response was quite different I ate that ass up. I then told her I never said I was mad at you but what I'm not going to do is have you belittle me Into making it seem like I have no sense of knowledge when I do. first of all I didn't do anything behind your back you need to take it up with him more than me. you do the same sis. I bet she wasn't talking to her husband like that I could also tell he had probably cheated on her before anyways based on how she was acting Plus when her and I went back and forth and a text message it lasted for so long pages back and forth to each other. she then texted me "Describing one's actions is not belittling. It seems you have a hard time taking ownership of your decisions and actions and when you're confronted with them you get upset. So you start attacking me about what you feel sorry for and taking shots telling me what he told you.Be careful who you come after, I told you that I am a child of God and to come after me with no cause will reap the consequences. Please don't call me sis. It is quite clear that you are not a sister, but a female who will try to cut someone when she doesn't know how to handle her emotions or the results of her decisions. Im taking the matter up with everyone involved." I sent her one last message that day and the bitch never responded I wasn't going to keep going back and forth with her ass I had more important things to do. I sent this and she never responded so I said I won and went about my day. "I never said I was going to cut you or fight you nor did I even cuss you out. I said it in a respectful way. Unlike you I wouldn't try to belittle a person if I'm so much a child of God..... I called you sis because I didn't want to say anything disrespectful, my mother taught me better than that. I'm good over here ma'am I'm not complaining I don't want your man that's your problem if you decide to stay with him that's your problem not mine. You need to take your own actions with your issues going on in your household and stop trying to use the Lord's name in vein to make yourself look better because that's not holy."

The next day when I'm at work on a lunch break her man was texting me all freaking day but I didn't check my phone until lunch we were very busy that day it was nice to see how the roles reversed and I wasn't blowing him up he was in fact blowing me up trying to get me back I knew he missed me. I decided to send her the screenshots of her man asking need to send him an optic not going to lie I did send an optic of myself Bet it was a regular headshot optic then I screenshot it everything and sent to her telling her that her man needed to be controlled because that was ridiculous.she then sent me this "Hello Brittany, I have warned you. Theo will get dealt with for his actions. The question for you is: Do you want to get dealt with along with him?You NO LONGER have the excuse of not knowing that he's married. Your interaction with him is A CHOICE now, even though you know the truth. Why would you send him a picture of you?? Why are you still contacting him??I have nothing else to say about this matter. You didn't know before, but now you do. We reap the consequences of our actions. I was getting so tired of her always bringing up God Sending me all of these damn Bible verses and stuff she needed to be sending her husband Bible verses on adultery.

The sad thing was about it all her husband was literally using the key I gave him to my townhouse at the same time slots he used to come over early in the morning at three in the morning having sex with me and my dumb ass was allowing it. One day Kai and I went to Walmart together we always went shopping together and everywhere together for that matter we pretty much seen each other every day I also lived up the street from him as well and we were at Walmart on Collins Rd when I receive a text from Theo saying that he saw me at Walmart but when I texted him back asking why he didn't come over to me he never responded back like that drove me crazy,I would often even ask myself if that was the type of man I really wanted to be with he couldn't even respond back to me in a good enough time and always had excuses which I knew the excuses were he was with his wife So the next time Theo came over to get exactly what he wanted from me which was sex I asked him when he texted me saying that he saw me in Walmart why didn't he come over to me and he said because he was with her I couldn't even say anything he then started talking about how she had mental problems and all of this stuff if I ever hurt my husband talking that bad about me towards another woman that he was cheating on me with I would be so sad and and disappointed in him all of that lying for a piece of ass. One time I ran home on my lunch break I just wanted to eat lunch at home and I had to get some paperwork because I was buying a house in middleburg FL it was crazy because we hadn't even lived in a townhouse long I just happened to go to Navy Federal Credit Union one afternoon with Kai and they told me I was pre-approved for a fifteen thousand dollar credit card so I said I'll take it then the woman tells me I was pre-approved for a four hundred thousand dollar house loan house but of course you never use the full amount of the loan that's damn crazy whether you can afford it or not because anything can happen. And I received a phone call which I already knew the first three digits after the area code I knew it was Jada Pickett Bitch She would piss me off because she was so fucking petty the bitch would literally call me ask me for information then hang up. That day when she called we've really got into a heated argument because I'm looking for paperwork to send over to Navy Federal Credit Union for my house and she called me asking where was her husband at and telling me how she pulled the phone records I literally told her lady I don't have time for this I have shit to do she then told me that I was going to listen to what she had to say I was just trying to understand who the fuck was she talking to. I then told her if I wanted to I could make her husband come over to me right now then she said you could do what I then told her that she heard me she then said you know what Brittany don't call me anymore or text me I said lady you called me she said yeah to hear what you had to say I was talking and she hung up I was talking and she hung up then I called her back she answered and I told her that was very petty and unnecessary she then told me so is me fucking her husband I asked her wasn't she a Christian then I told her she can't get mad at me because her husband is out of control he knew he was married he knew exactly what he was doing then I told her again I could make him come right now if I wanted to he literally used to leave work early to come see me and he was sometimes missing work to come see me which was why he was arriving home later and later but at the time of course I didn't know that he was married then she told me to come and get shit so I asked her when did she want me to come get his shit. Even the time before when I had emailed Theo on his work email which I knew I shouldn't have done and it was definitely too far I send him nudes to his work email and when he finally took a look at it he sent me all these messages telling me that he lived a drama free life and asked me why would I do that to him I then told him because he wasn't responding back to me and that was a red flag he wouldn't even allow me to come over to his home anymore even before I was doing that. He had texted me telling me that he would never disrespect me like that ever he then said like come on you don't do certain things and that's one of the things you don't do.

She then started trying to make me feel bad telling me that I wouldn't get any child support money from him at all due to the amount of kids he already has and how behind he was she then told me that she was going to get a lawyer and I asked her girl a lawyer for what like you look a mess. I told her I would see her in court then I then schooled her letting her know that when you're married to someone who is on child support in certain states especially when the person paying the Child Support owedand or if itis was behind they also take the money that is owed from the spouse as well but I told her if she wanted to go to court we definitely could I had a lot of money that I didn't know what to do with it. What also was irritating me was the simple fact that every time I went to that Walmart and Jada Pickett bitch saw us and by us I mean Kai and I didn't appreciate how she would call me or text me she did that way too many times before the situation had gotten even crazier she called me saying that she knows we saw her and Theo with their daughter I then told her I really didn't nor did I care and they don't own the store. She was really getting on my nerves to the point where I sent her more screenshots but my dumbass sent her screenshots of me with my face in the optics and matching bra and underwear optics that I had sent to her husband with his phone number at the top.

Even when I would text Theo at times he was doing the same bullshit before with the responding when he felt was convenient for him that shit wasn't going to fly with me. I even showed him my pre-approval letter from my home. I had downloaded a texting app just to text him and he then asked me why was I being so nice to him I then told him if he didn't care what was the point of me caring grant said I did go off on him not too long ago but you can't lay good pipe on someone and then just walk out of their lives I was emotionally attached to him and that dick. When I asked him when could I get what I was entitled to he then told me that he had to think about it he also said that his situation wasn't good and it wasn't fair to me I then asked him why did he care he replied back saying why don't I care I then told him well you didn't care before so why should I care when you don't. he literally had me begging him for his dick and there were millions of dick in Florida but I only wanted his and he knew what he was doing. He just kept telling me that he would think about it. He really had me head over heels and he knew it which was why he was treating me a certain type of way one time I had texted him asking him who else was he fucking and he said Mondays are always busy for him and that I was using such strong language with him. Theo had definitely put me through a lot of shit that I didn't deserve but the issue was I wasn't telling myself that I didn't deserve that from him I was accepting and allowing the behavior and his actions which was why it was so easy for him to manipulate me and brainwash me the way that he did all he had to do was kiss me or make me wet and I would forgive him all over again time after time. I definitely won't ever forget the time when my doctor called me with my sexual transmitted diseases test results and anytime I was having unprotected sex with anyone my ass stayed at those care spots every three to six months to make sure that I didn't have any sexual transmitted diseases because the Hiv, Chlamydia, AIDS, syphilis rates were way too high to be having unprotected sex, sex definitely required trust which is what I learned quickly. One time I had tested positive for CLA Medea while I was with Theo I couldn't believe that nigga gave my first time having a sexual transmitted disease grant said I was having unprotected sex but people felt so realize that having a sexual transmitted disease doesn't make you a hoe doesn't mean that you sleep around is sometimes the person that you're sleeping with and they're nasty ways I had never had an STD a day in my life we had literally been together in the beginning for four months before I even have found about his wife. Even after I found out about his wife him and I were still having unprotected sex hell thinking back on it we never had protected sex so that means that he was fucking someone else as well. When I tried to tell his wife about it her stupid ass didn't want to hear it I had absolutely no reason to lie I don't know who lies about getting Sexually transmitted diseases. that's nothing to brag about let alone tell people about I was so embarrassed I had to get a shot in my ass even wanted to get pretreated in case I had anything else that could be treated and cured just in case so I didn't have to go back to the care spot if I had anything else as well. I can never ever ever forget about the time when my actual doctors office called me with my test results and yes I did get tested multiple times with Theo especially after finding out that he was married and he would come back to me to have a protected sex with me I could only imagine him having unprotected sex with his wife as well the doctor called me telling me that I had herpes I already had HSV one which isn't sexually transmitted at all that just means I get cold sores from time to time on the sides of my mouth because my mother and father allowed some nasty ass people to be kissing on me as a baby and or kid. But HSV two was sexually transmitted I literally stared at the phone with tears coming down my face trying to control myself from not screaming as I started crying more and more I then asked the doctor if there was a cure for herpes even though I knew there was no cure for it you can only treat it and he told me there was no cure for that and that I would have to take medicine to help out with the flare ups The craziest thing about it all I had a few friends who had herpes HSV two as well as HIV and again yes I was having unprotected sex but just because you have unprotected sex doesn't necessarily mean that you're going to get sexually transmitted diseases. After all I had had unprotected sex with Jay as well as Garrett and I never once had any sexually transmitted diseases hell when I was with Jay I never even got tested for any grants that I was going to the doctor they were taking blood work and urine samples from me so even if I did have something they would have definitely told me.

As I talked to the doctor while I'm crying in shock and in disbelief I asked him was there anything that I could do for the herpes to get rid of it I even was crying telling him I had money and maybe I could get some type of treatment or something to get rid of it I told him I couldn't have herpes. He told me unfortunately ma'am there was nothing I could do except take medication to help out with the flare ups I had told him it was crazy that I had that because I didn't see any bumps or anything else that would have indicated that I had that after all I had a few friends who had that and one was a nurse a registered one at that. When I get off the phone with the doctor I texted Theo I blew his motherfucking phone up text message after text message after text message telling him how nasty dirty and trifling he is asking him why the fuck did my doctor just telling me that I tested positive for herpes. The bastard was literally trying to tell me that he didn't give that to me and it takes a while to know that you have herpes I then texted him asking him when did he go to school to become a doctor a doctor that works in a fucking hospital in or office talking like he knows. I told him having a PhD degree Being called a doctor isn't the same as being a actual doctor working in a hospital and or doctor's office. He then told me he didn't give me herpes I didn't know what the fuck to believe. All I could do was sit in my closet and cry meanwhile Leilani and Bri are both downstairs in the living room of our townhouse watching television and eating snacks I cried as loud as I could in my closet hoping that they wouldn't me.

The fucked up part about it all is moments after I had sent all those text messages to Theo my doctor literally calls me back to tell me that they gave me the wrong test results I should a sue the hell out of those people the amount of stress and anxiety they put me through the fucking pain and suffering and black hole I was about to fall into like I was literally about to destroy this man's life and he was actually right he didn't give me herpes at all. Which meant I actually had to apologize for once again showing my ass and acting crazy.

It is now October of twenty nineteen Kai had helped me pick a house to buy I honestly was getting very tired of looking at homes and my real estate agent he was OK he wasn't the best but he wasn't the worst the problem that I had was I wanted a four bedroom house two story but I didn't want homeowner association or any CDD fees and I swear it seemed as if my real estate agent wasn't listening to me when I was telling him all of that that was the issue that I had with him the house in middleburg it didn't have CDD fees however it had HOA fees I had never ever ever wanted to move into a neighborhood with HOA or CDD and I've always said that for years I didn't understand why my real estate agent was showing me homes that had homeowner association fees and CDD fees. I hate it when people didn't listen or respect my wishes especially when I'm the person that has to pay the mortgage and all the other bills that follow there's nothing worse than moving into a neighborhood that has homeowner association fees, dealing with a whole bunch of Karen. I also wanted to stay in Clay County which is the same county as my father they had better schools and the areas were just all better not all of Jacksonville was bad or ghetto even the area we had lived in where our townhouse was at they had nice houses and apartments but it was the environment that was the issue for me it was just ghetto our people were bringing it down unfortunately. One time my real estate agent got annoyed by Kai and literally asked him if he was the one buying the home or me he was making suggestions towards certain things in each house we looked at that was out of date like the air conditioning unit stuff like that I was not replacing an air conditioning unit unless it was actually broke Kayla always was over the top I was as well but also I was my dad daughter and one thing about me I'm not going to waste unnecessary money when you buy a home you get something called a home warranty so that anytime something in your home breaks you pay a deductible to get it fixed instead of having to actually pay full price to get something repaired in your home my home warranty for the deductible was only eighty five dollars every time the home warranty company had to send someone out to fix anything in the house Which was the same company that Kai and his husband had had they were definitely very knowledgeable and they taught me a lot. When searching for the perfect home I was also not trying to be that far away from my father since my father was also getting older in age and I was his only child. I even had took a first time home buyers class because the house in middleburg that I decided to get when we first looked at the home they had a paper on the kitchen countertop saying how you could take a first time homebuyer class so when I made the decision eventually to buy the home because it was everything that I was looking for and everything I wanted In a home the four bedrooms the two story all the space at each of the rooms. One thing about looking for a home to buy you have to visualize yourself you have to visualize your furniture and everything that you have being in the house hoping that everything would fit and that was one of the issues when I was looking in certain homes I had a black leather sectional couch there was no way that it was going to fit in some of those homes in the living rooms they had and I wasn't trying to make any adjustments either. The crazy and funny thing we weren't even in the townhouse long but I mean who would actually pass up the chance on buying their first home especially with a military bank?

I had even sent Theo the pre-approval letter asking him when was he coming to move in with me but he responded back telling me that he was at work and it was busy I then said ok Theo. Before I even had the keys to my house I sent a picture of the one in middleburg to Jada Pickett bitch telling her that I was buying a house she then said good for me then I asked her when did she want me to come and get my man shit and she never responded. The messed up part I had told my father that I was buying a home and how I had got pre-approved for a four hundred thousand dollar home loan with Navy federal granted he didn't buy his home through Navy federal. But he wasn't even happy for me I hated how my father always tried to belittle me and make it seem like I had no sense of knowledge I hate it with older people did that like I know what I'm doing and I hang around people in their thirties and at that time Kai and I literally saw each other every day we talked all throughout the day on the phone and texted all day he and his husband had a house so I had nothing but faith in them that they knew what they were doing they had bought their home when they were my age granted I got a better deal than I did their house was also older and way nicer but those older homes are normally more durable anyways. But my father had sent me a text message saying how most people wait until they have enough money saved up to buy a house little did he know I had thousands of dollars saved up for my house I didn't like how he treated me as if I was a kid and I definitely had some knowledge on mortgages and other things with being a homeowner I mean after all Kai and I used to work in the mortgage department so after a while you take in all of that my father never truly bragged about my accomplishments or anything else that I did in life which made me upset but also have saddened me. Who doesn't want to brag about all the good that their kid(s) accomplished? So I had told my mother that I was buying a house and going to get more furniture for my house I then had asked her for her advice on the bedroom furniture because if I was going to have four bedrooms the guest room was going to need a bed dresser and some more stuff to go in there I asked her if I should do brown furniture for the guest room as she told me yes she said I've always been smart. And I know how she likes things and she said she had faith I knew what I was doing when it came to the decorating at least my mother was happy for me and bragging telling people.

I didn't want to talk about the house anymore with my father until I actually got the keys to the house which is normally the right way to do things I just thought my father would have been ecstatic for his only daughter who was twenty one years old buying a house you don't necessarily hear about that too much well at least I hadn't. That was the thing that upset me about my father he could never just be happy for me or tell me congratulations with anything that I ever had accomplished. And oftentimes my mother would have to take up for me telling my father that I was grown and I didn't live with him anymore and it was my life and my choices and decisions to make but he still didn't want to do that he just loved being in control of everything and everybody which got on my nerves. Kai kept trying to persuade me to stay in Jacksonville but I told him buying a house is a long term and big decision especially since I had two kids in my house I told him when you buy a house when you have children you have to think about is the environment is the area safe does that city have the best schools and everything else plus I didn't want to be that close to him we already were seeing each other almost every day which was slightly annoying. At the townhouse sky and Steven would always come over and one time I didn't want to be bothered with him even though he told me he was going to come over after he got off work he worked at the TD Bank call center and

I heard him knocking at the door and I knew it was him but I didn't want to answer the door I had just finished having a playdate one time with my girl Jasmine and her two kids and Leilani I had made tacos and of course toddlers make messes which I had to clean up and sweep and mop so at that moment in time hell I was tired myself plus I still had to give my child a bath and get her put in bed so I didn't want to have company literally as soon as they were leaving out he was walking in which annoyed the shit out of me. Him and I had definitely saw each other a little too much and it was definitely time for a break hell I didn't see anybody that much except for him and Theo.

I was getting very annoyed with all the house paperwork that I had and what had to be filled out I also didn't know that once you're buying a house with the bank where all of your money is at you can't touch the money I even had my credit card that I had been using since I couldn't get any money out of my bank account with Navy federal some think I failed to tell me so we had Been using money that I had stacked up in my safe and the credit card but I didn't want to use the credit card too much because they were looking at my credit report which my credit was great and I didn't have that much on my credit yet. I did have to write a letter so Navy federal stating why I had what I had on my credit which again wasn't a lot at all and to be honest buying a home with Navy federal seemed so easy I can't speak for others experiences but at least for me it was,. The credits and the income did it for me. Plus there were so many cities to move to in the state of Florida there was no need for everyone to be up under everyone. My closing date literally kept getting pushed back on the House which was pissing me off because I didn't want to pay at the townhouse especially when we were going to be leaving there pretty soon then again the woman who told me I was pre-approved to buy a house at Navy federal told me that next to having a baby buying a house is the most stressful and honestly she really didn't lie all the back and forth all the late night calls with the mortgage people and my real estate agent and instructions that I kept receiving it was starting to really get on my nerves and my real estate agent was getting on my nerves I didn't go off on him but I didn't text I told Brian that this was pissing me off and chi busted out laughing talking about how you fussing out your real estate agent I then said because he isn't doing his job I actually should have listened to Kai and fired the real estate agent but I was on a crunch time I had to be in this house with Navy federal you typically get ninety days to find a house grant city possibly could have been extended but again I didn't want to have to pay the rent at the townhouse especially since I was buying a house that I was going to be moving in soon my closing date kept getting changed and I was starting to get very stressed out. One time when I went to Navy Federal Credit Union to wire some funds I literally asked the man if he was sure because I had to get that in a check form fifteen hundred which was my closing cost and he literally had no idea come to find out he didn't know what the fuck he was doing my check got wired to the wrong account and I told them when I found that out they better figure it out because I'm not sending another check for fifteen hundred Maybe had the man not trying to be in trying to flirt with me being an airhead he would have been paying attention to what he was doing I wasn't impressed at all I only wanted one man and that was Theo and somehow someway I was going to get him back he wasn't going to go back to his wife while they ride off in the sunset together while I'm sitting back slightly miserable we don't do that. I think Theo then realized I was the prime example of why you don't cheat all your spouses because some people are crazy and I was that some people that was crazy you can't be out here laying good pipe on me and then try to go back to your wife. That's why you don't cheat because there's women out there like me who will catch feelings and start acting crazy.

My closing date was set for Halloween of twenty nineteen which was exactly when I had closed on my house Leilani, Kai and I were literally at the title company for hours Which was slightly getting aggravating because my toddler didn't want to sit which was completely fine and understandable hell I didn't want to sit so I had to give her my phone so she could watch YouTube to keep her occupied while we were at the title company I was all types of nervous also it was Halloween and we had been at the title company already for a total of three hours I had loved Bri at the town-house with our puppy. I told Bree that I would take her and Leilani out for Halloween to the zoo every year the Jacksonville zoo had a Spooktacular event I had been there once or twice with Leilani but never with Bri and I thought it would be something she would enjoy considering the zoo was huge and I had never seen all of the zoo in the day. While we waited for the phone call to confirm that everything went through and was good for me with the house Kai and I decided where we wanted to go to eat we were in Fleming Island Which was where the title company was that we had to go to plus I knew where everything was in Clay County after all I grew up in Clay County it seemed like because my father lived in Clay County I asked Kyle if he wanted to go to Ruby Tuesdays I told him if I get these keys and everything goes through we're going to splurge at Ruby Tuesdays to celebrate I really had appreciated the simple fact that he had took the day off from his job just to help me because he already had knew that we were going to be at that title company for a while plus him his husband and family were always helping and looking out for us they did a lot for us so from time to time I like to return the favor.

Once we moved into our brand new home in Middleburg FL I had bought a four bedroom house with two in a half baths I only had paid two hundred and nine thousand dollar home. Which was very affordable because I was from up north so houses cost way more than that my home was built in two thousand and seven my closing cost was only fifteen hundred dollars and I didn't have to pay a down payment because I had great credit at the age of twenty one years old I was so glad I actually listened to my parents when they told me not to mess up my credit because credit is very important when she become an adult. I had everything that I needed for the home everything was ready before we moved in with the exception of a few things so I decided to meet up with Kai while the girls were at my dad's house I went to chis house to pick him up then we go to the Walmart on Collins Rd the one up the street from him and Theo and his ugly ass wife we literally see Theo was walking out of the store when we were going into the store so at one point in time I had gave Kai Theo's phone number and he saved it underneath my name as work next thing we know Kai's phone rings it literally said Theo I tell him to give me his phone now when I answered the phone I said hello then Theo said this is Theo and he said his last name he was always professional over the phone. Kai never told me that he accidentally hit the work number which he had listed underneath my name which was Theo"phone number he had literally called them a total of five times so they were returning the phone call. It pissed me off because I actually had to fucking deal with this lady I was ecstatic about my brand new house fuck them I wasn't even thinking about them. So Jada Pickett bitch starts telling me how her husband told me he didn't want me and it was just for the moment he only wanted sex from me temporarily and he didn't love me and couldn't see himself with me long term. Then the bitch would hang the phone up I definitely thought something fishy was going on because granted Kai did called them a total of five times according to his call log but why would they be returning the call a few days later on the same day where Theo literally sees Kai and I walking into the store because that wasn't suspicious at all. As soon as she heard a woman voice she took over that phone call real quick when I asked Theo what did he want and why was he calling me because that was my work phone number. I didn't know if Kai did it on purpose or not I mean after all he was gay and messy it's one thing to be gay but it's another thing when you're messy as well after all had he never opened his mouth none of that would have ever occurred anyway. I'm not going to lie she didn't hurt my feelings although she tried but I was really in love with her husband I mean those aren't the type of feelings that I can just allow to go away overnight stuff like that takes time all I ever wanted was unconditional love by a man who was truthful admit well by me I hated liars and once again I was caught up with another married man which definitely sucked it seemed like every since I had been with Jay after him all I could attract was married men It was as if I had been cursed for being with a married man when I was with him all I ever wanted was to have a family the perfect family even when Jay died all I ever wanted was a stepfather and father figure from my daughter since her father was deceased I wasn't trying to replace him but it seemed as if I could give my child everything she ever wanted and needed except for a father I love the temporary men the temporary happiness the temporary sex the temporary life that I had and I had to keep telling myself it was temporary and to enjoy the moment while I could. Theo had literally been around my daughter and my sister The night before I had even found out about him being married. After he had gotten off of work he came to my townhouse I had dinner prepared he sat at my table with me eating my food which I had made chicken, cornbread, collard greens, white rice and I had one for him and I. I couldn't believe that he had lied to me I was very much hurt and betrayed not that he owed me anything but he definitely misled me in so many ways.

The craziest thing about it I was talking all this trash about Theo but as his wife said if he were to come to my door I would let him in and that's what happens when we become emotionally attached to a man which she definitely was right because he had a key first of all so I technically didn't have to let him in that key was going to let him in. I had decided Leilani, Bri and I were going to go to Miami for our family reunion on my dad side of the family majority of my older cousins and everyone else was going to be there plus I had never been to Miami before so I decided that it was time for the girls and I to get a break and a change of scenery from Jacksonville plus all the drama that I had going on in my life I had texted Theo telling him I was going out of town on vacation to Miami with some of my cousins and I was going to be gone for a few days so I told him that I wanted my dick. He told me that he would put it on me but I had to promise never to threaten him again see how he had no respect for this lady even after I found out he was married he still would come back to me and I felt so bad because I was allowing it and letting him granted I was in love with him. He then asked me what day was I leaving to go to Miami because he had to have me before I left to go out of town I told him the date and the time the girls and I were going to meet at my father's house so I told him he needed to come over to this townhouse extra early.

Days later when it's time for us to go to Miami I let the girls sleep in longer considering that the three of us had already packed our suitcases the night before plus I already had to get up extra early way before they did so I could get my dick from Theo. He always would play these mind games with me and tease me no one knowing that he was going to give me some anyways I hated that. When he came over he had used his key I was already awake I had showered and put on some lingerie for him Even though it was going to be taken off of me slowly but surely I always try to look sexy for him especially since I had a baby face and especially after I found out his real age so it didn't seem awkward I tried to make myself look a little bit older than I was but then again I always felt as if I was older than I truly was I was twenty one but in my right mind I felt as if I was thirty one years old not by maturity but by pain and what I had endured throughout my life it made me so much mature though than I had to be. He threw me on the bed then he asked me if that was his pussy then I told him yes daddy and told him that he could do whatever he wanted to me. When Theo came inside of me I laid on his chest and he was rubbing my back and hair. We talked a little bit and he told me how he loved when I had the French tips on my nails and toes he said it was sexy and a turn on but to be honest I always got French tips on my nails and toes that was my signature look when it came to getting my nails done it definitely was sexy to me but plain and professional as well.

Theo then hugs and kisses me then tells me that he was about to go because he had to watch His time I couldn't believe that I was sharing a man with a woman but she was no better than I was to some women a piece of man is better than no man I never needed a man I just wanted that man. She was one of those wives that no matter how many times her husband cheated on her that was her man and she was going to stick by his side more power to her I could definitely tell that wasn't his first time cheating based on how she was acting towards me. As Theo walks down the stairs and I follow behind him so that I could lock the door I heard Bri she was up and getting ready so that we could go we had to go to my father's house where we then would alright together to Miami to the airport where he was going to be leaving his car then we had to get a passenger van passenger van that could fit everyone I swear something about my father and his side of the family booking hotels and or rental cars I swear something bad always happened it was like they had bad luck literally and figuratively meanwhile my dad's side of the family everyone had pretty much flew together to Miami meanwhile we had to drive to Miami which was a five to six hour drive I very much hated road trips especially traveling with a toddler I hated it I never got to get any rest or relax I was always in full mommy mode but I had hoped that when I got to Miami I could get my party on my cousin Cedes also was going to be traveling with her son who was the same age as Leilani and a month than Leilani. I was just looking forward to going to Miami because I had never been there before and neither have the girls been there before either so it was definitely a nice mini vacation I definitely had needed a break away from Theo his wife and all that drama that was going on I couldn't take it anymore. Our dog Snickers who Kai's cousin had gave us for free was watching Snickers until we got back into town.

When LeilaniBri my dad and I had finally reached Miami airport we literally had the worst luck with the passenger vans we had to swap out three times meanwhile it was raining really bad there so the pilot couldn't land the plane which my family was on it was just a mess already. When the pilot was finally able to land the plane when the rain started to slack up we waited for them in front of the airline door they said they would be coming out of it was so many of them our family was huge only two of my older cousins had came who were in their late twenties everyone else was the adults which were our parents and aunts. And some of my younger cousins were there as well we had such a hard time loading up everything on the passenger van my cousin Cedes and I both had one year old so we definitely needed those car seats especially when we actually went to Miami Beach and everything I was not carrying a one year old all around while we walked Around South Beach once everyone is in the passenger van comfortable my father then tells me to put the address in the GPS I actually thought that we were staying at the hotel in Miami come to find out I accidentally had gave my dad the wrong address which took us downtown Miami we were in traffic for literally an hour then when we arrive to the hotel he then tells me that wasn't the right hotel and that we were supposed to be in Fort Lauderdale and my mind I'm like Fort Lauderdale you said Miami my cousin tip who was getting very irritated because I had landed us at the wrong hotel and the amount of traffic there was unbelievable then my cousin Cedes puts the address in her phone and we're good to go after that.

When we finally arrived to the correct hotel that was in Fort Lauderdale we had an issue with the hotel rooms Cedes was arguing with the guy at the front desk of the hotel after he told us that we had to all put down deposits for rooms saying it was a requirement and Cedes then told him it really wasn't because she had stayed at hotels before where you didn't have to put deposits down on rooms but she said whatever we got money. I was once again very annoyed because it always seemed to be something that was the first date there and we literally couldn't catch a break with every single thing I was already missing home and missing my man. I had even texted him letting him know that we had arrived in Miami but of course he never responded instantly. One time I did him how he did me and started ignoring him was even leaving him on read and delivered until he Texted me asking me" so you're ignoring me now"? I literally had him right where I wanted him until I had gave in responding back to him telling him that I'm busy just like he was. One time after we finished having sex on the couch at my dad's house he told me to make sure that I told the military men that I worked with that I belonged to Theo he just wasn't shit and the fact I was considering him my man he was a married man a lying ass man with a whole bunch of kids ass man.

But the first day we were in Miami we really didn't do much of course until the next day because that was the same day that we had just arrived and we were all tired and needed to freshen up even for dinner we all had decided to just get Taco Bell since it was right across the street from the hotel especially since we were all out it was so many of us to Taco Bell was so full on the inside we had to go inside to order and people who were coming inside to order left because it was too many of us which I don't blame them at all. Anytime we had family trips we would always all stay on the same floor at the hotel.

CHAPTER

10

It is now the next day we all go downstairs to eat breakfast I then get Bri to take some optics of Leilani and I then I get my dad to take some optics of Bri, Leilani and I. everyone else comes downstairs to eat breakfast eventually as well then we all try to plan out everything for that day so we just decided to all go to Everyone else comes downstairs to eat breakfast eventually as well then we all try to plan out everything for that day so we just decided to all go to downtown Miami Miami Beach to hang out shop walk around take optics and have a good time. It was literally so many of us in that passenger van it irritated me how my dad family always wanted to carpool together with so many of us we could have at least had two passenger vans I think that would have been more ideal considering how many of us there was and the simple fact that Cedes and I also had to put our strollers for our children in the trunk which just about took up all that space. But I was definitely enjoying myself I did need a break from work especially because pretty soon I was going to be preparing to go to the police Academy in Jacksonville FL I had always wanted to be a police officer Since I was a little girl plus I was trying to be a Jack of all trades. It made me think of a flashback when Theo and I were laying in the bed together and I told him how I was going to model for him in my police uniform once I received it and he told me he couldn't wait for that when we were laying in my bed together talking. Once I finish that flashback I had another mini flashback of showing him his college that he worked at they had an Instagram page and I showed him some of the optics of him and some of his colleagues and the one lady who always was taking pictures of everyone it was crazy because I noticed that he had a wedding band on his ring finger a black wedding band but I didn't think anything of it I mean after all I always had wore the ring on my ring finger from Leilani father that he gave me before he died so I didn't think of it and Theo also never asked me about the ring either. When him and I were looking at the optics of him on the Instagram page for the college he definitely had a wedding band on that I noticed I know he was probably shitting bricks especially because he knew he was married all along and lying. I kept telling myself that I had to leave this man alone but I couldn't I mean after all I was pregnant by him and I was so in love with him I was in love with the sex I was in love with the fact that I was pregnant by him. All I wanted was a father figure for my daughter since her father was dead and I wanted a man to love me for me and actually do right by me but I guess sometimes you have to really be careful what you ask for because you get what you've been asking for just not in the way that you thought you would. I was actually beginning to feel sorry for myself for the second time just two different situations way different.

I knew I was definitely going to have to keep that secret I didn't even tell anyone that I was close with I didn't even tell Kai because he just talked too much for me it's one thing to be gay but another thing to be gay and messy and when you get to that level I cannot mess you anymore.

Theo and his Jada Pickett Smith low budget looking ass wife Had decided to place me in a group chat with them were they both call themselves trying to tag team me and she was stupid anyways because more power to her but I could never stay with a man that she did on me and still continue to cheat on me even after his mistress found out about me but more power to her. There's billions men in this world wide take shit off of 1 man especially when you can replace a man? In the group chat they placed me in a group chat and Theo started it off and said this " Hey Brittaney,

This message is long overdue. I watch your mental illness spiral out of control. I have notated all of the relentless calls you have made to my wife, including myself. All of the text messages from past and present have been recorded. Your STALKING has been recorded! At the end of the day I am texting you right now to set the record straight! I love my wife and I was wrong for bringing your DEMONIC ACTIVITY into her life! I will NEVER EVER LEAVE MY WIFE! She is my ROCK AND MY COVENANT PARTNER. GOD put us together and NO MAN OR WOMAN can tear us apart! It is called HOLY SPIRIT FIRE! You are TAKING PERPETUAL STEPS TO BEING REPORTED TO LAW ENFORCEMENT FOR STALKING AND HARASSMENT! Lord knows if they pull your phone records from both of your raggedy phone numbers that you fabricate messages with. UNREAL!!! You know how that STORY GOES! At the end of the day, your plan to break up my marriage was WEAK. God put us together and your MENTAL ILLNESS is so sad. You just don't CARE about your daughter?!?! Again, I have given you ample time to get it together. Child protective services will put her in a safe home with a MENTALLY STABLE parent! All we have to do is turn over our phone records and PRESS CHARGES FOR STALKING WHICH IS A CRIME PUNISHABLE TO 10 years in prison. Look it up online! Again, I love my wife and you could never ever be 1% of the WOMAN OF GOD SHE IS! Finally, I am going to pray for this mental illness and depression you are suffering with. Here I go.

Dear Heavenly Father. I ask in the name of Jesus to break this mental illness and Demonic spirits off of this young lady. I pray that she gives her life to Jesus and repent for her sins. I pray that the Jezebel spirit is broken off of her. I pray that you can build up her low self esteem and insecurities. I pray the spirit of vengeance and retaliation off her. I pray that she finds a good bible teaching church for herself and her daughter. I pray she can find someone who can love her in her damaged state. I pray she finds peace in her heart to love others. I pray that she becomes the mother her daughter deserves. Lastly, I bind all spirits of witchcraft, sorcery, roots, devil worship and cast them into the pits of hell forever in the name of Jesus and no weapon from this moment in shall prosper against my wife and my entire family. It won't work. It is sealed now. God is good all the time. Hallelujah,PRAISE GOD!!! I JUST SENT THAT ALL CONSUMING FIRE straight to your house. Every choice you make from this point on will be dealt with by God! Vengeance belongs to the Lord and he fights our battles. We serve aFAITHFUL GOD. I think this is a good point to get up and take your daughter to a bible believing church. Get some word in you is the first step to HEALING! Be Blessed! Jesus loves you! -TG. Then I responded saying this "It's not my fault you were trying to meet up with me with your bitch ass. She called me day one, I'm not the one married and lying and misleading women that's all you boo... Worry about not being a hoe and them thirteen kids you have and pay that child support. I never asked you to leave your ugly ass weak willed knock off version of Jada Pickett. She crazy for staying with a cheating ass man like you it's too many men in the world. You can keep your wife honey and we don't do church because we're not hypocrites. Monday-Saturday your cheating misleading and sinning but Sunday the first motherfuckers in church hooping and hollering.. Now you want to have big balls but how long ago were you just fucking me? Don't bring my child up in conversation because I'm a better parent than you I don't just go out fucking everyone making babies like you. Y'all the ones who need help funny how you said you were going to go to Ohio to leave her before I exposed your ass.. Meanwhile she wants to kill you and can't stand the fact you cheating on her constantly... You want to leave her and talk behind her back about how y'all separated and not trying to claim her...

Theo then said " I am not going to be back and forth. Only responding to defend my WIFE! You right, she isn't a Fake Jada! You know what, she is the REAL CJAI GRAHAM! Often duplicated, but never replicated! My WIFE IS AMAZING AND YOU WERE THE BEST THING TO HAPPEN TO MY MARRIAGE! Thank you so much Because of you, God showed me my weakness and what I need to do to be a better husband and father. We are a ROYAL COUPLE and God had to get this mess out of me to use me on HUGE PLATFORM. Thank you so much, now get up and get you some word! Hallelujah. I am going to send you a song that is my motivational source everyday. Yes Lord!!!. I then texted back saying "We know she put you up to this lol she runs you and that household with your scary ass". What pissed me off the most was the simple fact that this grown ass man of a man was really trying to play me not even trying he did play me he really was talking bad about his wife he stepped to me no one Lee knowing that he was married in a committed marriage but lied to me in order to get what he wanted and it actually hurt me and I was pregnant by him. Theo then texted me this "Matter of fact, read a book on BUILDING LOW SELF ESTEEM! Anyone who calls someone one thousand times needs help. I don't think your sailor will appreciate you calling me You contradict your-self all the time. MENTAL ILLNESS KICKING IN! Are you BI-Polar?" So not only was this man coming for me trying to act like he didn't know who I was at all it hurt the most because he really had played me and got what he wanted and when he didn't want me anymore he tries to act as if he didn't know me or he didn't lie to me and his stupid wife was a part of it as well I guess to sum a piece of man is better than no man at all. I couldn't believe this he cheated but for some reason I'm wrong for telling his wife about her non perfect husband and her dumb ass taking up for this man they definitely deserved each other. Her husband Theo Graham who worked at Florida State College Jacksonville. I then realized that these two people were actually starting to get to me and I was getting very upset so I needed Kai and his husband Jamal to help me on what to type and because Kai had that background check and Theo also was laid in child support and owed and child support I texted him this next " What you need to do is pay that child support from Nikita Littlejohn." Fun fact I know her she said your behind on your child support but I'm a unfit parent? "Is that why you have no insurance on your Tahoe With that big dent on the side of it."

Then Jada Pickett Bitch said "Get a life, how about a fun fact on SELF ESTEEM!" I see I ate her ass up haha!! The truth is a powerful thing. Taking up for her husband like he wasn't late in child support driving around in a Audi And they had the audacity to be talking to me about God? God needed to tell him to get his shit together and pay that child support. I then lied and told Theo this "My life is great I'm not worried about you or Jada Pickett.. like I explained my man is getting out the Navy this week and we move in our house so I have no need for you anymore. I only messed with you because you were available. He then said "I don't discuss anything GOVERNMENT WORKER! I will make notations of that too."

Theo responded saying "The first thing he needs to do is take you to CHURCH!" They were the exact reason on why I never liked going to church hypocrites now how is Jada Pickett mad at me because her husband was cheating and chose to cheat with someone younger than her so then they start throwing up how I need to go to church and God this and God that pathetic. I had all the screenshots and optics. I was just so hurt that I had got played and as a result of me getting played it left me pregnant and alone once again. Jamal didn't make the situation any better they always had to play him and Kai could never be serious for once like they enjoyed me being miserable and sad talking about the professor was acting like he didn't know who the fuck I was which he really was and I couldn't get mad at the truth but I was mad at the truth.

The craziest thing about it all a few weeks later I had gotten to a car accident someone had hit my car with me and me only in it they ran into the back of me so hard my head hit the steering wheel my head was bleeding my lip was busted and my nose was gushing with blood. When the guy who hit me got out and ran over to me to see if I was ok I had blacked out as he ran over to me and that was the last thing that I remembered. When I had woke up I was in the hospital and when the doctor and nurse came in they told me that I was pregnant both the baby was gone and that I had a miscarriage. All I could do was sit there and distraught I couldn't believe that granted Theo didn't deserve a baby from me nor did he deserve me at all but that was still a baby and a baby that I had wanted even though I had all these thoughts in my mind about how I was going to take him to court and make his life a living hell I guess it happened for the best looking back but at that moment in time I was very hurt and sad ashamed and embarrassed plus losing a baby always hurts. Not to mention I was feeling as if I had a curse on me because two weeks later my car was parked at one of my friends houses I wasn't in it that time but when I walked out to my car it was torn up it had been hit while it was parked and the woman who hit it just happened to be the manager at the apartment complex who was nice enough to leave a note on my vehicle so I guess at that time that was my karma which was very crazy and I was wondering to myself if Theo had even received karma granted I didn't know he was married in the beginning but even after I had found out and I still made the decision to keep messing with him things kept happening to me all these car accidents kept happening to me my Nissan literally kept getting hit over and over again I didn't know what to do I didn't know what to say thank God that I had that USAA car insurance at that time.

When I had moved to middleburg I kept telling myself that I wanted a white man with some money as a part of my fresh start but again I guess you have to be so careful what you ask for. Literally this man who I met who was in the Navy he was stationed at the same base that I was working at he would ask me out from time to time every time he came to my department but I kept telling him no the only reason I would tell him no was because I thought I had a man who was playing me so I decided to give it another try with the dating stuff after moving into my house. The guy that I had met on base his name was Antonio he was 33 years old he had two daughters and he was fine as hell. After a while of me telling him no I didn't want to give him my phone number or go to lunch with him I finally decided to give him a chance all I ever wanted was to be in a relationship with a man who wanted me for me who loved me for me who wants it to be a stepfather and or dad to my daughter and who was going to treat us right and do right by us after all I had my own money I had my own house my vehicles were paid for I didn't need anything from a man I just wanted to be loved and to be treated right. After I let Garrett go who was actually a good man and loved me as well as my child but I messed that up by saying the wrong things out of my mouth it's not what you say to people it's sometimes how you say certain things to people I was so upset with myself and regretful because I really had a good man that God had sent me.

Antonio and I started going to lunch often whenever we were on lunch break at work grant said we worked in different departments I also worked in the same department as my father so I definitely couldn't get caught dating a military man who worked on the same basis I did plus I didn't know if my father knew him or not I swear I was always taking risk when it came to talking to men who worked on the same basis I did because when things don't workout between you and the person and you work at the same place you have to see each other every single day or you're going to eventually run into each other but I was one of those people I always had to learn things literally the hard way I would literally get a lesson that needed to be learned but for some reason I would never fully learn my lesson I would keep doing the same things over and over again I always had to learn the hard way in life. Are eventually decided to give Antonio my cell number since he was putting so much time and effort into trying to talk to me which as he should I never approached any man no matter how fine I thought they were that was something I just chose not to do it's better to let the man chase the woman. Antonio and I would text every day all day and even talk on the phone we even got to this point where because he had two daughters and I had two daughters because I did consider breed more so as my daughter overtime instead of my sister because I did every single thing for her I paid for every single thing for her that she ever wanted and or needed we would always have play dates at the parks we would take the girls bowling skating to so many places and it was so cool and fun not putting a title on whatever it was that we had going going but just enjoying the moment I always tried to enjoy the moment while I could. It always felt nice being temporarily happy with a temporary guy because I was still not learning my lesson each time that's why I realized soon enough I kept going through the same thing with these married men because I was never fully learning my lesson I was ignoring all the red flags I wasn't taking my time and on top of that I wasn't doing background checks which would have definitely told me that they were married. Soon enough I started to invite Antonio and his two daughters over to my home in middleburg sometimes I would go all out and cook a nice big dinner for everyone and other times I will order pizza and or go get chicken from Popeyes. Middleburg was a very small town however we did have a lot of restaurants but Orange Park, Jacksonville, Gainesville, Palatka, Green Cove Springs, St. Augustine and a lot of other cities were very close. Antonio and his daughters would even spend the night at times his daughters would sleep in my guest room that I had there was a television in there that worked and all. Plus Leilani really enjoyed playing with his daughters even though they were older than her they were only in elementary school but they weren't that much older. We used to even take optics in my backyard I had got patio set furniture and I had these two couches put out on my back patio and a fire pit for the winter time one day we were all dressed up and got professional optics taken. My mother was scheduled to come up to Florida for Thanksgiving and Christmas in twenty nineteen to visit us and I had told him Antonio bout it he literally said that was fine he wanted to meet my mother and father anyways but little did I know he was of full of shit. My dumbass had literally gave Antonio a key to my house the house I pay the mortgage and bills at the house my name was the one and only name on the deed how stupid could I have been? I just wanted to be loved and I was so eager to find a father figure for my child that's all I wanted it killed me knowing I could give my child everything that she wanted but I couldn't bring her father back all the money in the world couldn't bring him back we may have had our ups and downs but I didn't want him to die after all he had wanted a baby more than me but I can't punish a baby for the sins of the father that wouldn't be fair nor would an abortion have been fair even though I wasn't ready for motherhood but I was definitely killing it.

I notice Antonio was starting to respond to me when he wanted to and call me when he wanted to even return to my calls when he wanted to. He literally would get off the work sometimes the same time as me and the latest he had gotten off would be six I get that he had two daughters who he didn't have full custody over so that's what he told me or at least what I thought and believed at that time but I noticed with him he would be arriving to my house at midnight and one in the morning when I was sleep he would walk into my bedroom and get into bed with me as if I wasn't awake or unaware of that. He would wake me up with sex or by grabbing my waist getting closer to me while I was sleeping but I was a light sleeper and would wake up to that. I was going to his work events with him with our children and everything. Even Bree was attached to him he would call her his daughter in law he would even have talks with Bree about boys and what to watch out for but hell he never told me that I needed to watch out for him. When the month of November comes up I notice that he was really acting different and treating me different worse than he was already starting to when he would choose when he wants it to deal with me and I would sometimes call him out on it I hate it to be ignored and I hate it being treated like crap. My mother was scheduled to come to Florida the week before Thanksgiving because she wanted to also help me hang up pictures on the wall and decorate the house with a whole bunch of movie theater décor that she had bought for me from a store called Kirkland's my mother always had taste and could definitely decorate and I needed some help with the decorating.

My living room was a movie theater setup so I really appreciated all the movie theater décor that my mother had brought me as my home warming gifts since I didn't have a real home warming I didn't like having home events in my own home people come to your house tearing your stuff up especially when they aren't used to having things themselves plus it seemed as if every since I had moved to middleburg it seemed like I wasn't getting a lot of company from my so called friends any of them after all I knew everyone in Jacksonville and Orange Park everyone was claiming I lived far and kept saying middleburg was far but I'm like all the times I've drove to you guys just because you live in Orange Park don't mean that Jacksonville is that much closer it depends what side of town within Jacksonville you're going to that was the thing about Jacksonville people they were all for people coming to their home and bringing things and seeing them but they never could return the favor and me move in the middle burg definitely helped me realize who my friends were and weren't held even my Burger King crew alma Renee and dad hadn't been in my house within the first two years of me being there talking about I live far but granted even when I lived in middleburg still driving to Jacksonville to see them hell they lived far. That's why I was just like my mom's ex fiancé CJ I didn't bother nobody and I didn't want nobody bothering me me moving to middleburg definitely helped me get rid of a lot of bad eggs that were in my life that didn't need to be.

Even my father would tell me how Jacksonville people were literally everyone was saying that I live so far but I'm like y'all literally drive and go everywhere else I was from up north I had even lived in New York in a few other places so typically to travel to places you had to take tolls there was no way around that the one thing that I loved about living in middleburg was the simple fact that I had multiple ways to get home I had the street way I had the back rows I had the toll rose so many ways to get home and it was definitely time for change like I once said when I watched that movie till death do us part when she was pregnant and had decided to buy a house for her and her baby it made me think man I want to do that same thing and it was crazier because I actually had bought a home. But well my mother had finally decided to come a week early to Florida for the holidays which sucked sometimes I really hated having company she literally came into my house and was taking over everything as if it was her house but I didn't want confrontation I decided to tell my mother about Antonio why I did that I honestly didn't know at all she always had something negative to say and on top of that she talked so much certain things I didn't want my father to know and one thing about my mother if you pissed her off just enough she would definitely tell your business which is why I told her absolutely nothing about me that less people know the better even your parents and family I was a firm believer of that but I had showed her some optics of Antonio and she said he was alright looking but my mother was into pretty men. I wasn't and my mother loved only light skinned men and Antonio as probably the first light skinned man I had ever been with I typically didn't like light skins but I was always open to trying new things.

He was supposed to come over with his daughters a few days before Thanksgiving I found it very funny that when I told him my mother was in town he didn't want to come over or was acting as if he didn't want to come over with his daughters I'm like what's going to happen though like you've literally been here you've literally had a key to my house and the craziest part about it I didn't have a key to his place I had never seen his place before I was just being young dumb and stupid once again and my world was about to come crumbling down on me once again I swear I never learned my lessons I was never cautious when it came to men because I just wanted to have a man that was always my downfall a man I couldn't help but think that I was starting to become just like my mother always wanting a man I didn't need one I just wanted one and sometimes you definitely have to be careful what you ask for because you definitely get what you ask for just not in the way that you thought you would. One time I had even showed Kai some optics of Antonio and I he then told me that he looked like he had a small dick But I mean compared to Theo who was fifty three with a twelve inch dick so any man that I would get with after him who didn't have a twelve inch dick was considered small to me I was taking all of those inches. I didn't even know why I showed Kai he always thought someone was gay or had a small dick Plus after all he was the reason why my last relationship with Theo was ruined because he talked too damn much. I would never get over the time when I texted Theo after finding out that he had a wife begging him to come over telling him how I missed his dick touching my lips he then messaged me back telling me do you see what you did by doing what you did. It was the manipulation for me and I was still being young, dumb, full of cum. The messed up part Theo knew he had me exactly where he wanted me that's why he thought he could treat me any kind of way because he knew that I was going to come to him.

The crazy part about it all while I was on a mini vacation with my family Theo decided to take his wife on vacation which was crazy because he was just fucking me unprotected meanwhile while I was pregnant with his baby and he knew that before I had even went out of town to Miami I had threatened him telling him that I was going to put him on child support and he wasn't going to see his baby fucking around with me. He started going off on me whenever I would tell him how I was going to place him on child support and or not allow him to come around the baby once the baby was born which was slightly a turn on for me and sexy when he would go off on me. When we get back Home I have received a text from Jada Pickett bitch trying to be petty and make me jealous asking me if Theo had told me that he took her on a vacation I wasn't jealous I was just upset because I really loved that man and I wanted him to be my man I didn't want to share him and I didn't have time for the baggage that he already had. I also didn't want him to leave me I mean after all I was pregnant by him on top of that we had already been together for months plus married or not he was not going to leave me as a single mom we weren't even going to do that because after all he was the one who from day one wanted to fuck me without a condom.

Once again yet another relationship ruined on the account of my so called friend Kai granted I did need to know when these men were married or as much as we could find out on the background check as possible but the issue was I never asked my friend to do a background check on anyone that I was with granted I needed to be the one who did the background checks on the men that I was allowing to come over to my home where my daughter and sister also laid their heads as well but at the same time it was my call to do so on top of that some people don't like it when other people tell them things because then you end up being upset with that person for being too into your business I prefer to sometimes want to find things out on my own without the help of others so that I don't get upset with the person who was just trying to be a good person helping me. Once again I had gave kai Another man who I was dating's last name of course he had Facebook something I didn't have at all nor did I want to have at that time. When Kai did the background check and was stalking Antonio page behind my back but then again what did I really expect he had the first and last name so of course I should have known better than to think he wasn't going to go be nosey granted his Facebook page didn't say he was in a relationship and or married but that background check said he was married once again I had been as if all I could attract was a married man I was young sexy successful I had everything that I wanted except for a man all I ever wanted was a father figure for my daughter which seemed impossible I didn't know if it was because I was so into older men or what but every older man that I ever had gotten what it did me dirty I don't know I just couldn't see myself dating someone my age not saying that men my age didn't have their lives together but to be completely honest a lot of them didn't have their lives together which was why I strayed to older men majority of the older men I was with had themselves together which is what I liked and preferred I always wanted my men to be on the same level as me but I guess that wasn't helping the calls for me.

When Kai did the background check on Antonio he sent me over the long list showing that he was married he had three kids not two this man told me that he just had two daughters which I had met his daughters would feed his daughters we would have play dates together I did a lot for his children but once again another issue I started to realize I was ignoring was those red flags it was definitely a red flag when I wasn't allowed to go to his home no or see where he lived at it was a red flag when he didn't give me a key to his home yet he had a key to my home but I was ignoring stuff like that because I just wanted companionship and I loved the temporary stuff that a man could give me to keep me temporarily happy. I was already pissed off at the simple fact that Antonio had embarrassed me when I told my mother that he was going to be coming over with his two daughters for the holidays then he didn't show up at all and he excused that he used was he got a ticket for speeding then he went off on me for that alleged ticket that he claimed he had which was a fucking lie also stuff like that is public record. The thing I hated about men and their lies was they never tried hard enough to actually think of a lie that sounded right they would just say anything and go with the flow. Antonio and I were also having unprotected sex once again I still wasn't understanding why I was being so reckless when it came to having sex unprotected granted in my bedroom I actually had a sex drawer full of sex toys condoms and more.

When Antonio stood me up on Thanksgiving Day which I didn't hear from him at all I decided to text him with all the proof that I had based on that background check his record of him being married to someone by the name of Candace which I got Kai to look up her on Facebook she was alright looking. I even had decided to reach out to this Candace but just not yet I wanted to make sure I had her her correct phone number as well as email address to show Antonio was current and up-to-date so I could play mind games with him. I then had decided to text Antonio asking him if he was married and it was very funny to me how when I asked him that he replied back instantly to that and all of the screenshots that I had sent him. He then told me not to come between him and his children and then told me if I did we would have a serious problem it was already bad enough that he and I had worked on the same base but the fact that he was threatening me he didn't even know that my father used to run that base new every chief Lieutenant and officer damn near on that base hell my father was even a chief on that base before Antonio was even in the military how dare him try to threaten me the thing about working on a military base and or reporting someone who is in the military who works on a local base all you need is a first and last name and that'll definitely take you very far with filing a complaint and getting someone in so much trouble. He wasn't thinking about his children when he was bringing them to my house while he got some sex from me.

He wasn't thinking about his children when he was lying acting as if he wasn't married he even had told me that Candace and him were separated I then asked him if he knew what the word married meant because truthfully I didn't give a damn if they were legally separated separated not together not living together married is married no if ands and butts about it something else I've noticed in this generation people hate to get divorces I could never stay married to someone miserable as fuck to fake a marriage or a happy life just to say I'm married or I got married my sanity is worth more. I was just so confused on these men and why they thought that it was really OK to do as women dirty like people literally will kill you for doing them dirty I was a tourist after all I definitely had an anger problem I definitely hate it to get done dirty I was also definitely the kind of woman who would retaliate against all people who did me dirty and or wrong The thing is that people forget you cannot do people dirty and expect them not to react.

My mother had literally cooked a lot of fucking food for Thanksgiving Which I had bought and paid for that shit added up very quickly. and the way our family operated we always would put up the Christmas tree and decorate the house that we were going to be at for Thanksgiving which that year for Thanksgiving we were all at my house so my Christmas tree was already put up as well as Christmas decorations I never waited until after Thanksgiving to start putting up Christmas decorations because after all I had nothing but time and it doesn't take as much time to put up decorations or at least for me it didn't it just depended on what all you're trying to do and the person. But even when Christmas will come around the way my parents always operate it just in case we were going to be having guests and or extra children come to the house they would always have children's gifts wrapped as well as adults gifts wrapped and it would be label child or it would be labeled adult with a number on it so that was another trait I had took from my parents that I learned. So me thinking that Antonio and his daughters were going to be coming over for Thanksgiving I literally had already bought his daughter Christmas gifts which were very affordable all I did was buy Them both telescopes that I had wrapped and I was going to save for Christmas. When Antonio didn't show up and I told my mother he had got a speeding ticket and told me that we would try again the next day she then told me that that was called the domino effect and that too much was going on with him and I that day I hated to tell my mother things because she would rub things in my face especially when she knew that she was right or when she was just actually right and she would throw things up in my face I had never expected my mother to be a friend to me but all I ever wanted her to be was a mother even if I tried to talk to her about certain things she would give me the right advice sometimes but the thing I hated if you made her upset she would tell your business that's not a mother and I hated mothers who told their children's business people don't need to know everything about you and what you have going on in your household and or with your family that's where people go wrong.

I had secretly finally got into contact with Candace Antonio's wife I told her how I had bought her daughters gifts for Christmas she then told me that Antonio told her the gifts came from his mother and Antonio was initially from Philadelphia and his son who Candace told me about also lived in Philadelphia with Antonio's other baby Mama.I then had told Candace how Antonio and I had been having unprotected sex we were trying for a baby she then told me they both were having unprotected sex as well while trying for a baby and that he told her they were going to try to work on their marriage. There I was again sending yet another woman screenshots optics videos and proof after their husband having an affair I just couldn't catch a break when it came to married men. Granted I couldn't help that men will be men and lie and you can't control others or their actions the only person I could control was myself like my therapist once told me.

Even after I knew that Antonio was married to Candace and after speaking with her he was still coming back here to my house I then figured that I had him on a tight leash I even threatened to file a restraining order against him granted I eventually found a restraining order against him for domestic violence because he told me that he was going to shoot me if I came between him and his children plus he actually had guns just like I did but the issue was who was going to get to their guns first and who was going to outsmart the other person after all I was a mother and he wasn't going to take my life my child had already been missing one parent we weren't going do that. But I also knew how to keep Antonio close to me and how I could threaten him when I told him that I would follow restraining order he didn't care until I actually went online to fill out the actual restraining order paperwork for the county of clay which is where Him and I had both resided then I screenshot it and sent it to him.

He once again told me not to come between him and his children he also asked me what I wanted he didn't even realize that his wife and I had been talking I asked her not to tell him yet because I wanted to gain more proof for her to give her on top of that I did tell her how he actually had threatened me and he was still coming to my home using the key that I had once gave him to have access to my home which was dumb as hell on my part I was always moving so fast I was always catching feelings and falling in love way too fast it was more so of me being mesmerized by the sex.

When my sister Bri moved in with Leilani and I had even taken and then when their first helicopter ride also every weekend I will take the girls somewhere fun and special we would write down a list of ideas really Bri and I would of course because Leilani was only one granted I would ask Leilani where she wanted to go and write her ideas down on Pieces of papers as well we would then put all of our ideas in a box shake it up and one of us will close our eyes and pick from the box and whatever was picked from the box that's where we would go that weekend I worked very hard for my money and I also wanted to show my girls a good time to give them nothing but the world I definitely consider Bree as a daughter to me more so than sister she was very appreciative even my father had done a lot for her while she lived with Leilani and I. I just wanted to give my girls a great life so they didn't have to want or need for anything even my father had got Bri a life insurance policy that he was paying for and my mother never gave me any money for my little sister but of course I never minded paying for her. I had even needed a break from my older sister Ashley like mother like daughter I tell you she was just like her Mama was always begging for money She literally was asking me for money within the first time we started all chatting my mother Was the main person giving her money I'm not accused of the girl of lying about being our sister and our mother being her mother but we didn't do any DNA test just because you look like someone doesn't necessarily mean that you're related to them or that's your parents. My sister Ashley always asked my mother for money and my mother would literally give it to her then complain about it so I told my mother stop giving her fucking money just like that.

Ashley seemed to be all about what someone had to give her granted I was very ecstatic about having an older sister I really was she lived in North Carolina with her daughter but at the same time she was slightly starting to get annoying we were all in a group chat with her why my mother made a group chat for all of us I don't know but Ashley one time sent a picture of herself sitting on the toilet like just too much at times she was. Then she started to howl me up for money like I was her personal ATM one thing about me I always had money but I definitely did not lend out money on top of that she was trying to be money hungry she was asking if Leilani had ever gotten Social Security when her father died and stuff like girl that's none of your business that's not my money that's my child money from her father I don't lend money to people because people don't know how to pay you back the craziest thing about it all my sister Ashley literally had two jobs and she was always broke the reason she was always broke was because she had her priorities wrong she rather buy designer shoes and clothes for her and her daughter which is why she was always struggling with bills she didn't know how to manage her money I was younger than her and doing better than her but I was also used to having nice things I was used to having money nice things didn't have me and to each his own let I wasn't big on buying toddlers designer shoes and or clothes I mean they're literally going to tear it up anyways and outgrow it very quickly my child was one years old and was very tall for her age if I was six feet tall I knew for a fact my child was going to be just as tall as me she was one and taller than most one years old.

The issue that I had with my sister was she always had some type of excuse to ask me for money every time she asked me for money I always told her no because I knew she was lying you can't con a con on top of that one time she told me that her insurance company was going to drop her if she didn't pay them five hundred dollars which very much sounded like a personal problem Or they were going to drop her like get a better insurance company then on top of that she always seemed to want to ask me for money and how much did I make a year and asking how much my mortgage was or how much did I have to spare her like I was literally a single mother just like her I just didn't understand the logic of how a person with two jobs is always broke she literally worked at Verizon and she worked at Sperry'sthe shoe store and the outlet malls in North Carolina and she was living with someone and she was getting child support for her daughter After a while Bri and my mother started to get very annoyed by Ashley she was always calling and texting all throughout the day everyday. Whenever she called she was always trying to be nosey always trying to see what she could find out about bri's dad or our mom asking how our mom was when we were growing up but I was one of those people I knew the limits and I knew that there was a limit when telling people information granted she was our sister she couldn't really be trusted I didn't know her like that. Ashley was just like our mother all about what someone had to give her and money hungry. I did feel bad for my sister because we talked everyday and we were actually bonding. I wanted to meet her in person and I wanted our daughter's to meet.

The problem Ashley messed up at was when she was telling our mother way too much of her business like she told our mother that she was raped when she was a kid by a man who had aids but she didn't contract the aids because no sperm from him went inside of her and my mother accused her of lying then my mother once said that Ashley was a dike and didn't need to have any kid which I didn't agree with because anyone can have kids no matter what they are I didn't judge people or their sexualities nor did I care I didn't to each his own if it doesn't concern me or affect my life I don't care more power to you. I just didn't like how Ashley would ask about my personal finances and my child's personal finances certain things people just don't need to know about you nor should they be asking either. Other than that she was very cool and I genuinely wanted to get to know her better and even plan a trip to North Carolina. But she also didn't know that our mother was going to throw everything back up in her face.

The messed up part that made me upset with Ashley was if you didn't give her any information and or money she wanted absolutely nothing to do with you which was completely fine because I was starting to get to the point where I was sick of her lies and bullshit excuses. After all I was a single mother just like her and I actually had my shit together she always thought that someone owed her something or was obligated to do for her she wasn't the only person that had a messed up life just because our mother chose to give her away I grew up getting raped and assaulted just as she did but I wasn't walking around acting like people owed me anything I wasn't walking around asking people for anything either I was one of those I was way too proud to ask for help or ask for money or ask for anything else from people for that matter I didn't want to need people I didn't want help I never wanted depend on people either people always say that they'll be there for you and they never are meant it actually counts one time I had to tell my sister Ashley that when a person or people tell her that they're going to always be there for her it doesn't necessarily always mean financially with was where she fell short at but I guess you couldn't blame her she definitely had the traits of her mother.

I hated how she tried to always make me feel bad for her granted I did because Bri and I absolutely had the chance to grow up with our mother sometimes it was good sometimes it wasn't but at the end of the day I chose to go out there and make something of myself and I showed up differently to the world and in this world I definitely wasn't expecting anything from anyone I was always taught that whenever you want to try to complain about something there's always someone out there that's going through something ten times worse than you are with is absolutely true I just tried to make the best of life that I possibly could it just so happened that when my child father died I had to work ten times harder faster and better not for me not for him but for our daughter who deserved better especially for the simple fact that she no longer had a father.

After a while of living in middleburg once again I then remind myself that I needed to get with a white man and leave black men alone dating wise most people would say that I was generalizing but I really didn't care every man that I ever had got with was always on my level especially financially so I couldn't feel like they were trying to use me for money.

When I get towards the end of Antonio and I being over that's when a pandemic had first came out in February of twenty twenty one day I went to Walmart at about three in the morning that's when I was going there to get milk, pull-ups, Toiletries, and wine. Thank God when I went to Walmart at that time of the morning they surprisingly were not packed which was a great thing because when the pandemic had came out everything was always packed and everything was always sold out. So when I left home the girls were already sleeping and my mother was also home with them. I didn't really want to take the girls out no matter what time of the day I was going to any store because the pandemic was fresh out and I didn't want them to get sick or anything. I was literally dress down because who was actually going to dress up to go to the store at three in the morning? That's when I noticed this white guy staring at me I didn't think anything of it however I hate it when people stared and didn't speak after a while I start to notice that the white guy was on every al that I was on staring at me I thought that shit was weird as hell. After I go to self checkout to pay for everything when I make it to the parking lot the white man was already outside loading up everything that he had going in his truck which he had a lot of stuff he then notices me putting everything in the trunk of my car and decides to come over to me I try to hurry up and throw everything in my car and get in the car before he got to me but I was too slow I didn't even have my gun in the car with me. When the white man finally comes over to me he said excuse me and I said yes how can I help you he asked if he could get my number. For some reason I went ahead and gave him my number I mean granted I had just gotten out of a really terrible relationship and I told myself that I wasn't going to date anymore or give another man the time of the day for a while. yet there I was again not listening to myself I mean after all he was really fine he was tall, white, had a dad body and

You never know until you try I had gave him my number and I asked him what his name was he told me that his name was Chris and he ask what my name was I told him my name was Brittany he shook my hand saying nice to meet you and I said same to you then he told me he would call me and I said ok cool I get in my car and he closes the door for me.

When I was on my way home I was listening to some nineties R&B music I was very much in my feelings that's when I received a phone call from Chris in my mind I'm like damn it but I decided to answer we talked all the way until I had gotten home I said in my mind so much for vibe into the music while driving I definitely had a lot to think about at that time frame when I had met him I had just gotten into some trouble in my life for the first time with the law A few days before meeting Chris so I was currently on bond little did he know which I wasn't going to tell him because it wasn't his business I was also very much embarrassed to say that I had gone to jail for one hour then I got bonded out I paid for it. The thing that was upsetting was how sometimes telling the truth actually in fact doesn't set you free that saying can be a lie. Literally this man had road rage in middleburg which is predominantly white people and rednecks but I generally liked living in middleburg it was better than living in Jacksonville in the hood or in the hood anywhere else for that matter Clay County had the best school systems. Some white man had really bad road rage when the girls and I were going to our Walmart up the street from where we lived he kept zigzagging between me and another car beeping the horn acting as if he was going to run into the back of us slamming on his brakes swerving behind us doing the absolute most there's nothing worse than short men which eventually I found out he was short short men driving those huge trucks typically the ones that were to do that were the ones that have small dicks. I noticed he had all his windows down so as he was doing all of that when we get to the red light and the left turning lane I rolled my windows down with my head sticking out yelling and cussing at him after all I mean I had kids in the car he almost ran me into a ditch I already had anxiety so something about people trying to rush me or make me hurry up and move faster killed my anxiety. Like I hate people that act like they're in such a rush like you should have left home earlier but don't be out here doing the absolute most and I told him I had a gun because before even making it to the red light he was literally following me when I would get over in a lane he would get over in a lane because every time he would get so close behind me I would break check him I also had children in the car little did he know my windows were tinted. I then had told him that I had a gun and I was going to use it if he didn't stop following me it's not a crime in the state of Florida to tell someone that you have a gun especially when you are licensed to carry I don't even think that was a crime to tell someone in any state that you had a gun especially when you're licensed to carry. At the red light for some reason I decided to getout of the vehicle I always had an anger problem but I was one of those people it took a lot to get me to the point of being angry to see that bad side of me but the thing was I was the nicest sweetest woman ever until you push me to a certain limit which we all have a limit before we snap on someone. I got out of my car talking so much trash to this man cussing at him yelling at him everything but when I told him I had a gun he tried to tell me that to show him my gun like he must have thought I was stupid. He told me he had a gun so had I pulled out mine that then would have been considered a threat then he would have tried to shoot me or maybe even shot me again I had kids in the car so when I just decided to go back in my car and forget all about it and drive off like nothing even happened little did I know that he was going to the sub police station that was near and that man went in there and so like a Canary a bunch of lies I didn't think to go to the police station but I didn't think his snitch ass was going to do that after all he was the one that caused the incident in the place. I have found out that he went to the police station the Sunday two days after the incident happened when I get a knock on my door I typically didn't open my door unless I was expecting a package and or company which I didn't get a lot of company but I hate it when people didn't ring the doorbell it there was literally a ADT doorbell with a camera that's right in front of you I never understood how people missed that. But when I go to open my front door it was the police two of them at that are already knew what they were there for I was never a troublemaker But the cops had asked me what happened on Sunday I then Told them that I didn't know what they were talking about. It was crazy because that same day when the incident happened after I decided to leave the man alone I had actually went to Walmart with the girls and we have returned home when we did return home my father called me saying that the police was at his house because my car tag was registered in my father's name and his address not mine But the first thing he assumed was that I used the gun even though he actually didn't even know the story telling me that if I pulled out my gun or used it on someone that I was going to be in big trouble and I'm like you're accusing me of something before you even know the story great job dad is what I told him. Then the cops asked me if I had any guns I told them yes I was licensed to carry I didn't tell them about all the guns I had I just told them that I had a nine millimeter which that was my favorite gun that I like to use at that time.

CHAPTER

11

They then asked me if I ever pointed my gun at anyone I said no I didn't and had it ever have to come down to that moment I probably would have actually used the gun after all why pointed at someone or pull it out if you're not going to use it. They then asked about the situation that occurred at the red light which was near the police station and Walmart. They then wanted me to start writing a statement about what happened which was completely fine I mean I told the truth there was absolutely nothing to lie about at the end of the day they were going to do what they wanted to do I already knew there was nothing I could do except get a lawyer and tell my father what occurred which sucked one thing about my father when it came to doing things especially things that were bad or getting caught up in stuff anytime my father had to help me out he'd always bring it up he was one of those people no matter how old something was he would never let you forget about it and I hated that sometimes it's best to just let the past be in the past you don't always have to remind people of when they messed up or when they've done wrong in their lives I was one of those people I hated when people kept bringing up certain things especially bad things that occurred. I then asked the cop why was there two people for one woman I said all black people aren't criminals I say you hear a black woman that's the age of twenty one has a gun and it seems as if you're scared concerned or bothered by that as if it's a crime to have a gun at least I'm a licensed gun owner he then said he wasn't scared or concerned he just wants it to be safe then he started asking me all these damn questions asking whose home was it that we were living in I said my home I own this home I bought this home he then started asking what kind of work I did I then told him I have a government security clearance that I'm not trying to lose behind a man that's lying on me and I told him I had some other sources of income which I did but not from working. They were legal sources of incomes I then told him he tried to slightly play me I said you see a twenty one years old and all white neighborhood with a nice house and it couldn't be mine I said all you had to do was go on Google and Google would have told you that when you typed my first and last name I told him hell even putting in the address it shows that I'm the current homeowner and I've been here since Halloween twenty nineteen said but thank you for trying to play me I said no offense taken feels nice being young and successful though.

I wasn't at all concerned because after all my father was higher up career wise than the police was so we knew everyone judges lawyers so I wasn't concerned I just didn't want to go to jail whether it's for a day or hour a few days who wants to go to a dirty nasty ass jail? Especially behind some men that lied on me that white man definitely lied on me the man told me that the white guy had told him I pulled my gun out at him I'm like are you crazy I've been asked the cop don't you think there would have been multiple white people at the police station I said the police station was literally next to the left light so how could I possibly have done that there's also cameras on the lights I told him I don't have to lie because it's not that serious one thing about me whether I was in the right or wrong one thing about it though I'll tell you when I did something proudly and pridefully I never had to lie about anything there was literally cameras on the top of the light I told the cop to make sure he checked the cameras he claimed they didn't work I said I bet they don't I said anything to lock up and put up a black person huh I then told the cop one thing about it I have money so I'm prepared for anything and like the dollar bill says in God we trust.

The cop then asked me if I could show him the nine millimeter I told him I sure can I went upstairs to my safe to get it I told him I would be right back because I don't like people walking in my house with their shoes on from outside the outside is this gusting people spit on the ground and shit on the ground and there's dirt and mud outside I don't like that being trapped in my house after all I had OCD again. When I went into my bedroom I grabbed the safe and put it on my bed with the door open so that they could hear it or the you upstairs or downstairs everything always seemed to echo in my house I wanted them to hear me punching in the code to the safe when I grabbed the gun I put it in the gun case so they didn't try to shoot me or feel anymore threatened anymore than they already did.

When I walked downstairs I give them the gun case and told them they could open it because they were not about to shoot me won't get me he then asked who was all home with me I said damn no one I said y'all asked little too many questions then the cop asked me about the CIA which I did tell the man my dad works for the CIA which was true at the time he did. The only reason the cop had knew about that was because I told the guy that if we had any problems I could just call my father the CIA is above the police that's why I wasn't concerned I just knew that once I told my dad more about the story he was definitely going to be pissed because he was definitely going to need some assistance getting his young black daughter out of trouble plus at that time in twenty twenty. That's when the police brutality was starting to get out of control with black people mainly black men They were shooting and killing our black men left and right like dogs. Once again I was having a downfall on the account of a man a man was always my downfall in my life And this man I wasn't even dating didn't even know this man from a can of paint didn't even know the man lived in my neighborhood with his wife and children but I was soon enough going to find that out. Once I had finished writing my statement the male cop who was doing all the talking and the question asking took the statement and read it then told me I might want to add more in there I then told him I wasn't worried or concerned that was my truth I don't have to lie and I don't lie he then asked if he could talk to my sister and I told him no he couldn't she was a minor and he wasn't doing anymore talking to us until I got a lawyer I said it in the nicest way I could possibly say it I know at times when I talk and speak proper and use my big vocabulary words it could seem as if I was coming off as a bitch but unfortunately that was just my personality a strong minded bitch.

The cops took my statement And I walked them both to the door when they left I went into my kitchen to get a few shots of liquor how was stressed out I was scared I was panicking and I actually knew I had to tell my father the truth even though I really didn't do anything wrong this was a prime example of why you had to control your anger because you get into situations like this that are very messed up and unfortunate in fact when I attended the concealed weapons class which was four hours long at this gun range up the street from where my father lived the man literally told us all in the classroom a similar situation to mine but in the scenario that he used it was an altercation between two men the one man who had the gun who attended the concealed weapons license class at the gun range actually had a gun but the guy he was getting into the verbal altercation with had absolutely no idea he had a gun so when he called the police to tell the police he had a gun when the police came he actually really did have a gun and they hauled him away and took him to jail even though he was licensed to carry lying actually ruins peoples lives and I was so pissed off at how the man tried to ruin my life and lied it's one thing to actually tell a story but there's always two sides to a story and my story was the simple fact that I was actually being lied on by a white man who lived in the same neighborhood as me that's the thing with some people they're shit talkers and their problem starters then when they get those reactions they're scared. He wasn't scared when he was trying to tell me to show him my gun Which he must have thought I was a damn fool.

I cried as I called my cousin Dhoping that she would answer the phone her and I were very close we told each other everything that was the only cousin that I trusted other than her sister who I can tell a lot of my personal business to and knew that they wouldn't repeat what I told them out of all my female cousins in Alabama her and her sister were the only two that I trusted with personal information. I had told her what happened and she told me to go ahead and call my dad I told her I couldn't I was so scared but she was right if I was going to get some help I mean you can't do everything in life by yourself you actually do need help and in that scenario I really did need the help of my father because he had the power and ability to Get Me Out of what I had gotten myself in just because I had an anger problem granted it was the man's fault looking back at that situation it was very silly and I should have just drove off or drove into the police station and I guaranteed he probably would have actually left me alone or even parked at the police station and went inside to report him like he reported me it's one thing to report someone and be honest but it's one thing to report someone in lie lying ruins peoples lives him lying costed thousands of dollars to get out of trouble. In the state of Florida reporting someone who actually did have a gun wasn't a crime but telling the police that that person you reported actually pulled out their gun on you is ten years licensed or not especially when they didn't even use the gun but I never pulled the gun out on him.

When I got off the phone with D I went ahead and made the phone call to my father try not to sound like I had been crying and I told him the whole situation and I asked him for his help I wanted to have everything prepared and needed before it was time For me to go to jail. Money put aside bills paid up for a few months my mortgage paid up for a few months and a great lawyer not just any lawyer but one of the best lawyers in Jacksonville

FL because I didn't know what was going to happen and I was one of those people I always liked to be prepared you always have to be prepared for the unexpected. I told my dad everything that I did and I told him the honest truth and he told me that he would take care of everything he even asked me what was the name of the police who had came to visit me and I told him the name he said he would call the Sheriff's Office and talk to the police. Later that day when my father called me back he told me that he got in contact with the cop and he said that the cop told him that he wasn't going to pin a felony on me or write up the report the way the man came in there exaggerating because the cop also said he already knew the man was exaggerating he just wanted to talk to me first to see what I had to say about the situation to just make sure that it didn't actually happen because he said things like that happen all the time people piss people off and then they want to come running to the police station lying on a person to ruin their life. My dad told me that he told the cop that he really appreciated him and weeks later the cop had called me telling me that I did have to go to jail but only for one hour but before he said go to jail for one hour I was like are you serious I didn't do anything. He then told me that either he could pick me up or I could turn myself in I told him I would turn myself in my daughter and my sister didn't need to see me like that or anyone else in my neighborhood that's embarrassing He then told me that my bomb would be twenty five hundred you only pay ten percent of that so two hundred and fifty was what it was going to cost for me to get out.

I had called my cousin Daizhato tell her that I had to turn myself into the police station and she asked me why would I turn myself in I said well it's either he comes here to pick me up like he just told me or I have to turn myself in I don't want my daughter and my sister to see me in handcuffs granted my daughter was only a toddler and she wouldn't remember that but hell I'm going to remember that. that would really break my heart So I then told D that I would call her back and I called Kai I didn't know why because he was so messy no matter how much he did for me it would never make me feel better because I did things for him in return and he would talk too much people don't need to know everything about you people don't want everyone in their business knowing everything about them. But I needed someone to bail me out of jail I couldn't bail myself out I didn't know anything about jail or the laws and rules just because I work for the government because I had never been in trouble in my life before at least not by the law. When I called Kai asking him if he could come pick me up he already knew about the situation but it was crazy how no one was believing my side of the story he told his family his husband everyone kept saying that I was pointing a gun so I then had to prove my innocence to everyone else even though it wasn't really their business or place when Kyle came to pick me up he kept telling me I told you not to move out here with these white people I'm like y'all keep saying that like that's the thing they want us to be boxed in and one location all of Jacksonville wasn't bad even in the hood they had nice houses it was just the area the people made the area bad My black people made the area bad I'm like there's so many cities to live in in Florida and y'all always want to be boxed in and up underneath each other it's not necessary like it's ok to spread out you don't have to be that close to people. Jacksonville was nice and all but the same people complaining that there's nothing to do in Jacksonville were also the same ones who weren't trying to do anything with their lives especially get out of Jacksonville so where did you expect change is always good bless when I was pregnant with Leilani I always said that when I can get an opportunity to move far away from Jacksonville which middleburg wasn't that far but I was going to take the opportunity I wanted a fresh start in life I wanted to move somewhere where no one knew us and we didn't know anyone and Middleburg was perfect plus I wanted to be more closer to my dad.

When Kai had picked me up I asked him if he could stop by a gas station I had to get me a mikes hard and a blackened out to smoke if I was going to be sitting in jail for an hour might as well be tipsy with a head high. What pissed me off about him was the simple fact that he literally called his whole family to tell them he was taking me to jail and then everyone was asking me what was going on with me why was I acting crazy and all this other stuff he talked too much that's not a friend I didn't tell my friends businesses because I really didn't care it didn't concern me and even if it did that's between you and whoever you have to answer to. One time my dad even made a joke saying that when black people come up in life and moved to nicer areas that's when they start getting in trouble I then told my dad we've never struggled a day in our life so I don't even know why he brought up that scenario we've always lived in nice houses especially with my mother she's had some over the top houses nicer than my father's but the thing with him he had money but he didn't have to prove to people that he had money my father would literally laugh at people if they had to put too much money down for a house and or vehicle or if there were over paying for something because he would say I would rather brag that I have money then to brag about how much money I had to spend on something when it wasn't necessary and it was too much to pay in the first place my father was always a logical thinker I'm glad I actually obtained that trait from my father when it comes to money it's always a good thing to be a logical thinker whether you have money or not that's where a lot of these celebrities go wrong they spend because they have they don't care how much stuff costs because they have money which sometimes is not always a good thing.

The more and more I started thinking on the ride to green Cove springs jail in my mind I told myself I had to stop being friends with Kai because I couldn't deal with all that messiness and drama he had going on him and his husband were so miserable and it's like they could talk shit about everyone else but themselves after all Kai's Husband was gay and embarrassed to say at work he was gay because he was a CDL truck driver and he worked with a bunch of straight men who were hosed so he didn't want the guys to know that he was gay because he figured that they would treat him differently which I'd most definitely agreed with him on that I'll never get over the time when he asked me if I could be his wife add a event for his job because whenever he would tell his coworkers he was married he would always say a woman name not a man's name and in my mind I never said anything to them but I just thought to myself he's gay but he's embarrassed to be gay if you have to do all of that you might as well not even be gay but to each his own more power to him see how miserable they were and a lie they were living and they had their nerve to tell everyone else his business the thing was too I also told them way too much in my personal business because every time Kai's husband Jamal would get upset with him he would literally tell Their business I will never ever ever forget the time when I got called to defuse an argument they were having they were throwing glass throwing tables furniture everything at each other Kaiser mother was already there but they called me over as well plus I had to bring them some milk anyways since I was already at the store so I didn't mind.

But when I got to their house for some apparent reason chis husband literally told me that they had HIV something I had never even knew about ever he knew about and I had known them for years not that they had to tell me I mean if I had something like that I would definitely tell no one because people don't have all the knowledge on it so they look at you and treat you differently which was exactly how I was treating them but I was just so shocked and surprised it was even worse because they had asked me if I could be their surrogate so you guys were going to have your sperm be put in me and you have HIV that's something that you have to disclose to people I don't want that it just amazed me how they talk so much trash about everyone around them but they themselves were the true miserable people it made sense to me after a while one time Jamal even told me that guy called me a hoe not that I cared I don't think that dating around and getting to know men makes you a hoe it's not about how other people look at it it's about how you yourself look at it and see it I didn't care what people thought about me nor do I now because it's not about how other people look at you as how you look and viewed yourself and if you believe that that's true what they're saying about you. I just thought it was amazing how Kai would sit up and tell everyone business as if he was so perfect himself when they were both living a lie. The messed up part about it when they asked me to be their surrogate they were only going to pay me eight hundred dollars like what the hell is eight hundred dollars. There's literally surrogates that make thousands and thousands of dollars I was so glad I didn't do that I definitely wasn't doing it especially after I found out that they had HIV.

The whole family on Kai side was attacking me literally everyone was on the phone it amazed me that he was telling all my business when I knew what I knew about him but unfortunately I wasn't like them I didn't tell people business because I really didn't care like I always tell people listen I have my own problems I can't always help you with yours. I remember Tia who was one of Kai's cousins Asked me what was going on with me she told me first I killed the dog which I didn't find that funny at al In February of 2020 when I had to go to court with Antonio because I had found a restraining order against him because he threatened to shoot me and kill me if I open my mouth to his wife little to he knows she already knew every detail had all proof screenshots messages and more between him and I. plus I also found that restraining order out of spite I was tired of men thinking that they were going to do me dirty especially the married ones like you're having sex with me raw you're trying to get me pregnant and come to find out you're married like how is that going to work for us I was so tired of men doing me dirty that it made me file a domestic violence restraining order against Antonio. Like I loved him I had strong feelings for him and to think that he was just going to leave me and ride off into the sunset with his wife the same wife he was trying to get pregnant the same time as me and also having unprotected sex with then coming back to my house to have unprotected sex with me as if sexually transmitted diseases weren't a thing he must have been out of his mind they weren't going to ride off into the sunset together happily while I'm sitting back in the corner miserable that was a no go for me I also told myself for every man that I get with it does me wrong there's always going to be consequences that come back onto them unfortunately for me I couldn't wait for karma to get them I believed in karma definitely but karma sometimes took too long for me.

Even when I used to play with Antonio telling him that I was going to file the injunction knowingly knowing that I had already filed the injunction he just hadn't been served yet because that's when COVID-19 had first came out the pandemic. I would play mind games with him he would ask me and beg me to come over and asking what did I want from him he just didn't want to lose his kids and or get kicked out of the military I also had soon enough found out that my father knew his superiors. So I would play mind games with Antonio telling him that if he didn't come have sex with me or come stay the night with me or if we didn't go out on a date or do things that I want to do I was going to file the restraining order once she fell out a restraining order at the courthouse she can only go to the courthouse to file the restraining order and fill out the paperwork then they submitted up to the judge and the same day that you go to fill out the paperwork for the restraining order you have to call back after three in the afternoon to see if the restraining order was granted, denied, denied and mailed to you. If it was granted you would have to wait for the respondent to be served with the restraining order then the police normally call you to let you know that the respondent had been served at their job or home or whatever because when you fill out the restraining order it asks you where do they work at you have to put the address you have to put their cell number in or home or work number you have to put all types of information that you know about them their birthday what kind of vehicle they drive. It asked how did they look eye color, hair color, height, weight, Age and more. It was just so nice having that type of control and power over a man for once plus he was all scared even though I actually did father straining order Oh well he was still coming over we were having sex and everything I even wanted to set him up but the thing was I couldn't set him up calling the police to say he violated the restraining order because he hadn't been served yet because I had already asked. For me it was the fact that I had just wanted to be loved unconditionally and actually not being done dirty all these married men that I kept getting involved with really start making me sad and depressed it made me feel as if that was all I could attract and it made me feel like I was cursed for being with Leilani's dad a man who was married granted his wife had never lived in a house he bought and she didn't live in a state of Florida at all but it was just simple fact that he still had that married title. I had even gotten a attorney for the restraining order for court to represent me. I always would keep money in my safe a few thousands as well as birth certificates passports Social Security cards and more.

We had a really bad storm a few days before Antonio was served the injunction by the police of Clay County of course he was at home with his wife and I remember Kai would tell me to say certain things to Antonio to see if he would come over or how he would react I tried everything that Kai told me to do why I didn't know because his own marriage was on this last leg on top of that the advice that he would give people was just over the top and too much he was too much himself.

Antonio literally tried to extort me from money the crazy part about it all I should have been extorting him for money but after all he was living with his wife one time she told me that when I told her that I was way younger than them they were both the same age in their early 30s and I told her how I had a house and this and that and she got offended I guess because I was bragging a little too much for her talking about how she had a house as well but What was most funny about it all Candace claimed to have owned a house however when you're a homeowner or own a piece of property your name pops up it's public record And there was no record at all for Candace or Antonio that either one of them own property or home all I had was all there addresses in the past and the current address that I had for her was an oak leaf which wasn't too far from me at all. It never said that she owned the house normally it tells you if a person owns or rents and how long they have been at that address maybe she was just jealous that I was younger than them doing better than them again to each his own we can all do better. I even would let Antonio and his daughters come to my home and eat up my food and snacks and not say absolutely anything at all.

But I had asked Antonio the night of the storm we had if he could come over I told him I was scared and our power was out he then told me that his power was off as well I was like oh wow the crazy thing is about it I really allowed this man to extort me for money when I was the one that actually had found an injunction against him I literally gave this man twelve hundred dollars cash out of my safe What the hell was I thinking? This married ass man giving him my money my hard earned money money from my save that I had saved up and always put aside for rainy days. When he was served a Clay County sheriff had called me to let me know that Antonio had been served the injunction and I told him thank you for letting me know they always let you know the person has been served I then get a attorney she was said to be one of the best in Clay County when it comes to defending the petitioner who was me against the respondent who was Antonio for an injunction. I have met up with my attorney in person showed her all the proof and text messages that I had of him still messaging me even after he was served that injunction with his phone number which was the same phone number that I had provided on the paperwork when I was filling out the paperwork to file the injunction. On the injunction and even asked if the respondent had any weapons which Antonio really did have guns not sure if he was licensed to carry or not but I did over exaggerate I put that he had an Uzi That he kept underneath his driver seat and a 9 millimeter that he kept underneath his passenger seat I didn't even care that he had kids because at the end of the day I brought this man around my daughter and my sister he literally was telling me lies telling them lies one time we had a really bad one time we had a really bad breakup argument and I lied to him telling him that I was cheating on him anyways because he was talking so much trash and it was actually hurting my feelings and then my dumb ass went back to him crying and begging getting my little sister involved texting him from her phone like it was too much. I was mad at myself more than I was before for allowing him to treat me like that but also giving him money giving him a key to my home allowing him around my girls my sister watching me be treated like that and depressed over a man I had given Antonio all that money and I was still out of a man. I had even told Candace that I gave him $1200 with the screenshot that I sent her of him telling me to send a picture of the money with my face in the picture and more and she told me that she would get the money back even though she didn't then again she worked at a hospital not like she was a doctor or a nurse.

The day where Antonio and I had to both go to court Leilani was in daycare and Bree was at school court was early that morning I was rushing to get out the house granted I was closer To the green Cove springs courthouse then Antonio was but I was running behind and the dog snickers we had at the time I used to keep her in and the dog Snickers we had at the time I used to keep her in a cage a kennel inside the house where the fireplace area was in the living room until she kept getting out of the kennel pooping and peeing everywhere and I couldn't have that we had just moved into home Halloween of twenty nineteen is only February of twenty twenty. I didn't want my house being destroyed especially not by a dog we weren't even in the house that long. So I would keep her in the kennel in the garage she would have food and water in there which from time to time she would also get out of the kennel it wasn't my fault at all she's the one that kept breaking out. I was running so late and rushing I didn't even see that she had partially gotten out of the kennel in the garage from time to time she would get out and we would notice she was out and I would turn back around and go back home or she would try to run out through the car and I would have to open the garage and put her back in there. This one particular day I had no idea that that would be the last day I saw Snickers but I was rushing to get to court I was blasting my Cardi B songs trying to get hyped up because I was absolutely nervous I had never been to court before for fouling an injunction against someone I had really never even been to court before. When I got there in the parking lot at the courthouse Antonio was already there he had a black Lexus that had Philadelphia plates and he was in love with the Eagles because he was from Philly so he had a whole bunch of Eagles car magnets on the back of his car.

I gather my Chanel bag with all the folders I had with all the screenshots from him messaging me before and after he was served the injunction by the sheriff. I was definitely feeling myself that day I was a bad bitch one thing about it I always dress my ass off. I had on a blue dress that was kind of short on me because I was six feet tall after all and I had on black high heels I had a Black Chanel bag. When I walked into the courthouse I had to go through a metal detector that's first before you can even go to the elevators or any of the court Rooms. When I was cleared through the metal detector I had asked one of the police officers if I could be escorted to the courtroom that I had to go to for a injunction I then told them that the respondent was going to be walking in the door soon I had saw him outside looking at me which made me very nervous and scared for my life which I wasn't really scared for my life but I was nervous I knew he wasn't going to be able to do anything after all we were in a courthouse there were police officers And we were in Clay County the Clay County police officers don't play at least in Clay County when you call the police officers they show up unlike Jacksonville they take forever. But there were police officers everywhere what could you possibly do?

The police officer escorts me upstairs which we had to get on the elevator to get to the second floor as we're on the elevator together he asked me if I was ok and I told him no he then told me it's pretty as I am he's sure every-thing will workout for me and that I was too pretty to be with the guy who I had filed the injunction against I then smiled telling him thank you you have no idea when we get off the elevator he asked me if I still needed him or if I was ok I told him I was ok and thank you for escorting me. For some reason I actually thought that a police officer stayed with you the whole time but I mean he did ask me after all and I told him no so I guess not. When I stand outside the courtroom I noticed there was others waiting to go into the same courtroom that I was I was also waiting for my attorney to get there I received a text on my phone when I looked at my phone which I had made sure I put on silent it was a text from my lawyers saying she was running a few minutes late but she was almost there I responded back to her saying OK and thank you for the update. After a few minutes I notice Antonio in his military uniform and people telling him thank you for his service I'm like that nigga didn't do Shit nor was he shit. He barely was even at work half of the times we used to leave work early together a lot of times he wasn't Shit And had the nerve to be walking around in a uniform like he's God.

On top of that he had his two daughters with him I said look at that nigga there. One of his daughters ran up to me to give me a hug and she asked me what was I doing there he then yelled at her telling her to get over there with him and don't come back by me again. He was so dumb like you're not even allowed to bring children into the courtroom unless you're going to children and family court and even then sometimes typically you don't bring your children to court. He was probably scared that he would go to jail or get in some serious trouble which was why he brought his daughters to court with him I noticed though he always had his daughters because Candace worked at the hospital and her hours were all over the place. I one time had told him that I hoped his daughters never meet a man like him when they get older because he was a piece of shit and he wasn't worth shit and he wasn't going to be shit and then I had told him that's why his baby Mama and Philadelphia keeps their son away from him because he wasn't shit. which he wasn't you can't do people dirty and expect to get rewarded for it that's not how the world works. I could have easily started talking about his daughters but they had absolutely nothing to do with what their father and I had going on nor was that right to do either kids shouldn't be punished for the sins of their parents and or parents that's not right plus I wouldn't want anyone talking about my girls because I would have gone postal on them.

My attorney she finally arrives thank God that's when I stopped feeling nervous and scared for a moment she was said to have been one of the best injunction attorneys around that was all she really dealt with as far as court cases was injunctions it was also hard finding a lawyer who could represent me for the injunctions one lawyer even told me that a lot of attorneys don't like taking injunction cases because they're a pain in the ass I noticed they also charge quite a bit of money for cases But I had money and I wanted to get the man who had done me dirty one thing about me when I got pissed off I was going to get through every person to get to the motherfucker that did me wrong and dirty and when I got pissed off it took so much to me calm down. When it was time for everyone to go into the courtroom there was a lot of people waiting outside of the courtroom like us for injunctions. A guy had came into the hallway and told everyone who was therefore injunctions to gather around as he started calling our names to go into the courtroom I heard my name being called so my attorney and I walked into the courtroom then when he called Antonio's name he walked up with his children and the man told him that he's not allowed to have the children in the courtroom which is what I figured in new especially when it comes to it restraining order that's common sense so he had to make his daughters wait in the hallway I could never and told them to stay there and not to move or talk to anyone we literally waited so long until our names were being called and it was so crazy because granted he did really threaten me but I also mainly found the injunction out of spite there were actually people in there women that had bruises on their faces and we're pretty beaten up badly and men who had tried to run their ex girlfriends off the road or broke into their homes and stuff I'm like there's actually people in here with worser problems than what I had going on with him even though he did say he was going to shoot me and he actually was a gun owner from what he showed me when he stood in my house one day with his gun telling me that he was going to shoot me that's a number for me and I had the video footage of him telling me that on the ADT camera in my living room on the wall pointing at us the thing about the camera Was that it didn't always record with the blue light flashing and the camera didn't record all day either if you wanted the camera to record something you actually had to go into the ADT app and click on the button that says record then when the clip was done it was saved in your actual photo album or your phone as well as the ADT app but the camera didn't record footage for too long Plus when he threatened me and had the gun in his hand I want revenge illegally on him but I already had a pending court case little did he know.

Listening to others injunction cases made me very sad to know that there's so many women out there that really get physically, mentally, verbally abused by men they had all the respondents sitting on the left hand side of the courtroom and all the petition or sitting on the right hand side of the courtroom the petitioners are the ones who fouled the injunctions and the respondents are the ones who had the injunction placed against them. The girl who was sitting beside me was whispering to me and told me to not talk loudly as she whispered to me because there was cameras in the room and and the room the cameras reported everything. She then asked me if I had any gum which you're not supposed to eat or drink in the courtroom either I did have gum so I went into my purse grabbed her a piece and passed it to her with my hand on the ground almost so I didn't get caught. She then whispered thank you and I said you're welcome We talked for a bit while we waited for the judge to come into the courtroom he was definitely running behind and taking forever at that I noticed the girl had bruises on her face well you could tell she got beaten up pretty bad she even had a black eye and the messed up part about her case she told me that her boyfriend didn't even show the court three times in a row nor was he there that day so typically whenever the respondent and or the petitioner doesn't show up to court they restraining order automatically gets dropped and you have to start all over again go back to the courthouse found the paperwork again wait for it get granted again. If the sheriff's cannot locate the respondent so serve them the papers then the temporary restraining order that's in place until you go to court to get an extended one it's automatically dropped as well. I had whispered to the girl whose name was Shay telling her that I was nervous I was even cold and shaking she then grabbed my hand telling me that it was going to be ok and I had told her thank you.

When the judge finally had came into the courtroom we all had to stand up and then sit down we were told to. Listening to some of the other stories it was hard not to laugh at certain details because you could automatically tell which person was just being very overdramatic and the judge looked like he wasn't impressed by anyone's story at all hell he looked like he didn't even want to be there. Antonio and I were the fifth people to be caught up I noticed every time the respondent in petitioner recalled up to stand at the podium's the police officer would hand each party the restraining order paperwork do's and don'ts and allow one person at a time to be dismissed then wait a while then release the next person to be dismissed to leave. When it is finally Antonio and I getting caught up to stand at the podiums on opposite sides of the room my attorney walks up with me which Antonio didn't know I had he was probably like damn this bitch got money she actually got a lawyer that quick. I sure did it's always better to be prepared than unprepared plus I couldn't help but think what if he himself also got a lawyer just because people look like they're uneducated doesn't always mean they are sometimes the people that you think aren't that educated are the ones that surprised you every time.

My attorney pretty much did all the talking for me after all I was paying her Three thousand dollars to be there for a case that was just for a day. The judge had read what I said as to why I wanted to file the restraining order anytime you're filing a restraining order on the paperwork it always asks you why are you filing a restraining order and you then put all the details and everything that the person has said and done to you with the dates as well to help you with your case to be one less thing to have to explain when you go to court plus judging by whatever you put down as to why you want to file the restraining order that would then determine if the judge himself or herself was going to grant the restraining order or not so you had to put a good enough reason as to why you were filing the injunction. The judge read everything that I put on the paper Stating why I wanted to foul the injunction I definitely over exaggerates it a bit but Oh well all I ever wanted was to be loved and I was tired of getting done dirty and being treated like crap I had everything in life in a nice life and the simple fact that it was that hard for me to find a good decent man was crazy. But it took the life of me not to laugh will the judge was reading everything and the way he was reading everything he definitely didn't want to be there. As I look over at Antonio from the side of my eyes I see him looking mad and his head.

The judge then asked me if everything that I said in my statement was accurate and true I then said your honor. He then asked Antonio if everything in my statement was accurate and true and Antonio said no he was so damn stupid you're supposed to say no your honor or yes your honor. The judge then asked Antonio what was a lie he said all of it was a lie granted I did lie a lot in the statement but I mean again you definitely have to put enough detailed information as to why you want to file the restraining order because the judge is the one who makes the decision whether they want to grant it or not he actually did have the gun in my house threatened in me little did he know I actually had that proof which I also had given my attorney the video and I also had the video on my phone so Bing bong. The judge then asked me if I had any more proof or screenshots I then told him yes your honor My attorney then said your honor my client Has in fact proof in a video of Mr Villanueva threatening to shoot her in her living room in the home which she owns her ADT camera in her living room recorded the whole thing and my client does have her cell phone with that video if you like to see it your honor.My lawyer also said your honor we also have numerous amounts of screenshots from Mr Villanueva messaging my client before and after the restraining order was granted my client has all screenshots and her folder we'd like to present to you and the judge said granted for both then the sheriff comes over I can't him my cell phone with the video already popped up as well as the folder with all those messages.

The judge then looks at the video not impressed which he was looking the whole time in court towards everyone which was funny as hell I tried my hardest not to laugh like he just had just gotten over a hangover or something. The judge then looks at Antonio and says to him this is you right here in this video it looks like you to me with a gun in your hand but you told me that you didn't do it so you already messed By choosing to not be honest in court after you and miss brown Jackson had both raised your right hand Stating to be truthful well in a court of law. The judge then says he wanted to hear the volume he then asked me how does he adjusts the volume because it wasn't turning up when he was clicking on the side of the phone I then told him on the video if you tap the screen once there's a microphone once you click that it'll have volume to it the judge then did what I told him to we could all slightly hear commotion in the video of Antonio saying how if I came between him and his children that we would have a serious problem and he was going to have to take matters into his own hands while holding his gun. The judge looks at Antonio telling him that he seemed like a hot head and he was already proven to be a liar and lied under-oath once in the courtroom. Then the judge starts reading some of the screenshots from the folder out loud the ones that had Antonio's phone number on it he had read the screenshot out loud of Antonio trying to extort me for money if I made the restraining order go away and more the judge then looked very appalled. Even before we had went to court I had to stop having communication with the wife because since she knew

Antonio technically illegally she was a third party and you're not allowed to talk to third party people that have anything to do with the person you're filing the injunction against and vice versa.

My attorney also told the judge that Antonio's wife had also been contacting me while the restraining order was granted and before it was granted. The judge then decided to grant and extend the restraining order for six months I then told him thank you your honor I also said that I wanted my house key back and my money back the judge asked and Antonio if he had my house key which he did in his pocket he took it out and the sheriff went over to get the key from Antonio which he gave to me and I silently told him thank you then as far as the money the judge told me that I would have to take that up in civil court. I then said yes your honor and my lawyer said thank you your honor the sheriff then walked over to my attorney and I telling us to allow Antonio to be released first then he would release us so we go to sit back down as in Antonio walked past me I then said to him dumb ass bitch.

My attorney told me to be quiet when I said that to Antonio he stood in front of me and said what did you say to me? I then told him he heard exactly what I said I'm not going to repeat myself again. I then asked him what was he going to do about it and he stood there in front of me still. Everyone else was quiet and looking at us even the judge and the sheriff then walked over to us selling Antonio to move and to walk out now then the sheriff told me ma'am the room is recording everything that's said I said I didn't do anything he came over to me while trying so hard not to smile. I honestly didn't feel bad for what I did at all grants that I did lie about certain things that I put in the restraining order but Oh well at the end of the day you can't do people dirty and expect to get away with it there's people out there like me that are crazy and sometimes don't know how to handle their feelings and emotions who act off of emotion after all I've always had an anger problem I just didn't show it until someone took me to the point where I felt as if I needed to show my anger.

When my attorney and I get up to get ready to walk out together when the sheriff told came over to us telling us that we could leave the girl who was sitting beside me Shay had gave me a piece of paper with her name and number and I whispered to her that I would call her later. My attorney told me to be careful and I told her thank you so much for her services and help I greatly appreciated it she then told me no problem and told me to be safe I then said thank you you as well. When I get the elevator when I get on the elevator to go downstairs so that I could leave the courthouse the same sheriff that had escorted me upstairs told me to have a nice day he also asked if everything worked out for me I told him you have a nice day as well and I said you bet he then asked me what's the guy I found the injunction against the guy who was in the green military uniform and I told him yes he then asked if I needed to be escorted out to my car I told him I think I'll be ok but thank you then I leave to go to my car when I get in my car I was so ecstatic that I called Kai to tell him what happened but for some reason when I get to the stoplight and Antonio was literally in front of me and I told Kai that I was going to start following him. He then told me to be careful and I told him I'm always careful Then I hung up the phone I honestly didn't know why I was still telling Kai so much. I literally followed Antonio for ten miles he eventually noticed I was following him so he gets on the Interstate so I get on the Interstate going all fast forgetting that he had his daughters in the car he tried to swerve over as if he was getting off on the exit to lose me but he couldn't lose me I swear back over to I was just as smart as he was had it not been for those kids in the car with it actually ran into his car purposely.

CHAPTER

12

I was so upset and all that anger came back into my mind and all those thoughts that I literally followed this man to the police station I was like all that trash he used to talk about I'm from Philly I'm a thug I got guns I set up my baby Mama to get jumped and I was going to get her killed but it was going to the police station how funny I thought he was a thug I said to myself. I literally watched this man go into the police station with a restraining order paper so Before he walked in I looked at his daughter telling them that it was OK and I asked him what was he going to do and he said to tell me I said why he said because you're following me I said yeah but I have the restraining order against you .while he was inside the police station snitching I was literally driving back and forth past the police station not realizing that everyone could see me I didn't think about the cameras they had in the parking lot nor did I care that anger came back to my mind and I couldn't control myself so then I parked in between two police cars that's when two police officers walk out to me and the woman asked me what's going on I told her I had a restraining order against him she then said and now you're following him I said OK she then said which would make you in violation now then I said ok and then she asked me if him and I wanted to go to jail I honestly was going to tell her yes take us both to jail but he had those kids with him I always had soft spot for kids.

I then told her I was just upset telling her that I wanted my house key back even though I had already got the house key back and I told her I wanted my money back she then told me that he was in the Navy he had money and was making money and that you never give a man money I said well I know that now. She then told me that it wasn't worth it so I left. He was lucky that I already had a court case going on and I really didn't need to keep getting in trouble but I guess it was too late for that because later that day when I had followed Antonio to the police station the police from the police station where I followed him at went to my father's house which I was guessing they ran the tags on the car but everything was registered at my father's name not mine so I didn't care anyways but they told my father that I had needed to stop following him because if I did anything else again I was going to be going to jail but craziest thing about it I was the one who felt the restraining order on him which was granted for six months then it would be dismissed and I didn't want my father to know that I found a restraining order against someone I never told my parents everything I had going on unless I absolutely had to tell them. My father then called me about the restraining order asking who this man was I then told my father that he and I had both worked on base together he was in the Navy we were dating until he threatened me so I filed the restraining order which was granted and we had court in the story I didn't know I had to tell you this though I said to my father.

My father then reminded me that I was already in trouble and on thin ice that's why I didn't like telling my father things at all yes I shouldn't have followed Antonio to the police station but all that anger and rage that I had been holding in for so long began to fill up in my head all the promises that he made to me All the things he told me that I believed. He especially knew that I had wanted a baby especially after telling him He especially knew that I had wanted a baby especially after telling him the one when I was pregnant by Theo I had gotten in a car accident and the baby died that was in my belly I was very severely hurt but I guess that was my karma for being with a married man even after finding out that he was marriedI really wanted that baby just as bad as I really wanted to be in a relationship with Theo but I knew it was never going to work and liked the movies they never leave their wives but it's so easy for them to cheat on them. I guess Theo had gotten what he wanted from me so we were done and over with he just wanted temporary sex from a young woman.

My father then told me that the police told him if I Followed Antonio again that I would be arrested for violating the restraining order even though I was the one that found a restraining order. I noticed something crazy in my life whenever someone did me wrong or dirty and I retaliated I was always considered wrong as if I wasn't supposed to have feelings say and or do anything to the person unfortunately that's life. I was then about to really find out how dirty Antonio could play as well after following Antonio to the police station and getting off the phone with my father who was correcting me telling me not to do it again I called Kai to see where he was he then told me that he was at home and I told him that I was going to be coming over and I hoped that he had some rum punch. He then told me that he had rum punch and he asked me what happened I told him I couldn't say anything over the phone I had to wait to see him in person it was better just in case my father had my phone tapped and yes I said my father had my phone tapped because he would do things like that because he could do things like that he had that power and control to do things like that he knew people who could do things like that.

When I get to chi's house I told him that I needed to smoke up blunt and he asked me if I wanted him to hit up his cousin I then told him yes please I need to smoke I'm stressed out. I had told Kai how my father had called me telling me the police came to his house looking for me and my father told me that the police told him if I were to follow Antonio again to the police station contact him or do anything else that would violate the restraining order that I was going to be arrested. As I sit there with Kai talking to him more about the case where the man told the police that I basically had a gun at his face trying to shoot him which I was still very upset about and trying to understand. I received a phone call on my phone I didn't recognize the number at all when I answered the phone call it was Candace Antonio's wife so then she was violating the restraining order because she was considered a third party person I wasn't supposed to be talking to her and she wasn't supposed to be talking to me not sure if she had knew that or not at that time. When she called me she had told me she had more questions for me I then told her before she started to ask me any questions I asked her if she knew that Antonio and I have went to court because I found a restraining order against him because he threatened to shoot me.

This bitch basically took up for Antonio saying how that doesn't sound like him and why would he threaten me I then told her my dear no matter how long you've known someone been married and or dating someone you will never truly know everything there is to know about a person we all have different sides to us some you see and some you don't. She asked me what time did we go to court and I told her it was about 9 in the morning she then called Antonio a lying ass nigga Saying that Antonio told her that he had a appointment. I had even told her that I could send her the screenshot with his name as the respondent and my name as the petitioner I told her he also had their daughters there she went from zero to 100 very quickly she was going off on the phone of course not towards me but the anger was directed towards Antonio but of course he wasn't there on the phone so she was just expressing herself saying how she couldn't believe that put her children possibly in harms way and how he took her children to a courthouse where he could have been arrested for violating the injunction and actually threatening me I even had sent her the video of him standing in my living room saying that if I came between him and his children he would kill me and the video showed him with his gun.

I then told her that I had to go the craziest part about all of that is once I had gotten off the phone with her I received a no caller ID call next. I typically didn't answer calls like that but I had knew that the cop who I had to deal with for the case would call me from time to time and that would pop up when he did call so I decided to answer when I said hello I had put the phone on speaker Kai sitting right beside me listening next thing I know I was told that I was speaking with a sheriff from the police station who told me that if I continue to have any type of contact with Antonio that I would be going to jail I then told the sheriff I had no contact with Antonio at all but his wife did in fact just call me thank God for me I was a smart cookie and I had Kai record the whole conversation. I get that I filed an injunction out of spite but also the simple fact I actually was threatened but what I couldn't understand is why this man was trying to be petty and make all these false police reports which was in fact a crime lying to the police like you cannot do people dirty and be upset when they try to kill you or do something to you that is not how life works and I didn't understand why this man was now trying to ruin my life after all we worked on the same military base so I already knew what I had to do unfortunately I had to go to the man who could help me stop the whole situation and that man was my father.

My father had already knew that I had an anger problem as well as my mother and sister but I didn't care I wasn't a crazy person going around purposely doing things to people I was a crazy person when people messed with me and took me there which is typically almost any person. I had to call my father back with Kai sitting beside me in the phone on speaker hoping that my father wasn't going to say anything about Kai or anything else out of the way I typically would tell people when they were on speaker but of course I love being messy and love drama especially other people's drama which was why they were so miserable. When my father answered the phone I told him how I needed him to tell Antonio's superiors about him harassing When my father answered the phone I told him how I needed

347

him to tell Antonio superiors about him harassing me his wife harassing me and threatening me I even had showed my father the footage in my living room of Antonio threatening to kill me if I came between him and his children and him having his gun that was all the proof that I needed to get myself out of all of that trouble that I was in because I knew for a fact Antonio love being a part of the Navy and he didn't want to get kicked out who would want to get kicked out? But then again the ones who would get kicked out would be the ones who weren't used to having a little bit of money or the ones who thought they were popping because they had on a uniform but before they had the uniform they were nothing and weren't doing absolutely anything with their lives either.

My father told me to give Antonio's first and last name date of birth and he would take care of the rest he then told me don't get involved with anymore military men especially not the ones that I have to work on the same base with because none of them will do right buy me after all my father himself was in the Navy when he met my mother at a car wash so I'm sure he knew all about that. My father always try to avoid confrontation but he was very much upset after viewing the video of a man threatening me he didn't take that well at all and Antonio as soon discharged from the Navy weeks later. Man being around people who have power is a lovely and beautiful thing especially when they're doing right with their power my father used to be a chief on that base so he knew everyone you can't do things to people and get away with it seeing Antonio ever even knew that my father used to run that base and also worked on that base and knew everyone and that's exactly what he got. Hopefully he learned his lesson and he'll never do another woman dirty again.

When I Was drinking some rum punch at chis house his husband Jamal had just gotten home so that was definitely my cue to head out even Jamal was asking me what happened with the road rage incident and I told him like I told everyone else one thing about me if I did something good or bad I would literally tell a person that I did it lying gets you nowhere on top of that I was tired of trying to prove my innocence and explain myself to people who didn't pay my bills nor take care of me hell after all Kai and Jamal used to go to jail so many times before I met them let them tell it for domestic violence charges that's worse than that road rage incident when you have a domestic violence charge it's so hard for you to get a job people think you're violent and dangerous you can't even get that sealed or expunged off your record. I then told Kai that I was going to head out and go home on my way home I couldn't even blast my music or celebrate the simple fact that that restraining order was good for six months against Antonio. When I arrived home halfway and so pulling up in my driveway I saw that the dog was outside but I hadn't got a closer look yet when I pulled up I saw the garage door was on her neck I already knew that she was dead and I kept thinking to myself and talking to myself saying and asking how could no one notice a garage door and a dogs neck. When I got out of the car I started jumping up and down crying and screaming because I knew that Snickers was dead I had always wanted my daughter to grow up with a dog I couldn't believe that had happened I went from having a worse day to even worser day even though I had won in court It still somehow someway slightly backfired because of all those false reports that Antonio made and the report he made of me following him to the police station even though I really did do it not that I cared but all of those reports is really starting to make me look like I was the bad guy then the dog had died I love that dog we all did I had to call Kai to let him know that the dog had died While talking on the phone with him I was crying most importantly I wasn't scared to touch the dog I just didn't want to have to move her I knew I was going to have to open a garage door to get her but I didn't know if her head was attached to her body or not I then started to blame myself because had I not been rushing I would have noticed that she had partially gotten out in the garage door had her but maybe I could have saved her when it happened instantly the craziest part about it all Snickers had gotten out of the garage so many times in that garage door had never did that to her before ever I guess it was just her time to die I mean after a while when you keep doing something and you get lucky eventually you run out of chances.

Kai had slightly upset me because he never really took anything seriously I then told him I had to go I had no choice but to call my father who was on the way to get Bri from school for me She had needed to be picked up early. When I had called my father and he answered I was sniffling and crying telling him how the dog had died I then told him that I needed his help getting her because the garage door was on her neck and I didn't want to touch her or move her. My dad told me that after he got brief from school they would be on the way and he said he guessed they were going to have to cancel her eye doctor appointment I then told him OK as I sat in the car crying in my driveway.

When Bri and my father finally arrived to my houseBri was already crying in tears and screaming she had also never seen anything like that As far as a dead dog with a garage door on its neck. As I cried as well I went to stand beside Bri to hug her and wipe her face. I knew that I would eventually have to get another dog because I couldn't deal with a quiet house I felt that it wouldn't be the same without having a puppy the thing that sucked the most was the simple fact that I knew I could never replace Snickers no dog was going to be like her. It pissed me off that my dad said that I killed the dog grant said I really thought that I killed her but at the end of the day if it's your time to die sure time to die and there's nothing you or anyone else can do about it as I stated she had always gotten out of the garage before so the more and more she kept doing it she was limiting her chances.

My father had put on some gloves and got a black trash bag out of my garage he then put Snickers in the black trash bag that's when Bri and I started crying more. I wanted my father to bury Snickers in our backyard and I was then going to start a garden for her right there but he didn't have a shovel even though there was Lowe's and Home Depot Walmart and a few other stores right up the street I guess he just didn't think to go there at the time or maybe he didn't want to go there at the time but Bri and my father took Snickers somewhere to bury her I couldn't go I felt bad as is and I just had so much on my plate I needed to really stop and think or I was going to have a mental breakdown. I literally sat at home crying and I went upstairs in my closet to smoke some of my blunt that I had I would often notice a few people in my neighborhood would be outside smoking blunts but that was just something I couldn't do that saying in the privacy of your own home was definitely a thing for me we have police in our neighborhood I didn't know them like that I didn't associate myself with them like that and I wasn't trying to get caught up in any more shit than I already was in.

When my mother had found out about the road rage incident she called me cussing me out mad at me talking about I could have got her daughter killed and my daughter killed I then told her I had a gun and I asked her if she really thought I was going to let that man shoot any of us and get away with it. I also told her that anytime she could definitely come back and get her daughter I also told her my sister didn't want to be with her at all anyways. I loved my sister death I really did but let's be real when she lived with Leilani and I it was honestly putting a strain on my life just a little bit when it came to my work schedule because in Clay County the high school she was attending she literally would get out of school at one forty everyday except for Wednesdays Wednesdays they got out of school at one twenty so I would literally have to leave work during my lunch break to pick her up rush all the way to middleburg to drop her off at our house then rush to get back to work. I told my mother if she wanted to get her child she definitely could come back and get her at any time. I found it funny how my mother was also upset that I found an injunction against the man who threatened my life she even had talked to Antonio now that's a shady ass mother Whether I was right or wrong she was supposed to be on my side I failed the injunction out of spite but he threatened me and I had all the proof I wasn't understanding how many more times I could keep explaining that to people without people judging me even my cousin Dee had told me if I was going to file the restraining order out of spite to dismiss it and drop it because after all I wanted those people to dismiss that road rage case they were trying to get on me which was two completely different things.

That's exactly why you can't tell people everything even had those people told the police they didn't want to press charges against me or anything else the state would have literally picked it up some people don't think before they start speaking and they really should think and or do research so they don't look or sound crazy but back to Antonio the only reason my mother was able to talk to him was because I had always been on her cell phone plan I mean I could definitely afford to get on my own I just had never thought about it before it never crossed my mind to get my own plan but my mother was reading the messages she even was telling her friends that was the one thing I couldn't stand about my mother when things happen or go on within your own family everyone doesn't have to know including your friends my mother talked way too much she would tell our business to her friends her friend's business other friends. That's why my mother and I were never close growing up I hated living with her I always wanted to live with my father but of course my mother and father were too busy working for the government and being in the military that my sister and I always had to live with family and our older sister Ashley had the nerve to be complaining I get that our mother gave her up for whatever reason but we didn't always have it easy growing up either yeah my mother and father had cool jobs growing up my father even got to meet some presidents when he was in the military and started working for the government but The thing is when you're a kid all that traveling and stuff for free it's nice but it comes with a cost and the thing was children need stability that's how I viewed it as I got older when I actually started to understand certain things I would never want to be traveling with my family packing up my children to keep moving due to jobs.

As a child I never have stability and what upset me instead of my mother and father moving us all together as a family Bri and I would actually have to go live with my father's family which wasn't the best at all I hated Alabama it was so country the people taught country the state was boring there was absolutely nothing to do in the city where my father was from and his family resided. I would often get picked on for talking proper even though I was from up north like how ignorant can people be? I just couldn't believe that my mother was talking to the man I had a restraining order against which was once again a violation of the restraining order because she was a third party person he wasn't supposed to be contacting her and she wasn't supposed to be responding back to him she literally took up for him like why was it every time I defended myself against someone I was always in the wrong I never understood that like it was OK for people to do me wrong and dirty I was only twenty one was just starting to really get into the dating game I didn't realize how hard it was to date in my generation.

When my mother drove down to Florida after hearing about the road rage incident and how her daughter and granddaughter could have possibly been killed even though that wasn't the case at all she wasn't even in Florida yet and she was already getting on my nerves once again another person didn't believe me and it was my own mother I didn't pull a gun out on that man there were literally cameras on top of the traffic lights there was cars behind us yes I got out of the vehicle which I probably shouldn't have done that definitely wasn't the smart thing to do at the time but when I got out of my vehicle I didn't have the gun however my gun was in my carrying case on the passenger side floor In the car. Everyone who was accusing me of lying some weren't even concealed carriers and or didn't even know the gun laws to be calling me a liar you can literally tell any person that you want you have a gun and as long as you have a concealed weapons license that is not a crime at least in the state of Florida that's the only state I can talk about because that's the state I was residing in at that time.

It very much hurt me that my own mother didn't believe me it also hurt me she was taking up for the man who actually threatened to shoot me and Antonio could have literally shot me in my living room and killed me with his daughters, my sister and daughter outside playing. My mother when she got to my house she stayed in my guest room even though I think she could have gotten a hotel but of course she hated to spend her own money. I had over heard her on the phone with her friend Leslie telling Leslie how I had filed a restraining order against my ex boyfriend and telling Leslie how I sent him a sex tape of me having sex with another man who I was with before him and telling Antonio that that guy whose dick was bigger than his which it was very much bigger and that guy was Theo the professor who was fifty three andAntonio was thirty three had that same day that my mother was here decided to get my own phone plan I could always afford it it just never crossed my mind to ever do so considering that I would always give her the money for my portion of the phone bill.

My mom was also another person who just talked way too much she told everybody else's business but then when you would tell her business she would get very upset. Like the time when Jamal decided to call my mother and father and tell my mom how I told them she had multiple men in my house which she in fact did whenever I went out on dates and stuff I never allowed any man to come back to my home because I had two girls in my house I don't play that and my mother stayed with us for months until everything was over because she wanted to see if I was going to go to jail or not which was very messed up as well she literally started thinking my house was her house doing all these decorations running up my bills and not paying for any damn thing at all that is why I don't like people in my home people won't treat your house like you will and then she wasn't even working anymore because she was here for months even though there was a whole bunch of military bases and my father had the hookup and could have definitely got her working on another military base but she just didn't want to do anything at all she was lazy at times my mother had all these damn degrees and never use any of them because she always had govern-ment jobs so there was no need to use them she would just get paid a lot of money for having all those degrees but at times she can be very manipu-lative and lazy when she lived with me in my house I was so miserable she was always trying to tell me what to do she would pick stupid arguments asking if she can park in the garage in this and that she never really cleaned up dishes would be everywhere she broke my dishwasher and my brand new house that was brand new I had never used my dishwasher. I was at the point where I was going to evict my mother because I was really sick and tired of her even when I would tell some of my friends that I was close with at the time they would literally tell me not to evict my mother or that's your mother you shouldn't do that like shut the fuck up. mother or no mother she shouldn't do what she did my mother had literally put her hands on me called the police gave them my full government name and when they arrived they told her she had to leave like this is my house my name is only name on this deed I pay the bills here I own this house I earned this house by myself.

She was so upset when the police arrived and told her to leave because she was so rowdy you can't play victim on the phone and when the police arrived you seem to be the issue which she actually was the issue you also can't put your hands on people and expect people not to react I've always had an anger problem I was six feet tall and I had weighed one twenty five pounds my mother was way bigger than me she was like 190 like she could sit on me yeah I'm going to hit you back then you almost fall on my daughter like yeah thank God Bree was there and took Leilani and they went upstairs. At that point my mother had put the girls in harm's way and everyone else I was on bond again so once again someone was trying to get me in trouble. She even had called her sister and was telling her sister how I just hit her out of spite and all this stuff like I'm not a crazy person going around doing things to people but I had noticed in that situation every time someone made a police report it wasn't helping my case at all. At that point

I also told myself that I had to stop telling friends and family members my business and just things that were going on in my life I was so depressed I was waking up at five in the morning drinking liquor I would literally go to bed drinking I was even binge drinking just because I was so depressed because I didn't know if I was going to go to jail I had too many issues just going on I was spelling suicidal and depressing but I turn my suicidal thoughts off because after all my child was already missing one parent she didn't need to be missing two parents because that wouldn't have been fair to her at all we don't ask to be here and she didn't ask to be here so why would I kill myself because who was going to take care of her not my father not my mother my father would in fact send my child to Alabama like he did Bri and I when we were growing up they always send us away So go live in Alabama when we couldn't travel with my mother and or father because of their jobs or when they didn't want to be parents they were always absent I hated living in Alabama and my sister did as well also when we were both living there I didn't like the simple fact that we were separated that's why I always said I would let my sister come live with me and I did and she was much happier she got to do more things she got to travel and experience life in Florida which was definitely a vacation every day I mean we lived in Florida also known as the Sunshine State. I paid for everything my sister ever wanted her needed I never told her no I never told my daughter know either I always had money and I always just wanted to show them a good life and they got so experience a great life they can never tell anyone their life was boring or we didn't do anything did everything.

But I couldn't believe that Jamal literally told my mother and father everything that I told them in confidence that is why you can't confide to people because when mad they comes up everybody wants to run their mouths and start talking it's one thing to be mad at somebody but what does everything a person told you has to do with the current situation of why you're mad that's why you can't tell people your personal business people will always use everything against you like my great brother Tupac said trust no

one. I always talk breathe that people will always disappoint you and people will always to reach a certain way especially when piss them off. Like
who were they to get upset because someone doesn't want to be your friend
anymore that's so middle school the sad part is they were way older than
me acting like that nobody wants to be around messy people they were my
first gay friends who were males and last. My mother then told Jamal and
Kai that she didn't care what I said about her or what anybody else had to
say about her for that matter my mother had knew they had HIV because
I told my mother and father plus they were always telling my business so I
thought finally time to tell their business plus something like that definitely
needed to know I'm glad I never ate or drunk off of them or they never bled
on me or anything. I then thought that my mother was going to tell them
that's why they have HIV because that was something she would definitely
say to someone but surprisingly she didn't say that.

My father then told me to act like I was still friends with them so that they
wouldn't contact the bells bond lady which I was definitely for sure they
had contacted her because one time I had tried to reach out to her which
she had an iPhone just like I did I called and texted and she never ever
responded back to me or return any of my phone calls so they had to have
done something I thought that was very strange. She had always reached
out and answered my calls and text messages before because I would even
ask her if she thought that I would go to jail for what had happened and
all of that and she would tell me that I wasn't going to but I was just you
know really scared with the whole situation that I guess I was just believing
anybody or just the thought of other people saying stuff like that made me
feel better I guess especially since she told me she had been in jail before as
well and she was a bailbonds.

I also noticed that every male that I met that came into chi's life was always
gay and they always would come and go you never seen them anymore
that's because they were so messy even chis friend Ashley her and I got

really close together we would start hanging out a lot more talking a lot more talking everyday and stuff but I soon had to also cut her off I just don't like that messy stuff every time we got together she always had to talk about kind Jamal and how she followed them on Facebook which at the time I didn't have a Facebook nor did I want one or care about it either a private life is a better life and I would always ask her if you don't talk to them or deal with them anymore why do you still have them on your social media and why are you always showing me stuff about him I really don't give a damn. Every time her and I hung out she started to get on my nerves too because we always had to go out to eat where she wanted to we always had to go where she wants it we always had to meet up when it was convenient for her and never when it was convenient for me I worked just like she did it's not my fault she chose to work at a call center from home sitting at home in the same spot all day choose a better job she would always get off work at nine at night and want to hang out or go out to eat but I will always have to go to her she had only seen my house twice I didn't like that these Jacksonville people are definitely different they always want to hang out or see you when it's convenient for them never when it's convenient for you she always had to pick a seafood restaurant for us to eat at like those seafood restaurants I have money but I'm one of those people I tend to save and not spend money I tend to choose wisely when spending money I'm a logical thinker when spending money which is why I had so much money at such a young age I was smart about my money and I still am.

Ashley also had a lot of stuff with her as well like she could literally call me at three or four in that morning to wake me up like I didn't have to get up to go to work soon and like I didn't have a child granted my mother and sister were there still that wasn't the point. But the thing about it that made me upset I couldn't call Ashley at three or four in the morning. Also I've realized with her that every time we hung out she definitely wasn't ugly she was also in her 30s as well she was big but she was big and beautiful like she could dress her ass off every week she had a new hairstyle she always kept herself up. But I didn't appreciate how every time we went out somewhere all the attention would be on me with people coming up to me saying how I look gorgeous or pretty or they like my shape and figure not saying she was hating because she would then tell me I did look good and I was glowing but at the same time it was like she was envious again she wasn't ugly at all she was just bigger and she also had diabetes but I didn't appreciate how she also tried to make me feel bad for her like if you're unhappy with your waiting how you look I mean all you can do is change it there's no need to feel bad about that. Plus she always was eating I'm like for someone that's unhappy with their weight she sure doesn't try to change her eating habits or her diet we got to eat sometime yes I ate a lot as well but I was tall and skinny and I worked out three times a day so it was ok for me to do that I also had a high metabolism her on the other hand we've got to eat she will order so much food just for herself I will look and say damn I wasn't one to judge because to each his own and it wasn't me I really didn't give them but The thing is I was also one of those friends who would actually be encouraging like hey Boo we can workout together I know you live in Jacksonville and I'm in a different city but you know we can get up in the mornings and after we get off work and you know go walking around the neighborhood a mile around it while talking on the phone But she never wanted to do that so to each his own that's her problem not mine but at least I tried to actually be a encouraging friend.

Sometimes Ashley would really get on my nerves because she had tendencies like Kai did. One time when they both came to my house before I had got in trouble and my mother had moved in temporarily we were all drinking and I had made some finger foods while we drank wine and talked a bit at that time I was still dating Antonio so I was showing my supposedly man off and everything showing her optics of us two together. Kai told her that Antonio was married granted I had found out that he was but I was going based off of what he told me for the simple fact that he was separated I had never been married so I didn't know how it worked with separations legally or not legally and whatever else and chi even had told her about Theo he just talked so much could tell everybody else this business. When he had told her about Theo and I showed her some optics of us together she was like he is fine but he was dead wrong for what he did to you and then she started jokingly saying to me he was taking that old dick weren't you and I said I sure was all twelve inches.

But I really just had to get away from Kai and his family and all their problems they were all messy with the exception of a few of his aunts and ghetto granted I did have good times around all of them like they would always cook and have get togethers and parties and they were definitely nice and fun to do but it was the drama. Plus chi was always talking about people I'm like you have HIV you and your husband don't know who gave it to who your teeth are yellow your pants hang off showing your ass crack which is not attractive at all you look a mess and you're too old for that that's very unappealing your fingernails are always dirty which I've never ate his cooking at all because I never ever seen him wash his hands I would eat before I arrived and you have the nerve to be talking about people? Kai talked too much for me I'll never get over when Kai and his husband wanted me to be their surrogate for only eight hundred dollars on top of that they forgot to disclose to me that they had HIV. I only found out the had that because of a argument they had which I had to go to their house and diffuse. Kai's husband was the one who told me they had HIV every time Kai's husband got mad at him he'd break up everything he bought for Kai. Most importantly when he got mad at Kai he would call up everyone of Kai's friends including me and tell us that Kai told our business and he didn't lie he would repeat everything and Kai would never apologize or anything. They were both just tofu and they weren't friends. Granted Kai's husband gave me one thousand dollars and I had never had any friend do that before nor did I ask for it. When I was closing on my houseonly because I wasn't aware you couldn't touch your money in your bank account with Navy Federal.

So back to the white guy Chris that I had met at Walmart he had called me after I gave him my number and drove off we talked all the way up until I pulled up at home I couldn't talk while I was unloading the car I could have but knowing me I was so clumsy I didn't want to drop my phone plus I was over men and tired of all the drama and bullshit that came along with the men. Chris had asked me where I lived and I told him the name of the neighborhood he then asked if I owned or rented my home I told him that I owned it he then began to tell me his parents lived up the street from me and he had a friend who lived in my neighborhood who he was very close with. I then asked Chris how old was he and he told me that he was thirty three years old and he lived in Jacksonville he had a apartment but he worked with his stepfather often his stepfather owned a roofing company in Jacksonville that was very popular and well known even I had heard of it a few times. I really wasn't looking for a relationship at all I already had enough on my plate as is but for some reason I don't know why I didn't just tell Chris that I wasn't looking for relationship I mean after all though I would even be slightly mean to him and for some reason he didn't take the hint it was asked if he was turned on by me being mean to him.

He literally came through the neighborhood the next day and he called me to come outside telling me that he had some stuff for me I stood on my porch while I waited for him to come to my house I had never told him my address however sometimes I will park outside the garage and the thing about my neighborhood there was only one entrance in the neighborhood and one exit out. When I see a truck that appeared to look like the driving it was actually Chris he parked in front of my house by the curb when I walked over to him he had brought me some waters, pull-ups, and flowers. I told him thank you so much I really appreciated it which I did it was hard to find water because that was the very beginning of the pandemic coming out so of course when people hear that there is a pandemic they're going to stock up on everything as much as possible it's also hard to find cleaning supplies as well as wipes and pull-ups he even had the right size pull-ups which I didn't even tell him what size my daughter wore however he knew her age.

I was noticing that Chris and I were starting to hang out a lot and moving a little too fast granted we didn't have sex for the first six months that we were together but that meant absolutely nothing to me I mean after all when I had first met Garret him and I didn't have sex for months because I was pregnant and even after I had Leilani we still didn't have sex for a while so I wasn't impressed. One night that Chris and I had hung out together I had met one of his closest friends by the name of Don he only had two friends one friend was Don and the other friend who lived in my neighborhood Who was married with kids. Chris and I would have truck picnics and We would go to his stepfather's office which was also up the street from me and he would make a fire we would then just hang out and talk about a lot in general. even though you can go to jail for not even paying parking tickets which one of my cousins Dee Had went to jail for not paying parking tickets which when I found that out it made me feel a little bit better.

One night Chris and I had hung out he had finally decided to tell me that he had a girlfriend but he was miserable and the relationship was ending I couldn't help but think Oh my gosh not again granted he wasn't married but still I just wanted a single man I then asked him if he had a girlfriend why did he even ask me for my phone number and he told me because he liked what he saw and things with him and his girlfriend were ending I then told him that I couldn't be with him talk to him or consider dating him until I knew for sure that he was going to leave his girlfriend because I didn't play that shit anymore. I had been there done that way too many times and I wasn't about to get played again. So until he decided to leave his girlfriend who was ugly as hell we were just friends for the time being Chris had also told me that he only dated black women all his life he always had a thing for black girls which was nothing wrong with that at all we all have preferences I love the fact that he was white but he wasn't ghetto or country he was just right.

There would be times where I wouldn't respond to Chris and I would ignore his phone calls because I didn't know what his intentions were and I definitely wasn't going to be played by a man again I was tired of that Shit. I had noticed with him that he wasn't giving up at all he would leave flowers outside of my house, food outside of my house, pull-ups and toys from Leilani, wine and or liquor for me, Cases of water, cards with money and I just didn't understand why. I couldn't understand why he wanted me I couldn't understand what was it about me that made him that crazy after all I had never had that before Nor did I tell him that I had never had that before I was for once trying to be in control of my time when I gave my attention and more. After all my attention was on the pandemic that was going going at that time my child and my court case. I couldn't even think about dating I was tired of getting done dirty ending up sad and lonely and having to start over again but a man was always my weakness.

I didn't want to tell this man about my court case who actually brags and or tells people every aspect in their personal life after all I didn't know this man from a can of paint but soon I would soon find out more about him than what he had told me about himself in the very beginning. The next time we had saw each other was that his stepfathers Middleburg office which was again up the street from me Chris would make a bonfire we would drink Liquor and talk. Chris decided to tell me that he was a police officer something he had never told me in the very beginning I couldn't help but think that he already had knew about the situation that I had going on so I decided to tell him and when I told him about the road rage incident he told me that he had absolutely no idea about it even though he was in fact a police officer in the county that I lived in. he then told me not to feel bad or sad about the situation because he had also went to jail for kidnapping his sister's ex boyfriend and friends because his sister's ex boyfriend had decided one night that he was going to rape her and when she told Chris who also had an anger problem just as much as I did which I would assume find out he decided to steal a military vehicle go get his sisters ex boyfriend in the friends kidnapped them hogtie them then called the police then when the police came to the scene everyone was arrested including Chris so the fact that he told me he was a police officer was crazy but then again he also told me how his parents new lawyers and judges so when he told me that I definitely knew about the type of person that I was going to be up against. I said once to him he wasn't wrong for what he did I mean he was just defending his sister I would have definitely done the same exact thing for my sister and or daughter the crazy part about it all he had just gotten into the military when he decided to steal a military vehicle and kidnap his sister's ex boyfriend and the friends that's when he was also discharged from the military but I respected him for the simple fact that he did all of that for his sister. It also felt nice to tell that story to someone who wouldn't judge me even my so called best friend Tamia at the time because we're no longer friends but she even told me she didn't know what to say to me and she couldn't help me like who actually tell someone that I get sometimes if you cannot relate to people with certain situations then you couldn't possibly help or give them advice. But the thing about Tamia that got on my nerves about her she was always judging people. When in fact she didn't have a pot to piss in or a window to throw the piss out of she never could keep jobs she was always broken struggling she didn't even have her drivers license or permit and she was literally in her late twenties still in her late twenties. I've always hated people like that like how can you even open your mouth to talk about anyone when you don't even have anything going on in your own life how does work?

When I had told him about the road rage incident he then told me that he knew a few lawyers who could definitely help me with the situation even make it go away but I told him I would have to get back to him I mean it was technically still fresh and I didn't know what would be the case at that time but I did tell him thank you and I appreciate it. As we drink more of our liquor in front of the bonfire that he had made outside in the cold weather Chris then told me that he wanted to be with me and he could definitely see himself with me. I told him that I didn't want a man who was married and or had a girlfriend I told him I had been down that path way too many times just because I was ignoring red flags and I wasn't doing background checks that's when he told me that he did a background check on me he then asked me who was the man whose name was on my deed I then told him that I bought this home by myself with no help so the only name that should have been on that background check should have been my name so I didn't know what he was talking about nor who he was talking about.Chris then tells me how he did a background check on me asking me whose name was on my deed with me he was like I think it's your ex I said no it's not because I bought that home by myself no one was on my deed at all no man or anyone else for that matter I then told him I don't know where you got that from I also told him you know I haven't been in the house that long so I can't claim that I own the house yet on Zillow or anything else I then told him maybe that's the old owners. At that time Chris was living at one of his parents houses that was also up the street from where I lived just until his apartment in Jacksonville got ready for him to move in.

As we had talked more and more that night I had told him that I had to go granted I was right up the street from home we always would hang out at his dad's office but it was getting late and I was a mother which she knew so my child always comes first whether she's sleeping or not so when I get up I gave him a hug and he literally kissed me and I told him he has to get rid of his girlfriend first if he wants me I said we're not doing that at all he then said he could do that. I then told him I would have him and I were together dating and he finds someone Who's attractive I asked him was he going to go up to them and ask them for their number no one Lee knowing that he's in a relationship and then be out hanging out with them like him and I were doing I said because I don't like stuff like that dating me is a full privilege because I come with my own everything and I don't just get with anybody. He then told me that their relationship it's basically over anyways and the more he starts telling me stuff about her like how she goes to church and all this other stuff I'm like so if you're not into women like that then why did you get returned first place I'd rather be alone and miserable by myself than to just say that I'm in a relationship because it's not that serious especially in this generation is so hard to date and it shouldn't be like everybody comes with baggage and issues and problems.

He then told me that he would never do that to me I told him that actions speak louder than words I also told him I really wasn't looking to date anybody talked to anybody go on dates with anybody or have sex with anybody like I was really just over men I was over dating like I had a lot of issues going on plus I had a whole new criminal case going on so being with Chris was the least of my worries and he had now knew about that criminal case I had to make sure that I didn't go to jail for 10 years. When I finally go home that night I continue looking on my laptop for the best criminal lawyers in Jacksonville FL money wasn't the issue at all I just wanted to get one and have a meeting with one and see what everyone had to say about my situation definitely didn't want to go to jail or prison I had already been to jail for an hour before I got bonded out by Kai who had told the whole world and as I started drinking and thinking more and more to myself I began thinking that I definitely needed to cut Kai off as a friend because he wasn't a friend he was ineffective messy ass bitch who talked trash about everybody else only because he was miserable with a sexual transmitted disease that wasn't going away and could kill you. I really couldn't get over the fact that they were actually calling me a hoe him and his husband Jamal they just really talk too much for me one time Kai was telling his whole family one night in front of me how I was with Theo who was a married man is showing the pictures on Facebook and stuff like you don't do stuff like that if I wanted your family to know my business I would've told your family my business and then you get mad because I tell you I don't wanna be friends with you anymore and your husband try to call my bills bond and get me back in jail because when you're on bond you have to stay out of trouble until it's time for you to go back to court my court date kept getting pushed back because of COVID-19. Like they were genuine people even going out with them they would pay for everyone pay for people who didn't have money they were very helpful but it was the drama that I couldn't deal with.

CHAPTER

13

It is now the next day which I definitely woke up with a hangover because my mother was also in town staying with us. She was telling everyone that I was going to be going to jail and or prison because I pulled out my 9 millimeter gun on a white man which wasn't the case at all I told the man I had a gun and I was so tired of explaining this over and over to people one thing about it I always hated having to explain myself to people at the end of the day no one was in the vehicle except myself my sister and daughter so we are the only three who know what happened really I should say only two which would be my sister and I would be the only two. My mother had even told one of her crackhead as having friends named Vanae She was ghetto and she was also a ex crackhead so listening to her I was not. My mother's friend Vanae Even told my mother that I was going to be going to jail because of what I did honestly I wasn't even scared I had already been in there for one hour which was nothing I wasn't even in a holding cell the police officers were flirting with me they were asking to give me tours of the jail they were letting me talk on the phone to Kai as much as I wanted to until I got out of there so that's what jail is like and people are actually scared to go to jail that was nothing The thing is when you're in jail you have all the power especially if you're going to be in jail for months or weeks you have power everyone has power the inmates the correction officers you can easily get anything that you want with your looks, sex, control, power. But I honestly wasn't scared at all.. But then again I guess when you've been in jail and or prison for quite some time it can tend to get rough for you but to each his own I don't know anything about that I was in and out and I loved it. The crazy part about it my mother's friend again was a ex crackhead lost custody of her children all eight of them which means she was busy in these streets with all those different baby daddies so why in the hell would I wanna take advice from a person like that? She was a criminal her damn self not to mention the simple fact that she was in and out of jail and prison her whole damn life drug possession, gun possession, Attentive murder Child Protective Services cases, child neglect I could go on and on so who would actually listen to a person with the likes of her?

My mother was also always so quick to call the police on me when she was living in my house not paying a single bill not working and running up all my bills but I guarantee she wasn't telling her friends how the night when I spray painted Kevin's car that the police came to my house looking for me while I hid underneath my bathroom cabinet because I was that skinny and I could But when the police asked my mother if I was home she told them no then she asked them if they had a warrant for my arrest and to search the house and they told her no. Which was a lie because I was home but that was also a crime and she could have definitely gotten in trouble for that.

Granted I had been to jail twice I absolutely thought that I was better than my mother's friend people are so quick and eager to judge those who have been to jail but fail to realize I didn't go to jail because I'm this crazy person going around just in the mood to do things to people there's always reasons why people do things cause and effect I get tired of people thinking that they're going to do things to me and get away with it especially men that was always my problem it was always men. Granted my mother hey got me in a Department of Children and family case in the state of Florida I still thought that I was better than her friend and a lot of other people especially those who choose to doubt me it wasn't my fault that I got in that case it was my mother's fault because she decided to put her hands on me then call the police trying to act as if she was a victim and me having an anger problem at that time I defended myself it was completely my mother's fault my father sister and daughter were present when that happened my mother kept thinking that she was going to keep poking me and hitting me and pushing me and I just snapped I threw the sweet tea up in the ceiling of my living room downstairs so which pissed me off every time I walk past it because I'm like I'm in here messing up my own stuff and property that I have to pay for you're supposed to tear up other peoples property not your own I had told myself. I was so grateful that Bri had the common sense to take Leilani upstairs to her bedroom and close the door so she didn't have to see that and Father was just standing there for a while he always hates it confrontation he was just telling us to stop my mother was pulling on my wig she broke my French tips.

She even had called all her friends lying to them over the phone telling them how I lashed out and hit her that's the thing about people there's always two sides to a story but only one person is going to tell that story correctly unfortunately but one thing about it I've always hated liars and if you're going to tell my business and tell others what I did make sure you get my story right. I couldn't believe that my child was placed in a Department of Children and families case I wasn't a bad mother just misunderstood granted I had been to jail twice I still wasn't a bad mother or person I was the kindest sweetest young woman around I would even give homeless people Especially those with children fifty to one hundred dollars. Because that always hurt me to see a homeless mother with her kids by herself. I would always remind myself how lucky I was to have what I had growing up to have what I had currently had and was putting in place for my daughter and sister because everyone isn't lucky. We always take life for granted every single day but I couldn't believe my child was now going to be placed in that situation all thanks to her grandmother because she was so jealous of me which is so sad when you know your mother is jealous of you. My own mother trying to destroy me out of spite even when I had first bought my home and my mother had came down to see my home which was in November of twenty nineteen she was hanging up all these pictures putting holes all in the walls putting holes all over my fireplace and acting as if this was her home my mother had always had nice houses always used to decorate them very nice and well but the issue was she could never keep the houses she was always one of those women who were very successful and had money but always tried to live her life like the Joneses My father always told me just because you have money doesn't mean you always have to spend your money anything can happen and it's always better to be prepared than underprepared. My mother even told me that I was acting as if I was Kim Kardashian because I bought a home I literally over heard her on the phone with one of her friends telling them that like if I want to brag and tell the world that I bought a home at twenty one then I will do so I was also on social media helping others and showing others that it's very possible to do what I did the legal and correct way which is something that a lot of people don't do I was helping people people looked up to me and it felt wonderful plus that was one of my biggest accomplishments I always said by the time I was thirty I wanted to buy a house in Florida in the country and I did it at twenty one that's a great accomplishment anyone would want to brag and I had every right to but of course people will hate never did I think out of all the people that were hating on me at that time that my own mother would be the primary hater which very much hurt my feelings and hurt me I always looked up to my mother my mother had so many degrees she was very high up in the government status.

But my mother in fact secretly hated me and she did a very great job at it I was never close to my mother like I should have been anytime I would tell my mother certain things she would always go back and tell my father even when I would tell her don't tell him or something she never was the mother that I needed her to be but for some reason she thinks that because she would buy us nice things or give us a lot of money that that's supposed to make up for what she lacked in the most which was being a mother. She always had men around she always took us while she did what she did with these men she always judged me she always look down on me. That was exactly why I wanted to move out of her house after I graduated high school early to move in with my father I always was way closer to my father than my mother one my father never physically abused me in the black community I feel like the physical abuse with parents beating their kids is crazy and out of control and we actually did fun things we traveled we did so much more plus my father had more money than my mother way more. When my mother came to see our new house I even was letting her decorate and go all out even though I didn't want her to after all this was my big accomplishment I wanted to decorate something that I was finally able to call mine. My mother was even telling her friends about how I had went to jail twice like she just talked way too much certain things sometimes needs to stay within the family like growing up black in the black community all the adults would say to the children that they needed to stay in a child's place and stay out of grown folks business. My mother needed to stay in her place instead of my business she talks way too much especially if you upset her and I didn't appreciate that who actually goes around telling people they've been to jail I didn't even tell my own friends they only two friends that knew at that time was Tamia and Nay.

My mother had even told her sister Keisha who lived in California all of my business the same sister who fucked my mother over not once not twice not three times but more. And as you know the same sister who eventually filed an injunction against my mother for her harassing and stalking she which is exactly what my mother got I was so happy. Her sister only came around when she needed money her adopted sister at that which a lot of people didn't know about. Her sister always asked for money from my mother and never ever ever paid her back they even had lived with us at one point my aunt Keisha and her son Caleb. They only would come to visit us when I was a kid when they were in trouble. I didn't go to California with Bri and my mother considering considering that injunction against my mother was served to her at my house which was very embarrassing and I was so tired of seeing the police at my door. My mother and Bree had drove to California from Florida what a long drive I couldn't imagine I hated road trips plus I didn't want to go when she claimed that she needed a break from me and being in Florida it was very much crazy to me how my mother had made so much money and had so much money in her savings but she was always spending and proclaiming to be broke she was no good at managing money too old and grown for that I was younger than her and managing and saving money better but I guess when one parent has common sense the kid will still do just fine. But my mother and Bri told me everything was great in California they were sending optics all day every day in videos even face timing me so that I could talk to my aunt Keisha I loved my aunt Keisha to death I really did especially as a kid we were very close.

Even the time when my aunt Keisha caught me under the blanket with Nay kissing in my bedroom and she had snatched the blanket off our heads then when I got smart with her when she said something to me she told me how she was going to tell my mother that I was kissing under the blanket even though she never did tail I guess she just wanted to tell me that she knew what we're doing under the blanket. But everything seemed to have been fine so to this day I still didn't understand why my aunt Keisha had filed the injunction against my mother I guess she did it out of spite my mother claimed it was because my aunt Keisha asked her for money the messed up part about it all not that I care but my aunt Keisha had even found my mother ex boyfriend on Facebook and was telling him everything at a spike I really didn't care when my mother was telling me because she got exactly what she deserved everything that she had put me through I still cannot and will never ever to this day get past the simple fact that I was placed into a Department of Children and families case because my mother was such a hater and the social worker was a complete bitch it was if she was on my mother side. One time my mother claimed the social worker told me that I had to leave my home the house I pay the bills at the only person paying the bills at that but told me that I had to leave my house and move in temporarily with my father I also knew that my mother had wanted my house for herself which was crazy because all those houses she had how are you in your forties jealous of a twenty one year old like at least I actually had my shit together and wanted to do something with my life unlike a lot of my old classmates and or friends at that time.

It was already bad enough that I was already in one that I was already in one DCF case Department of Children and families case before my mother had got me in the second one the first one was because the police officer told me that he had to report it to Department of Children and families to ensure that my daughter was safe because I've technically placed the children in a bad situation even though it's defending myself and defending the girls as well but whatever. The social worker Ashley was a bitch And the crazy part about it I always felt like her and my mother were plotting against me in so many ways it was as if she was helping my mother as if she was on my mother side. Ashley even had told me that I had injunction against Antonio who I followed to the police station who then about a report about me following hints at a police station which he did I was there then I had the road rage incident with the white guy by the name of Adam who we found out lived in the same neighborhood as me then my mother had called the police when she put her hands on me that one time while in my home so the social worker Ashley told me that all these people keep filing reports on me and it's not making me look like a good person at all it wasn't doing me any justice it was making me look like I had an anger problem which I in fact did have an anger problem and I also truthfully told her I had an anger problem one thing about me I'll tell you straight forward if I did something end or said something which was always a good thing to me

I didn't care for that social worker at all she was basically telling me how I was going to have to take a twenty six week anger management class but I was willing to do anything to keep my child from being taken away from me because I don't know what I would have done had my child got taken away from me but I would have definitely did everything in my power to get my child back even if I had to pay off lawyers and judges or whoever I wasn't going to let my child go into temporary foster care unfortunately I did have an anger problem and I was going to prove anyway I could that I was not an unfit mother it was just so upsetting to me that people can do things to me and get away with it and when I react I'm wrong always that has always been the freaking case for me couldn't understand why. Before my mother had came to Florida the social worker Ashley told me that I was going to need someone to stay with me temporarily who could monitor me with the girls I couldn't even believe she had said that to me like monitor with kids as if I was as bad dangerous person and at that moment in time I definitely had way too much to lose I was in school online and everything. This was also right at the beginning of the year when the pandemic was first coming out so that made things a lot worse everyone was pretty much out of work. The saddest part even about it all my so called friends who were always around when Jay and I would invite them to our home or invite them out to eat or go to their places and bring all this liquor and food and not require them to pay us back or anything because that was just the type of people that we were they weren't even there for me nowhere to be found. It was already embarrassing as is to say that I had been to jail but it was worse to say that I had a Department of Children and families case who wants to tell that to anyone and bitches nowadays when mad day comes up they like to tell all your business and try to break you down the less you tell people the better.

I had told Renee that I had needed to talk to her about what was going on in my life and to see if she could possibly help I was so desperate I was willing to pay people the same amount of money that they made at work as long as it didn't exceed past eighteen an hour. Renee had made me feel a lot better when I called her up over the phone and she had told me that she herself has had a few department of children's and family cases. After all she did have a lot of kids even kids my age and older than me but she told me not to worry and to just cooperate I was going to ask her but I knew she wouldn't be able to I couldn't possibly imagine couldn't no man run me hell no. But when I listen to her Department of Children and families cases that she had they were way worse than what I had so it definitely made me start to feel a lot better so I decided to call DayDay she didn't answer which she never answered the phone so I don't even know why I even called her at that time I didn't want to text about it and I was trying not to have paper trail even about the department of children's and family case because again when mad day comes up people tell your business and that was proof right there I really didn't want to text Day-Day about it but I had no choice at that time I had to do what I had to do and when I had text her asking her if she be able to help me telling her that I could pay her the same amount of money every day to monitor me with the girls that she makes at work I just need someone to help me she then asked me what was going on and said don't lie either so I told her everything that was going on.

I figure people will never do anything for you without knowing the full story and what's going on which was completely fine I was just desperate she then told me that she couldn't help me I even told her that I could pay her more money hour than she makes that work she wasn't making much anyway she was working at a store making minimum wage but you can't force people to do things for you nor make them all after possibly do is ask and I mean the worst you could say was no which was pretty much what she said but in the nicest way or whatever. After that I wasn't going to go through my list of contacts telling everyone in Jacksonville my business because certain things like that that's not something that you tell everyone that was a very sensitive situation for me so unfortunately I had to reach out to Bev but at that point we were very much closer and on a better mentality I hated that I had to tell her about the situation even though I don't think I did anything wrong at all it was technically self defense and I was defending the girls and myself so I didn't really care who had to judge me because at the end of the day no one was there but us so people's opinions don't necessarily matter to me at times especially when they don't even know the full story because they weren't there it killed me that I had to ask Bev but unfortunately I knew I had to ask someone and I was running out of options and people to call plus that was her niece her deceased brothers only child so I knew she wasn't going to say no and plus when I called she always answered the phone instantly for me. It hurts to have to tell her what happened but I needed help my child was not going into temporary foster care or any of that I even had déjà vu of me taking a stack of cash out of my safe in my bedroom with passports, Birth certificates,Social Security cards and leaving with my child.

But I had started thinking about the outcomes and how I would then be considered a fugitive on the run with the kid armed and dangerous I thought about so many other things and how worse a situation could have gotten had I chose to make that decision.

After a few days of doing over the phone interviews with different lawyers and weighing out my options I finally decided to go with the lawyer name Matt. He was said to be one of the best civil and criminal attorneys in all of Jacksonville he had great reviews and after speaking with him he definitely knew what he was talking about and it all made sense to me . so I had to set up an appointment later that day to meet with him when I did meet with him he didn't say what all the other lawyers said I also told him that I wasn't taking any plea deal or anything that involved jail time because I didn't do it I also told him one thing about me unfortunately if I did something I would probably tell you that I did it whether it was good or bad that was just me I wasn't scared of anything or anyone including jail you do the time you do the crime you do the time but in my case I didn't do the crime state of Florida it's not a crime to tell someone that you have a firearm especially for the simple fact that I was licensed to carry people shouldn't provoke others then they won't have to worry about people telling them that they have firearms and in case they actually have to use it against themselves to protect themselves so in my eyes I didn't do anything wrong. Matt told me that he couldn't promise anything which I completely understood and that was also a pitch that he's required to tell all clients and or future clients as a attorney for the state of Florida . I had even done some of my own research before going in person to speak with him because I never trust anyone else is information except for my own plus I like to know what I'm dealing with what I can ask about etc.

I didn't have to go to court or anything considering the simple fact that Matt was going to do everything for me as far as appearance and more over the phone conferences for my criminal case also COVID-19 was slightly getting in the way of any and everyone being able to go in person to courthouses and more, the crazy thing about it I never lost hope or faith throughout the whole situation because I didn't do it and I knew that justice was definitely going to Play out in my favor I just told myself over and over again not to lose my faith and courage . I was definitely doing a lot of drinking with the alcohol and I was also smoking a lot of weed which at the time or any other time wasn't good at all to do I was already under enough pressure with my mother being there and I was very depressed I asked Matt if he could please just help me I told him I have money I could pay up front for everything.But all as Always my father has to come to my rescue the problem that I had with my father is when I never asked or required anything from him he would just simply do which is great in all and most people's eyes but it wasn't great at all to me in my eyes my father would do things for me like give me money and or other things that I never ever even asked for then he would require me to pay him back I had my own money my father thought I was dumb and he questioned my knowledge and he would sometimes belittle me as if I had no sense of knowledge and understanding but I simply did I hated being treated like a child I hate it when others questioned me . my father had no idea that I even had all this money in my bank account from me just simply stacking up my money because he thought I was a young and dumb young woman in her early twenties that was going to mess up her credit and get all these loans and credit cards grants that I had credit cards I didn't mess my credit up from them at all . all he had to do was have faith in me then again my father was never proud of me he never ever told me he was proud of me he never showed that he was proud of me he never bragged to others about being proud of me which very much sucked after all I was the one that found this lawyer. After all I didn't want to go to jail or prison so I had to get the best of the best and I was told he was very much the best of the best after all this was my life I was a mother that took care of my sister as well and I wasn't going to allow everything that I had worked so hard for in my life to be thrown away because of the lies of some white man who can't control himself when driving a redneck truck and has to do the absolute most is actually sad that a lot of men that drive those big trucks have small dicks and are also hotheads I could see that.

Once again my father had to save the day for me when I didn't ask or require him to he had decided to pay all the money that I owed the attorney which was completely fine but I didn't need his help nor ask him for his help because my father would do things like that then he wants all his money back but who asked you to do things in the first place I've always hated people who do things for people which is completely fine to do for people but if you're going to talk about what you've done for people you might as well not do for people at all that's my motto. Not only did I use this attorney once but I used him twice so I think altogether my father paid ten thousand dollars for the attorney andthirteen hundred dollars to fix my ex boyfriend's car which had to be painted all over again because I decided to spray paint his car when I had a Nair outbreak and I go to the hospital the Doctor Who I trusted because he has that degree in those credentials told me that it looked like I had a herpes outbreak on my vagina when he looked down there it burned it burned to pee I have bumps everywhere come to find out it was just an allergic reaction and outbreak from using the Nair to shave so I basically spray painted my ex boyfriend's car thinking that he gave me herpes and it wasn't even herpes see the thing with me I was always the nicest person in the world until someone did something to me or pissed me off granted I should have waited until I got my STD results back which would have showed that I didn't have herpes and everything else was negative but of course I acted off of emotion and not clearly thinking so my father literally had to pay for a car to get a fresh paint job a nigga's old ass raggedy ass car. I was really trying to analyze how that man named Kevin was in the Navy he was literally stationed at the same base that my father used to be chief at in Jacksonville my father was chief at the base in Jacksonville and other base was in Jacksonville Orange Park border. But he was in the Navy and broke then again I can't actually analyze that because it's always the ones that go into the Navy they get all this money and blow it because they don't know how to manage their money and they're not logical thinkers then they go around crying about how the military doesn't pay them anything like if you guys feel that way get out the military the military isn't the only way to be successful in life so I don't even know why people think that. I spray painted then threw ketchup packets on it while out on bond from the other case thank God when I went to the Jacksonville jail they didn't find out that I was on bond because had they found out I was on bond I wouldn't have gotten released on ROR. So basically all this unnecessary money was being shelled down and spent because I couldn't control my anger and handle my emotions I've always acted out of anger without thoroughly thinking it through thank God that I didn't spray paint or key

Theo's Audi because I thought I about it and we would've been struggling well me.

When I went to the Jacksonville jail I had to stay overnight in that nasty dirty ass jail on top of that I was on my period and I didn't have any shower shoes and also there was a pandemic out there. Once again the person I was trying to erase out of my life forever I had to call to come pick me up out of jail even though I talked to him throughout the night and that friend at that time was Kai The funny thing about it he was actually in fact with me when I was spray painting and throwing ketchup packets on Kevin's car. My father even told his husband Jamal that had they called my bells bond to tell her I was out on bond and got rearrested that my father was going to tell the courts how Kai was there with me which he was laughing and being messy per usual while I'm doing something that could have ended badly for me. While I was in the Jacksonville jail I was crying and all I could think about was my child and my sister and how my mother was in my home-work I didn't want her to be acting as if that was her home redecorating making messes breaking up stuff that she didn't have to pay for my mother broke my brand new dishwasher she put a hole in my wall by my front door at the bottom and she was tearing up the guest room because she knew she didn't have to pay for anything that's exactly why you can't have anything nice being around other people because they don't care when they aren't the ones who have to shell out money to pay to replace things people will never treat your home and or property like you will.

I was in my cell with two other women one was forty her name was Janice and the other one her name was Shaquita she was in her early thirties. We were all just talking about how we were all going to get out tomorrow we talked the whole time and the sale they were very cool we told each other what we did and they both had been in jail before so they both told me not to tell anybody else because people in jail would get you in trouble and tell the tell the inmates the guards and or other inmates what you did try to flip your story lie and more. Honestly everyone was really nice and cool and helpful they were even asking if they could have some of our stuff since we were getting out tomorrow anyways. I couldn't wait to get home and go home to my daughter The next day was going to be Easter of twenty twenty all I could think of was getting my daughter some gift baskets going home. The thought of being told when to wake up for breakfast which was at four in the morning if you don't get your breakfast you just miss it for that morning until lunch and dinner is served the food was very disgusting but I mean after all when you're hungry everything tastes good. I had women come up to me asking if they could have my French tips asking if they could have my wig and all this other stuff that I wasn't used to because grant said that was the second time I had been to jail I have still never been in trouble before I mean after all I spray painted a car I didn't kill someone or worse.

Janice had told us she had been in and out of jail practically her whole life which she was forty years old and looked at she was too damn old to still be getting in trouble and for stupid shit. she was also on drugs and stuff something I couldn't relate to I had never did drugs in my life I don't even consider a weed a drug. I had never tried anything other than weed nor have I ever in my life had a desire to try any other types of drugs other than weed. Shaquita told us that she stole seven teen hundred dollars worth of food out of Walmart and there were other women with her they ended up leaving her behind which was very messed up and sounded like a setup but I was really trying to analyze how she stole seven teen hundred dollars worth of food out of Walmart she then told us how she was struggling she didn't get her food stamps and she had a kid so when it comes to stuff like that if I was in her predicament I would steal for my child medicine food if I needed to it was broken had no money or help but that's a lot of money and food to steal to this day I can't analyze how she stole that much food. The fact that there was one sink in the cell one mirror that was dirty and had rust all over it one toilet and of course two bunk beds and one twin bed. When we all take a look at our cards that we had they said felonies so I was then at that time I fell and I couldn't believe it me to this day I still cannot believe that I went to jail not once but twice in the same year a month apart.

When I finally get some thinking time when it's about that time to eat dinner I told myself in my mind that I had to absolutely stop having unprotected sex with people which is partially why I was in that situation because had I not been having unprotected sex with Kevin I would have never thought that he gave me herpes I also wouldn't have had a reason to spray paint his car and throw ketchup on it. I told myself I had to stop telling Kai everything and being friends with him he was too messy for me and too old to be messy. And Kevin claimed he wasn't the one who called the police come to find out one of his neighbors had security footage that caught the whole thing I hate people that don't know how to mind their business like how does that even affect you yes I spray painted his car and threw ketchup but the point was he didn't know why and he's calling the police but it's whatever you live and learn. Kevin didn't even have my last name I also had met him on a dating app something that I told myself I would definitely stay off you see I just wanted unconditional love and a father figure for my daughter it was so hard to find it really was I kept telling myself over and over again I'm not crazy I wasn't crazy I was misunderstood on top of being misunderstood people would often say that I was too young to realize I was being played and missing red flags but at the end of the day even had I seen the red flags people are going to be how they're going to be you cannot change a person no matter how hard you try people will always eventually show you who they truly are in the beginning you're always going to have that temporary happiness and be happy but The thing is we cannot always be happy and have it our way all good things come to an end eventually that's for any and everyone.

Kevin had no idea how much power I still had and I was in jail literally my father was a chief at not one but two military bases in Florida including the one where Kevin worked that at the time so I told my father his first and last name because Kevin didn't know my first and last name I've always had two last names however I've never gone by my two last names and that was why no paper trail. Granted when Kevin I guess told the cops how I resided in middleburg and at that time I was twenty one I was pretty much the only African American young woman that was twenty one in middleburg who owned a home so it wasn't that hard for them to find me plus since I had already been in jail the first time they probably showed him an optic of me which was the mugshot 1 which I look really good that day so I'm guessing that's what happened. But my father called Kevin chief who my father in fact knew and was very close with and told him that one of his guys is trying to press charges against me so now we're going to press charges against him even though I did spray paint and throw ketchup on his car and I was wrong but I told him that I was going to pay for it when he called me about it I also told him to call off the police I give him the money whatever I had money but when those cops arrested me I had to do what I had to do for me. And the chief told my father that he would take care of it and make him dropped those charges that he tried to pin on me and lied on his neighbor when he in fact himself was trying to do things as well. That's how we operate plus my parents knew everyone that worked in federal government lawyers judges and more. We would also pay off anyone if we needed to in order to get where we need it to be or to get out of a situation that we need it to. I wasn't going to allow anyone to make me lose my security clearance granted my father pulled strings for me to work for the government I had worked hard to keep my spot. No one can ever take that away from me granted my parents had money and connections I actually knew what it was like to work hard for things and I actually Worked hard for what I wanted.

How can I even forget the first day when I had went into the Jacksonville jail? They asked me if I could take my wig off and I told the guard I couldn't because it was so on I'm like lady I was getting out the next day they made me take off my engagement ring that Jay had gave me I always wore it. They made me take out my belly ring they made me strip. And to think that I had become a correctional officer at twenty three. Except I wasn't a bitch I've hated the correctional officers and or female police officers that just feel like they have to have this attitude and fill all superior because they have weapons and they're in uniform. Then they wonder why inmates set them up whoever thought that as a correctional officer inmate has no power they're absolutely wrong and they hadn't been a corrections long enough at all. And it was always the black women that had to fill all superior and uniform and would get attitudes for absolutely nothing the woman that had checked me in and everything she next had to take my mugshot picture which took her way too long I literally told her Clay County didn't even take that long I was in and out within an hour I said y'all are so slow for absolutely no reason I then told her I'm so glad I don't live in Jacksonville let's just get oh the crime rate in Jacksonville was way worse than Clay County that is why I would always say Clay County was way better than Jacksonville and why I never liked living in Jacksonville it wasn't all of Jacksonville but a lot of areas in Jacksonville were very bad hell the news station was really just mainly in Jacksonville and always only covered Jacksonville not even the other cities that were close to Jacksonville and every time you hear something about Jacksonville is always someone getting killed children getting shot up while sleeping innocent people in the sacred of their own home being shot up and stuff not an ideal place that I'd ever want to raise a family nor live which was exactly why I moved to Middleburg then all my so called black friends would be like you out there with all those white people I'm like I rather be out here with the white people than my own people my own people are too ignorant to get oh they like to shoot up people innocent people to get to the person that had done them wrong. Living out in middleburg in the country you hear gunshots but never once as a bullet ever hit anybody house out here that I had heard of and all of the three years that I had lived in middleburg and when you hear gunshots it's called we're hunting because there's woods out here you see deers in your back-yard and everything out here I love it.? Then everyone that I know who lives in Jacksonville is always complaining about how there's nothing to do in Jacksonville but yet they're the same types of people that have yet to try to move out of Jacksonville so how does that work for you?

Then some random inmate when I was finally being escorted to my cell Had handed me a note also known as a kite which was very illegal to do while you're in jail and I also could have gotten in so much trouble had I been caught with the note I didn't know what to do with it so I tucked it inside of my sheet and blanket and pillow case that he had given me. I could definitely tell that he had been in there for quite some time. Even some of the other young women who I was around they were joking me when we were all talking asking me what did I possibly do to have been in jail one girl even asked if I stole from Victoria's Secret while we all laughed about it she also said I don't even look like I would get in trouble or do something to be in jail. She then told me that I looked like I had money and I was rich. I didn't even respond at that point because it was no one's business all I was worried about was getting out the next day. When I had told Shaquita and Janice about it they told me to flush it down the toilet and hurry up before someone sees me. I had absolutely no idea that it was illegal to take a note from someone in jail when you're in jail too and I mean after all Janice would know she had been in jail a few times in her life.

When the black woman goes to take my mug shot optic after the strip search one tear had fell from my face then she loudly asked me was I cry-ing that pissed me off so much I kept thinking in my mind having a déjà vu moment saying to myself she's so lucky that I'm in jail and she's in uni-form because I would kick her ass. I couldn't believe that I had yet allowed myself to get caught up and sent to jail because of a man I seriously couldn't catch a break a man was always my biggest downfall and I realized that I was becoming my mother because a man was always her biggest downfall she could never keep one she could never be treated right by one and I was starting to notice that the same thing was unfortunately happening to me as much as I hated to admit that it killed me to have to admit that but it was true I had began to follow in my mother's footsteps. I was so ashamed and embarrassed for myself for the simple fact that I knew I had an anger problem and I allowed another man to get the best of me I also have felt myself because I would also always have these talks to myself whenever I was by myself about how I needed to start wearing protection and stop having unprotected sex with all these men especially for the simple fact that Theo had gave me chlamydia once but it came back again even after I was treated for it and it was completely gone. After all I was a mother even though my child won't ever remember what happened and that her mother was absent for a few hours due to being in jail I will always remember that in one day I will have to tell her that story so that she will take heath and not follow into my footsteps. I felt like I had felt my little sister who had always looked up to me and wanted to be just like me with being young and successful. After all I was supposed to be showing her the right way and the right path of life and I was going down a very bad path that was already bad enough I had went to jail in the same year a month apart I couldn't believe it and I never thought I would ever go to jail.

Janice, Shaquita and I had practically talked all day and night we never left out of our sale but everyone was just wandering around and coming into our cell talking to us surprisingly everyone was very nice compared to how they portray jail on television but I guess jail could get rough especially when you've been in there for a couple of months and or years. This one white chick had came up to us asking us if we wanted our breakfast the next day hell she even knew what we were having for breakfast the next day I'm just like damn she's probably been here too long. It's a damn shame when you start memorizing breakfast lunch and or dinner not that she was missing any meals. I told her I wanna eat my breakfast I eat a lot might be skinny but I eat. All throughout the night Janice Shaquita and I were talking about what we were going to do when we went home to our kids the next day and hell to be honest after a while you get very bored sitting in jail I had taken a few naps that day too. The next morning this one girl was trying to start trouble with us talking about you bitches had been up all night talking and loud at that I didn't realize people could hear us through a mail slot which was on each cell door which was cut out but it didn't seem like we were that loud so for some reason Janice decided to do the talking for us telling the girl that if we didn't get out later that day we were going to jump her and the girl responded back saying we didn't know if we were getting out or not and Janice said we definitely getting out we got money and we didn't do shit like you that's why you still here. One thing about me I might have been skinny but I could definitely fight and I was crazy I was just like left eye from TLC I wasn't the one to mess with. Nor was I going to fight some bottom bitch lowlife who had absolutely nothing to lose because she had clearly been in jail for a while we were getting out that day so not worth it. After Janice told her that the girl got real quiet I honestly couldn't wait to get home jail was dirty it was filthy I didn't even shower I was on my period and everything I didn't walk around without shoes on the floors were disgusting I couldn't deal with it my OCD couldn't which was another reminder of myself to keep my ass out of jail control my anger problems.

I couldn't deal with having to wake up at 4:00 in the morning to eat breakfast just the matter of the fact of being told when to get up to get breakfast lunch and dinner I couldn't deal with that every day and if you didn't get up to get your food or if you were asleep you just miss out. After we had ate breakfast we had to get ready for court it was bad enough being in a jail outfit but it was worse having to wear shackles on our ankles I really felt like a criminal as if I had just murdered somebody and all I did was spray paint my ex boyfriend's car that's not a serious crime at least it wasn't to me and on top of that I paid the bastard and he's lucky I paid for him a new paint job for his old ass car. I also told myself to stay off of dating apps I had met him on Tinder plus he was in the Navy full of crap.

The whole jail system was just so slow it took forever for them to call us after eating breakfast I was getting sleepy again Janice Shaquita and I would often take little power naps and take turns taking the power naps then waking the next person up to be on watch to pay attention when they call our names. The Jacksonville jail was so slow they took their time and it seemed like they took their time on purpose because we had nothing but time. I was so nervous because we had to see the judge and I didn't know what the judge was going to say or do considering I was already out on bond at that I wasn't even supposed to get rearrested again or in trouble. As we all sat around waiting this one police officer pulls aside Shaquita, Janice and I I was so scared before he did any talk and we all asked him if we were going to be able to be released from jail the same day as he pulled her names up and told us yes and he also told us he was going to slip something to the judge so that she would release us we all said thank you very much as he looked on the list for our names one by one and Janice started crying and the cop told her no crying no tears and just don't come back I was so relieved but then again some of them couldn't be trusted after all people will tell you anything they feel you want to hear not what you need to hear at times I've learned that a lot in my life in the past to know better.

When they finally let us all walk into the courtroom where the judge was at it was on a weekend I didn't even know they did stuff like that on the weekends with courts but the room was filled with a lot of us inmates dressed in the same color uniforms with shackles on our wrists and ankles. The judge was a white woman who seemed to be very stern and she looks like she didn't play I was so nervous. As I watch other people go up none of them really did any talking at all the judge did all the talking and just told you if you were going to be going home or not when I finally get called up I was so scared I was shaking on the inside and my heart was pumping ten times faster than it normally would and the judge told me that I was going to be going home That same day I was being released on ROR. I then said thank you your honor and walked away. I was then taken back to my cell Janice and Shaquita hadn't been called up yet so I was saying in my mind I hope that they were also getting released as well I honestly really liked both of them everyone in jail isn't a criminal it just depends what you did especially Shaquita I really saluted her for what she did for her son if I didn't have it like that even if I was working and still struggling I would have stole food for my child to gotta do what you gotta do sometimes I don't judge people to each his own we always say what we wouldn't do when would do until we're actually placed into that situation I mean I never ever thought I would ever go to jail.

About twenty minutes later Janice and Shaquita both walked back into the cell and they told me they were going home then we all hugged each other crying packing up everything in our room that's when some of the girls came into our cell asking if they could have our items and we gave them things that we hadn't used yet. We gave some of the other women items we hadn't used we all begin talking more and more as we ended up falling asleep from waiting to be released to go home not even knowing what time it was you couldn't even see outside the windows it was crazy because I had always wanted to be a correctional officer and or a police officer and at that time as I started thinking to myself I told myself in my mind that I may have to rethink those decisions because with those two charges I didn't know if it was possible for me to even be able to become a police officer and or a correctional officer but at that moment in time all I wanted to worry about was making it home to my daughter and I will worry about the rest when the time came up.

Shaquita Janice and I all decided to take naps until it was time to be released to go home because we already knew that that was going to take forever considering the fact that the Jacksonville jail was very slow they were literally slower than Clay County jail which is where I was at the first time I was in jail for an hour and I literally got right out they didn't have me in a holding cell they didn't have me in handcuffs they give me tours of the jail and flirting and everything. One of us had to stay awake just in case they called our names on the intercom to get up and get released from jail which was exactly what they would do they would call your first and last name on intercom.

When they finally called our names we had to be escorted back to check in to get our personal items I was giving back my ring, my belly ring, my cellphone, and my wallet. Everything was in my wallet that I had before I went into jail except the cash that I had when I went in jail it was very messed up that they literally had basically took my money and I had to pay a fee for being in jail and because I had that money in cash they took some of it and decided to pay for it for me No consent or anything but I didn't even care I was going home plus I had money. The police officer that was giving me all of my items back was flirting with me but I was with Chris at that time we were kind of on and off When I had turned my phone back on I had so many missed calls so many text messages from Chris he had blew my phone up he basically was giving me the business because I wasn't responding to him he was basically telling me how I was playing games with him and he didn't appreciate that and how he didn't want me if I was going to be ignoring him and not showing him any attention and giving him a little bit of my time that he asked for considering the simple fact that I was a mother. I couldn't even worry about it at that time or respond I was just wanting to get home to my child I could have called my father to come pick me up from jail but it would have taken him too long plus I didn't wanna hear his mouth I had enough going on in my mind and I was already slightly depressed and had a lot of thoughts in my head so unfortunately I called Kai someone that I should have left alone a long time ago and I probably would have been a lot better off he told me that him, Jamal, his niece we're going to be on the way and I was already more than sure that I had told his entire family what happened he couldn't hold water.

While I wait outside of the jail for Kai to come and pick me up Janice Shaquita and I all exchanged phone numbers telling each other that we needed to definitely hang out sometime Janice told us by because her ride was there to pick her up Shaquita and I had a little more time to talk for awhile as we talk we both told each other that we probably weren't going to be hanging out with Janice because she did drugs I try not to judge people in certain scenarios and situations but at the end of the day if I don't do something that someone else does I rather not be around the person at all because then people try to peer pressure you and to try and things all it takes is one time to trust something and you may get addicted to it. All I ever had tried was weed and I wasn't trying to try anything else it was already bad enough smoking weed especially while I had a government job. But her and I were only in our early thirties and twenties, I definitely didn't have the urge or need to try drugs either grant said I had a lot going on in my life and I was slightly depressed and even feeling suicidal at times and never had the urge to try drugs or take my life never even tried to take my life even though my mother Was making me suicidal I was just so sick of her she didn't want to go back to work she didn't want to do anything she told the whole world and she still tells the whole world to this day that I'm the reason why she lost her job even though she was probably going to lose her government job anyways I mean let's be real after all she was always taken our lunches she was always late she would always go on lunch get her hair done get pedicures And do all this other stuff plus at times she would be slightly tipsy as well or have wine in a flask and or a cup so Bri has told me before.

Chris and I started to get more and more serious even though I really wasn't into him though at first. I guess in the beginning I was just afraid to catch feelings for yet another man and be hurt betrayed sad and more. So I told myself that we didn't have a thing going on at all at least he actually wait uh six months to not have sex with me. He also very much had an anger problem just as well as I did so I definitely didn't know how that was going to work. He even had been around Kai a few times he also told me that he only did it for me because he doesn't really like gay men or being around them so I appreciated him doing it for me. Hi Chris and I had all went to the gas station and to grab some food from Wendy's when Chris told me that he had to go to his dad's office I love being in his truck he would often let me drive it it was huge and he would always drive fast and race and we would go mudding and driving through the woods. Chris would also pay for not only me but friends as well every once in awhile. He had met my mother and father a lot of times even my sister Bri and of course I bought him around Leilani few times. Everyone seemed to like him the only person who didn't know we were together at that time was my father I just decided not to say anything to him he probably would have been upset about it especially since my history with men in the past that I've dated and how I retaliated against them. Chris had paid for Leilani's second birthday party which was a carnival theme party at our house which was surprising to me that I had even had a birthday party for a kid at our house I was one that didn't like a lot of people in my home because people aren't going to treat your home like you would especially when they aren't the ones who have to pay for things and or replace things. But Chris pay for the bounce house and all the carnival themed activities that we had and the rest I made. I didn't ask him to nor did I expect him to he just did it he even gave me money and told me to treat myself which I appreciated it and I also wasn't used to that except for when I was with Jay.

Even then my father was upset when he found out that Chris had paid for the birthday party then he stated how he might want something in return but at that point we still hadn't even had sex yet so I wasn't even worried about it when we did sexual things it was really him who was doing everything to me and I was letting him. But I was also starting to catch more and more feelings for him he did a lot of things that I had never had done before or wasn't used to but I greatly appreciated everything he did for us plus it was nice having another man around who seemed like at the time he could be a good father figure. One time Chris I had surprise me and popped up at this restaurant that I told him I was going to be at which I was with one of my home girls at the time Sheena Her and I had met up at a restaurant called one night stand it was cheap tacos and cheap margaritas and I loved it we really only went for the drinks. The drinks used to get me messed up and I it The restaurant was on the South side of Jacksonville and a very nice area and my girl Sheena live right around the corner from it the one thing I couldn't stand about hanging out with her which I soon had found out was the simple fact she was all for me driving all the way to her but she would never drive to me talking about I lived like going out of town. The people are a different breed here in Florida they hate the drive to you but they're all for you driving to them that's what every person in Jacksonville that I've ever met and dealt with which is very annoying and why I eventually became an introvert. But Sheena and I sat at the bar at the restaurant we have went there a few times but this was our first time going there I had saw the restaurant was on Instagram and they had a special with their drinks Her and I are talking about our men problems and how she had two sugar daddies Sheena was thirty one at the time. Before I had went inside the restaurant I thought that I had saw Chris driving in his truck it definitely looked like him and his truck but I didn't think anything of it so when I go inside the restaurant a few minutes of us drinking and talking the owner of the restaurant comes over to me to ask me for my phone number but I told him that I was engaged and I had an engagement ring on. He then asked me if I was sure I wanted to get married and asking how long we have been together and stuff just all in my business like if somebody tells you know like just deal with it and go on with your life the owner wasn't even cute. A few minutes after the owner goes away Chris walks into the restaurant and in my mind I'm like I knew that was him the craziest part about it there's only two locations for that restaurant I never told him which location I was going to be at but I guess when he's a police officer full time he can do that it was sexy but it was also a turn off. When he walked in I was so shocked I got up hugged and kissed him he gave me flowers hand sanitizer a car with a lot of money in it and I introduced him to my friend Sheena I then asked him if he wanted me to get him anything for later because he always stayed at my house more than his own. He told me no babe I'm ok he said he had to get back to work he just wanted to bring me that. He hugged and kissed me again then he left when he left I looked at Sheena and I said girl he scared the hell out of me I didn't expect to see him I was also like how did he know which location we were at I didn't tell him which one I was going to. She started laughing and saying how she needed to get her a white man because she had two sugar daddies they were both black and in their fifties. The only reason I met Sheena was through my mother and sister when they were at red lobster one day and Bree told me that she went up to Sheena asking her who did her hair and Sheena says she did her own hair because she was a hairstylist and I mean she could definitely braid she even had braided Leilani's hair few times and she did a great job Even though she charged more than Felicia who was a friend of the family also I was very close to her two granddaughters who I was in fact older than but we all had attended the same Christian Academy she charged more and she lived further but she also had more patience with doing my child her that's the thing Lots of people can do her but not everyone has the patience to be able to sit there and do a child's hair which was the issue I was having with Felicia she was like a grandmother to me I was very close with her as well and I also confided to her a lot of times but when it came to doing Leilani her what pissed me off was a simple fact he would yell at my child and had no patience doing my child's hair so at the end of the day she wasn't charging a lot of money But it was the bitching and complaining that I couldn't deal with I didn't appreciate how she would often tell me that I needed to pop my child or have these talks with her to explain to her that she needed to sit still and get her hair done the issue I had with that the biggest issue I had with that don't tell me how to be a parent for me to have been a young mother I had my shit together and I hate it when older people corrected me or tried to tell me what I needed to do. I mean who the hell did she think she was after all she was in her late fifties and had her grown ass son in his forties stayed at home with all them damn kids that's not cute like maybe if you preach your son he'd be on his own and he'd have it together but meanwhile she chose to baby him.

She was always telling me that I needed to pop my child or hit my child second of all I didn't beat my child I didn't believe in that for the simple fact that when I was a kid my mother used to beat the hell out of me with whatever was insight because I'll never get over that I'm I went to school and told the teacher that my mother beat me with a brush I mean she really did it wasn't a lie in fact very much hurt. When I would go to Alabama during the summer time my aunts we use switches to beat me that very much hurt and that was very much only a thing in the South we didn't do that up north so I definitely didn't agree with hitting my child I definitely wasn't going to be hitting my child because she didn't want to sit and get her hair done at the end of the day if you cannot handle doing children's hair then don't but what I didn't like was the simple fact she kept trying to tell me what to do. As long as I can remember especially in high school I always hate it when people talk to me as if I had no sense of knowledge I always hated when people try to belittle me I always hate it when people try to judge me without knowing the full story. And this older woman was judging me I never judged her or the simple fact that she was in her late fifties with two children who were in their forties like damn how young were you when you had your kids not that I care but don't judge if you don't want to be judged back.

The woman even used to do my hair but I had to stop going to her for my so wins it wasn't even the simple fact that she charged a lot because money wasn't an issue at all granted I was always good with managing money and a logical thinker it was the simple fact of how she would talk to me and treat me one time I accidentally was short there was literally a few ATMs up the street I could have easily went to one and got her the money she told me not to worry about it so that was her own fault but she literally said to me I don't want to take all of your little money like lady little money are you really trying to insult me I was literally 21 with a security clearance working for the government meanwhile she was working at the hospital a person who takes peoples insurance not saying that's a bad job but at the end of the day don't come for me in assault me I make a lot of money the government job wasn't even my only source of income so I was very much confused why she was coming for me trying to be funny talking about little money. I didn't like stuff like that and it was very ignorant of her to make those comments like she was doing me a favor didn't have a her license the first and was trying to overcharge granted I just paid her the money she was charging me for my hair for the simple fact I never had known how to cut out the string from the so ends because I was always scared that I would cut my own hair so I would let her cut out the so winds I would also let her take out the cornrows she would do and I would let her wash my hair so I didn't mind paying more money it's just a slick remarks and comments that I cannot deal with and couldn't deal with at that time I was always told to respect my elders but sometimes the elders get out of line with their mouths.

She would always yell at my daughter which I don't play that so after a while we just stopped going to her was for the best she didn't even charge that much to braid Leilani's hair she would only charge twenty five dollars. Which is absolutely a very good price I wouldn't even mind paying thirty dollars which is what I was paying Sheena but she now also lived damn near hour away from me as opposed to Felicia who lived literally twenty five to thirty minutes getting on the toll road for me. But I wasn't going to deal with someone yelling at my child like if you don't want to do her hair anymore and didn't that's all you had to say but don't take your anger and frustrations out of my child I don't play that with anyone because I've always had an anger problem and I was not the one I may have had a baby face but that means absolutely nothing. That was exactly why at times I couldn't deal with my own kind of people I swear sometimes I couldn't. Even Leilani aunt Bev would braid in or twist her hair free of charge I wouldn't have minded paying by all means but her aunt would never allow me to pay so I wasn't going to turn that down but she didn't seem to do that great of a job to me and I would always have to throw in beads and or bows and other hair accessories to make the hairstyle pop and look pretty.

Felicia also had OCD which was something that I completely understood and I was medically diagnosed with. The issue was she would literally make me course out Leilani's hair then she would start complaining saying how there was hair on the floor which of course I was going to clean it up I'm not nasty we go to homes of others and clean up any mess that we made people won't be talking about how my child and or I came to their house and was nasty because I didn't play that as a young mother. But she would literally have me vacuum up her that was on her wooden floors after combing out and coursing Leilani her only for her to get right back on the floor again when she started combing and braiding the hair so I was very confused with that she wasn't the only person who had a nice home because I too did as well. Like my mother always said "Niggas that ain't never had nothing in life". I also couldn't stand how Felicia was always trying to tell me that I needed a man I was a strong minded young woman I already knew how it would end for me whether I had a man or not a man was always my downfall and men were always my weakness especially older men who were on the same caliber as I was so I was never eager to look for a man and I always try to take breaks from dating and talking to men I was interested in.

I hated how she always tried to tell me that we're not here on earth to be alone and all of this other stuff granted she was alone and she was also a single mother I was very confused by that I hate it when people were in my business and asked too many questions because one thing about me I could always get an engagement ring the issue I had was keeping the engagement ring and making it down the aisle but one thing about it if I had any intentions on being abused and and or trying to fake it to make it then I clearly would have probably been married at that time but unfortunately for me I wasn't going to keep putting up with shit from men. I didn't just need any man I needed a father figure a good role model of a man to my two girls and around my twogirls. I never had an issue with finding men who were on the same caliber as me and older and fitted the body description that I loved and was obsessed with it was the baggage that came along with them it was the simple fact that I was obsessed with older men but I didn't fully pay attention to their game and the red flags.

I'll never get over that I'm Felicia also insinuated that her son and I were together first of all I don't judge people who've been to jail it just depends on what you did to learn yourself into jail because I too had been to jail twice bet her son wasn't even close to my type first of all he was in his 40s staying at home with his Mama I get we all have to start somewhere and we all start from the bottom some of us at least to work our way up to the top I very much get that but 40 years old living at home with your mother that isn't cute especially when it comes to the men second of all he was so obsessed with trashy trailer park ass white women They always looked like they were strung out on drugs and he had way too many kids for me not as many as Theo but I mean he was trying to slowly but surely get there I don't think there's anything cute about a man who has a ton of kids who cannot provide for them financially and by all these different women that's not attractive nor cute it should very much be frowned upon on.

Her son was also on probation and yes I had been on probation for four months then I paid it off completely so that I could get off early but the issue was he also had an ankle monitor on and for some reason he was always gone partying and stuff to this day I'm still trying to understand how he was partying and clubbing and going to all these events with an ankle monitor on I'm more than sure he was lying to the people telling them he had some type of important event to go to even though it wasn't important at all but I'm very shocked and or surprised they didn't get his location or track him but his priorities were not in order granted he was fine and he was in his forties like I liked them specially height wise and weight wise but he wasn't my type nor was I going to sell myself short I even made more money than him but I didn't appreciate how Felicia insinuated that him and I we're a couple and could have been a cute couple she even one time said to us when we got back to her house that she thought we rolled off into the sunset together because of how long it took us to get back to her house because he had wrecked his car for like the third time he always went to jail for DUI's which is why he had the ankle monitor on two grown to be getting DUI's two grown to be getting in trouble in general.

But also when Felicia did Leilani's hair she always required me to drop her off and come back to get her because I seem to be a distraction to my child and she would always cry for me even if I was sitting literally directly beside her while her hair was being braided so I would often sit outside on Felicia's front and or back porch or just go shopping up the street to the Town Center. So one day Felicia said that she had to take her son to see his probation officer which was literally far as hell and on the other side of town deep into Jacksonville in the hood somewhere. I didn't feel like waiting at that time so I told Felicia that I would take her son all the way to that side of Jacksonville and my SUV Lincoln MKX which was a gas guzzler I loved that SUV it was luxurious it was nice inside and out and I had got a great deal on it but a gas guzzler it was and I had just filled my truck up and I didn't plan on going all the way that far on the other side of town wasting my gas her son didn't even offer to give me gas and yes I get that I offered to take him over there but I only offer to take him over there so that by the time we got back to his mother's house my child her would have been completed by then which in fact it was but that wasn't the point if someone took me that far I would have given them gas money no doubt about it especially since he worked from home from some type of call center and always had money to go out partying and clubbing so I was definitely for sure he had some type of money also instead of Florida when you're on probation you have to pay that fee every month you also have to pay for the ankle monitor if you have an ankle monitor when I was on probation I didn't have to get drug tested nor did I have an ankle monitor on.

But on the car ride there her son and I we talked a lot about our jail experiences and just how it changed us and we were talking about our dating lives at that time. The worst part about it that day when Felicia was supposed to do Leilani her before I even agreed to take her son on the other side of town her son had some white trashy woman who he had snuck into Felicia's house there and Felicia was beating her with a broomstick I hated being around when other people had arguments and or altercations occurring just ghetto and I didn't like my child being around that nor seeing that either because I didn't know that white woman knew what she was capable of doing granted I was armed and dangerous but that wasn't the point my gun was in my trunk. So while taking her son to his probation officer we talked a lot about that situation and I was telling him how much I adored his situation and I was telling him how much I adored his grandmother Mother mother which I very much did she was very cool honest and upfront it was just at times that slick mouth I couldn't deal with. And after I had took him to his appointment with his probation officer I had to make a few stops especially since I seen the stores and we were going to pass them anyways I was like let me go ahead and do it now. I definitely didn't want her son though he was a cool person to talk to and very attractive but he wasn't my type it was slightly an insult to me for the simple fact that she insinuated we wrote off in the sunset together her son wasn't on my calendar at all not even close I in fact actually was making more money than him as well.

Sheena might have been slightly hood and ghetto but one thing about it she could do some hair. While we were at one night stand she called her daughters to check on them and Leilani. Her daughters we're in middle school and her cousin who was nineteen was also there watching the girls while Sheena and I hung out which was very much needed. When her and I finally received our food we started talking about how it was nasty which it was so Sheena had paid for the lunch which I appreciate it so I told her I would pay for our drinks at the mall the malls in Jacksonville had stores that sold wine and liquor which you could walk around while drinking it in the mall. after that we went to the mall call the avenues it was a very nice mall that had way more stores than the one in Orange Park. I had drove my own vehicle because I hated to carpool because when I'm ready to go I'm ready to go and Sheena drove her own car. She was driving fast I wasn't tipsy or drunk but I also didn't wanna get pulled over for speeding for the simple fact that I had about three to four drinks.

When we get to the mall we do a lot of shopping when I finally opened the car that Chris had gave me he gave me three hundred dollars in cash and I read the card which on the outside of the card it said for my beautiful black queen it had a black woman and all on it I loved it it was a little things that always got me. When Sheena and I get to the mall we go to bath and body works they had a rope we walked all the way around these other people went underneath the rope and cut us and Sheena said out loud hell naw and they moved out the way I died laughing. I told her scaring them white people while laughing. It felt nice to have someone to hang out with because I was the type of woman I would cut somebody off very quickly. We did a lot of shopping even had got some food for the kids to go.

The next day Chris told me that he wanted me to meet his parents since he had practically met my friends some family my daughter my sister. His parents also lived up the street from me they had a nice house it was beautiful and private. They were lucky that they didn't live in a neighborhood that's like a dream house for me that I want no neighbors private gate three car garage. It was about eight in the morning so Chris and I go shopping I told him that I had some nice clothes to wear but he insisted that we go shopping for some clothes to wear to his parents house. He also told me that they were going to be cooking for me and asked me what types of foods that I like I told him that I'm not picky you know I eat a lot and drink a lot in my mind though I was like man I have to eat somebody else is cooking I really did not eat other people's houses people are nasty have pets in their kitchen people don't wash their hands I've seen it all and heard it all which is why I prefer to cook my own food. But I was willing to give it a try I mean after all we were engaged we weren't telling our parents or family members at all. I really didn't allow anyone I was dating to ever meet my parents until I knew it was serious granted it was serious we were engaged we hadn't even been together that long before we got engaged but I guess when you know you just know it wasn't like we said we're getting married tomorrow or something.

We went to a few stores like Burlington and Ross to see what they had I had already had it jumpsuit that I was wearing it was black with lace on it and professional I always had a tendency to dress up even when I wasn't at work that was just my style my wardrobe had definitely evolved over the years I used to always show midriff and skin which nothing was wrong with that considering of how young I was but time and place for everything I believe. Chris had bought himself a blue shirt then we stop at a gas station and grab some mikes hards we love drinking those next to drinking a four loko The mikes hards would give you a nice buzz. I used to drink those with Jay all the time. Chris dropped me back off home so that I could get ready he also told me that his mother told me that I could bring Leilani and let her swim in the pool but I told him maybe another time I had to see how his parents would feel about me and act around me and towards me first before allowing my daughter around. But Chris did buy Leilani some toys out of Burlington one thing about it he was always buying gifts for her and giving me money to add into her bank account for her even though she was already set with her dad's Social Security and money that I would put in there from time to time for her she never needed or wants it for anything but I was just that type of mother I always had to go home with something for my child I could never be empty handed I would even also get Bri things as well even though they didn't need anything. While Chris was driving to take me back home he grabbed my hand and started kissing it.

When he dropped me off home before I could open the door he gets out and opens the door for me then he grabs all the stuff out of the back seats for Leilani and Bri He takes everything to the front door for me opens the door for me then he told me he would see me later and I said ok we hugged we kissed he grabbed me on my ass I smiled and then he walked away. When I go into the house to get ready I received a text on my phone when I finally decided to check it because it took me a while sometimes I often wanted to take breaks from my phone plus I have been gone all morning so I had to spend time with my daughter and sister I always talked to them ask them how they were feeling what they wanted to do for the weekend it was also a virus out so I really tried not to take them places but we would do a lot of activities and things at home.

When I checked my phone it was my sister Ashley it was funny because one time when I was still dealing with my second court case she told me to take care of myself and that she loved me and she wasn't going to be talking to us anymore and he or she was talking to us she was a con artist like her mom like mother like daughter she only came around when she needed her once at something and the something that she wanted was always money something I never gave her hell I was a single mother just like her granted I had a better career than she did she was terrible when it came to saving money so that was her own fault if you can't even save money and keep money in your pocket why would I lend you money how are you going to pay me back if you're always broke that's why I don't lend money. Plus last time she told me she had to get away from all the drama even though she would only know what was going on because I would tell her I'm like girl you're asking what's going on so if you don't like drama or wanna be around us stop asking about our personal lives she was so damn nosey she wasn't complaining when she was asking what we had going on that's why you can't tell people stuff. I didn't have anything to tell her nor did I even want a relationship with her she lied so bad just like her mother.

Leilani Bri and I play the PS4 In my room we play Grand Theft Auto and hang out for awhile that's when Bri asked me how are things going with Chris and I and that she just wanted to see me happy as her big sister I always do things for everyone else and make sure everyone else is ok except for myself which was very much true I would literally splurge on the girls splurge for things for the home make sure all the bills are paid up for a few months or even weeks and I would literally put myself last and forget to take care of myself and let myself care and self health was very much important but I didn't care as long as the girls had what they needed they were always my first priorities my sister was literally like a daughter to me I did everything for her because her mother was too sorry to even send money for her when she lived with me from the very beginning. I told Bri that everything was perfect and that it was just different being with a white man because I had never been with a white man before. She then told me to have fun at Chris's parents house as I get up to shower and get ready and pack my bag. I decided to where a black jumpsuit With my red Gucci sandals and I had french tips on my fingernails and toes. I had also wore the engagement ring that Chris had bought for me except no one knew that we were engaged nor did his parents ask about either.

His mother and stepfather had literally had all different types of foods for me they had made ribs with beans they had potato salad they had different types of sushi They had BBQ chicken for me and I really appreciated it. Chris stepfather began asking me what type of work that I do and I told him that I work for the government on a Navy base in material management with my father. Then his stepfather asked me if my father had ever been in the military and I told him yes my father was going into marines then he went into the Navy. Then again a lot of people didn't know that my father was going into the marines first but my father told me that they took too long so he decided to go to navy. Chris's stepfather made a joke saying if your father was smart he wouldn't go into the marines then we all started laughing. And then they began asking how old Leilani was and I told them. Then Chris's stepfather was watching him and I Chris kept puckering up his lips indicating he wanted a kiss but I didn't know what his mother and stepfather would say even though we were grown so I blew a kiss to him and his stepfather had noticed and asked us what we were doing I said it was an inside joke to him. then Chris mother asked me if I wanted to go into the pool with her and I told her sure she then pointed to the guest bathroom that I could use to change into my bathing suit I had put on the bikini in the guest bathroom but I decided when I walked out to at least wrap up in my towel.

I walked outside and Chris mother asked me if I wanted anything to drink alcohol wise and I told her sure then I asked her what was she drinking and she made me a Jack and coke she then told me that she used to be a bartender and Chris had came out and asked me if I wanted to ride to the gas station with him to grab some mikes hard for him and I that's typically what we would drink. I told him that I would stay with his mother and continue talking to her he then told me ok and he gave me a kiss. Chris mother then asked me if I wanted anymore kids and I told her at least one or two more I love children and that I was soon going to be a teacher. She then told me that She had Chris at a very young age which I could definitely tell because Chris was thirty one at that time and his mother what's in her forties. I didn't judge I mean after all I got pregnant at eighteen going on nineteen and I didn't have Leilani until I was twenty years old. His mother even told me how she got food stamps and was on welfare when she was pregnant with Chris and even after she had Chris. The only thing I didn't like about Chris's stepfather was the fact he made a comment saying he doesn't understand why "we" have to go around looting and burning down our neighborhoods. He was referring to the Black Lives Matter stuff but I was confused on who we were. I wasn't looting or protesting. I told myself in my mind I was just going to talk to Chris about it later, plus he said his stepfather was a asshole anyways.

It is now the next day I decided to cook a Big Breakfast for everyone whenever I cooked anything I always would wash the dishes as I'm cooking so that towards the end there wouldn't be so much of a pallet of dishes all over the place I had had a brand new dishwasher that I had never used my mother used it a few times and somehow someway she broke it the craziest part about it the dishwasher as well as all the other appliances for my home were literally brand new when I purchased the home she would literally do things out of spite. Luckily for me I had a home warranty so as opposed to paying a few hundreds to get it fixed I would just pay eighty five dollar adaptable and the home warranty company was sent out someone to fix it thank God I had that a lot of homeowners don't know about home warranties and the importance of having home warranties is also cheaper to have a home warranty. I had text Chris asking him if he wanted to come with the girls and I to get out of the house and I slightly before had filled him in on the situation of what was going on with my mother and I and he told me that we were going to be getting married in December on the tenth and that my mother was going to have to leave my house because he was going to move into my home so I wouldn't have to move into his house and sell and or rent my house out and he said he wasn't going to be dealing with that nor sit back while I suffer because of my mother. He even didn't care for my mother much because of all the situations I told him about and everything that transpired while my was here.

Chris also taught me why you can't tell people everything about you or certain things about you because when bad day comes up people always bring up everything you said and throw it up in your face he was definitely one person to do that to me. One time Chris and I had both got into a argument and He asked me if I was done with him and I said yes next thing I know I hear a loud slam outside when I peep out the window it was Chris he had threw something in the back of his truck which was loud and scared me I jumped so hard because he definitely had an anger problem I think worse than me. Another time we had an argument and I texted his stepfather his stepfather then responded back to me telling me that I had to stop doing whatever I was doing to make Chris upset because he wouldn't stop until I stopped that was the type of person that he was it was as if he was scared of him what a punk of a man. The messed up part was at the time of the argument I was still on probation I only had to be on probation for four months which was absolutely nothing. I have still gotten off easy with my case one I didn't do it I wasn't convicted it was a misdemeanor I didn't do it and there was no proof thank God I wasn't convicted I was definitely moving up career wise and I didn't need to be convicted of any crime I did do the other crime which was spray paint in the car I still wasn't convicted of that either and that was also a misdemeanor even though I did it but whatever my lawyer was one of the best and I told him I don't care what the outcomes are I don't want any convictions I don't want any felonies most importantly I don't want to be convicted or go to jail or prison so if you could deliver that I told Matt I will pay you any amount of money altogether $10,000 For both cases which wasn't bad at all to be honest. But when I had pissed off Chris one night he literally texts me back saying aren't you on probation you're supposed to absolutely stay out of trouble it would be a shame to have to get you in trouble I couldn't believe that. And to be honest white people are the ones that turn on you real fast they'll be real cool until you make them mad they be ready to destroy your life at that point I didn't do anything to him all I probably did was slightly provoke him because he was running his mouth because he told me that he may have had to get tested for herpes because his ex actually tested positive for it at that point in time we have been having unprotected sex so yeah I'm going to hate you I literally told Chris if you give me herpes I will hate you for the rest of your life no I'm not going to want to marry you no I'm not going to want to be with you I'm going to have nothing but hate towards you I told him that to his face and I told him I would ruin your fucking life. He couldn't even say anything he was just looking at me crazy I knew we both had anger problems however I didn't know which one of us had the anger problem the worst.

I then asked him do you think I want something I can't get rid of I then asked him also when was he going to get tested. He told me that we could both go together to get tested I told him right about now I don't wanna be around him I told him he makes me sick if I have that I'm going to be sick I'm going to die scream yell not want to live or be here I told him that's not something that goes away I said a shot in the ask aunt cure everything. It was just too much for me we were arguing back and forth and text I told him I hated him I'm going to hate him. He was trying to hug me and hold me I told him don't fucking touch me I will snap in here. So see? no matter how much things always were great there always had to be something or someone that ruined things for me. I had told Chris to get out of my house he asked if I was sure and I told him I was positive please leave he got up and left. I sat on my couch downstairs crying as I start taking shots of drinks to numb the pain because I couldn't believe that I could possibly have herpes I was so scared to even go get tested but I mean at least he said he was willing to go with me to get tested but hell it was his fault.

The last man that I got with was Tony the problem with me was whenever I learned a lesson I never truly learned it because I would always keep doing the same thing over and over again which is why I got into the predicament the last situation. I met Tony at work at the government job he wasn't in the military he was a civilian me. I'll assume going to find out that he was married they all always seem to be married I think another issue that I had was that I never took my time when it came to dating always rest and jump back into it. The craziest thing about it everyone knew that he was married except for me when he approached me he didn't have a wedding band on and this is the problem right here that I felt to realize time and time before because I fail to do background checks I fail to take my time I was so eager to have a man in my life not realizing that a man will come and go that a man is going to do what he wants to do with whomever he wants to do and there is absolutely nothing that I could have done to make any of these men tell the truth it just very much hurt me and I was in such distraught because the simple fact I was allowing another man to do me dirty again and I was accepting it which was why I figured and taught myself it kept happening to me I kept allowing these men to be married and deal with them in fool with them. Again I never seem to learn my lesson then on top of that I was having unprotected sex with this man allowing this man to come into my home smoke weed with me in my home I never let anyone smoke in my house except for me because I was the bitch In my house that was paying the bills one thing about it my sister and my daughter never seen me do it nor did they smell it. I was literally having sex with this man at work in my car on our lunch breaks letting him come to my house we would even sometimes smoke weed together on our lunch breaks I was literally allowing this man to consume me and help me ruin me. With this man though he claimed that he was going through a divorce and he claimed that I couldn't come to his house when I finally found out about him being married and I decided that I in fact was going to inform him that I knew he was married and when I did I didn't appreciate how he was still not telling me what I needed to know.

This was the same man who was in my house the same man that I had cooked a whole meal for and prepared and took the time to do so for the same man who was sitting on my couch with me smoking blunts with me while watching the movie a thin line between love and hate the same man who was saying how Martin Lawrence was wrong in that movie the same man who was sitting beside me knowingly knowing that he was married but he had failed to tell me. The same man who was sitting beside me on my couch telling me he was on the phone with his mother and he told his mother while sitting beside me that he was at his girlfriends house and he would stop by her house on his way home.

Not to mention the simple fact that February of twenty twenty two I literally saw this man when my daughter and I were shopping together in the store Ross in the Town Center of oak leaf forgetting that he resided in oak leaf I had no idea that I was going to run into him not that I planned for that to happen but it was whatever I mean after all we didn't live far away from each other at all. Leilani and I were shopping around grabbing a whole bunch of things that we didn't need for the simple fact that we were just killing time because my entire house was being painted so I figured it would be better if we weren't home while they were painting the house because that was already day four and it was just stuff everywhere in my OCD couldn't take all the mess everywhere I needed to definitely get out of the house especially for the simple fact that my father was there while they were painting the house. I had saw Tony first before he noticed me and I started to back up but the shopping cart which my child was inside of when I did so she looked at me and noticed me and said hey and in my mind I was like damn it because I didn't want to talk with him or engage in any type of conversation that he had to say I was already starting to have flashbacks about how I tried to help him I tried to basically build this man up again from when he would tell me stories of his wife and how she was a piece of crap and she was trying to take him for everything he had he was already struggling even then when we were together but there I was being a supportive girlfriend that I thought I needed to be and should have been offering him to move into my house offering to give him money and help him because I knew I could do so and do that even though he would never allow me to help him in that way or give him any money. I just hated the fact how he wasted my time like at the end of the day he knew that he was married and he still decided to come and talk to me knowing he had baggage with him that's the thing that I didn't appreciate like if you're in a situation why come and waste someone else's time and disappoint others like I had already had enough disappointment in my life with all the men that I had previously been with and it seemed as if I couldn't catch a break yet another married man like when was the married man thing going to really stop? These men in this generation are very selfish they're all almost married and they just have so much baggage with them.

As I backed away as I told him hello while I gave Leilani the phone which I was actually on the phone until he started talking to me and I passed it to my child to talk to the person I was talking on the phone with. Tony started telling me how I still look good and saying how I always look good he starts saying how I look like I had money but he was like you've always had money in my smart about making money talking about let him hold some money he playfully said to me. He then asked me how was I and what did I have going on I told him that I was engaged and I was pregnant and his face instantly dropped. I couldn't believe that nigga flipped the script on me talking about how could I go get engaged to someone else when he loved me and how come I didn't wait for him. I told him I waited for you long enough and it seems like you're still the same Tony always thinking about yourself always making everything about yourself I said when I was with you you definitely had a good woman I tried to help you uplift you do a lot for you I was even trying to build you and make you become a better man and turn into someone else that you could have definitely been for the better and for the better if your children but you didn't want that then so I couldn't wait for you any longer I had to wash my hands with the situation. I hang up the phone with the person that I was on the phone with at the time who was a friend I thought I was close with that I had met on an app called tiktok named Selena. I then put my phone on youtube Kids for

Leilani she loved YouTube and she knew how to maneuver it while I talked to this dumb ass. Then Tony told me that my ass was fat still and that I really looked good and he missed me and he's definitely been doing a lot of thinking about me he then asked me if I could take him off the block list and asked me why he was blocked.

I then told him that he did me so dirty and wrong and I had nothing but love for him at that time but now that Love Is All gone. He then asked me was I really going to marry someone else and then try to play me saying that I always could keep a man I told him hell yeah I was going to marry someone else because the man that I was with he loved me for me he didn't treat me wrong he wasn't married he treated my child right he cared about my feelings. He actually wanted to make me a wife meanwhile Tony you never ever communicated with me and the simple fact that you knew you were married all those times we were hanging out together and . you told me that you felt bad but yet you still let me walk around thinking we were really a couple while everyone else knew that you were married that's embarrassing. I told him this man has been taking really good care of me I don't have to beg or ask him to Take Me Out on dates or to do things for me like I had to do with you Tony. Then tony told me that I knew he was broken struggling I told him I didn't know anything because you never communicated and you chose to keep secrets even when I tried to uplift you like a woman is supposed to do with her man that she's with whether he's doing good in life or struggling but wouldn't let me. He then asked me when was I going to leave Chris for him and I told him he must be out of his damn mind I deserve to be happy and I deserve the happiness that I currently have and I'm not going to allow you or anyone else to mess that up for me or ruin that for me I've prayed and begged cried for this to happen all of everyone it was a great man and a father figure and it's finally happening and I refused to allow anyone to get into the way of that do me.

CHAPTER

14

Tony then brought up how I used to go to lunch with this one guy who worked with him not me but the guy Fernando and I were very close he was also very fine but married even though he didn't tell me I had already knew that because after all people talk but sometimes we go out for drinks it was very friendly at 1ˢᵗ and harmless. Tony then told me how I could be petty at times in the past like when I told him that I was going to fuck his boss but I wasn't actually going to have sex with his boss I was just telling him that because I knew that I could get under his skin that way I knew he didn't like stuff like that it felt nice always having power in the upper hand that's why you saw him like that and say that like that I think go the understand why he would get so upset about it considering he was married but Tony told me to this day he still doesn't talk to Fernando because I told him that we went out a few times which we did lunch and dinner for drinks all the time. One time Tony did tell me that I needed to be careful and watch out for him because he knew Fernando liked me but I wasn't trying to listen or hear anything that Tony had to say he was married and he was a liar but he was actually right I did need it to not be around Fernando as much as I was because one night we were eating at Buffalo Wild Wings at the bar drinking and talking and Fernando had kissed me knowingly knowing that he was married and I knew he was married. And for some reason I told

Tony about it I guess one because it happened and two because I wanted Tony to hurt and to feel how I felt when he decided to tell me he was married at the last minute.

I told Tony that was old but since he wanted to bring up the past I told him I remember all the times I would bring him breakfast and lunch to work all the times I would cry and beg him to Take Me Out or even just to go out with me in public in general all the times when I kept calling and texting and got no responses or answers. I told him I was miserable and that wasn't love at all I told him when you really care about people you don't do things like that had he really cared he would've told me that he was married they won or better yet he would've just left me alone after all he was the one who approached me I never approach any man if a man wants me they have to definitely come over to me and prove to me why they want me and talk to me the craziest thing about it I really didn't give any and every man this time of the day or my attention. The craziest thing was I was the successful young woman in her early twenties, Who had it all didn't need a man I just wanted a man I wanted a father figure for my daughter I wanted to have a family something I never had. I wanted to give my daughter a two parent home granted a lot of times we see married people and think that their lives are so much perfect and or better than ours because we're not married as a single mother especially in today's society on social media mainly I see so many women gets judged for being a single mother but what I had to eventually teach myself was the thing that being married doesn't always mean that you're happy being married doesn't always mean that you have it all being married doesn't always mean that your marriage will last forever being married doesn't mean that you're better than others who aren't married married people endure a lot just as well as a single person and or a couple that's just starting out dating.

Plus at the rate I was going I had eventually told myself that I didn't want to get married even though I was even then in a relationship when Tony approached me but I just told myself I've always wanted this it was never an issue for me to get engaged ever the thing that I had that was an issue was keeping that engagement ring making it to walk down the aisle and walk to the courthouse to say I do I never made it to that point ever I was always close. But on social media in this generation some married people are always so eager to judge a single mother at the end of the day I cannot help that I was a single mother because my daughter's father died and unfortunately there was absolutely nothing I could have done to prevent his death it would have been nice to have been able to prevent his death however everything happens for a reason and had he survived or I prevented his death I don't think that I will be a single successful black young woman. You see him passing away made me turn into a strong minded young woman that I need it to be not for myself but for my daughter Jay passing away made me see that I needed to do better in life as a young woman entering her early twenties. I loved him with everything that I had within me and I would never stop loving him but I always think about the what ifs and sometimes I tell myself that if he were still alive it doesn't necessarily mean that we would have still been together after all it is now the year twenty twenty two so his birthday was February twenty fifth he literally would have been thirty eight years old and the age was never an issue with us at all even though he had people in his ear on his side of the family telling him that I was way too young for him but what they fail to realize yes I was young in general but spiritually mentally and physically I thought I was way older than I was I've always thought that.

But I hated how people judge me for being a single mother in society without knowing my story we all have a story on while we're a single mother and or a single father which is why you don't judge books by their covers until you get the story and even then it's no one's business my pregnancy was very much planned with Jay and I granted I didn't want a baby he did and sometimes that's the thing when you're with older men but I told myself that I love this man I gave my all we kept trying to get me pregnant and it finally happened when we stopped trying to get me pregnant so I was definitely devoted and dedicated to having a baby for this man and we were also having unprotected sex so unfortunately those are the ramifications of having unprotected sex you have to deal with those consequences that come with having unprotected sex. But him passing away made me stronger out of everything that could have possibly ever happened to me in my entire life that had to be number one on my list for one of the worst things that I've ever endured the amount of pain and suffering that I endured the thinking about my child never having a father again and thinking of how I would have to replace him even though I can't replace him no matter how hard I had tried to there was never going to be a man that I met that was on his mentality which there was absolutely nothing I could do about that. But people are always judging you for being a single mother and me personally to have been a single mother who was only in her early twenties I was definitely killing motherhood by my damn self at that and I loved being a single mother for so long and I had gotten so used to being a strong minded independent woman and I loved it yeah at times I would get tired overwhelmed weary stressed depressed sad my anxiety and depression will definitely come out at times my therapist had even prescribed me on some anxiety and antidepressant medication but I told him that I didn't want to be on it anymore because at the end of the day if I need medication in order to function and in order to get where I need to be in life then I don't need to be on it nor do I want to be on it I don't want medication to be the only reason I can tell someone yes I'm ok.

That was another thing I was in therapy I had been attending therapy sessions with the same therapist at his office for years and out of all the therapists that I had ever went to I absolutely loved going to seek counseling with this therapist in particular the women counselors I feel are too judging. But the male therapist I have been seeking counseling with always kept it real and always told me what I didn't want to hear and or what I needed to hear and I really appreciated that he would teach me techniques and skills for the next time I felt myself getting angry. He always had solutions for any problem that I had even if he couldn't relate to the situation he also told me that as a black woman I will always have it harder than any other race which he was absolutely right and I'm glad he knew that because it was in fact true black people in general will always have it harder in life than any other race

Tony had even told me how he followed me on Instagram at tiktok I'm like aren't you a stalker he then asked me if I could pull strings to get him into the correctional institution that I was at. I told him that I don't pull strings for people I don't vouch for people nor do I help people get into the same job that I'm in because all it takes is one time for them to mess up and that comes back on me you're using my name I have never done something like that for someone and I do not think I will because sadly people will always disappoint you even when you think they won't. Little did he know and everyone else know it took me a long time to become a correctional officer which was absolutely crazy I couldn't believe it I was good enough at twenty three years old to be a teacher with my criminal history but I wasn't good enough to be a correctional officer. I was literally a teacher in Clay County they did a background check and I had to pay one hundred dollars for that which was very risky because I thought to myself what if I don't get this job I'm out of one hundred dollars but I was willing to risk that because I told myself I always wanted to be a teacher I loved kids I even wanted to have more kids. Which was very crazy because growing up I always told myself that I would be the one to not have any kids at all. But I've really had the run around to become a correctional officer because of my criminal history which was very crazy because I only had two misdemeanors I had the criminal mischief charge I was found guilty because I mean I did do it but I had a very great lawyer but he was able to make a deal to where I wasn't convicted of the crime even though I did it and I received a withhold adjudication.

Then all I had to do was pay Kevin to get his car a new paint job, Which I hated to do that old car but I did spray paint his car so unfortunately it had to be done and then I couldn't have anymore contact with him and I was on probation with that case for four months. The craziest part about it the improper exhibition charge was worse than that yet I wasn't even on probation for only four months with that but whatever I was just trying to get off easy especially all the money we paid well my dad paid. Then the other charge was improper exhibition of a firearm that was also a misdemeanor I received the withhold adjudication I wasn't convicted of the crime All I had to do was surrender my firearm and I was able to keep my concealed weapons license and I couldn't have any contact with the guy Adam even though he lived in my neighborhood but he soon enough had moved out that neighborhood The crazy thing about it months later he was arrested for narcotics that's exactly what he got I was so ecstatic especially when I found out that he moved out my neighborhood. I was even able to buy myself a few guns after everything was completely over with my concealed weapons license I was so glad they didn't take that away. But I definitely had gotten off easy with both cases. It was just very crazy to me how I really was getting the runaround to be a correctional officer ever since I was a little girl I always said that I wanted to be a police officer and or a correctional officer in the state of Florida it's easier to become a correctional officer stay in the same position as a correctional officer for about a year or two then you can switch over so being a police officer you actually can become a deputy after two years of being a correctional officer.

I was going to all of these correction officer institutions going to all these interviews filling out the same forms online over and over again because sadly even when I would call at institution to ask them if they thought I had a chance or not they would always tell me the same thing oh we don't know anything until you submit your application I'm like but basically what I'm trying to tell you is I'm wasting my time doing that Which is what I would tell a lot of them I mean who wants to sit there and fill out the same information over and over again like you don't need my application to tell me if I'm going to be able to be good or not when I'm sitting here willingly telling everyone the type of charges I had. Some places would lie and some would be up front with me one place even told me that it hadn't been long enough on my record I'm like I get that but they're still misdemeanors I would even tell them like I'm literally a teacher I was in therapy I had completed my terms for the twenty six week anger management class. I didn't even finish the twenty six weeks because I wasn't required to granted I really loved going to anger management one of the women who attended the anger management class that I was in literally her and I became the best of friends she was Forty years old at that time and she also lived in the next neighborhood over from me I had just loved hanging out with her because it was nice having somebody who could actually relate to you she could relate to me by going to jail granted she had been more times than me in her situations word worse and she also Had been in a few department of children and family cases it was just nice talking to someone who can relate who wasn't going to judge me class I always love hanging out with older people I would always go to her house with Leilani so she could play with her daughters and we will be in her garage drinking white claws and just talking and her name is Devin. We would always hang out at her house have cookouts talk chill and because our neighborhoods were next to each other I would stay at her house until midnight with my kid having a playdate with her kids. We would even talk about some of our anger management homework assignments and or the sign assignments that needed to be completed before we went back to the next session but I really learned a lot in that anger management class it made me a better me slowly but surely I learned so many techniques when I'm angry that I wish I had known about a long time ago but I'm not even upset that I had to attend that class or the trouble because sometimes we need things in life to slow us down or to show us to get us to learn to listen to think before acting and I guess at that time that was exactly what I needed.

But I wanted the correctional officer job so bad that I was crying I was going back to the binge drinking I couldn't believe that I couldn't become a correctional officer because of criminal history I wasn't even a felon I wasn't even convicted of anything so it was almost like I didn't do anything but I guess that was a prime example of no matter how much you change people will always still judge you for your past and look at you as if you're that same person you could literally go into the military with criminal history you could literally be a teacher with criminal history I was living proof of being a teacher with criminal history clearly they didn't find it that bad enough to not let me be a teacher at twenty three years old. I was very livid I literally was working with children never went off on them never had a outburst I actually adored all the children that I ever had taught and of course as a teacher you're always going to have a few children that give you a hard time which is completely fine and we know that the thing about being a teacher you have to have a lot of patience and understanding if you and if you can't you don't need to be a teacher there would be times I would be in the teachers lounge eating lunch and the teachers some of them will be complaining about their students which is understanding but when I would teach at the elementary schools some of the other teachers would be like oh these kids need to be on medicine and they're out of control and complaining about how they were going to go home and get drunk and I'm just looking at them Mike wow maybe you don't need to be a teacher then because you have to have a lot of patience especially as a elementary school teacher yeah definitely.

One time this one lady set out loud how kids need to be on medication and I told her I disagree I said see as a mother and I said I had two kids at that time because I consider Bri a daughter I did everything for her paid for everything for her She would even call me her mom sometimes which I didn't care. I also told the woman who was older than me which I didn't care age had absolutely nothing to do with it I told her I don't agree with putting children on medication little does she know when I was a kid my parents especially my dad family because they simply couldn't control me they thought that putting me on Ritalin was the answer I hated Ritalin I would look like a zombie I didn't wanna talk I didn't wanna eat I didn't want to play or do anything I hate how people are so quick to think that fixing a child is putting them on medication I didn't agree with that at all like how would they like it or somebody put them on some medication like that that makes you not want to talk eat play or interact with people I'm sure they wouldn't like it I was really against medicating children especially for those purposes to get them to calm down or act better because at that point they're not even acting better they're not acting like anything because they can't even understand what's going on because they're high on medicine that Ritalin was nothing to play with I was on it for so many years in elementary school even some years in high school but no one knew my ninth grade year is the last year that I had to take Ritalin and it was crazy because I would always get pulled out for random drug tests at that time I wasn't really having sex I wasn't drinking smoking so that was crazy they always used to pull me out.

But people are so quick to put their children on medication to help them act right so they say then when the medication messes them up overtime the parents are crying and they want to sue the company that made the medication and gave it to them they want to sue the doctor bet they fail to realize they have to take some type of accountability because you wanted your child to be on that. After that day I never sat in a teacher's lounge again I just wanted to see what it was like and after seeing what it was truly like I said yeah bunch of white women that are very catty complaining about a job that they clearly wanted because they got degrees and took state tests to become teachers how ironic. I get that no job is going to be perfect and we're always going to have people that irritate us and But when it comes to kids if you can't handle the stress and pressure of being a teacher then you don't need to be one because if I heard a teacher talking to my kids or about my kids the way those teachers were I would beat they're ass respectfully.

But I was even a Public notary for the state of Florida so I was so confused on once again why I wasn't able to be a correction officer they were literally misdemeanors felonies are worse but I guess something I told myself was criminal history is still criminal history felony or not. The state of Florida also had to approve me to become a public notary granted I guess took the test online and passed it but you still had to be approved by your state hell I was a public notary, notary signing agent, wedding officiator, immigration notary. Even to be a notary signing agent that's real estate so you definitely had to be approved by the state of Florida for that separately from just becoming a notary because once again you're interacting with people. Tony had knew that I had been to jail I mean hell he had been to jail as well but he wasn't a felon but he also didn't judge me I mean after all how could he but it was nice just talking to people who could relate and understand. But I wasn't going to help him become a correctional officer he was going to have to go through the same steps and procedures that everyone else did it literally took me a year and a half to become a correctional officer because of my criminal history I got so many rejections and I told myself I cannot give up I was crying I I was binge drinking I was smoking weed I've kept telling myself every night I'm going to keep applying and keep trying they're so many correction officer institutions I went to ones in Lake City,Lake Butler, Ocala,Tallahassee,Putnam county because everything was so close to me living in middleburg all I had to do was take the back roads to get to these institutions there were so many. I would always be ready and overly prepared for the interviews for when the question came up about if I had criminal history or not I had my folder with my depositions statements, the outcome, written letters my anger management information my therapy information I even had a letter that I had typed up by myself stating how I changed and better person after getting in all that trouble. At one institution I had even received my uniform I did the drug test I got tested to see if I had tuberculosis I did everything they asked me to do and never heard back from them again. after a while of me following up I kept talking to different people over and over again I would give them the name of the person I had previously talked to they then told me that I would have to start the whole process over again I thought that was crazy. When I finally had decided to give up I waited months later to take a break from applying to all these institutions.

After a while I just told myself it wasn't meant to be I had enough Sources of income but I was also a Jack of all trades and typically anything that I wanted I always got so that was very much a slap in the face. It was definitely a lot of motivation for me when I finally did become a correctional officer because it taught me to never give up and I didn't give up even though it took a year to become one it was definitely worth. It was also a very dangerous occupation which I knew it was and my father how could I forget he would always remind me just how dangerous the job was even one of my friends from middle school Tati Would definitely piss me off at times I hate it judgmental asspeople like how could you possibly tell me anything when you live at home with your mother with your child and the father of your child is a piece of crap in which she knew before she had a baby with this man he was also a drug dealer like sometimes we have to make better choices and decisions sheshould've knew nothing good was going to come from that.I couldn't understand why she was so eager to judge me like at least I moved out of my parents house at least I get up and go to work for my child even though I never had to and I like to make something of myself and something to leave behind for my kids when I'm gone.I try not to judge people but when someone decides to take shots towards meI'm going to do it just that and harder.

My father would piss me off because he would tell me that as a mother it's a dangerous job which yes law enforcement is very dangerous I was well aware of that but that was my passion and my dream I'm not going to give up my dream because I'm a mother and I've told myself and taught myself that one too many times just because you're a parent doesn't mean you have to give up your hopes and dreams that's why so many mothers and fathers eventually have regrets the older they get in life.But then again my father always did want me to go into the military but I told myself that I did enough listening to my mother and father throughout my entire life and trying to please themI was so over that I was an adult and I had to make my own decisions and choices and what I felt was right for me not what everybody else wanted me to growing up I was slightly miserable because of that after all it is my father's fault slightly that I got sexually assaulted in college because I didn't want to go to that college not to mention the fact he put me in debt forty thousand dollars for sending me to a private college because at that time I couldn't use his military benefits to go to school if it wasn't for him sending me there I wouldn't have gotten sexually assaulted in the first placeI definitely one hundred percent blamed my father for that.My father wanted me to go into the Navy but I just did not want to go into it I wanted to at first because I wanted to be just like my father as well as my mother but then I soon discovered that I could never be either one of them because I'm me.I hate parents that try to make their kids make up for what they've missed in their life or parents that try to live their life through their kids.

My father was definitely annoying as hell not even just with a correctional officer job. Since I had been working at Florida State prison which is a maximum security men's prison the same prison where Ted Bundy and a few others were executed. We were the only prison in the state of Florida that Does executions we have lethal injection as well as the electric chair. I'm not going to lie I really enjoyed the job and I liked it a lot especially considering how long it took for me to get into the job in the first placeI had even sat in the electric chair and seen the death house pretty cool experience a once in a lifetime experience at that. Since I had been at that prison I had seen so much in just the first month of me being at the prison but I also learned so much as well.We literally have-a bunch of transgenders on Lima wing One of them is in prison because he decided to put cement and his butt which caused him to be in a wheelchair for quite some time when

I first started there's well as other people's killed some of them he literally had twelve counts of that not to mention the simple fact that he thought it would be a good idea to be a plastic surgeries illegally performed plastic surgery on his own face which he looks a mess he also was performing plastic surgeries on other people's faces.Plus in the state of Florida whenever inmates are entering in the prisons and they've already started the change within their bodies the state of Florida does have to pay for the rest of the procedures for the inmates.One time I was working in October dorm which is medium custody inmate only And one of the officers which who I was working with had found contraband on one of the inmates the dorm and when she took it from him he started to get louder belligerent and tried to run up on not her the person that took the contraband but me three times I literally told him that he put his hands on me I'm going to beat his ass with a fire extinguisherI would have grabbed because that was the first and only thing insight considering that he was way bigger than me and I have every right to defend myself if an inmate puts his hands on me. One of the inmates grabbed the inmate back who was loud and belligerent and that was probably the best thing he could have did for that inmate that day because I don't play those gameshe could have had a weapon on him or anything.

One time I was working on Lima wing again and the runaround on that wing asked the Sergeant if he could show me some optics of what he did to a child molester who was in prison the runaround only killed child molesters which I'm not even mad at him anybody who's willing to do something like that to a child is sick and disturbing anddeserve whatever they get when they go to prison. The Sergeant agreed to allow the inmate to show me the optics of what he did to the inmate who was bragging about molesting children that runaround killed the inmate I grab my blue gloves you always put on gloves when touching any contraband or any of the inmates property in general and I began looking at the pictures it was crazy because it was just like something that you see like on law and order or police television showsI wasn't even disturbed or disgusted I was actually able to even eat lunch after looking at those pictures of how he killed the inmate the runaround staff the inmate fifty times and the inmate died with his eyes open the pictures were very graphic. The runaround was even taken up for me when some of of the male inmates were saying provocative things to me.

One timeI was on foxtrot wing and the run around on that wing was trying to establish a relationship with me three times I told him to get away from me and he still kept trying to push his luck granted I've been to jail twice so at certain situations I try not to judge because how can I but I'm not a killer or rapist or anything plus on top of that I'm the correctional officer so if I tell you to go away as the inmate you need to do what you're told but I guess they were trying to see where my loyalty was because I was also new at that time but I still didn't play that a lot of people don't realize and understand that if you sleep with an inmate you literally go to prison yourself inmates cannot consent to sex just because they are legal ageI'm gonna have my life ruined on the account of an inmate some of them have absolutely nothing to lose in the first place some of those inmates have aids, herpes, syphilis, tuberculosis and more. He kept telling me how soon he'll be getting out of prison and how he lived in Miami and he wanted me to keep in contact with his sister and mother so I thought in my mind let me set this inmate up because he's not listening and getting it so in order for me to show that I'm serious and get my point across I thought to myself if I set him up he'll tell the other inmates and they won't try me either which seemed like a smart idea at that time before I realize how crooked some of the sergeants lieutenants and other officers be.

I had told the Sergeant with who I was working with on the wing that time about the runaroundAnd he told me to get the note the runaround wanted to give me.I hadn't even read the note from the inmate when he had given it to meI put it in my pocket so that I can give it to the Sergeant just so happened that a Lieutenant came on the wing and that's sergeant old the Lieutenant about it so the Lieutenant pulled me to the side and ask for the note then he put the run around in handcuffs and put him the dayroom by himself. This inmate literally lied on me and I'm one of those people I don't care what you say about me but when you lie on me we have a problem a serious problem because I'm going to get you before you get me. I have worked on that same wing with the runaround again the last Sergeant who was on the wing when the runaround was showing us rats and stuff because that Sergeant allowed the runaround to get into our business and personal conversations the runaround knew that I was engaged and I had kids and all this other stuff. Even though people are in prison and they can still do a lot-and get their family members and gang members to do a lot of people even people at this prison have been followed home by the inmates family. Other correctional officers have had hits put on them at my prison by the inmates so not for one second do I ever underestimate any inmate but I just I'm not scared nor was I. When the Lieutenant was talking to the inmate he told the Lieutenant that I told him I had kids and stuff which I never technically told him he heard the conversation but I didn't think it was that serious so it's not like I'm saying where my kids go to school at and all of that so why does it matter? That same Sergeant who allowed that run around to be around us listening to our personal conversation in the first place was the same Sergeant who told me that I was sexy as fuck he was always asking me out on dates he even talked about me to this run around because the runaround told me and I knew for a fact he wasn't lying about that because there's Sergeant was always sexually harassing me asking me what when was I going to cook collard greens which seemed to be a tad bit racist like just because I'm black does not mean I can cook collard greens even though I can that's not the point. this sergeant was fat white nasty sloppy and ugly even if he was attractive you don't shit where you lay.

Anyways this same Lieutenant decided him and his girlfriend who was a correctional officer were going to have a conversation with me this

Lieutenant literally said to me that it's like when you go to a club and talking about how when you start having conversations with these inmates they get into their feelings and they get to liking you and stuff in my mind I'm like is he really taking up for this inmate like what that's crazy at the end of the day I thought I did it right thing because I was setting up the inmate and then I told on him to make an example out of him so he could go telling his other inmate friends how I'm a snitchand tell them not to try me but I could see that slightly backfired for me and I didn't appreciate it I definitely didn't appreciate the Lieutenant's girlfriend Trying to talk to me like girl talk one on oneI had literally worked on a military base before but nothing but men and everything so it was very unnecessary especially considering the fact I saw his girlfriend smoking a cigarette in the electrical room which is a crime and illegal but they don't talk about that.I've also had inmates try to ask me personal questions.One inmate when I was walking down the wing to the wing check even asked me how much did my ring cost on my finger then he says to me your man must love you and I said shit I hope so. They wanted the president to be so professional and my personal opinion there is nothing professional about working in a prison the inmates cuss at you the inmates talk trash to you the officers cuss the captains the measures do lieutenants the sergeants hell even a warden and assistant warden cussed.Even an inmate had added me on Facebook one time from the same prison where I worked at-so it was definitely very dangerous but I just wasn't scared. Let's not forget about the amounts of times I see penises all day which was annoying and I hate to say this but some of them inmates had huge dicks. I just wasn't pressed about it I would have to tell some of the inmates to put it away one time I was doing a wing check on Juliet wing and this inmate had literally just finished masturbating. I literally saw the cum on the tip of his dick.

I honestly would tell my mother some of the things that happened at work were pretty much all of the things that happened at work but I would never tell my father because he would try to convince me to quit and he would get on my damn nerves if I was that scared to work in a prison then I didn't need to be working in one at all. You could literally get fired at my prison for being a coward and it's in the handbook.It took me a year to get that jobI was not going to quit or leave because it got hard and difficult with everything that was happening and going on howeverI was very offended when I was sexually harassed by a Sergeant for so long and I wrote incident reports even told the warden and turned it into the warden and nothing was done about it then they'd be mad if I sue them.I would even have issues with some of the correctional officers just being plain out nasty even when I was in the Jacksonville jail overnight myself and I would ask certain questions to the correctional officers they were very rude now I see why so many of the correctional officers get pee and poop thrown on them and spit on.The pay was pretty good even though I didn't really care about that but it was definitely one of those jobs you really have to enjoy it and want to be in law enforcement because even sometimes working on the wings inside the prison I would feel like an inmate for the simple fact that you're locked inside the wing from the inside and the outside would be boring cold time goes by really slow I would be binge eating and counting down the time.It was also a job where I realized I had to really control my anger problems because I did have an anger problem especially if I didn't want to become an inmate I was once told every inmate is a decision away from making a bad decision and hell I was too.So I guess I could see my father's concern in my personal opinionI always thought that being a correctional officer was way more dangerous than being a police officer granted police officers are out in the streets but they're also armed there's been times I've literally run the chow hall by myself and there'll be forty inmates in there I've literally been on the rec yard by myself around thirty to forty inmates and all i have is a damn radio on my belt.I would often think to myself what are those inmates wanted to rape me or beat me up or just anything could happen and it's like I don't even have any OC spray or a Taser or handcuffs how am I going to defend myself against that many inmates. Chris and I would slightly get into disagreements because I would tell him that I felt more superior than him-as a correctional officer because the simple fact I didn't have weapons and I still felt like a badass that made me feel like even more of a badass because I didn't need weapons though either anything could be considered a weapon especially in the sense of having to defend yourself.But realistically any job in law enforcement is considered dangerous we were both in dangerous fields and I honestly just want it to be a police officer like him.Even my mother would make comments towards me saying that they couldn't pay her enough to have a job like this and she doesn't see how I could be a correctional officer and be around a bunch of men.When I told my mom and showed her the inmate who sent me a friend request on Facebook she said that he was fine as hell.

But my dad was always trying to tell me what to do he always acted as if I had no sense of knowledge and he would always talk to me like I was a child growing up I hated when anyone would try to treat me like a child because I did not have the mind of a children when I was a child.my father would always try to tell me how to be a parent what I should do what I shouldn't do it was very annoying it was one thing to already be a single mother but it was another thing when people try to tell you how to parent especially when you have the parenting thing down packed.even Kai's Mother said that my dad treats me like I'm his wife and or girlfriend even my mother has said that my father treats me like I'm his wife and or girlfriend which is very disturbing and highly disgustingI was so disgusted just hearing them say that but honestly they slightly had a point. I was getting to the point where I was tired of my father and honestly he was making me want to move even further away from him than I did live because of how he would treat me he was always calling he was always coming over he was always wanting us to come over to his house and I get one day my father and mother are going to die but they really needed to understand boundaries even my therapist said the same thing and what I would repeat what my therapist said to me about them needing to learn boundaries they would get very upset but I guess people often do get upset even at the truth. I'll never get over the time when my father sent me a text message when my mother was staying with me and I know she was the one who told him that I had a man over but it was my house and I was a grown ass woman. My child wasn't even home but my father sent me a text message telling me to get my dumb ass up and go get the baby I thought that was very inappropriate how weird is that for your father to tell you not to be laid up with a grown ass man when you're grown and in your own home.

That's why I couldn't be around my dad that long plus sometimes he would make me want to bust him in the head like let's be real that's very disturbing what grown ass man tells their grow ass daughter that she doesn't need to be laid up with a grown as man the same man that I was in a committed relationship with that's very weird. One time my mother even insinuated me and my father had a relationship going on that was very disturbing and disgusting often my mother would even get upset and jealous if my father would give me money and not her the difference between me and her is I was responsible with my money and I wasn't always trying to scheme and scam my dad when I would ask for money sometimes my father would just give me money but again I was responsible I know how to manage money I've always knew how to manage money my mother not so much she literally spent all her money and then she'll come asking me and my father for money and we're tired of always having to give her money especially giving someone money who doesn't have the intent of even paying you back very inappropriate. I'll never get over the time my mother said to me that me and my dad have a weird relationship and we seem like we're having sex that was the most disgusting thing I've ever heard literally when she said that I threw up like that is disgusting I can't even think about something like that nor would I. What would also upset me when people would think in public that my father and I were a couple I've always looked like my dad he's always been my twin very disturbing.

Even inviting my father to Leilani's baseball games as well as her practices she was literally a three year old toddler playing that sport sometimes she would get antsy sometimes she just wouldn't be in the mood I get it-she has her own personality as well and I also didn't want to make it seem like I was forcing her to do something she didn't want to I just was trying to allow her to try new things in lifeliterally asked her if she wanted to play baseball and she said yes so technically it's not forcing her and plus at baseball practice anytime she was ready to go we would literally leave especially when she would get to crying and so the point where she felt she did not want to participate anymore which was completely fine.One time I had invited my father to her practice and she was distracted by her granddad being there she's always crying for her granddad and wanting her granddad next thing you know we had to leave because he had distracted her to the point where she was crying for him so we left and when we got to the parking lot my dad pissed me off because he was like probably because you'd be hitting on her that's why she wants to come home with me and all of that stuff. I put my child in the SUV and I like to have ran y dad over that's why I didn't want him there in the first place there's like no break from him you talk to him every day and we see him a few times in a week like you don't need to talk to someone that much and see someone that much that was the issue right there very annoying he always wanted to be a part of stuff and didn't realize he was ruining stuff and ruining the moments.

Growing up my mother forced me to do modeling and she would take all the money that I would make from it. She was very selfish.my father and I would always have to give her money which was very tiring and annoying especially when you know and have a gut feeling that that person doesn't have the intent to even pay you back which my mother never paid us back every time she asked for money I would always give it to her because I thought that that's what a daughter should do specially when you have money to do so but hell my mother worked for the government she had a way higher government status than I did and she was always broke always struggling because she always had to go out to eat always has to go shopping always has to buy the best designer purses and bags trying to live the life of the Joneses. My mother would always ask everyone for money and I know people were so tired of it hell I was tired of it my father was tired of it it was embarrassing nobody always wants that to give their money away especially to a person who never pays you back and isn't even good at managing money themselves like my mother literally needed a financial advisor the way she spent money was ridiculous I did always get my good spending habits from my father though he had a lot of money but you would never know he had money because he didn't tell people what he had and how much he had he always told me and taught me that sometimes just because you have does not mean you always have to spend your money that's where a lot of people go wrong nowadays. My mother most definitely a liar a manipulator-she would often talk about me then turn around and ask me for favors she was always trying to get money for things she didn't need but wanted.She definitely would always get what she wanted my mother would often throw things up in my face if I told her any personal business which is why I tried so hard not to have to tell her anything if she got mad she was definitely going to tell the business she even called me out once on Instagram which was very childish ignorant and our business had absolutely nothing to do with social media. It's a damn shame you can't even trust your parents especially your mother a woman to talk woman and woman about things-and be there to support you but not mine she would judge me. My mother also kept my sister Bri and I involved in a lot of sports and extracurricular activities.Don't get me wrong I really appreciated a lot that my mother did for us but at the same time she would use things against us like if she bought us Chanel bags and she starts talking about everything she does for us I would often make comments saying we didn't ask you for it which is absolutely true we didn't like I hate people are so quick and eager to say what they've done for you but it's like you didn't ask them to at the same time so it's like don't make it seem like you're doing me any favors because you're not.

She would even often talk about Chris and how she liked him but she couldn't see herself with a white man so that's when I then told her that I didn't think she liked him I just liked how she tried to make it seem like she liked him for him and the fact that I was happy but in reality she liked him because of the gifts he used to buy her gifts was always about what a person had to give her.even though I wasn't asking for permission from my mother or fatherto get married let alone to be with a man in general Chris loved me as well as my child was so nice that he is specially accepted my child considering the simple fact he didn't have any kids nor did he know what it was like to be apparent I know he always wanted to be though it was definitely a very nice feeling and I knew I loved him and I was definitely ready to get married however there would be times where I would start reminiscing about The I guess because I was so in love with him in the sex was so good and I hate to admit it as much as I loved Chris and he loved me but I did have a fuck up I'm not proud about and I was going to keep it my secret and never tell him because I told myself I couldn't go down that path again. I literally waswith one of my ex is named Mario.I literally had took Mario with me on a cousins trip to Tennessee with my cousins and everything from Alabama and we were having unprotected sex and everything while Chris and I were on a break and I thought I was pregnant I'm always very fertile.I was just really reminiscing about some of my exes mainly it was just the sex, I've always slightly been a sex addiction when I'm not hornyI'm thinking about sex and I'm always wet.

I was always happier with Chris he was literally the first white man that I've ever been in a real relationship with and not to be generalizing but I feel like that I'm happier with him than I was when I was with black men a lot of people would say I was generalizing or they would say it was the type of men I was dating however I've always only dated men that were on the same level as me especially financially because I don't ever want to have to build a man or feel like I have to buy a man especially when I know I don't need a man.One day when I got off of work from my correctional officer job I would always get off at four in the afternoon and I would go to work at six thirty in the morning well I had to be there before six thirty in the morning. Although my hours were from six thirty in the morning to four in the afternoon.I worked in Raiford Florida so that was about thirty minutes away from my home.And one afternoon I had to go to vystar credit union to check my balance and take out some cash because their app was down so I had to literally speed to get to the bank before they had closed while I was in the bank this one woman was randomly talking to me because we were told as correctional officers that were not supposed to go out in our uniform and public but I was one of those people I didn't care I was not going home to change and then running back out to the store when I was already passing by the store in the first place or they would say you can go to certain stores but you're not supposed to go grocery shopping like it made absolutely no sense and it was crazy even police officers and military people don't have those rules of not being in uniform it's just the fact you shouldn't get a confrontation while in uniform. I always ran errands in my uniform and I never took off my badge because I didn't care they were so extra sometimes for no reason and I get it's a safety issue on why they don't want us in uniforms but who's actually bringing changes of clothes to change just to go to a store?

When I left out of vystar I received two text messages from an unknown number that was not saved in my phone so I took my time responding back to both of the phone numbers when I did respond I asked who was it and the person responded back saying Mario the only Mario at that timeI knew of was my ex but I was playing like I didn't know who it was I was like which Mario and he responded saying the one that you would least expect to hear from that's when I told him to send me a picture and he did then he asked me for a picture so he had send one and I sent one back then he started saying how he missed me and all this other stuff which I knew was bull shit. I then said but you're just now hitting me up I also told him I was surprised he was hitting me up considering how everything ended between him and I after all I had felt her straining order against him if someone felt or straining order against me I wouldn't even want them messaging me or talking to me at all and even though the restraining order had already expired because it was last year ago still he's a better person than me I could never.in my mind I felt like he was just hitting me up because he was still single and he wanted sex for whatever reason I never once told him that I was getting married silly me. There would be nights when Chris and I would be cuddling watchingmovies or Chris and I and the girls will be eating dinner or playing board games and Mario would text me but I never saved. There was no need toI also knew that I had no intentions on getting back with him after all I was getting married that's what I always have wanted and prayed for and it was finally happening I kept telling myself that I wasn't going to allow Mario to interfere with my relationship especially not to mention the fact how he did me when we were together.

I can't believe that I actually allowed lust to almost make me lose the man that I love and he still stayed with me. Chris and I were the type of people we had each other Sloane passwords however never really went through each other's phones checking for anything because there was no need the trust was strong. Plus if he wasn't working he was pretty much always at my house he barely went to his house like that. We consumed each other the sex was great we always had sex we'd always kept it interesting where we had sex we always change positions use sex toys one time Chris and I were in my garage and my mother was visiting in town and she was in the kitchen cooking and he was eating my pussy out in the garage and I had an orgasm and I was loud as hell he would always make me orgasm when he ate my pussy in fact the only man that could ever make me orgasm when eating my pussy. Sometimes we'd even do role play during sex he would be the police and I would be the inmate and he would put handcuffs on me and everything I love stuff like that I love being chokedI loved rough sex it kept it very interesting. I could literally be having an orgasm and screaming his name and he still would keep sucking on my clit. So I couldn't understand what the problem wasI just couldn't believe that I was going to be getting married soon and everything was moving so fast and everything between us had moved so fast after all we weren't even together that long before we got engaged but I guess when you know you just know.I felt so bad even more for Bri because I was supposed to be that big sister that sets a positive example since she had been living with me she got to see how I was badly treated by men And how all my relationships always failed and ended badly.so it's a be with a man that actually didright by meI loved because the simple fact my sister got to see that there are happy endings somewhat when you finally get what you wantI also like that she saw me in a healthy relationship with the man who was actually doing right me.But once again I had to mess that up I always seemed to mess things up.I also tried to teach my little sister my life lessons that I had to learn the hard way but she was one of those that just didn't listen or she acted nonchalantI wanted her to know that life is not a game and will knock you back down with that type of attitude that she had which made it so hard for me sometimes to even allow her to stay with me.I'll never get over the timeI fought my little sister and I did beat her ass because her mouthI told her she goes in society with that type of mouth she'll be dead or in jail which is true and real.Of course when that happened she contacted our mother which I didn't care because if my mother was a real type of mother I wouldn't have had to take her child in the first place which I didn't mind because it was my sister but at the same time it wasn't my responsibility nor was I obligated to do anything like that.Which I in fact told my mother that on the phone and to her face because I was sick of her shit my mother always used people to get what she wants it which was money.I remember as a child I would literally have to lie to my father and Bri would have to lie to her father to make it seem like we were going on field trips and so on with our schools to get money to give to our mother.

I hate to admit it but Bri was becoming like our mother all about what you had to give her and do for her as long as you're buying and spending on her she's fine but the moment you stop she didn't want to be bothered as much.I would often tell her she was becoming our mother as well as very ungrateful because I didn't have to do half of what I did for her even when my mother sent her to come stay with us she didn't send any money for her and she never would give money for her I will have to buy all her wants and needs which I didn't mind because that was my sister but again I wasn't obligated to do any of it. Bri would complain that I was being too hard on her sometimes-she would say I was always yelling at her but the truth was she was lazy she never wanted to listen to me she never cleaned up and when she would she didn't do it to my standards on top of that she would call our mother for every little thing and I was so sick of it and I told her she could always go back living with our mother miserable broke hungry.I had my own problems that I was dealing with like sometimes my depression and anxiety would take place couldn't even tell you why I would be depressed or sad. Meanwhile everyone is thinking that I'm this happy person who successful and proud and yes I was happy and successful the happiness would come and go but it was just the depression that was kicking my ass I was even on medicine and I decided to take myself off of the medicine because my motto is if I need it in order to function or to not be sad then I don't want to take medicine to not feel that way because eventually the medicine is going to stop working. Hell sometimes I would have thoughts about popping pills with alcohol especially when our mother had moved in with us when I had gotten into all that trouble that was the worst time of my life if it wasn't for my child I probably would have killed myself. When our mother had moved in with usI was drinking bottles and bottles of liquor bottles of wine daily all day every day from the bottle.

I wouldn't respond to Mario sometimes I would always ignore his calls because I just wasn't trying to get back involved with him the thing about him that I didn't like was he appeared to be a Rolling Stone.when he and I had went on the Tennessee trip one of his side pieces had called him and he claimed that she was pregnant but he didn't know that the baby was his or the guy she cheated on him with so he had to wait for the DNA test results. That had really sobered me up at that moment because that was something that he should have told me he shouldn't have waited for us to go on a trip together and he met my family had he told me that before that Tennessee trip I would have actually broken up with him because that's just baggage that I don't need in my life. Not to mention the simple fact that he literally had a picture of him and the girl as the contact photo.Plus he already had a son anyways and his brother lived with him his little brother.I soon found myself with Mario having sex we had sex three times before I got caught.We literally also had unprotected sex like I just wasn't thinking and using my head you watch TV shows and movies about people cheating and doing the dumbest things and then I was doing the dumbest things what was I thinking to be having unprotected sex with a man when I'm with a man engaged at that. Mario had a long dick he would always eat my pussy and I would suck his dick while he was doing it.He would be very rough when we were together he would sometimes cause me to bleed due to how rough he was during sex.I remember during the Tennessee trip and before we went on the Tennessee trip when I was with Mario I would constantly get yeast infections which meant it was him. Some of these men out here barely go to the doctor and they have the audacity to be having unprotected sex with people.

I was literally meeting Mario in a nearby hotel not too far from my house we had sex three times in the same weekI felt so bad that I would cry every time I came home because I couldn't believe that I did that to a man who loved me excepted my child it was going to marry meI felt so bad I betrayed him.I was wanting to tell him about what I had done but I decided that after those three times I wasn't going to allow myself to have sex with Mario anymore.so I started at ignoring Mario and I was even lying to Chris telling him that I had to work later I had to notarize some papers for some clients. On the third day of me a Mario having sex he started telling me howhe just found out that he has another son and the sun is five years old but he didn't know he had the son talking about how he has to pay the little nigga three hundred and ninety dollars every two weeks telling me how he doesn't see his son that he just found out about nor does he really want anything to do with him at that very momentI saw how he didn't change he was the same selfish person that he's always been and I couldn't be with a man who couldn't take care of his responsibilities like if you feel that way maybe stop having unprotected sex with everyone. I asked him if he was going to start spending time with his son that he just found out about and he told me no because it'll be too awkward and he said the little nigga cost too much already and I told him that he's still the exact same person that he was.I also told him that I was getting married and I'm even upset with myself that I'm standing here in a hotel room with an ex you never go back to your ex that's a rule in the dating world.Mario was even telling me how hewanted us to get back together and how he loves me and misses me and I told him he doesn't love me he loves himself and he loves what I can do for him and to him he then asked me what is it that I can do for him. I told him suck his dick and make him cum. I then told him most importantly I can take his dick because he would go really deep in me it was slightly hurt but I'm a pain freak so I take the pain.I then told Mario that nothing good was ever going to come from us which is crazy because I remember my ex Antonio told me the same exact thing when I was begging him and pleading him to stay with me and get back with me he was telling me noth- ing good was going to come from us and he was absolutely right and I was absolutely right about what I said to Mario. As I made my way to the door of our hotel room to leave Mario comes behind me and grabbed me and starts holding me I told him I didn't wanna do anything anymore I told him I'm going home and I told him what we had was over that's when he pulled my dress up I started eating my pussy he then picked me up pitting me against the wall while eating my pussy.I wanted him to stop so badly but I didn't because it felt so good and I was enjoying it.But I told him to put me down eventually then I told him I already got what I wanted I just wanted to taste the water again a little bit and have the last remainder of my fund before I got married and I told him that I won't be needing him anymore but I told him thank you then I finally left. When I went Home the next day I pull up to my house and I see That Chris was sitting in his truck in my driveway and there were items on the front porch that no one had ever gotten he would always leave me flowers and gifts outside on the front porch.I thought to myself why didn't Bri get any of the stuff off the front porch but then I also remember how I instructed heron not to open the door for anyone even though she is of age but I will also tell her To stay in the house unless she's taking the puppies out Because I just didn't trust people but my neighbors were pretty alert and aware and some of them had my phone number and would keep an eye out on my house especially when we went out of town.

I kept telling myself in my mind when I pulled to act naturalI then remembered I was so upset when I left the hotel I didn't even shower-so I had another man scent on my body I thought to myself maybe Chris won't notice.why I tried to play him like that considering he was a police officer.I get out of the truck to go over to his truck and I say hey babe what are you doing here he then said to me just coming to check on you to make sure that you're ok especially since you weren't at work when I called them since you were working extra hours because I was going to bring you some foodI then told him that I got off early andI went home and went to sleep I put my phone on silent and then I had decided to get up and go for a drive because I was feeling depressed a little bit. Chris then told me that I'm smarter than that and if I keep pissinghim off we're going to have a problem.I then said honey what are you talking aboutI'm just tired and he leaned caressing e as if he was going to kiss me and he smelled my neck and ask me why did I smell like Cologne then told him you know from time to time I wear men's Cologne. Last when Chris asked for my phone and I told him that the phone was dead so he takes out his phone and he calls my phone which was in my purse which was on my person because I thought he was going to come into the house with me when I walk over to him he calls my cell phone and it rings he then says to me it doesn't sound like he's dead to me because it's ringing. He gets out the truck standing in front of me and he asked me if I loved the man that I was with then I broke down crying saying that I didn't mean it. It was a mistake and he then tells me that meant to do it and that he's leaving me.Chris then told me that he hopes it was worth it and I grabbed his arm and I told him please don't leave me he snatched his arm back and told me to get the fuck away from him.I was on the ground crying and begging him not to leave me. He then compared me to his ex wife who cheated on him and which I knew about and now I had messed up.He then told me that the wedding was off and his face started turning red and he got in his truck and he told me he was leavingI called him for hours every day all day he was still coming around leavingLeilani pull-ups outside the house and cases of wipes leaving envelopes for Bri with some allowance. Not to mention days after having sex with Mario I literally got another yeast infection I felt really disgusted after that considering that I always would get yeast infections with him we're together in the past that means that he's a nasty nigga. I also went to the doctor to get tested for any STD's.Chris wouldn't talk to me he was also ignoring my texts and calls I even would call the station to talk to him but they would always tell me that he wasn't in which I knew was a lie but I guess I don't blame him I wouldn't stay with someone who cheated on me either.

I also couldn't stand the thought of someone ignoring me and not talking to me it made me feel a certain type of way but then again I couldn't sit around feeling sorry for myself after all I was the one who did the dirt so I had to live with it. I was telling myself I finally got what I asked for and

I messed it all up like I always do mess things up that's one thing I can do best in a relationship doesn't feel so good being cheated on but I couldn't in fact play victim anymore especially for the simple fact that I had just cheated.I was begging Chris every day to talk to me I was telling him we could work it out we can go to counseling whatever he wanted to do and he still was giving me the cold shoulder I then told him in a text message out of anger that hetoo has had his past come back like when it's ex-wife was texting me and messaging me and calling me.I told him about the time that I had to get tested to see if I had herpes because he had to get tested to see if he had herpes because his ex wife tested positive for that the bitch probably didn't even know she had it already in her.When I texted him that he called me really quickly going off on me yelling and he then told me that he's never cheated on me though.I then told him while crying it's fine he can leave me when I said that he asked me why so I can go with my ex the one that cheated on me and has all these kids popping up.He then said the one who wouldn't let you come to his house but he's coming to your house and has a key to your house he then said the one that went to prison for drug trafficking He said the one that smoked cigarettes he said the one that isn't even your type to begin with then said since when he liked thugs. I then asked Chris since when did he like welfarerecipients since that's what his ex-wife was and ghetto.

Chris told me if I didn't have the girls he would kill me for cheating on him and I told him if I would've had herpes I would've killed him and his ex bitch. He then asked me how are we going to fix this and how do we come back from this my mind I'm like damn he sounds like my ex Antonio who asked me the same thing when I found out he was married but still wanted for some reason to stay with him.I told Chris we can go to couples counseling we can do whatever he wants I just didn't want to lose him we were already in way too deep.He then said that he wants to arrestMario for having sex with me. He said we can do counseling but we also had to take it very slow because now he has images in his head of another man being inside of me when he looks at me. I told him whatever he wants to do and I told him That I didn't want to lose him I told him we're supposed to be a power couple.I told him there's so much we still have to complete but we have to do it together like me running for mayor I need to have my man beside me when I do so. He said that it was a lot and it was a lot to think about but we can start off with counseling. Luckily for us my therapist offered counseling for couples I had text my therapist to get a date and time for counseling in person. When he responded back to me he said he had something in the next three days available and I had told him that that would work.Then I told Chris he had availability for the next three days and I asked him if that would work for him and he said yes.Chris told me that he loves me but I really hurt and betrayed him and it's going to be hard to get back to how we were.I then said babe I know and I'm sorry I don't know how many more times I could say it I don't even know what else to say because I know it wasn't right no matter what I say it won't ever make it right. He told me that he loved me but he had needed more time.

not even to mention before Mario came back around my other ex Steve camearound and the craziest part about it allI had a dream about Steve one night.I tried to look him up on Facebook but I couldn't find him and it was so crazy because the next day after I had that dream about him he literally added me on Facebook and when I accepted the Facebook request he sent me a message on Facebook Messenger.Judging by his Facebook name I realized the reason I couldn't find him when I went to search him on Facebook was because his real name is Steven which I forgot but we just called him Steve anyways he and I met each other when we went to this Christian Academy in Orange Park in which his aunt and uncle the first lady in pastor owned he grew up with them after his mother died. I remember when I went to church with them at times and one time Steve wanted us to have sex at the church and I told him I might be going to hell but I'm not going to hell for having sex at no damn church. It's quite crazy how Steve did me dirty when we were dating I was in tenth grade and he was already a senior and he was graduating after he graduated high school he went into the marines and when I graduated high school-we were supposed to be together in Hawaii which was where he was stationed at for years-he ended up cheating on me and moving the girl that he was cheating on me with into his apartment.All he had to do was break up with me he also had a temper just like I did and the thing that would piss me off is whenever he would call me if he had a bad day he would always take it out on me as if I had something to do with it.One day after I had gotten off of work Steve had called me We stayed on the phone for a few hours catching up he told me how he was kicked out of the marines because he assaulted one of the higher ranks And the guy press charges and Steve also told me how he went to prison for 30 months then told me how he violated probation and he had to go back to prison.It was crazy because it's like after I've been to jail like I don't judge people just depends on what you did honestly but it was so crazy because when he went into the marines he really did allow for it to change him and he did always have an anger problem soI saw something like that happening plus you never put your hands on people unless they you first.He told me how he was struggling and stuff but he told me he drove trucks so when he said he drove trucks I assumed he had a CDL license but I was wrong we were even supposed to get together to have sex because it was crazy all that time we were together or we would talk that was the one thing we never got a chance to have sex. he sent me some videos of him masturbating he also has a big dick. He then told me how he lived in Jacksonville and how he wanted to see me we were supposed to link up a few times but we never did on his accounts because he never told me that he didn't have a car the most important thing he was supposed to tell me and I was telling him I could even come to him but he wouldn't respond he would respond when he wanted to and he was always smoking weed and just drinking and I get why because he's really struggling in life so I just decided not to even get involved with that so I just left him alone and I had his phone number since he had given it to me but

I decided to change his contact name to don't answer but then eventually I decided delete his number and what didn't happen was probably for the best and probably never will happen. Even when Steve and I were together at the Christian Academy there wasn't that many of us at all so the only high schoolers in the whole school was Steve me and this other girl named girl named Angel. Angel also like Steve and Steve would sometimes tell me to make sure that I don't tell her that me and him talk in exchange pictures and stuff which was crazy. Inside of the classroom where Steve was in one timeI can never forget the time when I was sucking his dick and we almost got caught.plus every day he would get dropped off we would kiss in the cafeteria.Angel was kind of jealous of me and she liked Steve but she didn't know that we were together so she would say things about him that would really get under my skin because me and him were a couple.

Tati as well as my friend Dev would piss me off They were both so eager to judge me for being a correctional officer but at least at the end of the day I wasn't depending on the government to take care of me and mine. I wasn't asking for handouts I wasn't asking people for anything honestlyI was always too proud to ask for help even when it came to needing a break and having some mom time to myself.Dev was the last person to be telling someone what to do especially when she was in her forties depending on roommates and or a boyfriend to help her afford her rent and her house her overpriced rent at that even my mortgage was less than her rent at her house. She was always trying to tell people things but it's like how can you when your life is also in shams doesn't work that way that's why I don't tell people things I rather just go to therapy people always have opinions and negative things to say and then they're so quick to say well I'm just telling you the truth sometimes when you tell people things that does not mean that it's always the truth that was just their personal opinion that you felt was the truth. Dev also had a lot of children as well a few Department of Children and family cases that she continued to keep getting in as well as arrested even after we completed our anger management class.Tati had a lot in her life that she needed to take care of as well like I get being a correctional officer was a dangerous job but I didn't need people to keep telling me that at the end of the day it was a job a well paying job it was a career it was something I could retire from. I was just tired of people always trying to tell me what to do tell me what I need to do tell me what I don't need to do.

Something even tells me that Dev reported me to Department of Children and families because I had this close a lot with her as she had also disclosed a lot to me but what she told me never left from our little circle I would never tell my fiancé I wouldn't tell my parents or any other friends for that matter. Especially because it wasn't my place. The day she had called me over to hang out at her house I was confiding to her about something very private and the more and more I was she kept making these like weird faces like something was just off about her and she was the only person that knew about What I had told her. I sometimes really didn't want to hang out with her because she was always one of those people she never wanted to go to your house or anyone else says you always had to go to her. The crazy part about it she literally lived in the neighborhood before my neighborhood and all the years I had known her she had never been to my house. Every time I go to her house all we do is gossip and talk and really it's always her venting smoking cigarettes and drinking liquor and when she drank too much liquor her mouth got very reckless for her to have been in her forties she couldn't handle her liquor at all. I was typically the type of person I would never tell someone every single detail or thing about me a lot of people didn't even know that I had another baby but because I wanted to keep it a secret granted I posted about it on Tik Tok and sometimes on Facebook but I didn't want selective people to know.

But I hadn't been in trouble every since those cases with the law. That was until my friend Selena someone who I met on tiktok which I also told myself I very much had to be very selective on who I give my phone number to

Because bitches are crazy and people always have intentions. But I also on tick tock had a notary business that I was advertising I taught people how to be legit and buy a home like I did I had Google classrooms for those who want it to learn how to become a public notary in or a notary signing agent for those who want it to become homeowners. I was also charging these people for the google classroom sessions And I was very much making a lot of money after all I was tiktok famous I had 38K followers on there. A lot of people who followed me on that app lived in the state of Florida And some of them would come up to me so tell me that they followed me or say that I was pretty or they were proud of me and or asked to take a picture with me. So my phone number was on the app but for the business purposes only my phone number was also on Facebook and Instagram as well but on my business pages Only. She was considered a friend at least at first we would video chat almost every day talk on the phone every day and also text every day but the thing was she didn't work she stayed at home and took care of her daughter who was autistic and had a few other health problems cute as can be though and she would take care of her husband who was in his 60s then she had a son that was my age. The only reason her and I began talking in the first place was because she sent me a long ass message one time on tiktok Which she was very lucky I responded back to her at all and gave her the time of day because there were thousands of messages in my inbox I had never read them all nor could I was just so many with people asking questions about becoming a notary becoming a homeowner I mean unfortunately you can't reply to everybody that would take so much time out of my day to try to do that.

She was very much cool at first but like I stated we talked every day she didn't work or anything I did a lot my daughter was in sports and activities and for some reason I had time for everyone and everything still no matter how busy I was. When Selena had messaged me on the app tick tock she was telling me her personal business day one didn't know this woman from a can of paint telling me how she was getting abused sexually and physically by her baby father not her husband the father of her daughter and how he was a firefighter telling me this crazy story about him her story kind of sounded untrue and also too good to be true it sounded like a lifetime over or something but I tried not to call people liars because I mean in this generation and nowadays anything is possible but she would tell me how he would sneak into the home she shares with her husband and two kids Then tell me how her ex husband Shane who was the firefighter would break into their home and sedate her then raped her then get her pregnant because he wanted their daughter's DNA. Again I didn't judge I didn't question it I was just going with the flow if she was lying that was her business and her own problem I really didn't care absolutely nothing to do with me. She told me a lot of personal stuff and I would tell her a lot of personal stuff something I told myself I definitely had to stop doing because soon enough the personal stuff I was telling her she would then use against me not to tell others but to tell the police the same police agency that my fiancé worked at.

Selena was very cool taught me a lot and I taught her a lot she was in law school she had always wanted to be a lawyer which she very much stressed out about every damn thing especially the situation she would tell me about Shane hard to orders father who was in fact very fine Selena was white and Mexican and Shane looked like one of those hot guys from a soap opera. She had showed me his Facebook page and gave me his new wife's first and last name to look up on Facebook to see how she looked the woman wasn't bad looking at all she just looked older than him and her pictures looked airbrushed and they used way too many filters but she would tell me all these stories about Shane's wife trying to kill her once again I was never once called someone a liar because I hate it when people called me a liar especially when I was in fact telling the truth but some of her stories just sounded a little unbelievable like the getting pregnant every month how the hell do you get pregnant every month I was very fertile and always could feel when I was operating but I never got pregnant every month and

I get that our bodies are different but you get pregnant every month like damn does she have a period at all?

After a while I started to tell myself I needed to take a break from talking to her I didn't mind talking to her but you see I was in school online I had two girls to look after I worked a lot between running my own business at twenty three my notary business was booming I had all of my neighbors coming to my home for me to notarize for them day and night I would literally notarize for my last client at nine o'clock at night. On top of having my regular jobs hell I would even notarize for people at work and for my notary business I was number two on the top ten list for the top ten best notaries in middleburg FL. I definitely printed that out when I saw that and framed it I also posted on my social media accounts which gave me even more business also a lot of other notaries on social media especially Instagram were interested and knowing how I was able to become number two on the top ten list for the best notaries and middleburg. I hate it to seem as if I were a crab in a barrel but at times I would have to be because all day long I would receive messages from people on how to become a notary how to become successful how to make more money I'm all for helping people but at the end of the day no one helped me become a notary no one helped me become a, Wedding Officiator,Immigration Notary,Notary Signing Agent, Notary,Bail Bonds. I had to do all the research by myself I even had received a plaque in the mail with my name on it and it said appointed by the governor state of Florida and at the bottom it said public notary. I just hated how people were so quick and eager to ask for help without thoroughly doing their own research me personally I never trusted anyone's information but my own because one thing about it I had nothing but time for some reason even after being busy so I was definitely doing my own research. I never knew what I wanted to do next but no matter what I did I always had multiple sources of incomes and I always saved my money.

I didn't mind talking to Selena but at night time Bri wasn't the issue she was old enough she could stay up whatever she was doing school online anyways but my toddler once she went to bed that was my time to have me time to watch my shows, get drunk, talk on the phone catching up with people, resting doing whatever I want it to do while my kid was sleeping. I didn't mind talking on the phone to Selena the issue was the amount of time we talked on the phone I would literally be on the phone with this woman for four hours sometimes five hours I would literally fall asleep while talking on the phone with her and it would very much upset me because it's like damn I didn't want to talk on the phone that long to her. You could literally say you're getting sleepy or tell her you're sleepy she still talking and telling her stories every time we talked on the phone we both always had stories to tell each other especially her. She would ask to talk to my fiancé about her own problems and issues with her baby daddy Shane because he was a firefighter and a allegedly kept raping her every night he would sedate her then rape her get her pregnant she claimed she would lose the babies a lot of miscarriage just happened so he would keep sedating her a few times a month or every month to ensure that she was pregnant. She also told me that the state was helping him do so and That he had filed a restraining order because his job told him to file one against her. She also said that the police were crooked and knew him the firefighters were crooked and at the hospitals they knew him and they were crooked. One time she told me she had to take a break from talking to me all because I said Chris had helped me out with the situation because he knew one of the attorneys and he paid them to help me out and she said the thought of that was making her suicidal on how he paid the attorney to help me I said OK and he knew that attorney personally that attorney was a friend of his family but how did that affect you if people are crooked they're crooked I Can't help that you're too scared to do something about your abuser.

What was very funny to me was the simple fact that she claimed she had family that was in the mob but yet they didn't do anything to help her even though they knowingly knew how Shane used to sedate her break into her house and have his way with her. My family wasn't in the mob but we would never let that happen we would literally go to jail for something like that get out beat their ass go back to jail get out and do it again but to each his own. That's why I always had a suspicion about her and her and I have both told each other a lot of personal things that happened in our lives as kids and growing up something I typically didn't like to do because when mad day comes up people would definitely tell your business. So when she told me that I honestly just stopped talking to her and messing with her I didn't have time for that crazy stuff after all she was the one who reached out to me on social media to tell me her full life story not that I needed to see that or cared send a long ass page on tiktok. So literally when I stopped talking to her which she was my friend on Facebook my friend on Instagram and of course my friend on tiktok. She decided to foul a missing persons report on me and do a Wellness check on me she called the police the same police where my fiancé had worked at that time and ask them to do a Wellness check she told these people I was pregnant she told them I had a daughter she gave them my address she told him I was sick with COVID which I did not tell her I had COVID we all know I have sickle cell trait and microcytic anemia which time to time makes me sickly dizzy weak fatigue and more. She told these people how my fiancé worked at that police station she knew his first name but not his last name because she didn't need to know his last name and I had never told her that information it wasn't her business to know and for this reason exactly right here.

The only reason I knew At first about the police coming to my house which when they did I wasn't even home was because my neighbor who lives across the street from me she's from the Dominican Republic her and I were very close when Leilani was sick she had made me some natural home remedies which I really had appreciated and when I tried to pay her for it she wouldn't allow me to. Her and I were very close Her daughter had even once came to my house when I had pulled into my garage to ask me if I could take her up the street to CVS to get her mother's medicine and I told her sure and I actually felt grateful and lucky that her daughter came to me for help and that they trusted me enough to do that because her daughter was clearly going to have to go with me, so when I went to her mother's house to get the paperwork with her first and last name since her mother didn't speak English at all her daughter and or brother or husband always had to translate for her the people had ended up delivering her medicine so I add gave her my cell number and told her anytime she needed anything or the kids needed anything to just give me a call or text me and anytime her and I texted I always had to use Google Translate I new Spanish but not fluently enough. But one day I was at my father's house with Leilani and she had text me telling me that the police Were at my house looking for me it was four cop cars she then told me they came to her house looking for me and she said she was worried and thought something had happened to the baby or me. I was very much embarrassed and scared at the same time because I was like why the hell with the police be looking for me I was also on the phone with Bri and my mother at that time as well so I had told them what happened and my father had this distraught look on his face like he was mad and worried I'm like I don't know why you're looking crazy because I didn't do anything and I told my father that.

Then my father and Bri are going to tell me I said that last time and I did something I said hell yeah I told you I didn't do anything last time even though I did when I spray painted Kevin's car I said I was on the phone with Charlie you crazy one thing about it I don't put things past my dad sometimes he's definitely a damn snitch and he tells the truth too much he talks too damn much we were on the phone for all I knew he could have been at the police station and hell yeah I would think my dad would do something like that I mean after all my mother would do something like that and she had done something like that why would I tell you I committed a crime over the phone are you crazy. But at that time I really didn't do anything nor did I know what was going on as I'm sitting there responding back to my as I'm sitting there responding back to my Mexican neighbor neighbor I told her thank you for telling me this and told her I would find out what was going on I then told her I wasn't a troublemaker or anything and the only reason I had told her that was because the simple fact her kids would sometimes come over to my house she had a son and daughter who were in elementary school and because it was just Leilani I typically that were always here because Bri was gone every Friday we did movie night we will pick a kid friendly movie sitter not living room I would turn on the disco lights we would eat popcorn put them in popcorn buckets put different seasonings on them we would make cakes and or cupcakes eat pizza and do all these fun activities for movie night every Friday which I've really enjoyed doing with my daughter we would even play video games. My daughter loved watching music videos on YouTube and dancing to them we were both dance it was just a little things knowing that I could make my daughter happy with the little things we did at home at times and I very much enjoyed being a mother as well as all the activities and fun things that I did with my daughter. So hell yeah I was embarrassed because that Lady was allowing her children to come into my home for movie night My living room was also a movie theater so we had a lot of video games by the television we had the sectional leather couch with cup holders LED lights everywhere surround sound systems a projector I would even go all out and make forts and stuff I had movie theater pictures on the walls everything that it made it seem like we were at a real movie theater and it was fun that I took the time to do that.

I didn't want the lady to think like I was a criminal or something or I had did something bad she was letting her kids come here that's not a good image or look also before she had moved out here let's not forget about all the trouble that I had been in so anytime the police came here I was always embarrassed it's not about what we know of the situation or what we know is happening it's about how other people will judge you without knowing the full story of what's going on or why the police are there also just because the police are at your house which I told my father that day doesn't necessarily mean that something bad happened I mean police come to people's houses all the time and deliver messages about people passing away or to ask questions about the last time you've seen someone so it doesn't always mean you're in trouble my dad used to get on my nerves he was too worried about what people thought and to a certain extent I only was because like I said that Lady was allowing her children to come over here I didn't want her to think I was doing things I had no business criminalize getting in all this trouble which I wasn't. But I received a lot of Facebook notifications because when the year of twenty twenty two came in I told myself I was going to have more time to myself keep my phone on do not disturb and I did and I still do so I was looking at all the Facebook notifications without actually clicking on the Facebook notifications and it was Selena talking about how she had call the police to do a Wellness check on me and how she told them I had COVID and I was missing and how we talked every day and then we stopped talking every day and she was very scared and concerned for me she even told them that I told her my police officer fiancé had an anger problem as she was worried that if he may have done something to me I'm like this fucking bitch. I had a old one this woman so much. I told her how Chris and I were having issues with who was moving into whose house. I told her we kept arguing about moving into his house. We argued about when we were going to get married and hell we argued about me being pregnant, I knew Chris wanted kids of his own but I was tired of having babies for men. I was tired of feeling used and like I owed a man a baby because that's what he wanted even though I never wanted that.

CHAPTER

15

The only reason I had gave her my address was for the simple fact that she had told me she had purchased Leilani Christmas gifts and she wanted to mail it to my home which was completely finding me not that Leilani needed anything I even told her you didn't have to get hurt anything at all my child had everything just to be the only child she had a lot of stuff you would have thought I had multiple children in my home my child didn't want or need for anything every time I would tell myself when we go in a store that I wasn't going to buy my kids something I always fell in for her trap and did it. So I didn't think there was any harm with giving her my address even though she didn't send the Christmas gift because she claimed that she put her address on accident and I mean yeah I could see that happening I've done that before as well but I fixed it and I sent the gift when she told me that she had got it sent to her house she then told me that she would probably get the money back for the Christmas gift she purchased for Leilani because she said that she had bought her slime and play dough kits I then told her Oh yeah we don't use stuff like that but at the end of the day if you hesitated or suspected that I wouldn't let her play with it in the first place why the hell did you buy that? So I kind of thought that was slightly suspicious I mean did you really buy a three year old a play dough kit and slime kit? Leilani had once ruined my carpet when she was two years old Chris and I were sitting in the living room with her yes I allowed her to play with the slime and it had kind of got on my carpet and it took a while to try to clean it up I had to replace that part of the carpet because I couldn't get it up. The craziest thing was she was playing with the slime kit at the coffee table in the living room so I was still very confused when I saw that it had gotten on my carpet.

But I started to get suspicious on how she was saying she was just going to get her money back and stuff if that was the case you shouldn't have bought my child a gift at all that's why I told you not to buy her a gift she didn't need it I wasn't even upset that she said she would get her money back cool fine whatever my child is just the only child and she has everything she didn't need it that's why I told her not to get the gifts in the first place and I get she's being nice and all of that and I didn't have suspicion but when she said that I started to have suspicion granted had I gave her my address or not I mean it's public record I'm the only twenty three year old with my first and last name that owns a home in middleburg believe it or not all she had to do was put my first and last name on Google for the state of Florida in middleburg FL I'm the only person with that name out here that would have popped up she could have used a background check website and obtained my address that way as well I mean it's that easy people to realize. But as I was sitting there with my but as I was sitting They're at my dad's house on the phone with my mother and Bri telling them what happened telling them how all the messages were now coming in from Facebook from Selena saying how she was sorry if she calls any trouble and if I wasn't missing but because she had stopped hearing from me she decided to do it the Wellness check and missing persons report she then told me she was just very worried about Leilani and I and she knew I had been sick which I had been sick but it was my anemia I never told her ass I had COVID spreading lies I don't like that. I had never tapped on any of her messages to read them also I was receiving her calls and text messages but I wasn't clicking on the text messages considering the simple fact that she had an iPhone and I had my read recipients turned on So it would have told her that I read her messages.

But also I'm a grown woman and I'm not obligated to respond or return anyone's calls for that matter I'm grown if I don't want to talk to you I don't have to explain to you why I didn't want to talk to you I was also trying to take a break from my phone because you see I was always making time for other people even when I had my me time or office supposed to be having my me time and four hours and or five hours talking on the phone to her that was a lot especially when we already text throughout the day all day when I'm at work I'm texting this woman I needed a break and it was a boundary thing. But just because you don't hear from someone doesn't mean that something was wrong with them but I let it slide for the simple fact that I guess had I not heard from someone I would think something is wrong but I'm not going to call the police people will talk to you when they want to talk to you but we can't get mad when people don't talk to us people have their own battles and demons they trying to fight people sometimes need space. I needed a huge break for my phone considering the simple fact that I was always on the phone as is the amount of calls I would get from my notary business it was a lot. I literally had one thousand texts messages when I put my phone on do not disturb and the only people who can get through with the do not disturb being on was my mother father and sister and Leilani because granted she was three years old she also had a cell phone Leilani was in a lot of sports and extra curricular activities. At that time Leilani was in karate as well as dance classes In lake Asbury I just wanted to be one of those mothers that had my child involved in as much sports and or extracurricular activities as I possibly could put her in in a Ford because the simple fact I could afford it plus for my daughter to be three at that time she was always talking about how she was bored which I didn't understand why or how she could possibly be bored she literally was the only child and she got everything anything she wanted I never told my child no even though I would tell myself I had to stop buying her toys or buying her what she asked for I just couldn't in my right mind do it. I just always wanted my daughter to have the perfect life since her father was deceased and absent because he was deceased at times I would actually have mental breakdowns crying but I was also one of those mothers who was too proud to ask for help yes my father had lived aboutfiftyminutes away from us and Jay's family lived in Jacksonville taking the toll road was about thirty minutes away from us. I just didn't like asking people for help I was always a strong independent young woman and I had always wanted people to view me as a strong independent young woman so I never asked for help even if I craved the urge to need a break from my kid I never asked my father to babysit Leilani I never asked her dad's family to babysit her and when I did it was for reasonings as if I needed to get surgeries which I had gotten to a colonoscopy and endoscopy one time and her two younger aunts had babysat Leilani I get that her father's family didn't have money like that and they were always working a lot which I respected but at the same time I didn't like how they made the two younger sisters miss school for me to get those two surgeries just to watch Leilani instead of just saying they couldn't do it but I thank them and I very much appreciated it but communication is key. I still couldn't believe that Selena had contacted the police the same police that my fiancé Chris at that time had worked at at that point it really upset me because you're not being a concerning friend you're being someone who's bringing unnecessary drama and attention in my life that I didn't need. I would have never done that to her she could have literally caused me to get into another Department of Children and family case. From time to time she would tell me that I was like a daughter to her sometimes she would tell me that I was like a little sister to her considering the simple fact that her son was the same age as me she would sometimes try to give me all this advice and knowledge which was greatly appreciated it but I didn't need it I didn't like when people tried to tell me what I needed to do what I should do what I should have done what I could do I absolutely hated it especially for her to have been trying to tell me anything when she was married and unhappy herself. She was married to this older man unhappy in getting sedated and sexually abused by her ex husband? And she was calling the police on me? Hell I should have been calling the police for her for her help for her family and their safety and again I always hated to call people out as being a liar but the situation just seemed crazy it's like something you watch in a lifetime movie how can you have two children in your home your husband yourself and no one knows when this man breaks into your home like that just doesn't sound right especially for the simple fact that she told me that her husband was an ex marine my father was an ex marine and ex Navy man and he could hear anything and everything he could even hear for pin dropped so that didn't even sound right to me my father also had flashbacks from time to time so that definitely didn't sound right that her ex marine husband didn't know that she was being sexually abused by her ex husband who was breaking in their home but I never called her out on it or called her a liar I mean I never like when people called me a liar especially without knowing the full story or having the proof for evidence to call me a liar story was just very wild though. The issue was she was always trying to correct me in my life when she didn't have rooms too like you should actually have been lucky if I allowed you to come into my life my world my space my atmosphere because considering the amount of drama that I had with the men that I've ever encountered with and allowed to come into my world my space my life my happiness it always failed and I would tell myself time after time after time to never allow anyone else to come into my space my world my atmosphere plus friend wise I didn't need any friends I didn't want any friends I didn't care about not having friends anymore after all even though I knew everyone in Jacksonville and Orange Park and Virginia I just didn't care anymore. I was a mother so the friends that I truly hung out with the most were mom friends and every time I went out it was for the purpose of the children play dates mom dates mom friendly activities kid friendly activities anything that had to do with mom life was my idea of going out and having a good time. A lot of people also thought that I was very stuck up however I never from once thought I was stuck up or better than anyone I just always had my shit together and I always knew what I wanted life. I was a type of woman that if I see something I want or something I want to do that I'm interested in I'm going to do it I'm not going to tell anyone I'm not going to second guess, I'm going to sit down or take the time to do my research thoroughly.

That situation was partially exactly why I was always an introvert when I moved to middleburg Florida, I absolutely loved it I love living in the country I always said that by the time I was thirty. I wanted to have a big two story house in the country and I did it at twenty one. I didn't care anymore that people didn't come to visit me or wouldn't come visit me even though I had always visited them. I was happy my girls was happy we had everything that we ever needed I didn't want more I didn't have the urge to want more people always go wrong wanting more without being happy with what they have when it's others who don't have anything at all or nearly as much as they have. Just like when I had met one of my neighbors and her husband and their two children I love the reason why I'm an introvert I always get close and deeply talking to people I always would tell people too much of my business my lifestyle what I had going on that was always my biggest downfall the thing about people you upset people they will always throw things up in your face that you've told them in the past people never forget they're waiting for the moment when they can actually throw that up in your face so one of my neighbors who had met for the first time in the year of twenty twenty one.l Dedra And her husband his name was Marvin they literally lived two houses down from me on the exact same side as me and worked on the same base as my father and I Marvin was in the Navy for about ten years and Dedra was currently at that time in the Navy we only met because Marvin and I would have conversation from time to time with my next door neighbor Kevin who they had no longer than me considering the simple fact they all had lived here way longer than me we would always just talk from time to time be drinking beer and our front yard or I will come out and check my mailbox and have like small talk with them. So one time I had brought up the idea to Kevin and Marvin that we should all have a cookout together and we could also have play dates especially considering the simple fact that Marvin and Dedra sun was the exact same age as Leilani she was just a few months older and Kevin also had kids who were way older than ours but it was still a good idea plus we're always hanging out together we would all sometimes smoke weed outside on the back porch at Kevin's house he was definitely licensed and had a medical marijuana card only one who actually was licensed he loved white women trashy trailer park trash white women who acted ghetto but as he would say act black. Which I didn't know how you could act black because I mean I was a black woman but I wasn't trashy nor ghetto so I hate it when people said the logic of white women wanting to act like they're black like how could you act like something that you could never be and you probably never will be? But one time we all had a cookout at Kevin's house for some reason I was only person that had bought over stuff but I didn't think nothing of it because I mean after all I always shopped at Sam's Club and I always went overboard so I didn't care because I hated wasting food I didn't care if I could afford to buy food it was a matter of not wasting it because there was people out there that couldn't afford food every time I went to Sam's Club I would always go overboard with the grocery shopping the snacks so I would always give food away to people that had never been opened before close people to me at that so I had took a bunch of hot dogs and hamburgers buns over hell I even took a bottle of liquor over I was also the only person who had bought anything I mean granted at Kevin's house he was cooking it on his grill and everything and he had the liquor and told us to help ourselves and he also supplied weed so I guess it was all good. Me, Leilani and Bri were the first ones to get there I mean after all he was next door Kevin lived in the middle of Marvin and Dedra as well as myself but he had told me that I could go ahead and come on over which I didn't mind or whatever considering his children were there as well so I didn't feel any type of uncomfortable about going over there had I felt that uncomfortable I would have never went over there at all to be honest. Marvin and Dedra and their son and daughter had later came over because they had all been taking naps when they finally had arrived Dedra and I instantly clicked I was typically very cool I never thought I was better than anyone I was always outgoing and I was a people person I was never shy or scared to talk to people to venture out to ask questions any of that. Then again I had a notary business and I always just worked with people so you can't be shy and scared with the types of jobs and businesses that I had I was just typically a people person I love to chat with people networking was key for me. But Dedra and I talked for hours slowly but surely sipping on our alcoholic beverages talking about our lives our careers our children she was very cool and nice at that point in time her husband was very cool and nice I never thought he had a crush on me I felt very weird if he would come over to my home late at night though needing paperwork to be notarized and I would have talked with him like you know I'd respect for your wife I don't think that's appropriate and I don't think that you should come over here without her knowing especially not late at night kind of raises eyebrows and red flags it's not about how we look at the situation and what we know within the truth of the situation it's always going to be about how other people would look and view a situation that's what I've always taught myself you could actually be doing the right thing but unfortunately to other people they may not agree. He said he understood completely but he will still be texting me and yes in the past I had an Councilman with married men even though they should have never happened I used to blame myself for being young and dumb not being aware for not being smart for allowing these men to insult my intelligence to make me feel less of a woman less of a person because I got used and abused mentally sexually physically financially by some of these men and I was just too smart for that. I guess just for me when it came to picking men I wasn't all that smart like I thought I was and what upsets me the most and what upset me in this generation people are so quick to say you're at fault you're at blame no I disagree because at the end of the day you never see what you don't want to see on top of that you will never truly know a person and or know everything that there is to know about a person no matter how many years you've dated them how many years you've been married to them how many years you think you thought you knew them or know them it just can't happen way. Looking back I do one hundred percent take accountability for not taking heath and carefully accessing the men that I allowed to come into my world in space but I will not only take that accountability these men needed to take that accountability men in general that choose to go out and pray on innocent young looking women or just women in general needs to take accountability for their actions. There's a lot of men in the world that will literally do a woman wrong and not see absolutely anything in the world wrong with it yeah they needed to take accountability of how they enjoy using and abusing women how they did it allow you to see the part of them you needed to see but they showed you what they wanted you to see and that's the thing with people that I hate the most don't blame someone because they got done dirty let's start blaming the other person who chose to get up go out pray and seek on women to do them dirty. But Marvin will literally text me late at night and or every day they would be friendly conversations but I would have to keep reminding him from time to time over and over again it was very inappropriate it was extremely inappropriate. I was literally in a relationship with Chris and had he found out about that situation which I never told him about it not sure if he ever went through my phone but I'm sure had he he would have definitely brought it up he would have killed that man no if ands or butts at it Chris always had an anger problem we both had anger problems I'm not sure who was worse with the anger problems but at times it wasn't the anger that had me scared but it was the simple fact because he had that anger and rage in him which he had told me about time after time his parents had told me about time after time and I didn't take the heat of that but it was the simple fact that I would think over and over whether this man was to put his hands on me and it's crazy to have to think about that but when you're dealing with people who are on the same mental level as you especially when they have an anger problem you cannot help but think about those types of things I also had a anxiety pretty bad so definitely something that came up in my mind from time to time. It was crazy because I felt as if I never had anxiety up until I had a baby.

Marvin would be overly nice to me he would tell me how nice I looked and his wife wasn't bad looking she was OK but she was supposed to be a friend and her husband had no business texting me I didn't want problems in my own household nor did I need problems at all and to be honest I had no desire or urge to want him at all he was one of those men that thought that they were all that he wasn't ugly but he wasn't my type I don't like pretty men I never liked to date pretty men he seemed to be one of those men that thought they were better because they had a little money because they knew they look good but he was also married and I didn't want no married man nor any other man for that matter because the man that I was with wasn't just going to let me go especially not for the second time Chris was very much head over heels for me and he wasn't going to kill me on the account of someone else. Dedra and I would have play dates all the time with her son and Leilani we will go to their house they would come over to ours we will order pizzas we would have juices a whole bunch of snacks for the kids here and I would talk and catch up she would tell me some personal things and business I would tell her some personal things in business but see the difference is with me I was never one who was going to throw things up in peoples faces what they told me that just wasn't my character at all like what do people actually get out of throwing things up in peoples faces that you would have never absolutely not known at all had that person never told you to begin with? That was the thing that I didn't understand about people especially in arguments as like you throw something up in someone's face to try to see if they're going to have a reaction to see if you can get the best of them but had they never told you you wouldn't have had anything to throw up in their face at all that was exactly why I stopped telling people my personal business I had told the girl how I had went to jail and stuff before which jail didn't ruin me jail didn't break me jail made me stronger it's helped me a lot of things it slowed me down it taught me to control my anger problems hell it even motivated me to start an organization and program for those who had anger problems or still do just like myself it even made me want to become a motivational speaker by the year of twenty twenty two. Something that I knew I could actually do one thing about me I didn't tell people my business plans and another thing about me anything that I said I wanted to do or told myself that I could do I would just do the research and see what was needed and required and hop wanted that quick that was me I hate it procrastination I hate it to wait I was never patient with anything. Hell I even told this girl that I was going to be the next mayor of Clay County which I mean you can do anything that you put your mind to I think it would be very inspiring specially to the younger generation in this county that someone in their twenties had became mayor someone who wasn't committing fraud doing illegal things and whatever else that these politicians did I love politics I love debating with people I love respectfully placing people in their faces knowing that I got the best out of them knowing that I ate them up with my comments I absolutely loved it I was a bitch a bad one at that. Hell I was such a great friend because of how insecure this twenty-four-year-old young woman was Dedra. I wouldn't show midriff around her I wouldn't dress inoperative way even though I didn't have to do any of this around her or her man because if your husband is really your husband and faithful and loyal and only having that urge for you not saying that men won't look at other women it's not the looking part it's the actual act of touching another woman or having the desire for another woman but really I shouldn't have had to do all of that I can't help that someone is insecure hell I was being the greatest friend that I could be towards her because the simple fact she had two children and granted I had one at that time I was skinny before I had my child and I was skinny after but one thing about me I worked out every day. I had even offered to let her workout with me I never let anyone workout with me that was my me time that was my time to talk to myself meditate pray think about what I wanted and needed to do listen to my music that was my me time I would work out with my child was sleeping morning and night no matter what time I had to do it and we will take our puppy Chanel on walks I will put my daughter in her wagon and or allow her to ride her bike or put her in the stroller at times while I was walking Chanel my daughter would have her iPad and or DVD player and I would be listening to music.

The problem with me was I told people way too much of my business especially when drinking I could definitely handle my liquor I had a very high tolerance for drinking the more and more I seem to get up in age the higher my tolerance got for drinking because it was just something that I did every day I didn't think I was an alcoholic but I had always been drinking for a good percentage of my life More than I would smoke weed plus weed stayed in your system a little too long for me and it was one of those things I knew I had drug tests I knew I had too much to lose career wise so if you have to get fake pee or in or other people pee and all of this crazy stuff so you can pass your drug test and maybe you just shouldn't do it and that was something that I had to teach myself so I would drink more as a supplement. But one time Dedra saw a video on my tiktok which I wasn't throwing shade towards her I also had a lot of followers on tiktok thousands for that matter. People on that app who followed me looked up to me as a mentor Would ask me how to become a homeowner would ask me how to become a notary all of these things would join my Google Classroom seminars and pay for it as that and it felt very nice. People would always take up for me on that app would always share my videos with friends and or on other social media platforms and it very much felt very nice seeing that I would have thousands of videos that would get shared I would have thousands of shares and I loved it knowing that I could help people become homeowners joined the notary business all of this cool stuff and I absolutely loved it because I was always taught to be a leader and that was just something that I was always great at doing I never follow people but it felt very nice to have others follow me kind of made me feel like a celebrity.

But I had posted this video talking about how I felt as if some mothers who are married think that they're better than a single mothers which I felt like was true it wasn't all mothers who were married but a good percentage of them definitely always thought that they were better because they were married but see the thing with me I never needed a husband to validate my happiness to validate what I had in my life to validate what they had done for me and or could do for me I had never needed a husband or a man I just wanted a husband and or a man because all I ever wanted in my life especially from the time when I had Leilani was just a family and all we were missing was that father figure for so many years after having her. So as I had looked at a lot of the comments under that video a lot of other single mother said they could relate some got offended but in the comment section I went thoroughly into detail responding back to those who seem to have been offended who were married with children explaining why I said that and it was definitely a good enough reason of why I said that I even had told them about the situation with Becca and Jenna two white girls I had met we were all pregnant on base together and you know we became friends short term but they absolutely thought they were better than me because they had husbands because their husbands did everything for them see I grew up being taught to not depend on a man whether he was your husband or boyfriend and or fiancé because the one thing about a man a man can come and go one thing about a man they're going to do what they want to do and there's absolutely nothing that you or anyone else can do to stop them not the counseling not the having talks with them anything you can't make a grown person do what you want them to do you can't stop them from seeing and or having sex with who they want to. And yes I did agree with myself and some in the comments did as well with the simple fact that there are women out there who were married who actually thought they were better because they were married merry men are the ones the main ones that will really be out here cheating on their wives knowingly new one that they're married especially all the other men that I talked about in my past that were married.

I didn't think anything of it though I mean I had lots of videos on that app tiktokthousands of videos thousands of likes views and shares comments everyday all day even messages were booming I didn't know that Dedra had sold the video but most importantly I didn't know she had got offended by the video you see I didn't read minds but I also said that whenever I obtained a masters degree that it was going to be in counseling I could help everyone else with their problems except for myself I was helping myself with my problems but the thing was I wasn't taking my own advice I wasn't listening to my own advice. I had no idea that she had saw the video and got offended by it because she never told me that she got offended instead she decided to pout and not be an adult about it and we were just too grown for that like sure she was a year older than me but so? You have to tell people what's on your mind like it wasn't that serious to me at all so here I was texting this grown supposed to be woman who was a year older to me and one thing about me I didn't kiss as I didn't kiss anybody ass not even my parents even when my parents and I got into slight disagreements I would literally block my own parents I sure did and would for a day for a few days whenever and so they would beg my little sister to ask me to unblock them.

One time Leilani and I were leaving so that I could take her to karate class one afternoon after I had gotten off work for my teaching job and I saw Dedra so I decided to wave at her I noticed that she looked at me in my direction and kept walking into her garage and shut the door I didn't think anything of it I just said whatever because one thing about me I hated People that only wanted to talk to you and or deal with you when they thought that it was convenient for them I would definitely cut someone off in a heartbeat for that 'cause I didn't play that. So I was still making my videos to post on the app tick tock still blowing up and booming because at that time I was talking about my notary business how it became a public notary for the state of Florida how to become a public notary which you needed to do how to become an immigration notary how to become a wedding officiator and I was becoming famous on that app for that and going viral very often on the app for that. So another time I decided to text Dedra again saying hey how are you doing next thing I know I receive another text on my phone that came through very fast but it wasn't her was her husband texting me saying if you feel this way why are you messaging my wife and he had tagged the video that made her offended I then texted him back saying why are you in women's business and I said if your wife had an issue all she had to do was tell me I wasn't going to hit her I then asked him aren't y'all moving anyway so it doesn't really matter to me that's my social media I can post whatever I wanted I said I guess if she got offended then it must have been true I then told Marvin don't text me again or I will tell my fiancé who worked at the Clay County Sheriff's Office I didn't play that. One thing about me anything that I said to people I could definitely back up but because I had already been to jail twice in my life I just simply couldn't be involved in anymore altercations or anything with people because I had way too much to lose way too much that I had worked for to go down the drain if I did anything else I only had one strike left so I wasn't going to let anyone get the best of me and caused me to come out of character every time I had came out of character it always resulted in me getting in trouble and that other person being free I told Marvin that I would fail the restraining order and they would be served right at the naval base. Then I blocked him I then texted Dedra to tell her if she had an issue all she had to do was tell me her husband didn't need to correct me nor try to then she responded back instantly sending laughing emoji saying that she didn't need her husband to do anything she just told him about the situation and she told me if I was a real friend I would have tired to talk to her about it.

I told her I don't kiss nobody asks not even my parents I said we were both too grown as adults that are mothers at that I then told Dedra that if she had an issue all she had to do was tell me I told her I don't read minds honey if it was that serious we live literally on the same I told her I don't kiss nobody asks not even my parents I said we were both two grown as adults that are mothers at that I then told Dedra that if she had an issue all she had to do was tell me I told her I don't read minds honey if it was that serious we live literally on the same block street. I also told her That I wasn't talking about her and I told her for someone who was telling me how she was being picked doing that work talking about she couldn't say anything to the lady who was picking on her at work and or correct her because she can get her rent taken away and I had told her I had never in my life heard of anything like that I said my father had been in the Navy since the 80s he was a chief in a sniper it's always these newcomers who think they're better than everyone because they wear uniforms and think that they have so much validation because they're in a uniform and they're better than everyone in the world I didn't know why people always thought that the military was the only way to be successful in life because it wasn't after all you had to take a test to even get into the military back in the days you didn't have to take the test to get into the military they were happy and gladly to get people to go in. there were also drafting people for the military.

But I just found it funny how her husband was texting me that's just like me getting my fiancé to handle my problems but the problems are with a female that's a no no you don't do stuff like that 'cause I wasn't scared of her husband and I didn't know who he thought he was because after all my father was a chief on the same base that we all worked on so it wasn't anything for me to tell my father what happened and get them both in trouble but see I had that much power and they didn't know that my father had that much power But they didn't know that but you see a lot of people would say that oh you're abusing your power or you're getting your father to abuse power no I'm not because anyone who thought that they were going to threaten me or try to do anything to me especially when I had the authority to have something seriously done to them as far as getting them fired and or kicked out the service oh hell yeah I was definitely going to do that but see that's the thing let that be lessons the people that you can't go around saying certain things and or doing what you want to people and they're not be consequences you see every time I took matters into my own hands good or bad there was always consequences even if I literally wasn't even in the wrong and I was tired of people thinking that they could do things to me and get away with it so I figured that if I did things the legal way to get people in trouble it will workout better in my favor and sometimes it actually did so to each is own.

I just didn't like the tick for tat thing and appreciate how she was supposed to be so grown and instead of just talking to me about the tiktok post she didn't. A lot of people would say that she probably didn't owe me anything but at the end of the day it wasn't even about owing me anything if you were offended or bothered that's all you had to say like all the extra Ness wasn't necessary at all after all she's the one who got offended so it must have been true next thing I know I received another text message from her asking me how would I feel if she made a post about single moms I then responded back to her quickly stating that single moms aren't always struggling I say just because of mother's single doesn't mean she's broke or struggling because she don't have a husband I said but that's what society likes to tell people I said one thing about it I may have been a single mother but I was a single mother because my Childs father died there was nothing I could do to ever prevent that. I may have been a single mother but I was very far from struggling in fact I was a single mother who was And expiration to other single mothers my age younger and older as well and I loved it I loved being able to help people to show people that guests were single mothers that we too can do it we to are superheroes and or super women after all we were doing everything for our children by ourselves hell yeah I thought I was more superior than a woman who was married because just because you're married doesn't mean you're better than people that's where a lot of these married women get wrong and that was exactly why I posted the post and what I said and I was not taking it down nor did I take it down hell no if you don't like it that's on you I can't help this someone else got offended by something I said if you got offended it I guess it was true.

As a single mother I definitely went encouraged myself and tell myself that I can do it all I've been doing it all damn I did it all damn look where I'm at in my life look At the life my child has my sister has I was like a single mom with two kids and I was doing a damn thing you couldn't tell me anything yes I had breakdowns yes I would feel depressed tired and more but that's the power that was making me stronger making me the woman that I needed to be the woman that I felt like I could be and I was definitely doing it life was never supposed to be easy but one thing about it you always get through whatever you're going through. After awhile I just blocked her and then I decided to call up my mother and father about the situation my mother was upset and she was saying the girl is ugly fat her baby looks like a bookworm all this other stuff my father didn't like confrontation so I didn't even know why I told my father about the situation but he told me that if her husband texted me again that he was going to report them because one thing about it my father knew everyone on base and I also knew everyone on base who knew him because he was a chief on that base for so many years he was a chief not only on that base but another base in Jacksonville.

I had decided to take the situation to social media which is something that you really aren't supposed to do and shouldn't do because of course it never makes a situation better it makes it far worse than in fact already was when we had started. So I talked about the situation in a video on my tick tock that was about three minutes long just explaining to my viewers and followers that this is exactly a promise sample of why you don't hangout with people who live in the same neighborhood as you because when things go wrong you still have to see these people which is absolutely true because yeah they were moving soon to go to Texas because Dedra was being stationed there next but that wasn't the point where if they hadn't moved to Texas then I would have probably been on the investigation Discovery Channel on the show called love thy neighbor. I definitely wasn't scared of her I mean after all I was a criminal and granted we all had guns I wasn't scared of anyone I didn't need a gun to fight it's just in this generation and time if someone thinks that they're going to put their hands on you or something then hell yeah they deserve to be shot maybe in the next lifetime don't put your hands on people that's the thing life comes with consequences comes with lesson learns and sometimes there's not always second chances in life so you have to do right.

I also had said in my video everything that happened how Marvin had texted me on his wife's behalf which was a no no and I said I she got very offended instead of just telling me what happened I mean it was that simple of a fix then she came out of nowhere in the comment section on my video lurking saying that I was the friend she was talking about and all this other stuff and after all one thing about it my family was on all my social media as my friends and they were definitely always going to jump in anything that was happening so one of my cousins Dee From Alabama her and I had always been close thickest thieves since we were kids we always had each others back and after all we knew everything about each other and never threw anything up in either one of our faces. She came in under the comment section to respond to Dedra where it said I'm the friend that you're talking about then my cousin asked her what was going on and Dedra sentence long ass message talking about how I had said what I said in a different video talking about women who are married with kids and how they think they're all that. Then I commented to Dedrain the comments section telling her that if she was that upset then it must have been true and I told her no husband should ever be checking a female that's her no no.

I also had told her If I had an issue with her I would have just told her instead of acting stank and doing all that she was doing because it wasn't that serious I also told her that the post wasn't directed to her I was talking about in general and from past experiences which I had explained in my comment section but I also didn't need to explain myself to her or anyone else because it was my videos I told her she didn't like it then she could go elsewhere she there was a block button and unfollow button. She then told me that a husband is supposed to take up for their wife something I know nothing about and never will so I then responded to her and I said oh so you do think that you're better than everyone I said no wonder why you got so offended I then told her I don't need a husband nor have I ever needed a husband to validate me or be there for me I said one thing about it a man can come and go I said these married men be the main ones out here cheating on people I said I didn't need a husband nor a man for that matter I said because one thing about a man they will come and go they'll do whatever they want to do and there is absolutely nothing you can do to stop that I said a ring don't mean forever nor does it mean happiness I said but more power to your sister

I also had told her that I love being a single mother I've always loved being a single mother because one thing about it being a mother maybe a better me that situation that had broke me for years had me depressed suicidal and saddened for myself and for the sake of my child made me of strongest woman I could ever be and I love the new me I needed a change I needed to be this better person to me I had involved so much in my life and I loved it my wardrobe of all my upkeep of my nails my hair everything else evolved this bougie young woman I was becoming I loved it. Most people would call me materialistic but I mean after all tomorrow isn't promised hell I have a 20 year mortgage and I was making good money what's the point in making good money if you're not going to spin and enjoy the good money from time to time one thing about it I worked so hard so I mean there was nothing wrong with treating yourself and I always tell people there's nothing wrong with treating yourself it's ok to have money and nice things as long as those nice things and money didn't have you. And most importantly no husband that I could say I had ever was the reason for my success and I loved it I would often hate when solicitors would ring my doorbell and or knock on my door and before they would even start talking to me they would ask me was my husband home that used to kill me and eat me alive it really upset me because has no one ever seen a young successful woman owning a house without a husband? Like has anyone seen that before because all these solicitors that were coming to my door they wereAsking if my husband was home so calmly and nonchalant and I would tell them I'm my own husband this is my house I don't have no husband there isn't a husband here it's just me. Yes I had Chris but he wasn't my husband I didn't even know at times if I was ready to make him a husband yes it was something that I had always wanted but I love being independent I love saying I had everything by myself and work hard to get everything by myself without a husband I didn't need a husband I didn't need a man to validate me I didn't need a man to buy a house for me to buy cars for me to do anything for me I didn't need a man to pay my bills either hell I had money I wanted a man but I never needed a man a man can come and go a man will do whatever they want to do and there is absolutely nothing that you can do to stop nor change that so no I didn't need a husband no I didn't have a husband and I hated being asked the question.

When I had first met Chris for quite some time I would always wear the engagement ring that Jay had given me just because I wanted to act as if I was still engaged and or married so that the men would stay away from me but for some reason that never seems to keep them away. But I literally told this girl all of this on the video because like I told Dedra you can only be upset or allow yourself to get upset at something that you absolutely knew was positively true. She then told me to come outside and fight her mind you in the comment section underneath my video then I told her in the comment section that that was exactly why white people thought we were ignorant and ghetto and had no class I then told her that was exactly why those white people didn't want black people in their neighborhoods at all. And I didn't think that I was generalizing or being racist at all. Whenever I would go on Facebook and or Instagram or some social media app if the video was about black people men and or women robbing someone or trying to steal from someone or even doing so even just fighting in public the white people in the comments section would very much be racist they would say things like look at the black people that's why we don't like them in our neighborhoods that's why I paid extra to keep them away they're like animals why people already think all these negative and bad things about us as is and then she's talking about come outside and fight girl first of all I had French tips on my fingernails and toes and I was not fighting anyone that is why I have a concealed weapons license and why I had guns because if anyone thought they were going to be touching me at all in or my child or my sister that you're going to be on someone T shirt in the grave in the casket because I didn't play that I was too bougie for that had too much class for that and that is just ghetto and not tasteful that was exactly why white people thought those things they thought about us as being animals and ghetto and they were partially actually right even though their people did things as well like you know shooting up schools and killing for absolutely no reason and all the other things that they did is I didn't know why they were even saying stuff like that about the black community.

Hell even one time the first day I literally met Chris mother and his stepfather his stepfather was talking about the black lives matter movement and he was telling me that whenever I went to Chris's birthday party with them on the yacht to not say anything about black lives matter because one of Chris's sisters dated a black man and only dated black men and she was very big on black lives matter and stuff. Then Chris his stepfather looked at me and told me he didn't understand why we had to do the things we do as far as burning down neighborhoods and looting was very much upset me and maybe want to get up away from that table and go home like the movie get out it made me want to get out that really had upset me but then I told myself they can't help it they never will be able to help that that's just how a lot of white people are they say things that they don't think are racist like oh I'm not a racist I have black neighbors like you think just because your neighbors are black that you're not racist like that didn't even sound right nor has it ever sounded right and they always use that Logic. It really upset me though because I'm like did he really say this to me? I hate it when people what classified a whole race and or organization as being bad like first of all who the hell is you people like it's not all the black people all black people aren't ghetto all black people aren't ignorant all black people are uneducated all black people don't live in the hood and or come from the hood all black people don't speak Ebonics so I hated stuff like that but I guess that's what I got from moving to a white area county and neighborhood.

I also had to teach Chris so much so many things like I loved him and I actually was fine with being with a white man that wasn't the issue at all even though people are so racist and cruel but I definitely had to teach him and train him on a lot of things like washing his hands sanitizing his hands after touching doors especially out in public my OCD was just too bad I had to teach him how in the black community we don't wear outside clothes that we had on like out in public sitting down in public places and stuff in the house on our beds and stuff that was a no no. If I go to eat at a restaurant I don't know how many other peoples butts were sitting on that booth before I sat there whether they claim they sanitize data wipe it down whatever they do therefore when I go home I'm going to change clothes and put on something comfortable to sit down on my bed and or my couch or furniture in general that's just something the black community does . I had to train him on taking off his shoes before coming into the house after all he worked at his stepfather's roofing company and he was also a police officer The kids and I always walked around in the house barefoot with socks or something but at the end of the day I don't want to be tracking in dirt, spit, shit and anything else from the outside into my home so yes people have to take their shoes off even if you didn't have socks on or feel comfortable walking around in my house without socks on I give guests brand new socks I give guests shoe covers whatever but your bottom of your shoes are not touching my floors and definitely not my carpets. Some would say that I was doing the absolute most which I didn't care at all at the end of the day if you felt that way then don't come over some of us just have nice things and we don't want others coming into our home tearing up what we worked hard for but I guess when people don't have what you have at times it's so easy for them to say ignorant things like that because they don't care.

But yeah I wasn't going to fight her We had a lot of police officers in our neighborhood so that would be dumb plus on top of that yes she was in the Navy or whatever but I mean I was in school I was obtaining degrees I was doing a lot in life plus I said I was trying to run for mayor so I don't think that's very tasteful to be fighting people in street fights and stuff it's just not cute at all I had already been to jail twice with something I told her she then decided to bring it up in conversation in the comments underneath the video of me calling her out. My viewers and followers had already knew that I had been to jail one thing about stuff that you do like that in life you can always come back up from things and teach people the lessons and stuff and I wasn't embarrassed about it. That was the thing about being young or just in life in general will always do things that we get lesson learned from I was completely fine with that I wasn't a felon I wasn't even convicted of the crimes so that's perfect it's almost like I didn't do it well at least I didn't do one. Not judging felons but at the same time it's way harder when you're a felon there's so many things you cannot do people have absolutely no idea there were just two misdemeanors and I could get my record expunged so it was no biggie I just chose not to get the record expunged because I had never had any problems other than with the correctional officer job. It was the fact that she put out there that I had been to jail underneath the comment section to try to hurt me Which was very funny but see I still won because when people realize that they cannot hurt you or do things like that to you when they realize they can't get that reaction from you you win every time.

That's when my cousin DaizhaStarted chatting in the comment section because she was taken up for me and I had also already told her about the situation And she then said that I wasn't wrong which I didn't even need people taking up from me it was the matter of the fact that I should be able to post whatever I want to post on my social media you can literally block me unfollow me do whatever you need to do. Then I had told Dedra that I was going to have my father get her and her husband in trouble she then told me that my father didn't know her and I said but I have your first and last name and a optic of you so it's definitely not that hard to get people in trouble especially when you have all the credentials. Dedra even started commenting on my other videos talking about how I look goofy and She even said that's why I couldn't pass my ASVAB the test you have to take and pass in order to go into the military I said I didn't pass it because I didn't want to I've already explored the world with my father when he was in the Navy so there was no need to see it twice. I told her I actually enjoyed having stability for my family and I and I loved it I didn't want to travel for work not having stability having to go from state to state and country to country yes fun when you're by yourself or not when you have to keep packing up a whole entire family it gets very tiresome but I told her more power to her.

I then told her at least I wasn't fat and overweight after having a baby that's when it really hit her she then said how am I coming for a black woman and I hate it in the black community when people would bring up race like what does race have to do with anything? She got very upset talking about she had two kids and I told her I had a kid and I don't look like that I said thank God for that I even sometimes didn't like going to her house at times because the simple fact they had a camera in their living room and I also had the same exact thing but it was the simple fact that her husband would be up work listening to our conversation one time he came out of nowhere and started talking to us from the camera all types of creepy I have the camera in my living room as well but it's for assurance purposes. I told her she's so unhappy with how she looks so then instead of doing something about it which is working out she chooses to pout about it and cry about how she's unhappy with her weight I told her I was a real friend even offering and volunteering to allow you to workout with me something I didn't do with anyone I do not. I then told her she's so bold with me but she couldn't even defend and take up for herself at work letting some old bitch get the best of you and have you go home stressing and pulling your hair out there but more power to your sister.

I told her closed mouths don't get fed I said you could respectfully place her in her place you don't have to be ghetto loud belligerent and Speaking Ebonics to place people in their places it's unnecessary and it also gets you nowhere then next thing I know she blocked me but smart told me I had already screenshot all those messages just in case I needed to use them to get her in trouble on base. On tiktok when someone blocks you all the messages and all the comments that they ever had commented under any post all go away. After that situation I vouched to never befriend anyone in my neighborhood and or anyone else for that matter it was hard having male friends because they always wanted sex from me or ended up liking me and or confessing their love for me and it was hard for me to have female friends because some would be jealous because I had a nice mom body I had the abs and show midriff and it looked very attractive when I did so some would just hate on me because of everything I had accomplished in my life hell I was even the type of friend I would help you try to accomplish what you were trying to do that was just something that I did but also I never did it for everyone and that was the thing about me. Granted I could be a bitch but I could also be nice but because of everything in my past I had to be a bitch I had to be strong minded I couldn't allow myself to be weak and weak willed. Especially not in the eyes of others I couldn't allow others to see that from me. However, in my neighborhood I was very cool with my neighbor across the street from me she was from the Dominican Republic. She would always take care of the girls and I when we were sick. She would also always feed us and make these homemade remedies for us. I was also cool with another neighbor his name is Mack. I was cool with his wife and their kids. Mack Was also very cool with my dad they would often drink moonshine together and talk a lot. He would also tell me in my dad if I ever needed anything or ran into any problems that I could come to him I was like a daughter to him.

I would try to have my me time at night time when my daughter was sleeping I would do homework I would be great in papers I would be doing research I would be exploring my next business venture I would be watching my shows and or catching up on my shows I will be finding new movies to watch I would have me a glass of wine or two or even some Scotch. I would be working out I would be prepping dinner for the next day in or week I would be washing clothes I would be putting up clothes sometimes while putting up clothes I would even drink and watch my show multi-tasking because when you're a single mother multitasking is key and that's something that you very much learn to do and I mean honestly it became very beneficial for me I would be drinking a glass of wine and my daughter's room sitting on her play mats folding and hanging up her clothes while drinking a glass of wine watching my shows and as a single mother that was something I taught myself you had to do which was Do all that you wanted but you make arrangements. There was no need for me to be complaining so I never did I held all my thoughts and except when I went to therapy because at the end of the day I didn't want a kid at all I was always the one that said I hated kids I didn't want kids of my own but I was also the one that had kids later on down the road but I also got pregnant because that was something that my fiancé at that time wanted and I also thought that it would make us work it would make us stronger it would make us get married but he died plus on top of that I soon have realized that when I had became pregnant we argued more more problems came about his wife kept contacting him.

So here I was as a single mother trying to tell myself to ignore my feelings and hold everything in until I go to therapy but I was actually cracking people will look at you and see the outside of you and see that you're temporarily happy you're temporarily smiling you're temporarily good in life and you have your shit together but little did people know that was me on the outside but no one ever knew how I actually felt on the inside on the inside I was actually cracking I needed a break I was having mental breakdowns every night I was crying I was depressed I was suicidal I was sad although I love my daughter and I gave her the best life that I feel I could have possibly ever gave her but there would be times I would be sad because her dad was no longer here with us I never wanted a baby he wanted a baby and I gave him what he wanted and as a result of giving him what he wanted who would have thought that he would have actually eventually passed away granted he told me that he was going to die before me I just thought he was talking and reminiscing because he was also one of those guys that played entirely way too much even looking at him in a casket and a hospital bed it didn't seem real at all. There would be times I would talk to myself while folding clothes washing clothes washing dishes cleaning up the house cooking whatever whatever and I would tell myself sometimes like is hard being a mother is hard being a single mother at that it was hard doing everything on my own sometimes I felt as if I couldn't do it but I was doing it and that's all that mattered I may have been a single mother but I wasn't a struggling single mother and that's all that mattered to me I had my shit together I just had tribulations along the way.

Sometimes I would wake up or just get to reminiscing about Jay and I would have hatred towards him I loved him to death I really did but at the same time I would sometimes wonder to myself did I get used to have a baby because from the first time I had ever ever met him that was all that he talked about he always wanted a family he wanted kids and I had finally given him that months later after being pressured and pushed and him asking if I was ovulating or if I had had a period if I had missed my period it was just too much for me. I often talk to myself and have these conversations with my therapist as well state and how I feel like I was used to just have a baby for him to have a legacy because he actually knew in fact that he was going to die which he in fact told me he was going to die before me I just didn't take heath or listen to him and as a result of that that left me as a single mother granted I love my child to death I'm happy that I had her she's my joy she's my world and I would literally die and or kill someone for her I literally became a better young woman when I had my daughter she made me a better me she made me want to be a better me she made me want to work hard to leave something behind for her for my legacy she made me want to buy a home to leave behind for her so that when I die she has something paid for to live in. At times Leilani's granddad which was my father even told me that he was leaving his home which he eventually paid off before turning 60 years old he was going to leave that behind to not me but my daughter and I really appreciated it I greatly appreciated it I had worked so hard for my daughter but not only my daughter but my sister so they can have paid off vehicles left behind they could have property left behind they could start off in life without having to struggle and mess up their credit mess up their names get these apartments with their boyfriends and or friends and mess up their credit I just wanted the best for my sister and my daughter I gave them the best I gave them as much as I could and in the mean time of doing so I forgot that self care is important self health is important I forgot to take care of me to put me first sometimes but I couldn't because I always had taught myself that I can't put myself before I put children first.

I taught myself that this is what it's like to be a grown adult and have yourself together in life I taught myself that life is just a game of monopoly or in life. I told myself that at times I may have seen like I was cracking and or I wanted to give up but I told myself I had to keep moving I had to keep pushing because there was people that were looking up to me and there were people that were watching me and those people that were looking up and watching me was my daughter and my sister so giving up cracking wasn't going to help the case there would be times I would literally cry scream drink talk to myself one thing about it they never saw any of those moments of me ever. They never heard about any of those moments ever no one else ever heard about those moments ever with the exception of my therapist. I was so caught up I thought about myself that I didn't realize my sister was sad and depressed that she needed counseling herself as well which she was soon going to seek counseling for herself I had never wanted to do counseling as a group and or family because I felt like doing that no one is actually going to express how they really truly feel because they're going to be afraid and or scared that the other family member is going to be ashamed and or mad at them for actually telling the truth or speaking their mind so everyone did separate counseling although I always felt separate counseling was better anyways because there may not have been certain things that you wanted your whole family to know.

As much as I did for my two girls I didn't even know for so long that my little sister was depressed and suicidal and sad and see that was always why I always put myself last I always would tell myself I can get sleep and rest when I'm dead in my casket I just really wanted my girls to have a great life they had a great life but sometimes money isn't everything money doesn't solve everything money doesn't solve all your problems and and to have solutions money doesn't make the world go round and one thing about it most importantly no matter how much money I had I couldn't bring Jay back and that was the thing that people like me had to realize and remember you can have all the money in the world and still be unhappy which I wasn't unhappy but at times I would have unhappiness as a trait come into me at times I would feel depressed and sad and suicidal it was sad to me that I didn't even realize that one of my girls was suicidal and depressed and that was my sister who I was supposed to be looking after closely watching although I was looking after her closely watching her doing everything for her paying for everything for her giving the best life that I thought I possibly could hell that time do I even thought that she was my daughter but I was forgetting to talk to her I was forgetting to ask her how she felt what was on her mind what was she thinking I was making all decisions and choices that I felt was best for us as a family three of us had that that I forgot to ask how they felt granted my daughter was now three years old at this time she was very intelligent to be three years old. She literally new a geometry was I had taught my daughter multiplication. when I had decided to homeschool my daughter I told her multiplication we were reading chapter books my daughter was very intelligent for her age to be three she also seemed as if she had an old soul something I'm pretty sure that she had obtained from me as her mother because I always had old so I always hung around those older than me dated men older than me I just genuinely love being around older people because they teach you things they give you so much knowledge strength and everything else that you felt you may not have had then but they eventually rub off on you and you obtain all of that energy and more. Leilani definitely had an old soul like her mother she even knew all the places that we ever want to sometimes when she was in the backseat watching her movies on the DVD player she would see certain places that her and I had been together and she would say hey mommy there's that carwash we go to or she would say hey mommy there's McDonald's I saw that on a commercial my child just was very intelligent and I loved it she even knew how to speak French and Creole somewhat I had only taught her what her father had taught me.

ACKNOWLEDGMENTS

I want to thank my daughter Leilani for making me a stronger woman I needed to be that I never thought I could be ever. I want to thank my daughter for saving my life after her father died had I not been pregnant with her in my belly I wouldn't have had anything to look forward to or Anything and or anyone to live for. Being a mother definitely made me become a mature woman that I wanted to be and always dreamed to be. Had it not been for my daughter I don't think I would have tried hard in life to be so successful at a young age to be a Jack of all trades everything I ever did was all for my daughter I'm proud of me and it makes me cry when my daughter tells me that she's proud of me especially at her age. Everything that I've ever accomplished in my life was for my daughter so she didn't have to struggle so she didn't have to watch me struggle because after all if I struggle my child struggles. So she could grow up having the perfect life that I always wanted to her to have even though her father was no longer with us.

I want to thank Garrett For not only saving my life but the life of my unborn child the saddest part of it all is that he will never know. Considering he'll never know I was going to take my life, I never told him that once ever. Unless he put two and two together but I didn't think that was something I needed to tell him anyways. A man that I loved a man that gave me temporary love And temporary happiness. A man that helped me get rid of temporary pain and suffering, A man I regret losing I really loved him he showed me a great time and that I need it at that moment in time he showed me that there are still some good men out there in the world who actually just want to be loved and show a nice woman love and the right way at that. I guess I'll never know how things could have been how I stayed and had he stayed but I'll definitely never forget him. I'll never forget all that he did for my child and I'll never forget how he was always there whether I needed him or not I'll never forget how he tried to show someone else's daughter love who wasn't even his daughter.

I want to thank Jay he showed me temporary love, temporary happiness,- Temporary pain. I will always have love for him as I know that no one could ever be him or replace him. I've tried to make myself forget about him so that I could move on and raise our daughter but the sad truth is I always remember him and have a pain in my heart because he's no longer here. He was my first love probably the only real love that I will ever have again. Most importantly he helped me create a beautiful little girl Who looks exactly just like him. I could never forget all the great memories I had with him and after all we have a child who acts just like him in certain ways. It very much saddens me that he never got a chance to meet our daughter. He showed me a lot and gave me a lot of knowledge that I needed to know that I use to this day. I miss him so much and I think about him every day, I think about if we would have actually gotten married if he were still here if we would have actually had more children together if he were still here.

I want to also thank every man who has ever came in my life it was either a blessing or a lesson hell maybe even both. Had I not endured so much pain and suffering dealing with the BS between all the men who ever came in my life who did me wrong I would have never became the strongest woman that I could possibly be today. So thank you all now I have so many stories to teach my daughter and sister to make sure they never have to deal with what I dealt To make sure they never accept Anything from any man that they get with. To make sure that they choose wisely and think smarter than any man they get with To always know their worth to always make sure they have their own to never have to depend on a man their married to or not. In all my twenty three years of life somehow someway a man was always my biggest downfall ever I definitely didn't want that for my daughter and sister.

Thank you to all the friends whether the friendship ended or was ongoing there was still a lot of knowledge I took in there were still lessons that I learned most importantly my friends made me become an independent woman made me understand and realize that I don't need friends I don't need people always around me me becoming an introvert was probably one of the best things that could have happened especially when I started losing friends and seeing how people really were. My friends made me realize that I didn't need anyone my friends made me realize I didn't even need friends I was perfectly fine with going places alone doing things alone exploring new places and things alone. People always say they'll be there for you but they're never there for you when it actually counts. I never asked if anything from anyone ever just time, attention, love, the truth.

I want to thank my little sister Bri for listening to everything that I've ever told her good and bad. for looking up to me as a role model however I don't want her to repeat everything that I've done in my life I want her to be better than me to be more successful than me to be more wiser than I was to never allow and take certain things from anyone.

I cannot forget my parents the ones who were sometimes the partial reasons why I endured so much pain and suffering. Sometimes they were the reason why I was ecstatic and had a nice life. But one thing about it everything that I've ever gone through because of my parents in or with my parents is why I'm the bad bitch that I am today. Like MC Ltye said "Only the strong survive,Only the wise excel". My whole life I had pretty much been through so much but I still somehow someway came out on top to being a young successful black woman a strong one at. I'm a firm believer that we all endure things in life good and bad but The thing is each situation that's bad you're supposed to learn and grow from it to know how to handle the very next one and be ready for the next obstacle each obstacle makes you stronger makes you wiser makes you more creative Makes you more prepared for the next. Even the good that has happened in my life has made me more prepared for the next good things that Well come my way in life that I've deserved and waited for in life.

And the best for last goes to myself I want to thank me all the good and bad that I ever endured in my life has always made me stronger made me smarter made me wiser made me better prepared for anything that comes my way I've had a great life and I've also had a sad life but one thing about it I'm always going to be ready for the bad things that had occurred and will keep occurring in my life we all have obstacles in life and we will always have obstacles that come in life but it's how you prepare and handle yourself for each obstacle. I'm so proud of the strong independent successful brave young woman that I had independent successful brave young woman that I had ever become become especially when I hit my twenties We all have stories there's always two sides or multiple sides to a story but this book was my story my true story some of the things that I endured in my life that actually made me stronger, wiser, Made me a better me a better person a better woman a better mother a better sister a better daughter a better friend a better person in general. No one can ever take anything away from me or that away from me. I'm here because of me and God. I've always prayed for everything good that I ever received and I finally got it and in my early twenties and I'm so happy for me I definitely deserved it. Like Ariana Grande said been through some bad shit I should be a sad bitch who would have thought it turn me into a savage.i felt that verse with everything within me. No matter what I've ever endured in my life I never gave up I never shut down what really doesn't kill you will in fact make you stronger. And this is my story the story on how all I ever wanted was love respect and a father for my daughter but I have accepted the fact that some of us will not get married some of us will not find love or have a man in our life that will do right by us but I've completely come to conclusion that I'm perfectly fine with being alone and single by myself at least I know my words I know I'm happy I know my happiness and I found happiness and have taught myself so much being alone by myself I've showed myself that I don't need a man to feel complete I've taught myself that I don't need a man to make me feel good I've taught myself that my daughter will always have one father and I cannot replace him nor bring him back all I can do is teach her the things to look out for when she starts dating tell her the stories and what I've endured and my dating world in life hope that she doesn't make the same mistakes that I made and if she were to I'd be a great mother better than my mother and be there for my child and daughter not judge but correct her and show her the way to go. I've taught myself that a man will come and go a man isn't the answer to all of my problems a man will always disappoint you and people will always disappoint you and there is absolutely nothing in this world that you could ever do to prevent being disappointed. I've taught myself that you can be successful and have everything without a man I've taught myself that in this sexist world women our bosses as well and I'm a boss. I've taught myself that I don't need a man to feel completed ever I've taught myself to love myself better and 1st before a man. I've taught myself the types of red flags to lookout for I've taught myself to enjoy life and not to worry about whether I have a husband or not. I've taught myself that some women won't get married I may be included in that category of some women who've never made it to get married and or will not make it to get married but one thing about it while I was on this earth I came here I grew up I've learned I've taught I'm learning I've obtained I've gained and I completed the assignment of what I expected of myself what I wanted to do with myself what I wanted for myself what I've achieved for myself for my daughter for my sister. I came I saw I conquered I did what needed to be done of me and was expected of me for me on this earth and no one else and if I were to go tomorrow I would be completely happy and satisfied with the person that I had become. I've taught myself that I'm the most permanent person in my life.